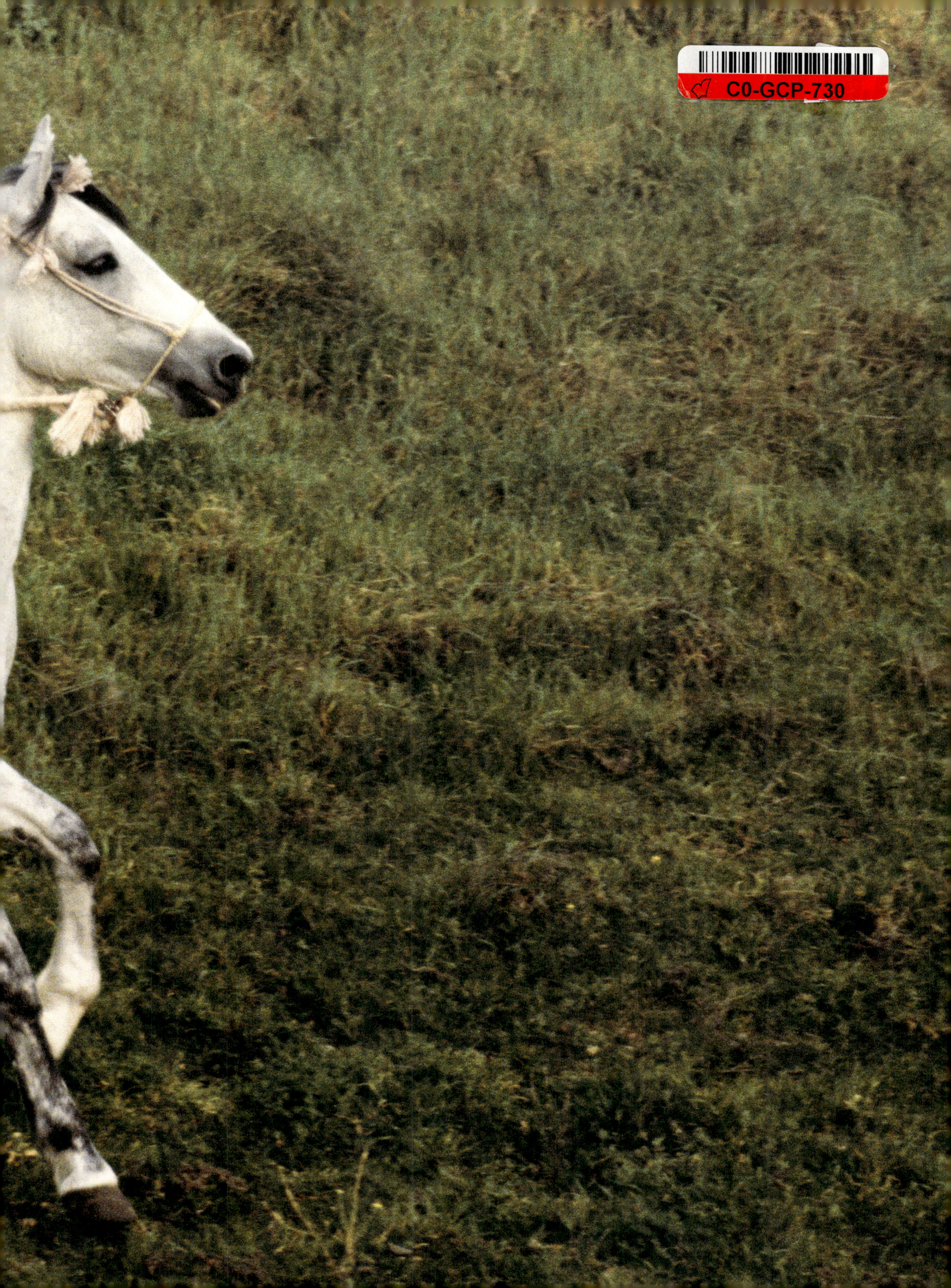

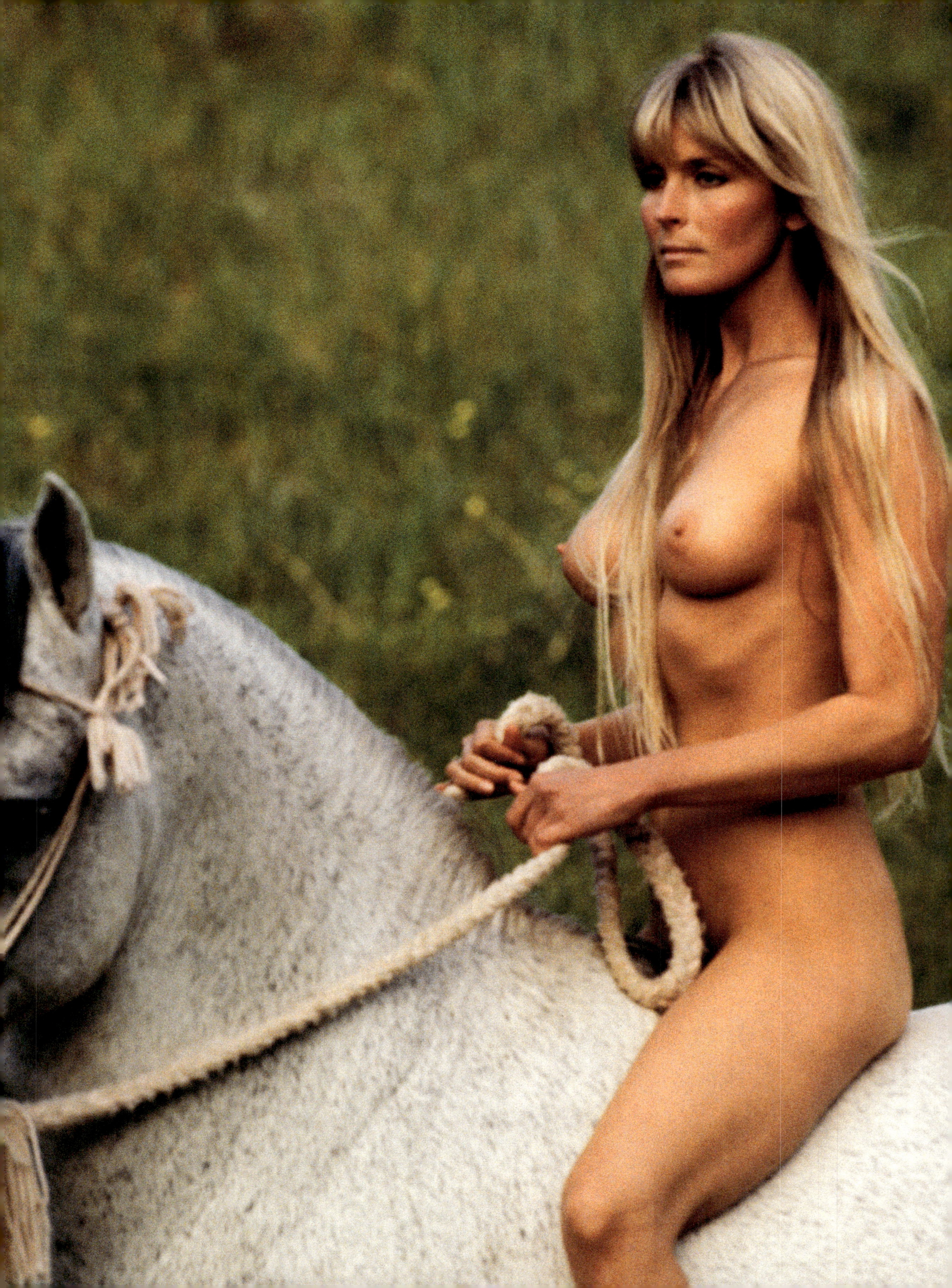

ALL-AMERICAN VOLUME TWELVE

# A BOOK OF LESSONS

BY

BRUCE WEBER

A NOTE FROM THE EDITORS:

*Don't lose your swagger!*

teNeues

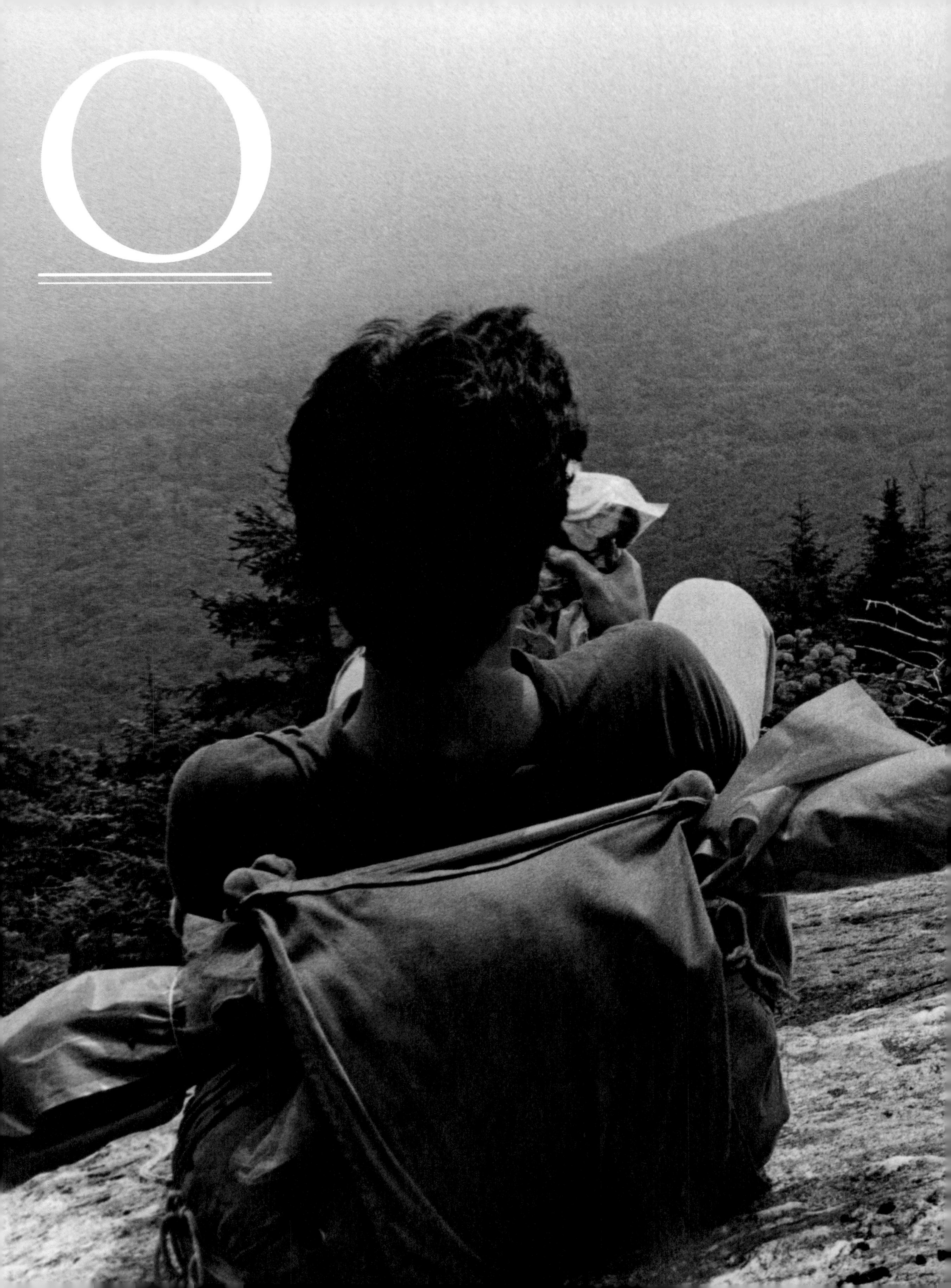
O

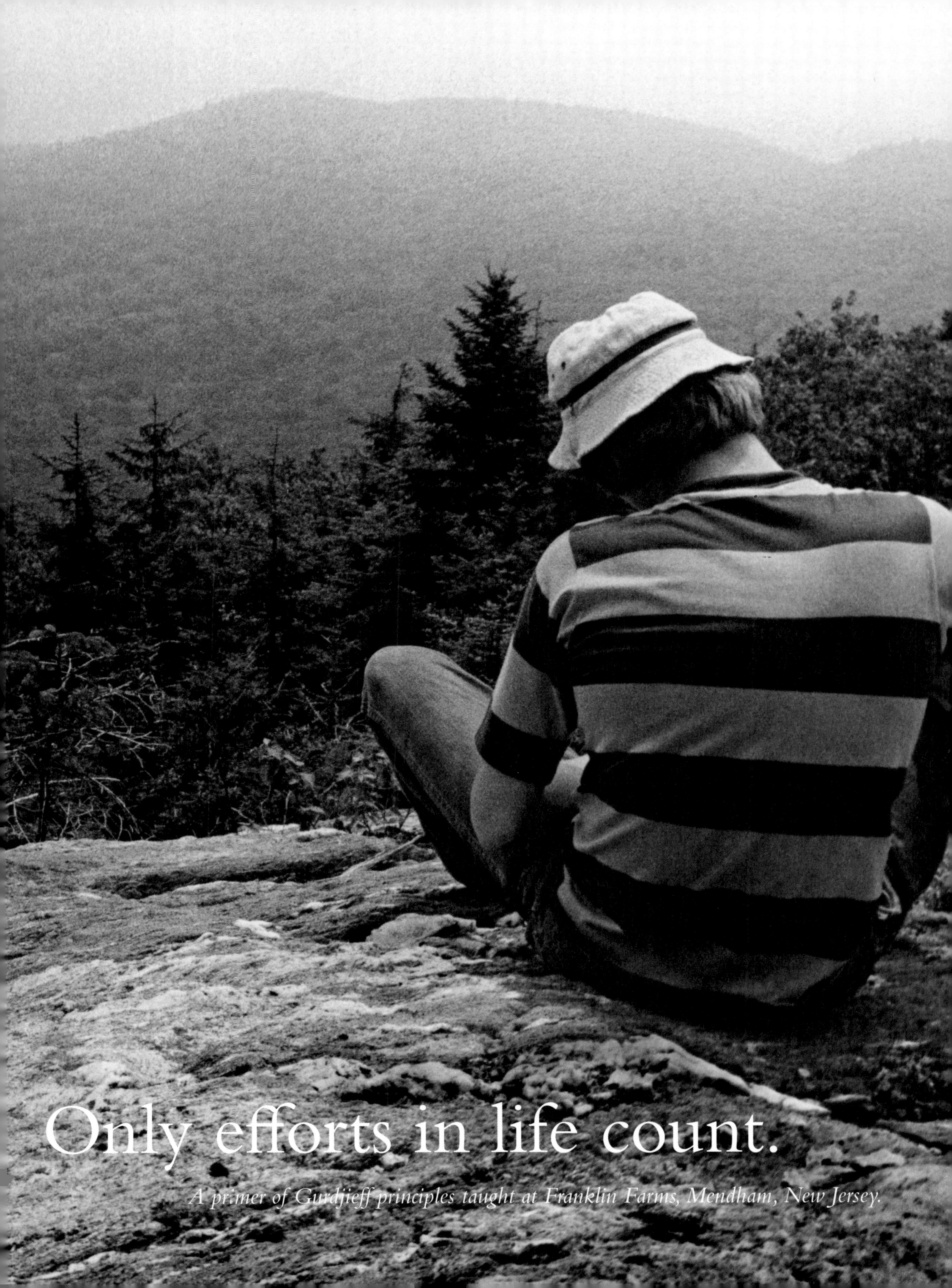

# Only efforts in life count.

*A primer of Gurdjieff principles taught at Franklin Farms, Mendham, New Jersey.*

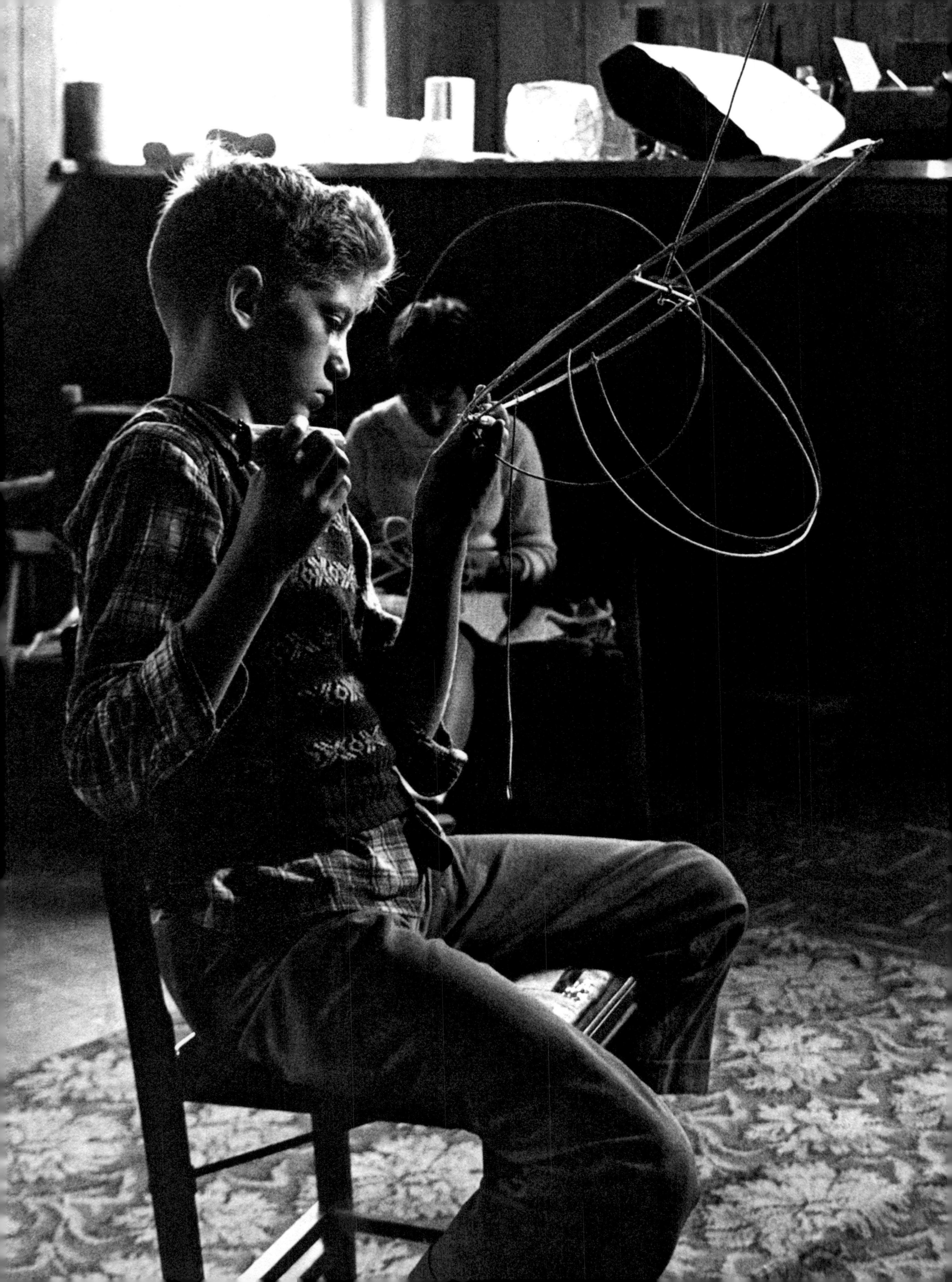

L

Love work
for work's
sake and not
for its gain.

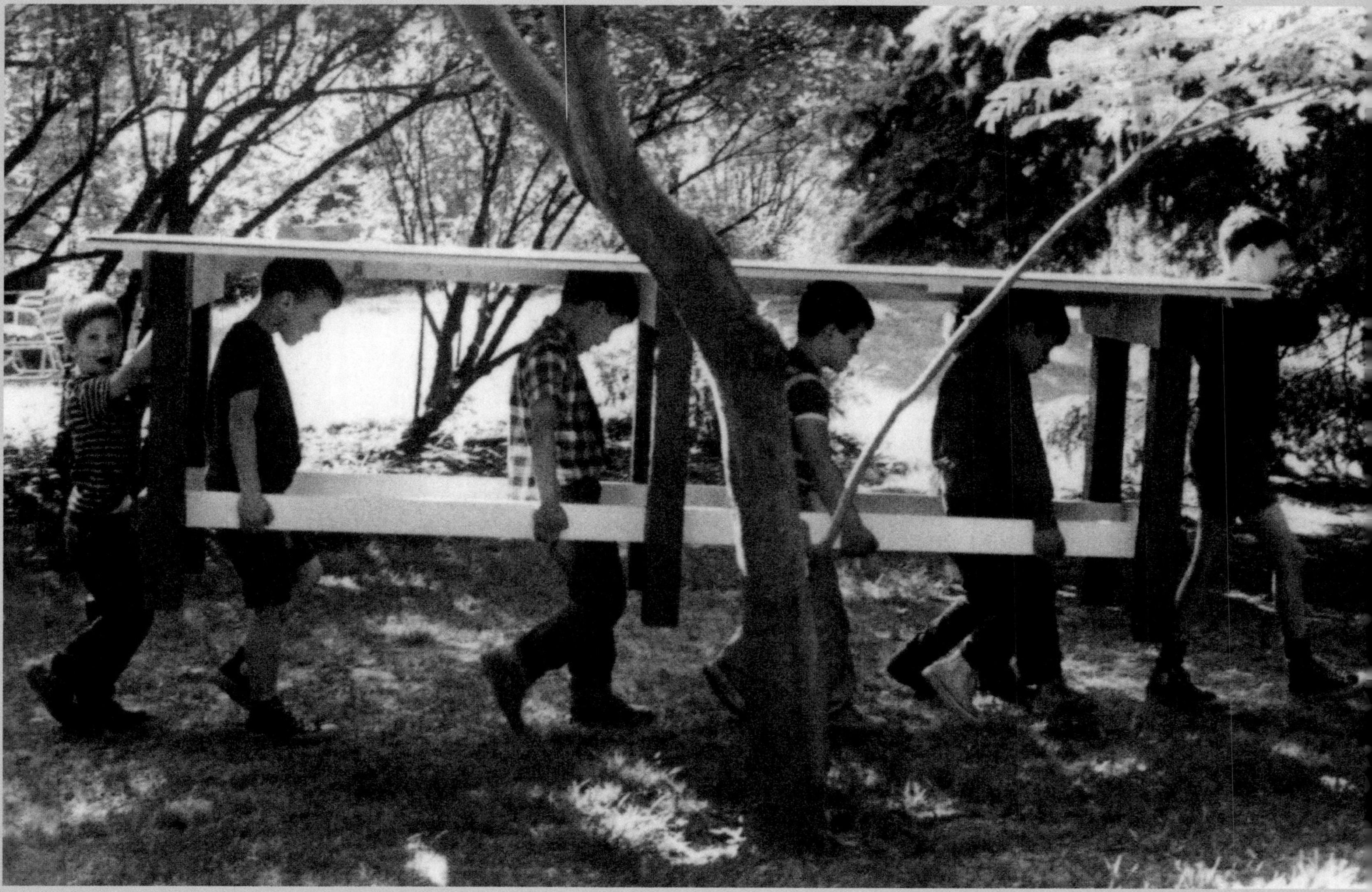

# R

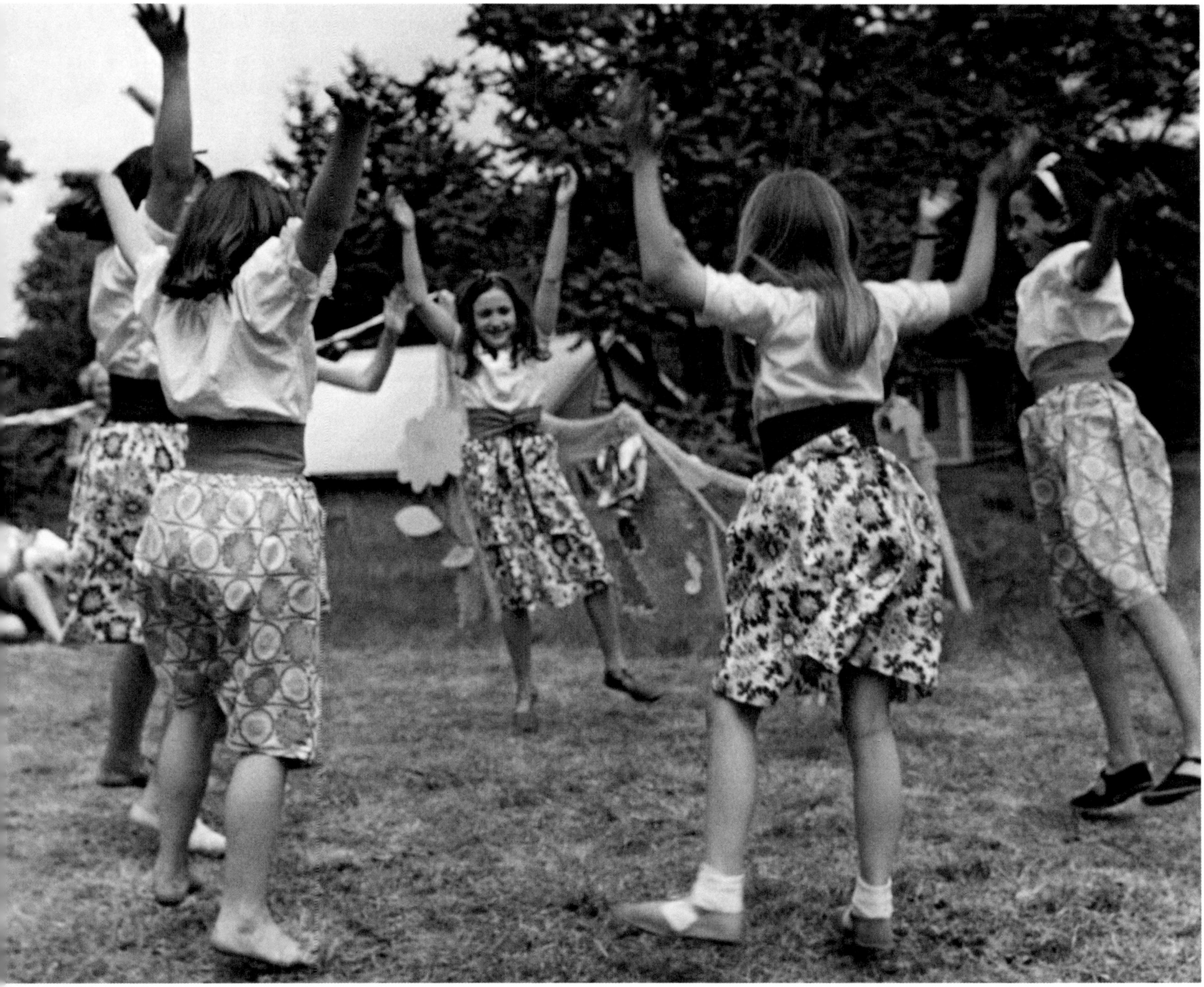

Remember what it
felt like to be a child.

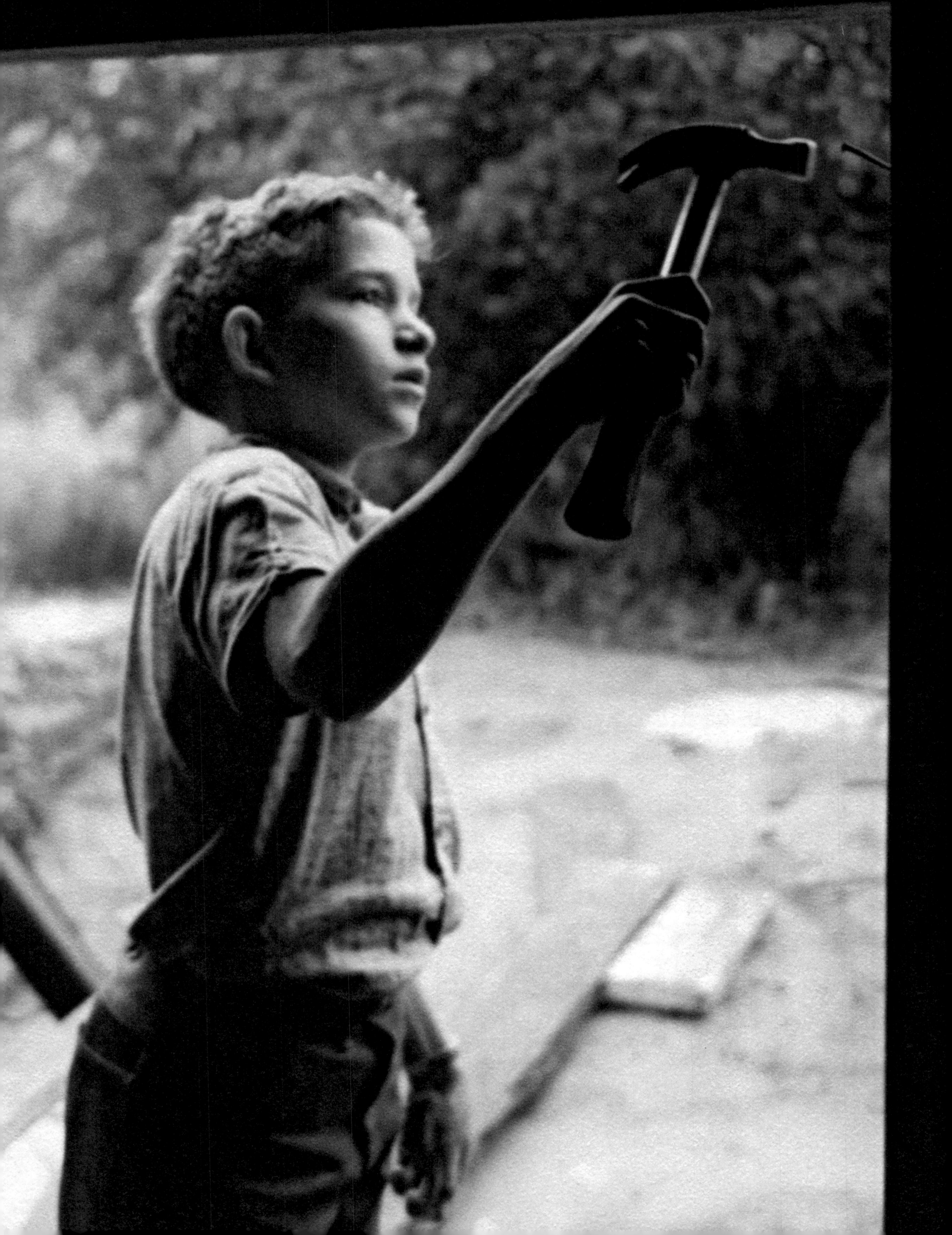

N

Nothing is difficult; only our thoughts make it so.

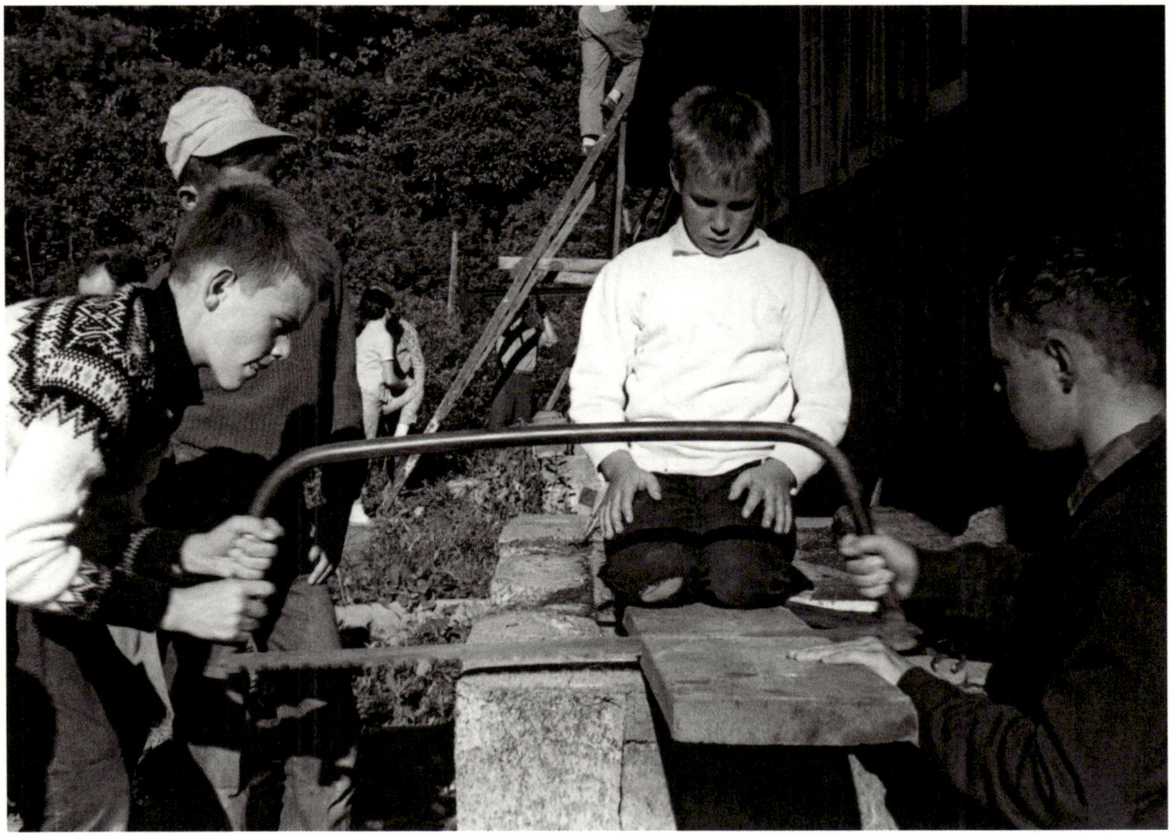

# M

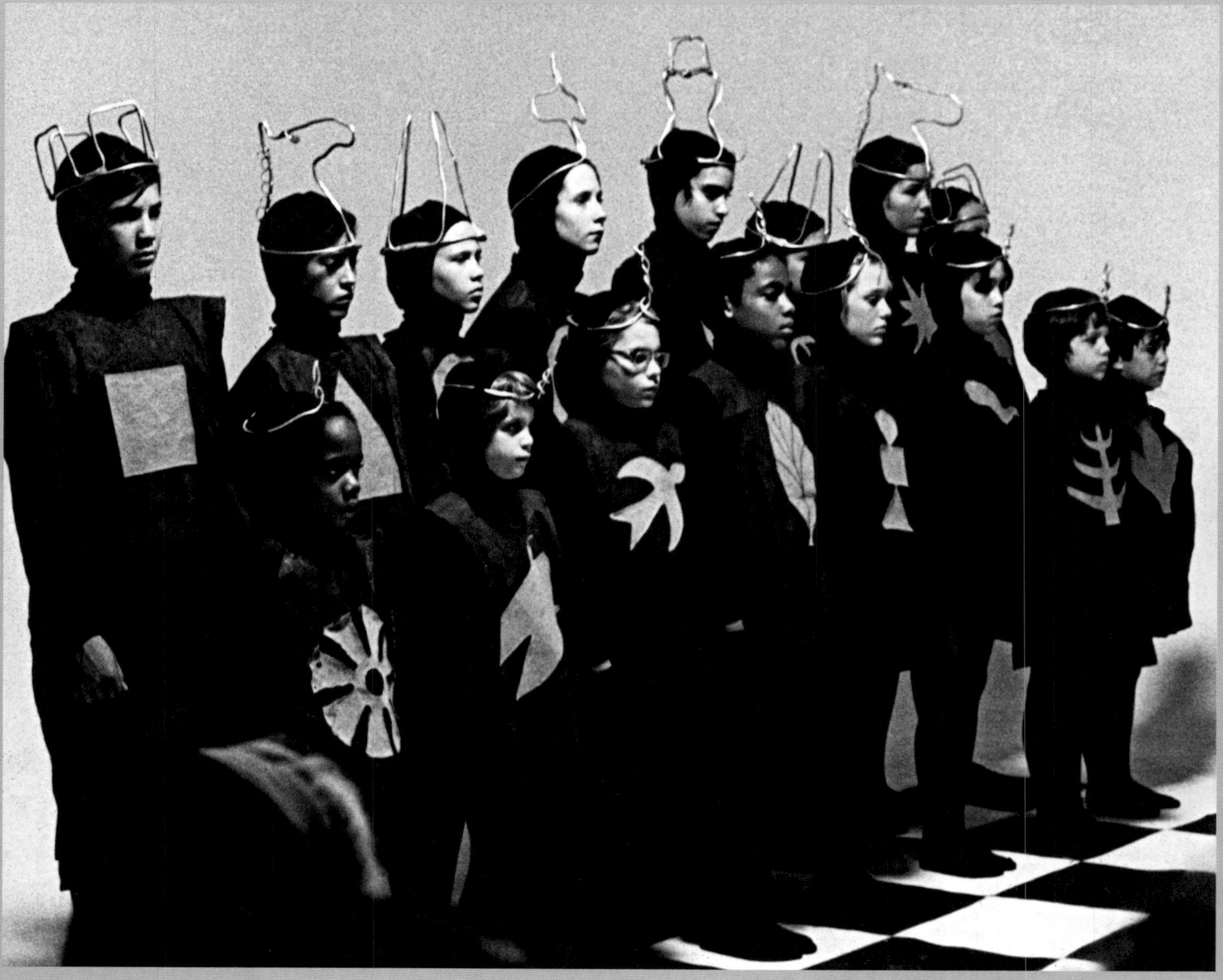

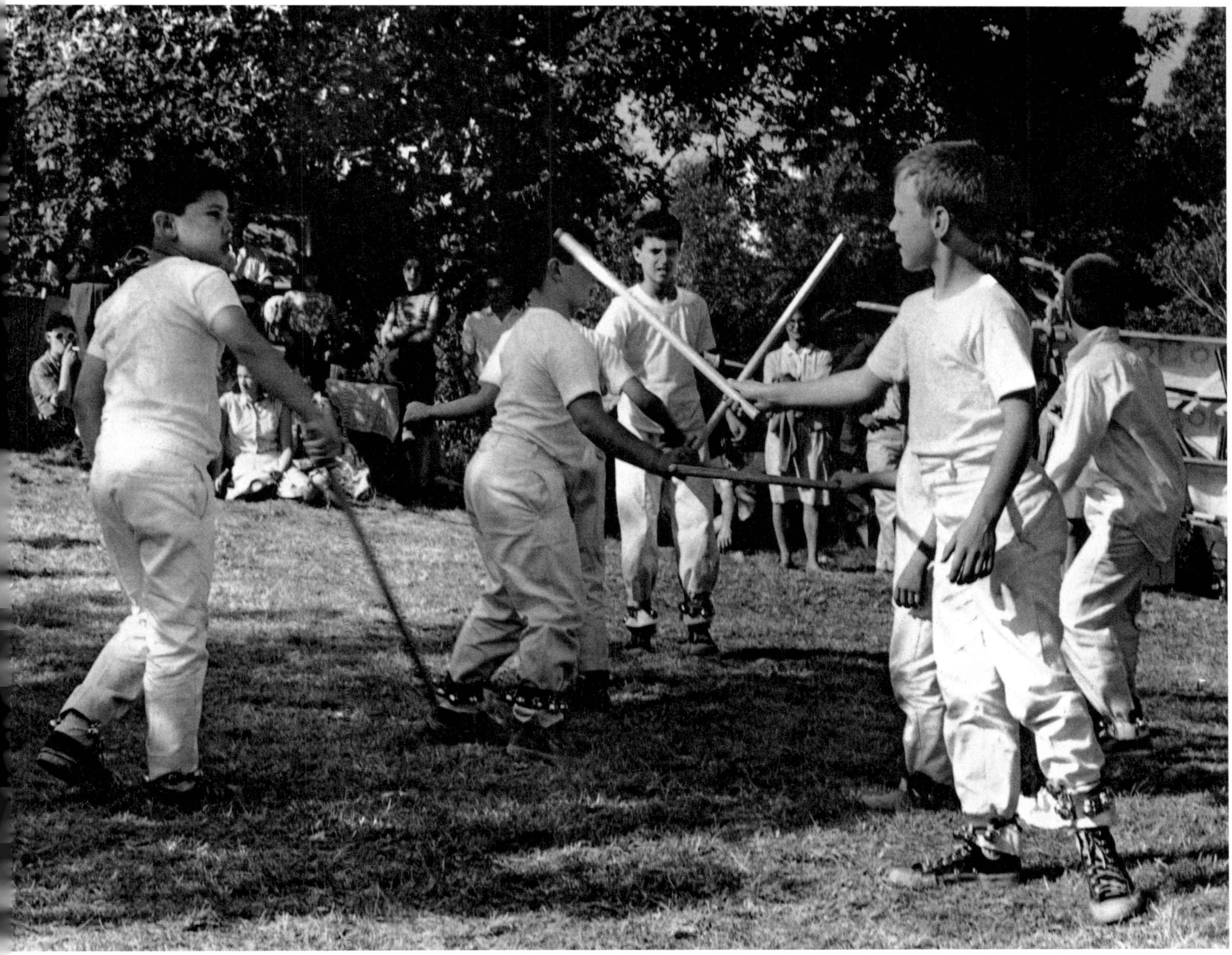

Make room for
the unexpected
and welcome it.

*If you wish your children well, you must first wish yourself well. For if you change, your children, too, will change.* —GEORGE GURDJIEFF

George Ivanovitch Gurdjieff was a Russian spiritual teacher who promoted a philosophy called the "Fourth Way" throughout Europe in the early-to-mid-20th century. He believed that most people existed in a hypnotic sleep-state, but that they could awaken to higher levels of consciousness and realize their latent potential through spiritual exercise. His methods sought to increase his pupils' attention and focus on the world around them. Gurdjieff's teachings drew from core practices of various ancient religions. But unlike faiths that considered solitude a key to enlightenment or relied on the instruction of a religious leader, Gurdjieff believed that self-awareness came through one's active participation in society and everyday life, through a deep questioning of the self and the pursuit of personal freedom.

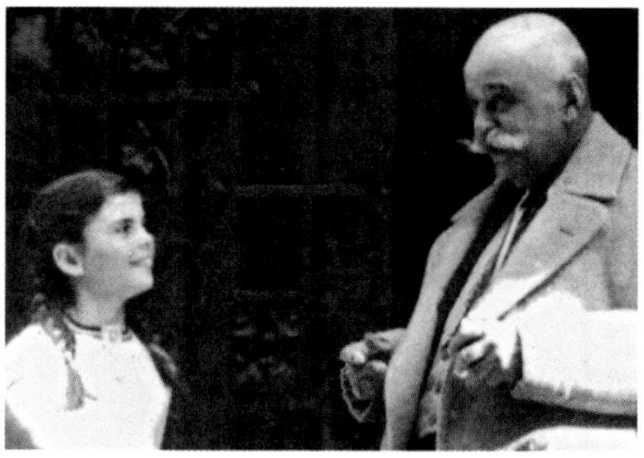

In 1943, a group of Gurdjieff's pupils from England purchased Franklin Farms in Mendham, New Jersey and set up the first school in the States based on his teachings. They converted the house and grounds into a physical implementation of his "Fourth Way" philosophy. Students carried out farm and household tasks as a part of their training, following Gurdjieff's belief that enlightenment can result from hard work.

Gurdjieff was particularly interested in children, the inner lives of their minds and their perceptions of the world. At Franklin Farms, kids were encouraged to explore his methods through a program called "children's work." Special activities were designed to develop their emotional and physical vigor. Like their parents and elders, the children were taught to question everything, explore a variety of perspectives and solve problems through stories and play. They also participated in household and farm work. They cooked for other residents, directed theatrical performances, and even built a home on the premises. For this last project, it was the kids themselves who gathered all the necessary building materials and installed the electrical and water systems.

As Lillian Firestone explains in her book *The Forgotten Language of Children*, the principles guiding this "children's work" required real trust in the power of young people's curiosity, imagination, and individuality. The adults at Franklin Farms came to believe that each child's desires and determination would allow them to do anything, no matter how difficult it might seem. Through teachings and exercises, they imparted this confidence on to the children.

The photographs here present a sampling of the activities children participated in at Franklin Farms as it existed in Mendham in the 1960s, and hint at the pride and confidence this "work" inspired. Franklin Farms has since closed, but children's work continues to this day through the efforts of the Gurdjieff Foundation.

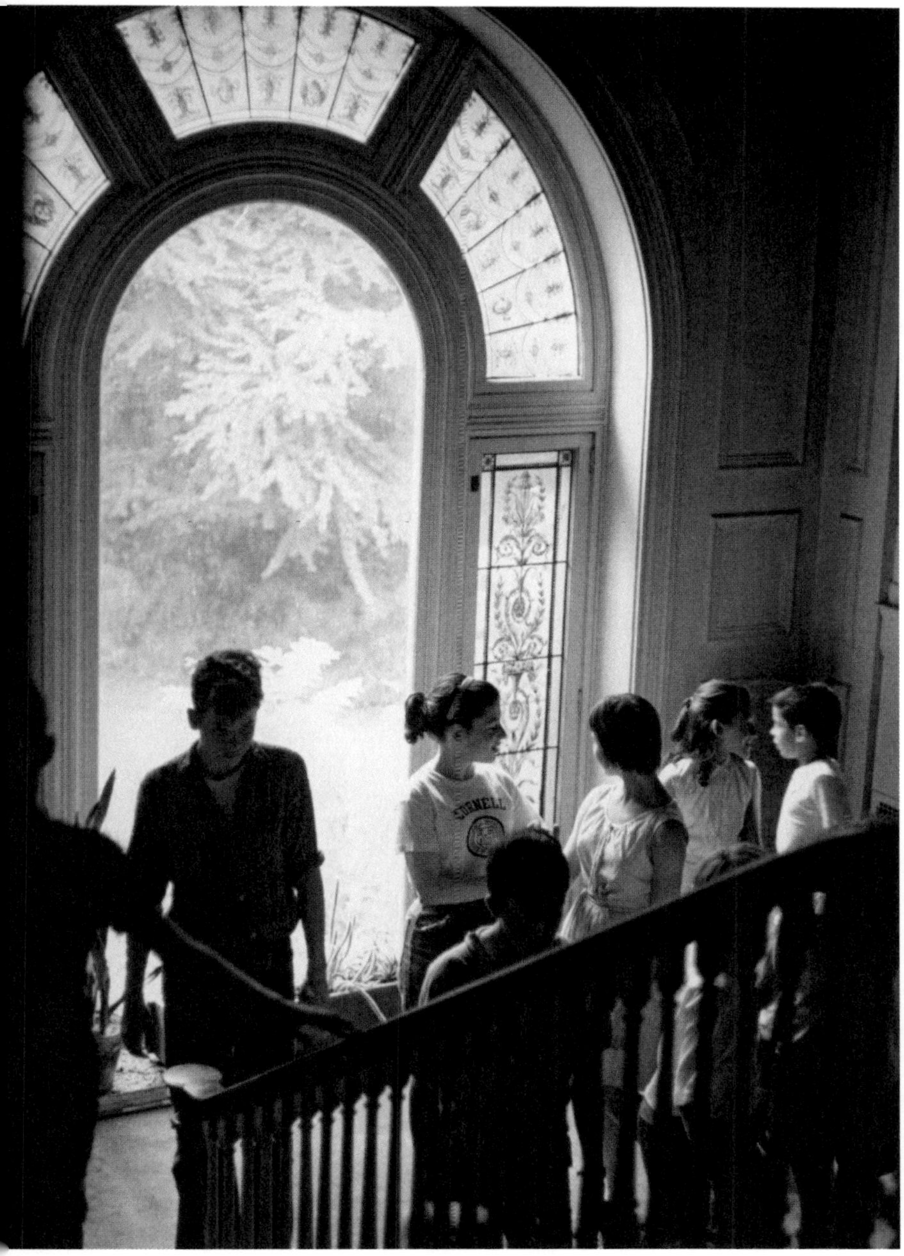

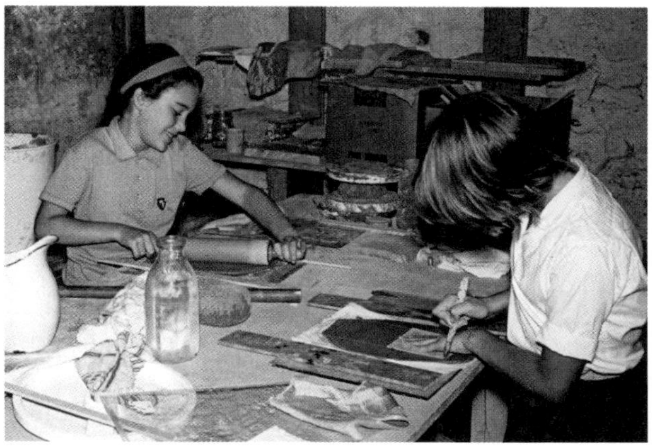

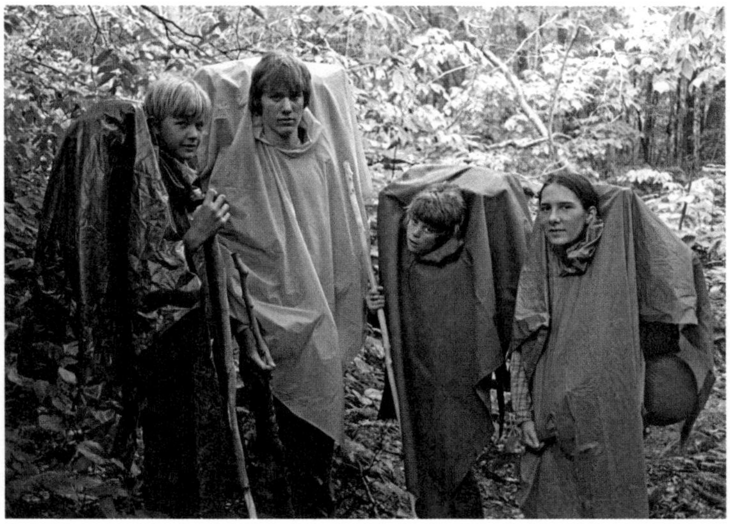

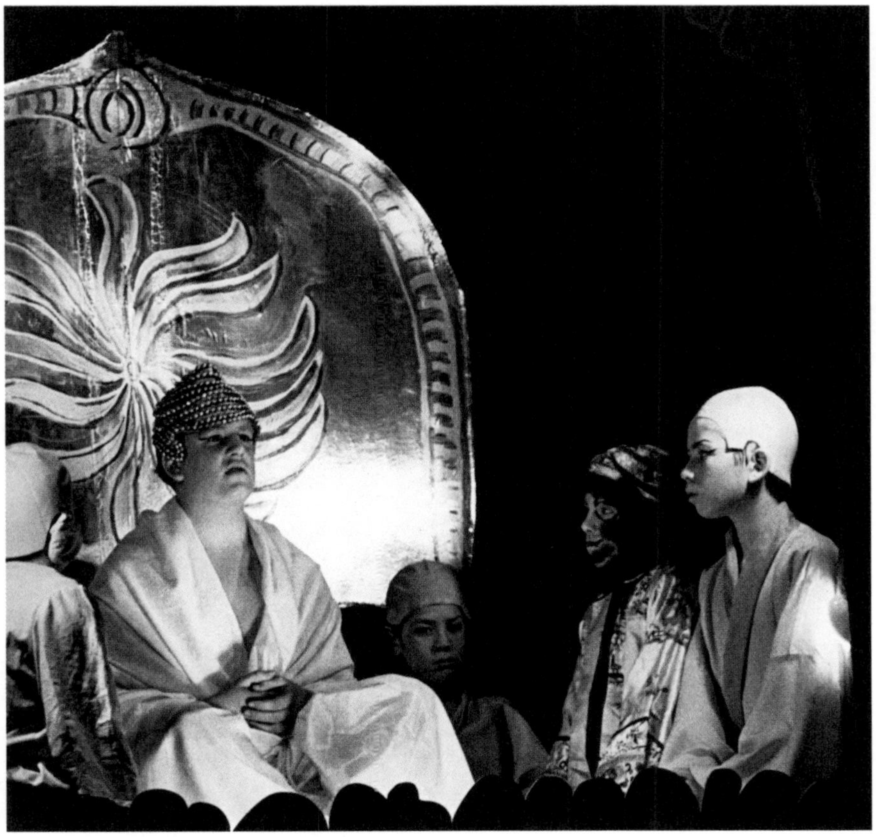

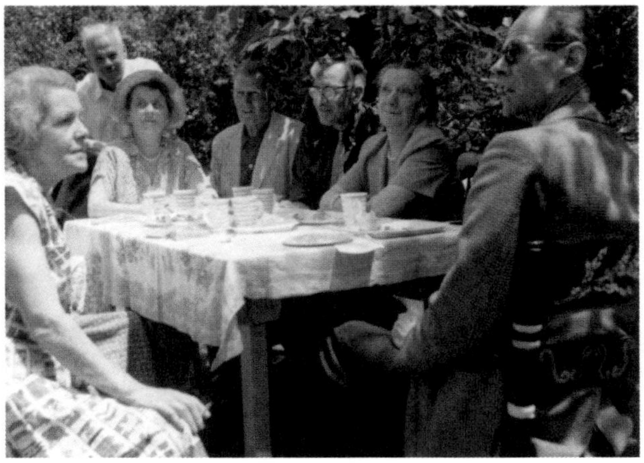

*While in the children's work, I learned how to hammer a nail, plaster a wall, saw, plumb, drill, listen, sit quietly, watch, hear, see…that I had something to say, that there were many different sides to me, that it rains out of nowhere in Arizona, that the mountains in Montana have to be one of the most beautiful sights on earth, that I didn't know America until I'd seen it–and the same goes for myself.*—CHRIS, ONE OF THE STUDENTS

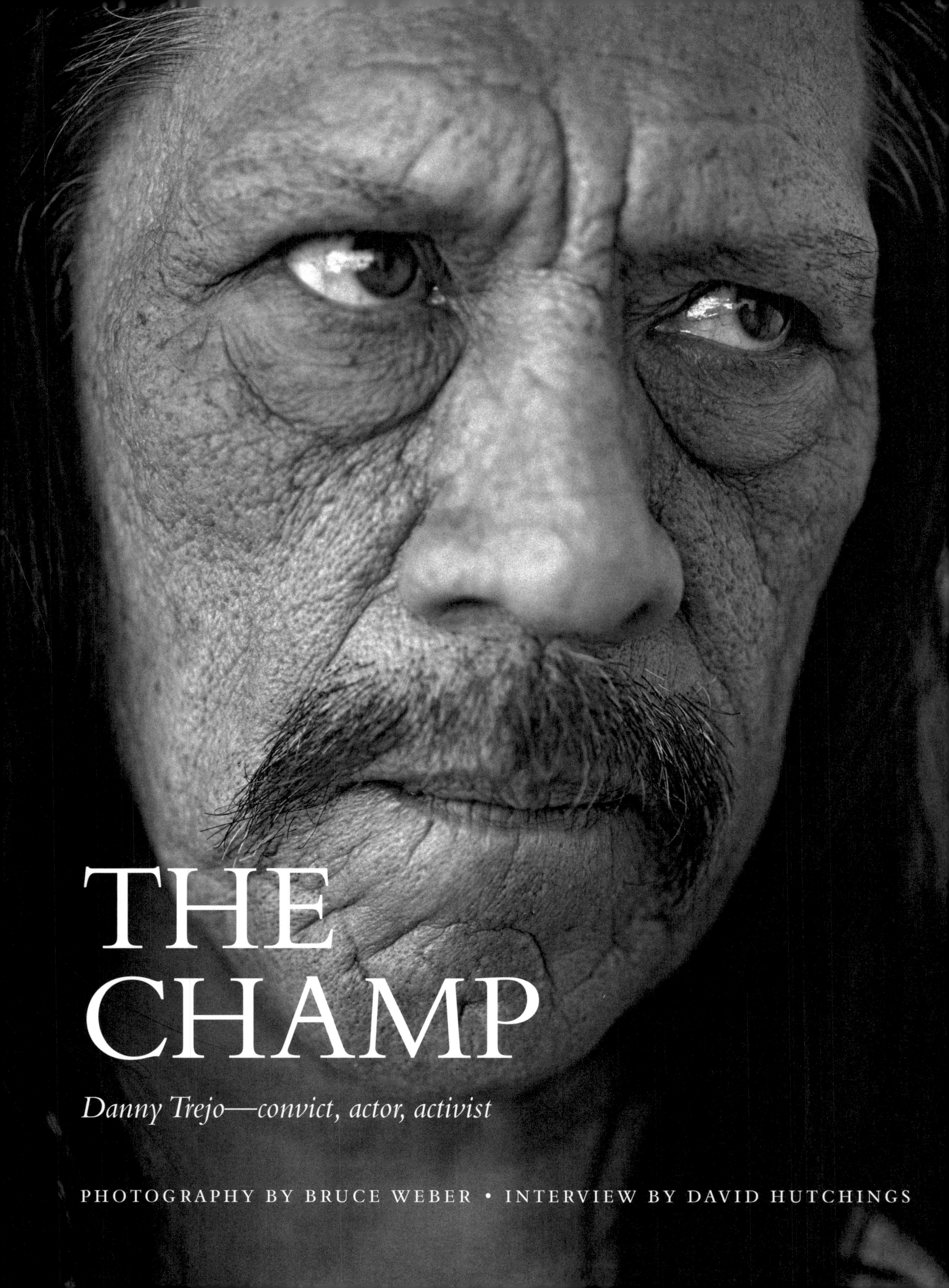

# THE CHAMP

*Danny Trejo—convict, actor, activist*

PHOTOGRAPHY BY BRUCE WEBER • INTERVIEW BY DAVID HUTCHINGS

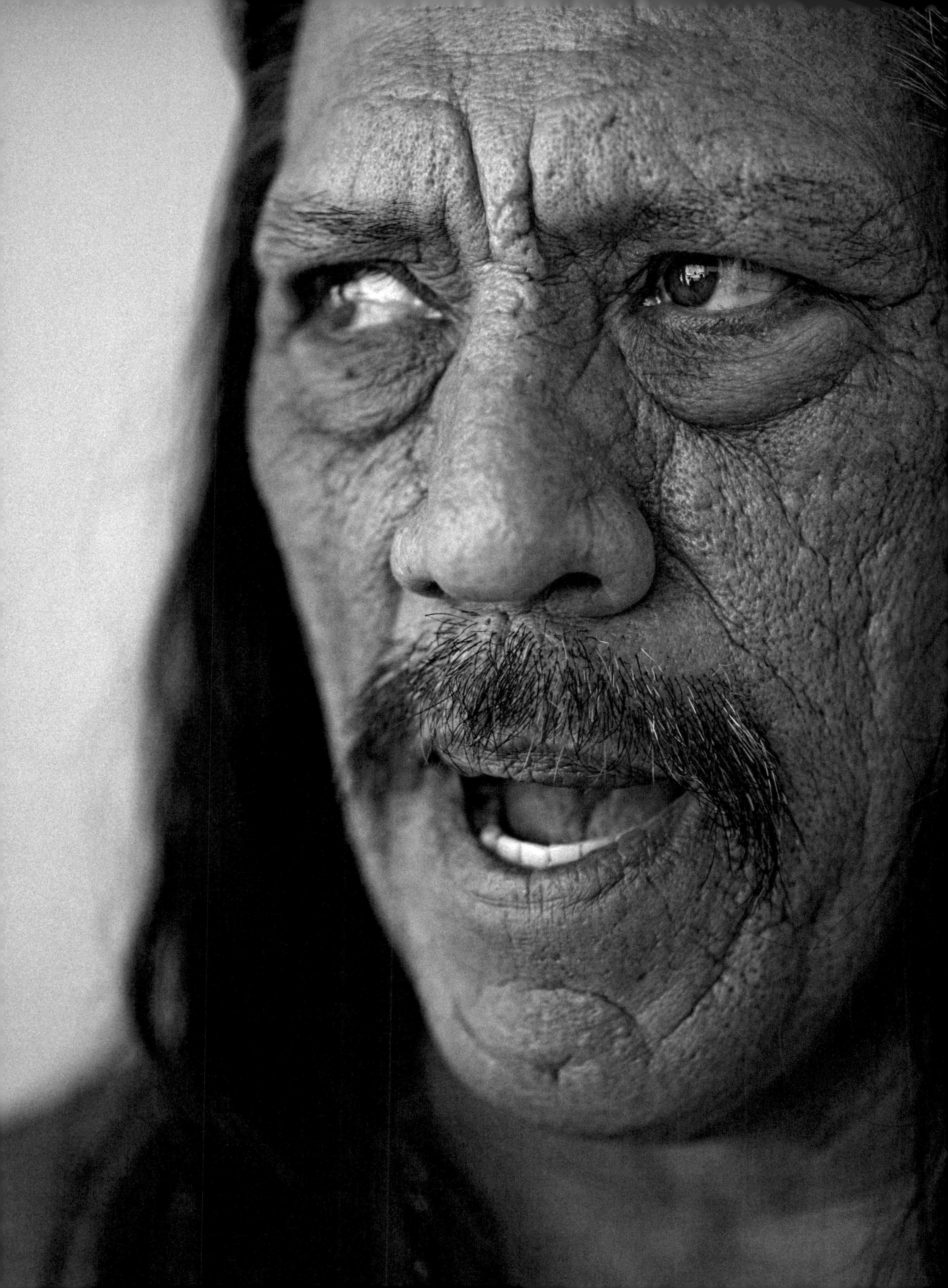

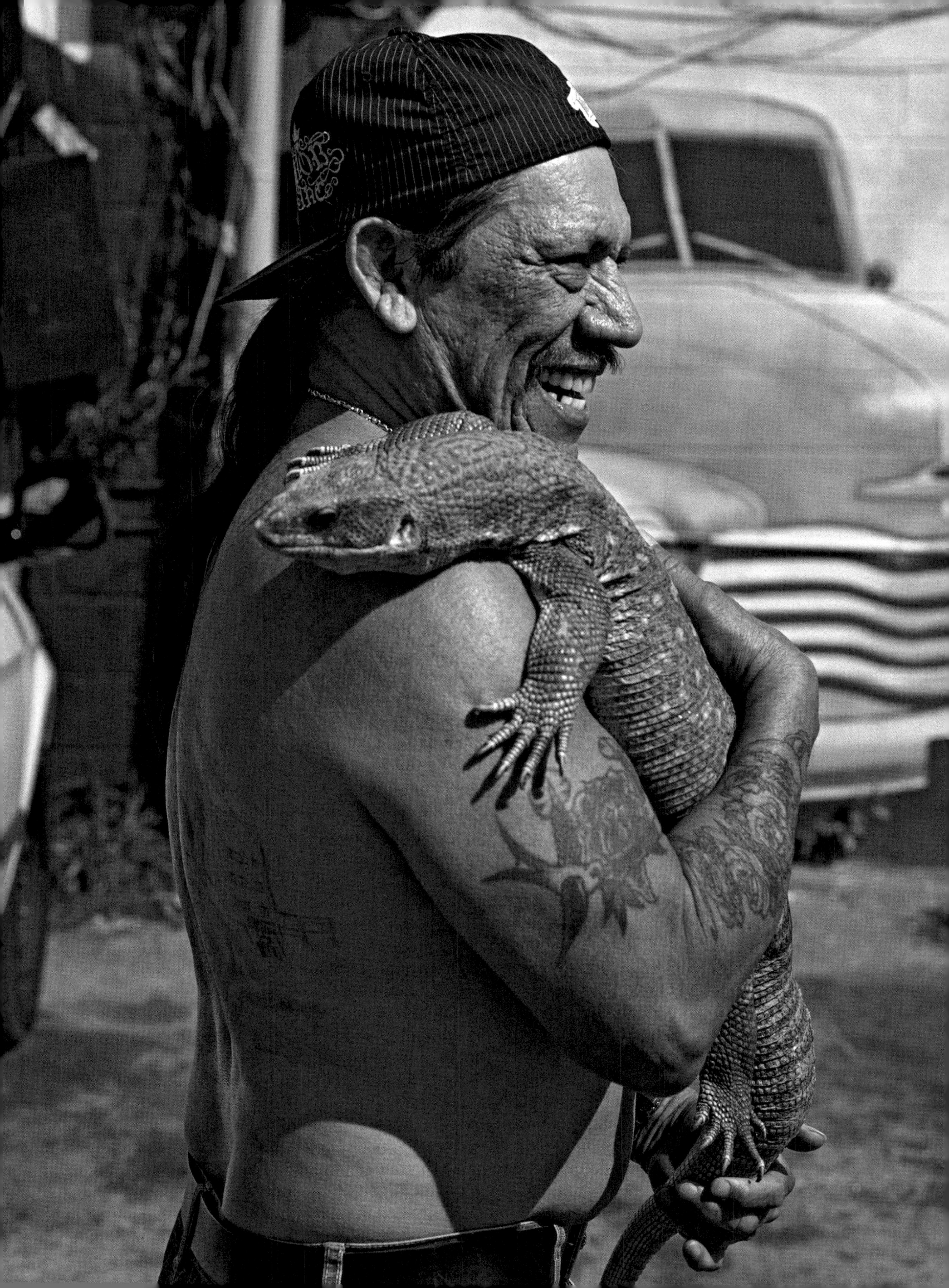

“Once I was in county jail with this creepy guy with a weird laugh who was brought in for vagrancy. He was one of them hippie types who takes acid and smells bad. His name was Charlie Manson. Later I heard how he manipulated these misfit, abused girls in the San Francisco area. That would never have worked with the Mexican broads I grew up with in East L.A.”

—*Danny Trejo*

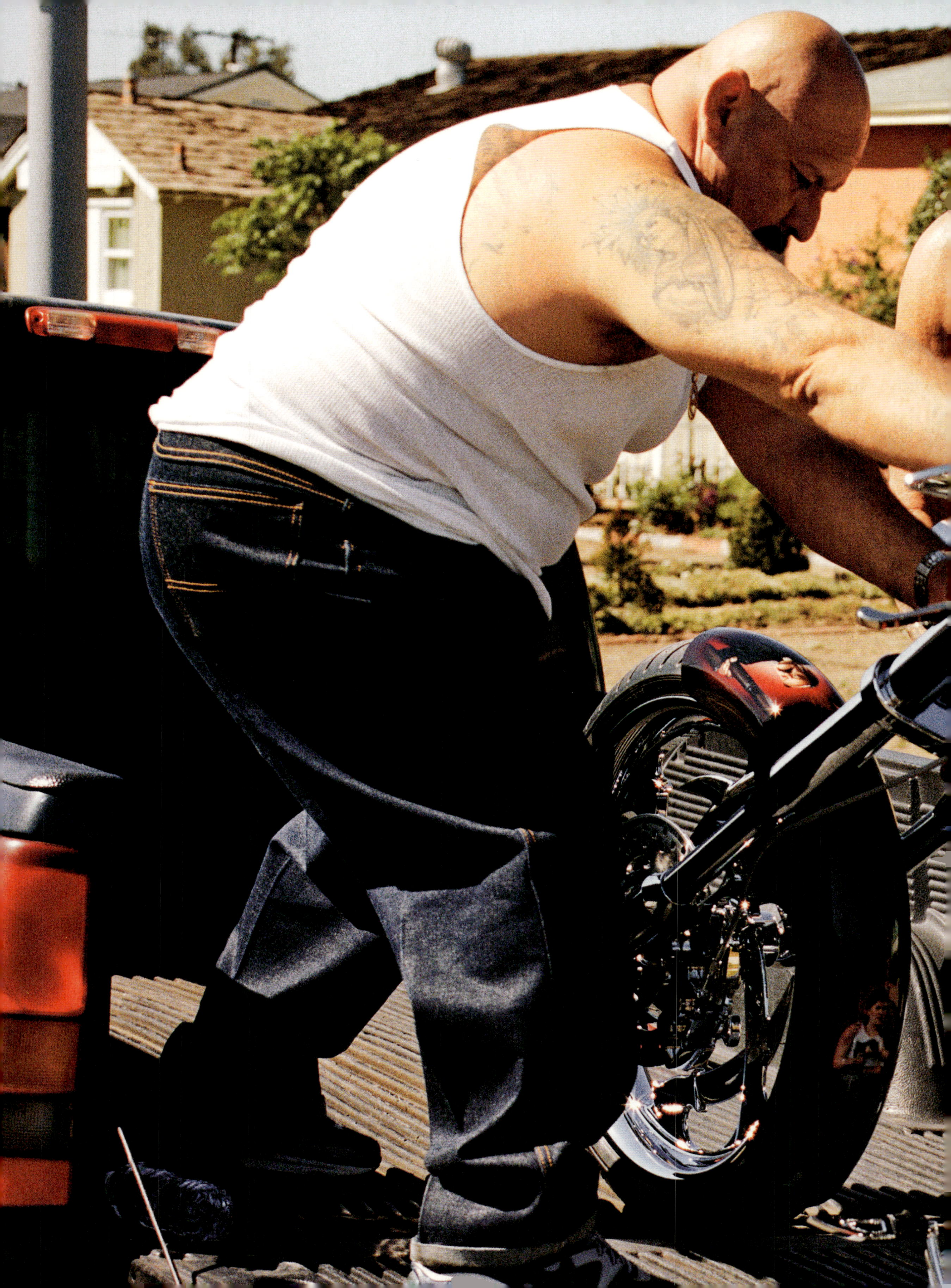

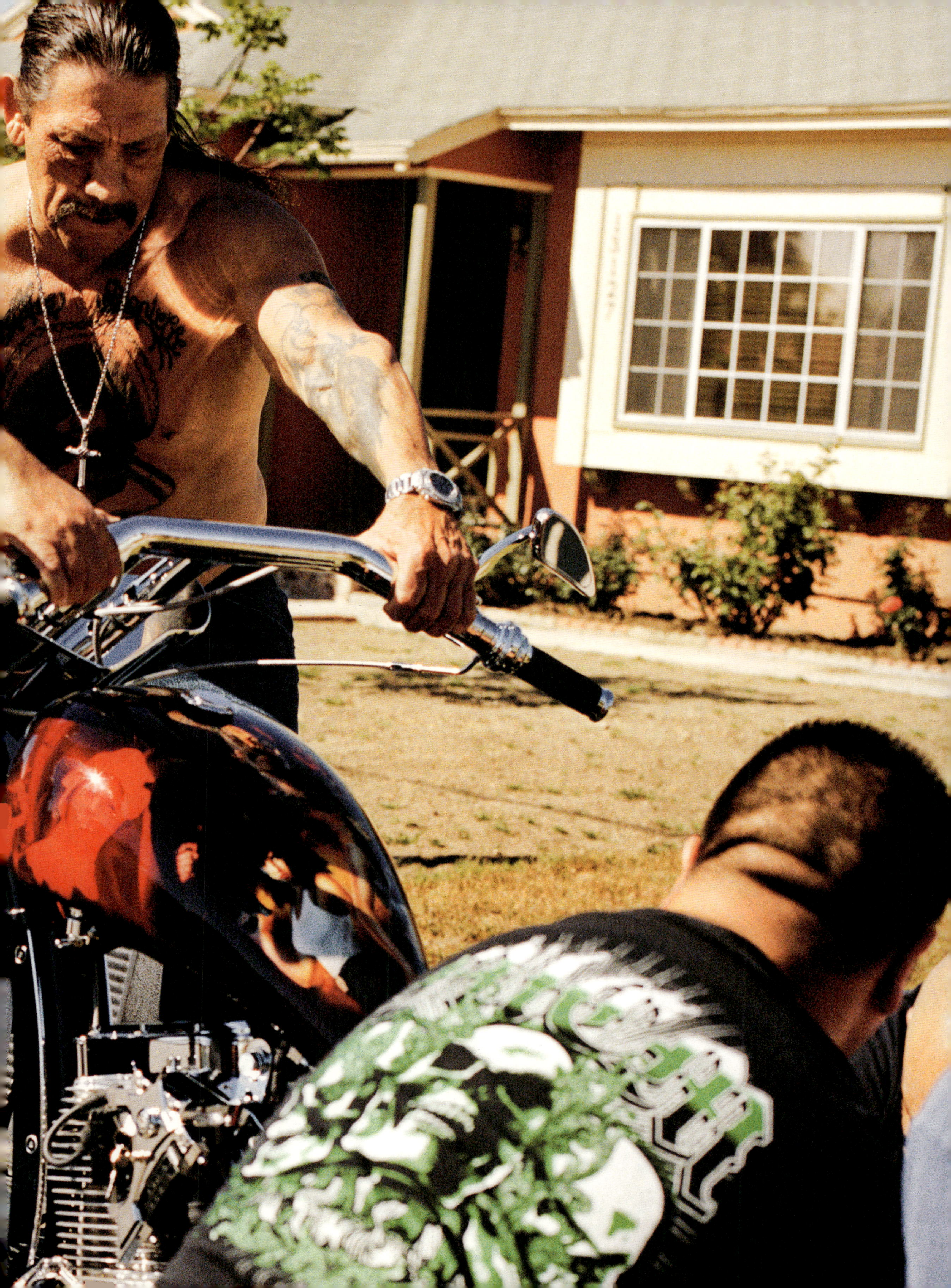

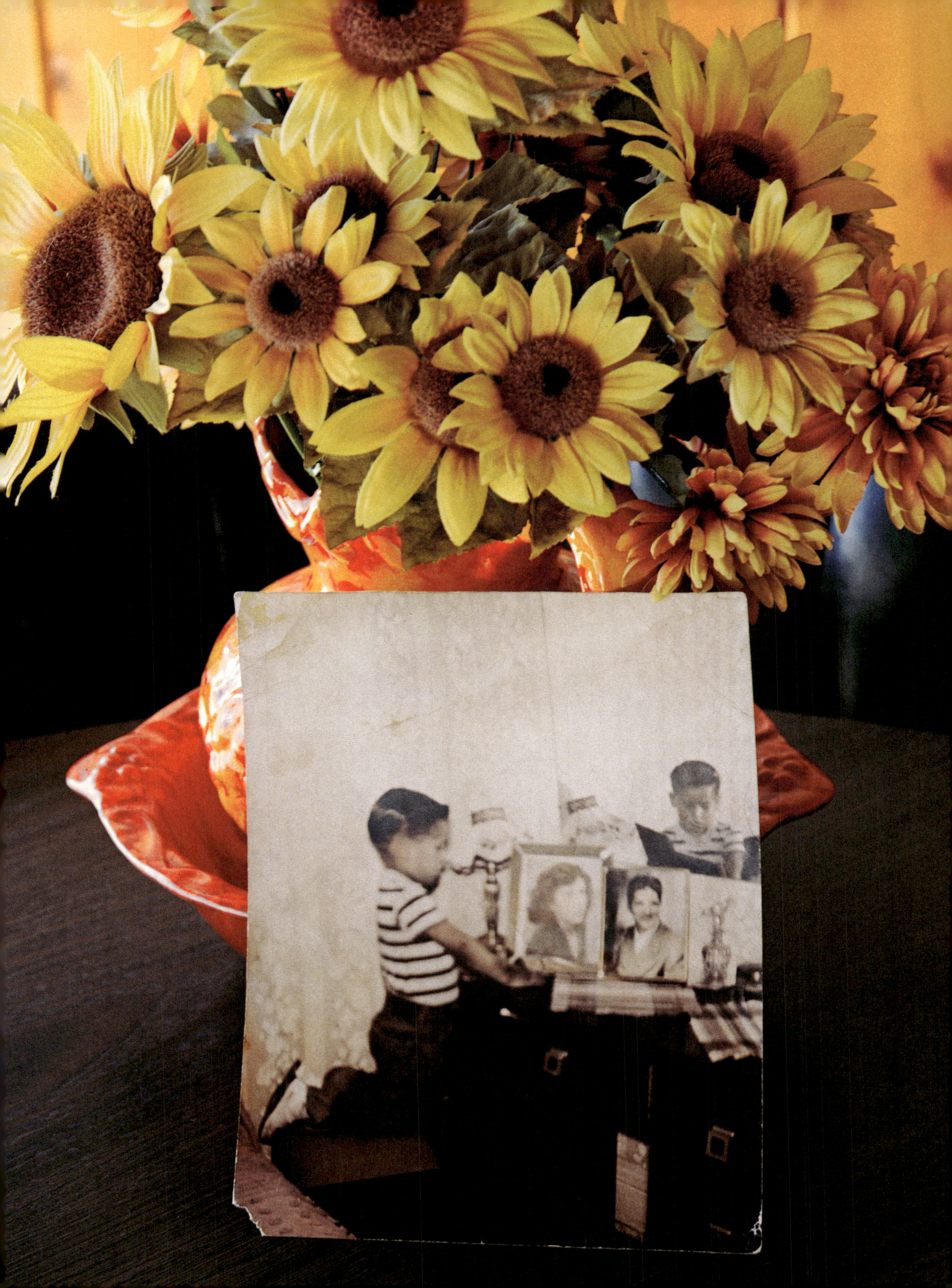

When Hollywood is looking for someone to play the toughest convict alive, there's one person they always call first—Danny Trejo. Danny has bludgeoned his nasty way through some 200 films—from *Con Air* to *Heat* to *Machete*. There's a reason why casting agents view Danny as the perfect convict. He has actually been one in his real life. Trejo spent years in California's roughest prisons before he straightened out his life and became a mentor to countless kids in peril. Here is the story of how Danny Trejo went from a total badass to a local hero.

"I grew up in two different worlds in Pacoima, California. At first I lived a Shirley Temple life with my grandmother and eight girl cousins. Then I lived with my dad and his parents in a John Wayne world surrounded by his five brothers. I went from 'we love kitties' to 'let's kick some ass.' I was 9 when my dad's 18-year-old younger brother came back from serving as a paratrooper, and that's when I started getting in trouble. Uncle Gilbert was my hero. He was a charismatic rebel, and the kind of guy who says, 'There must be a better way to make a living than working.' While my dad and his other brothers worked hard every day as laborers, Gilbert got me smoking weed. I was 12 years old when I first shot up heroin with him. In school I was put in a special class called 'social adjustment' with five other problem kids. Back then, there was no medication or training to deal with people like me, so we were just known as bad kids. I spent my days using and getting loaded on whiskey and 7Up in the park with my uncle. Those other kids ended up either dead or in the penitentiary.

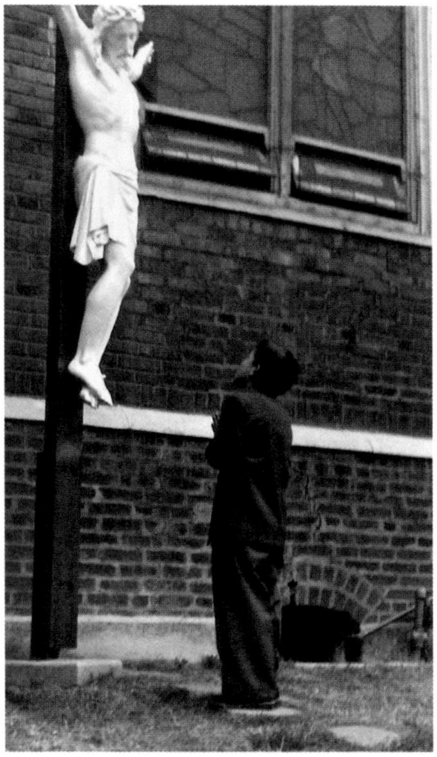

I committed my first armed robbery when I was 14. Once you start using heroin, you have to stay high, or you start getting sick. I needed to pay for my drugs, so I got a gun from a guy in the neighborhood and tried to rob a local market. However, when I pulled out the gun for my 'stick up,' the gun fell apart, and the lady behind the counter started throwing everything on the shelf at me. Still, I was on my way. I was arrested for drugs when I was 16 and again at 18.

My uncle was arrested for armed robbery, but I always got arrested (five times) for drugs. In 1965, I sold four ounces of pure sugar to a federal agent and got sentenced to 6 to 10 years in San Quentin. I was 20 years old when I first went in, but I got smart fast. What I learned early on is that prison is probably the only place on earth where you're either the predator or the prey. You decide. If you enter with fear, you better turn that fear into anger turned outward fast, or you won't make it. It's hard to bluff in prison. You have to be as tough as the toughest guy you are in with. I was a good boxer, and I won the lightweight and welterweight championships. But I kept on getting high on drugs and alcohol, and after I got involved in some riots, I was sent to Folsom and then Soledad prison, where I came close to losing my life. It was the Mexican holiday, Cinco de Mayo, and everybody was drunk as hell. We had a baseball game that day, and one of the free people (someone from outside the prison) got hit during the game and a riot started. I was accused of throwing a rock that injured a guard, causing blood, and when you are convicted of injuring a free person or guard, that can be a death penalty offense. I was immediately sent to the hole.

It was when I was in solitary that I started to change my life. I really thought I was going to the gas chamber, so I made a deal with God that whatever time I had left on earth I would dedicate to helping other people. I stopped drinking and I stopped drugs, cold turkey. Everything you've heard about how horrible it is to kick heroin is true. You have the shakes, every muscle in your body screams and you are blowing through all of your orifices. But I just sat down and got through it. The free person didn't press charges, and the guard said I didn't throw the rock, so four months later I was let out of the hole, and I joined AA and started an NA program. I also offered protection to other inmates. Family members sent me money to look out for their loved ones in prison, or guys paid me some money to keep them from being raped. Some might call this extortion. But when you are known as a predator, as I was, then people won't mess with you. I was a deep predator and I protected people, and they thanked me for it.

When I had served my time, I went up to the patrol board. They looked at my record and told me they expected to see me again soon, probably with a life sentence hanging over my head. But I felt differently. As soon as I got out, a buddy got me involved with a sponsor. I joined a 12-step program and started to find my way. I discovered that trying to play games doesn't work in the real world. It was time to be honest, open-minded and willing to try. I got out in 1969, and I have not had a drink or taken a drug since the day I was released from prison. I became a drug counselor, and for 17 years I've been working with kids, trying to help them avoid making the wrong decisions I made.

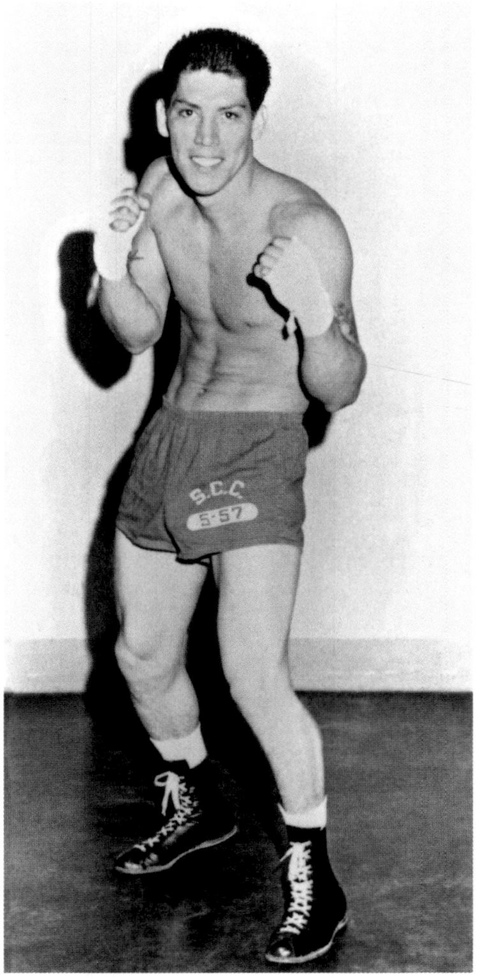


One night in 1985, my life changed. I got a call from a kid who was in trouble, asking me if I could come help support him. There were drugs at the place he was working and he was afraid he was going to slip. His workplace was the movie set of the film *Runaway Train* (with Jon Voight), so I went down there and started hanging out with him. One of the Assistant Directors came up to me and asked if I'd like to be an extra. I asked, 'Extra what?' He asked, 'Can you act like a convict?' The fact that I'd been in every prison in the state flashed through my mind, and I said, 'I'll give it a shot.' I was going to be paid 50 bucks a day to act like a convict! Then when I took my shirt off and they saw the tattoos on my chest, a guy came over and said, 'Hey, you're Danny Trejo. I saw you win the boxing championship at San Quentin.' They asked me if I'd like to make 320 bucks a day to train Eric Roberts how to box. I started boxing with Eric, and he trusted me. Then they asked me to be in the movie. That's how my acting career started. In many of these films I'm billed as 'convict number one.'

The greatest gift I've gotten from being in movies is that when I meet kids in danger, they listen to me. If I were a counselor talking to them about the dangers of drugs, they'd probably nod off. But when they hear I've been in *Spy Kids* and *Machete*, all of a sudden I'm cool and I have their attention. I've had principals come up to me in tears and tell me I've accomplished more in 45 minutes than they have in a year. There's no feeling in the world like going into a market and having a bag boy come up and thank me for talking with him at juvenile hall, telling me how it made a difference in his life.

My message to kids is always the same: education is the key to anything you want to do in life. Even to get a good job in prison, you need a high school diploma. Also, any problem you have, alcohol and drugs are going to make it worse. Many Saturdays I go to juvenile hall and talk to big groups of kids. Twice a month I speak to middle school students, and as a drug counselor I make sure that every kid knows they can call me, day or night, and I will be there for them. When I was filming *Machete II* in Austin, Texas, I went to a school where they were having gang troubles. I told the kids they're on a dead-end street, and I explained where they'll likely end up. But I also gave them understanding. I tell them God doesn't make mistakes, and that they belong in this world. When you show kids you care, that's your start. I do little things, like make them sit by someone of another color, and I make them look at each other and say hi. Then I tell them my stories of drugs and crime and prison.

I was 38 when I got out of prison, and that's when my life really started. I had kids late, and I love them more than anything in the world. I have told them everything about me, so they can't say, 'Daddy, you don't understand.' I *do* understand. My kids are grown, but I make sure I have lunch twice a week with them. I live in the city I grew up in, so it's all family for me. Sure, I wake up at night sometimes, remembering what I had to do to survive. I'm sorry that I chose the wrong mentor when I was young, but I think I turned into a pretty good guy. I wake up with a smile because I'm free. And if I'm known as a badass in movies, that's fine. I'm the real deal."

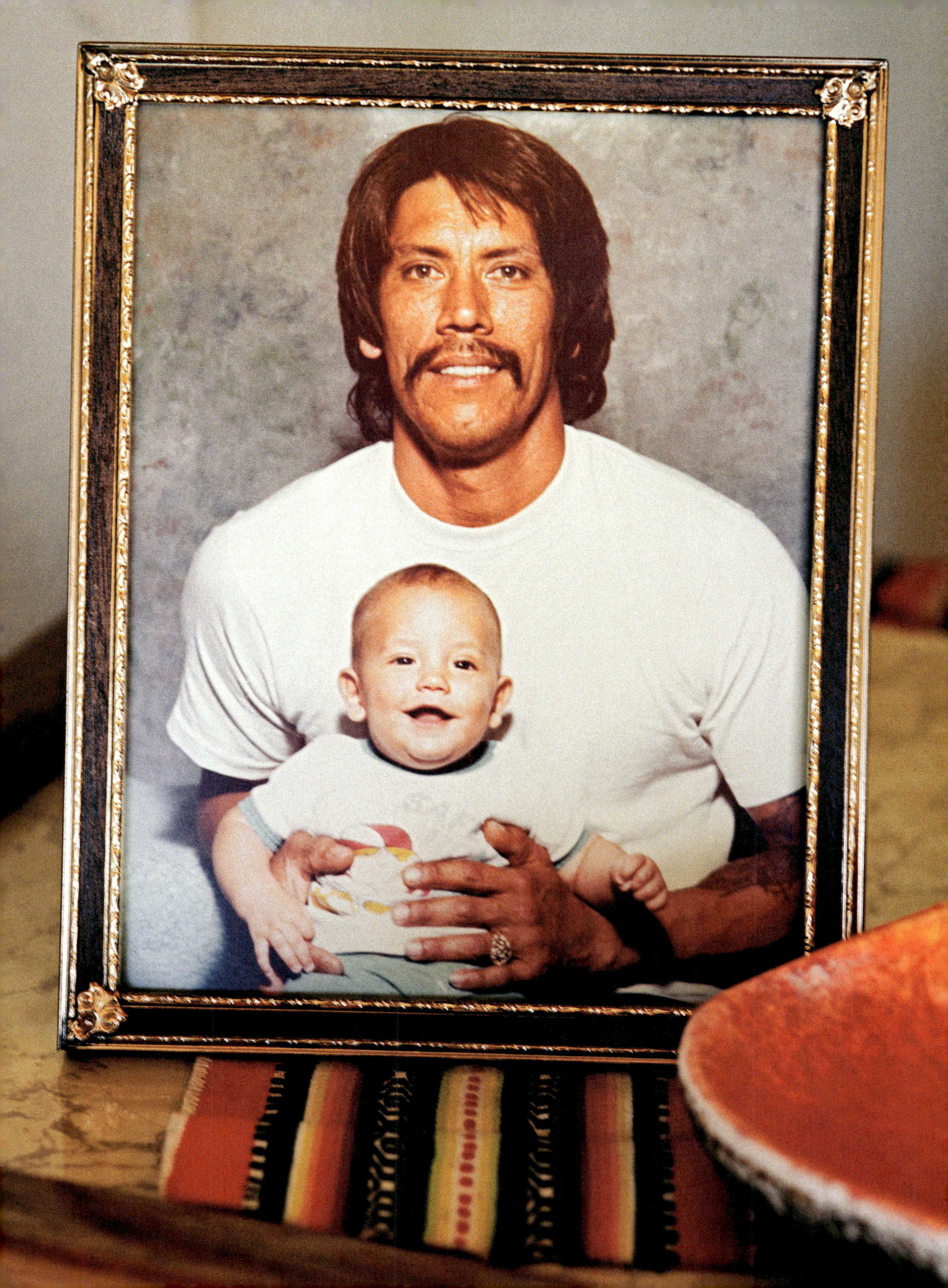

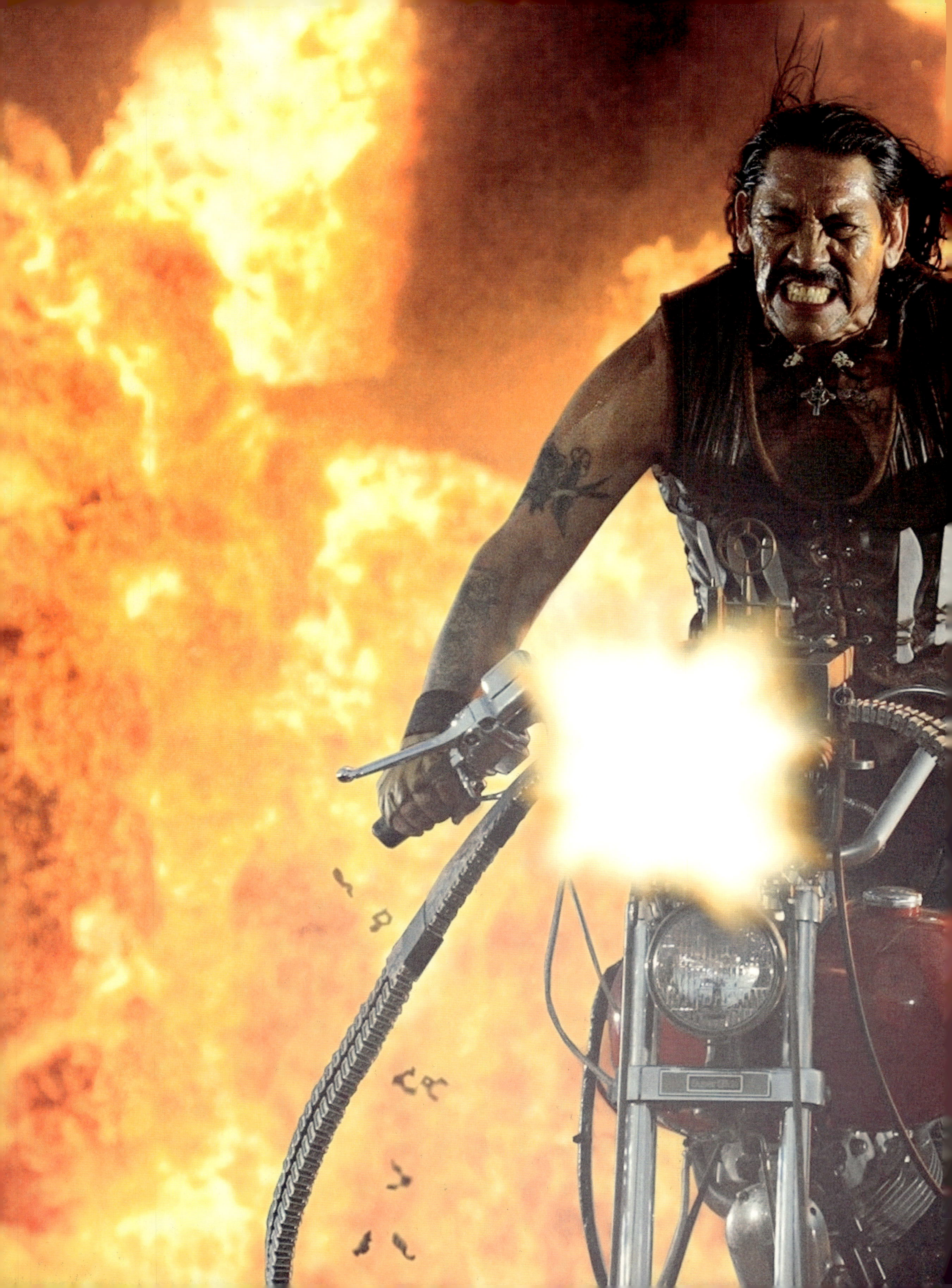

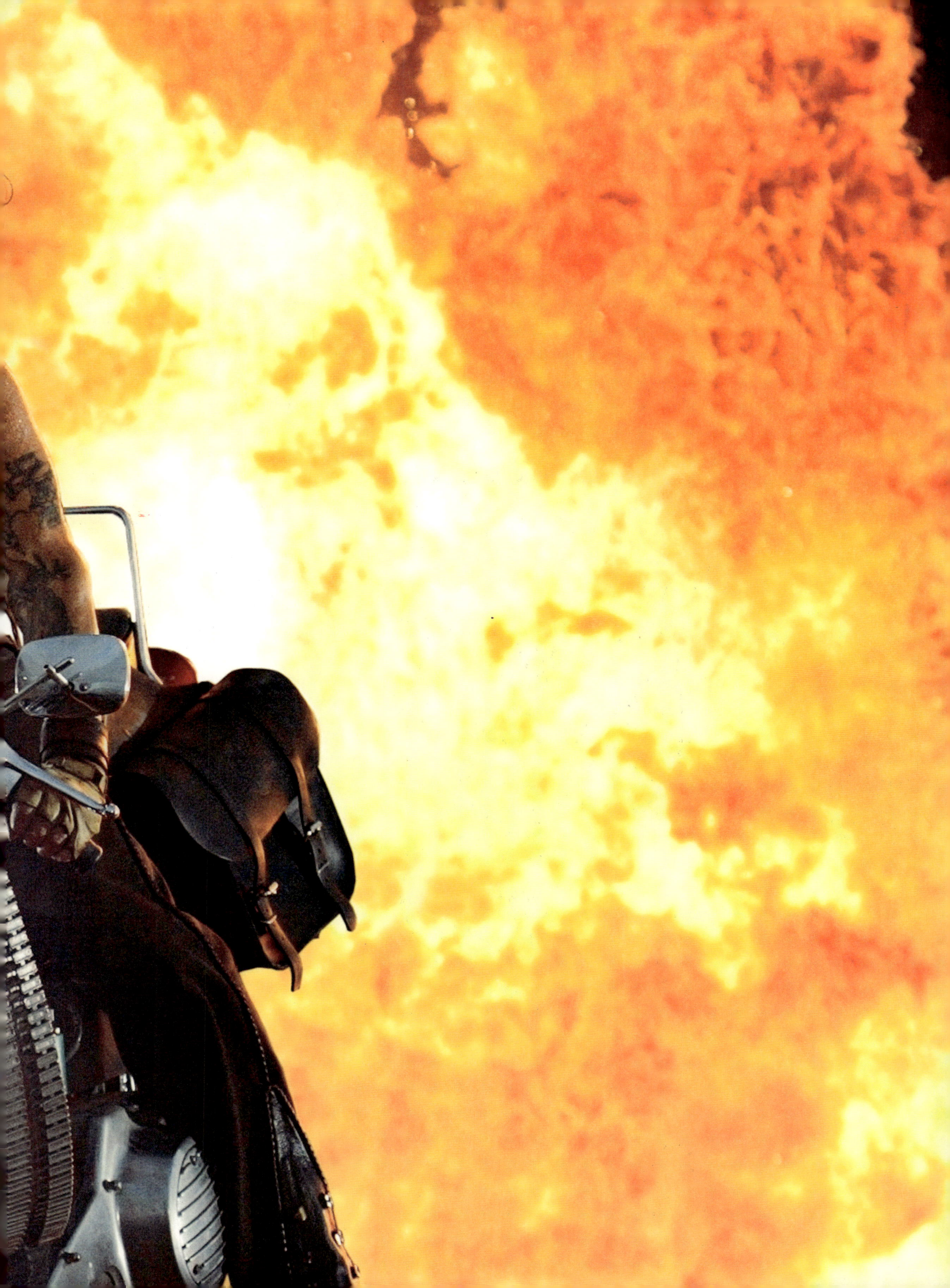

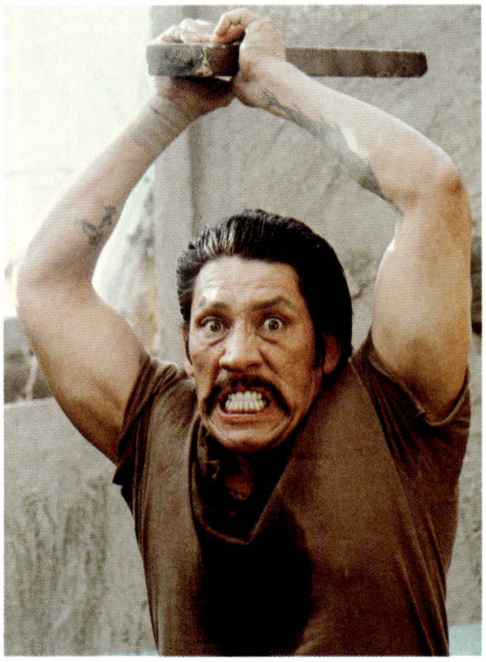
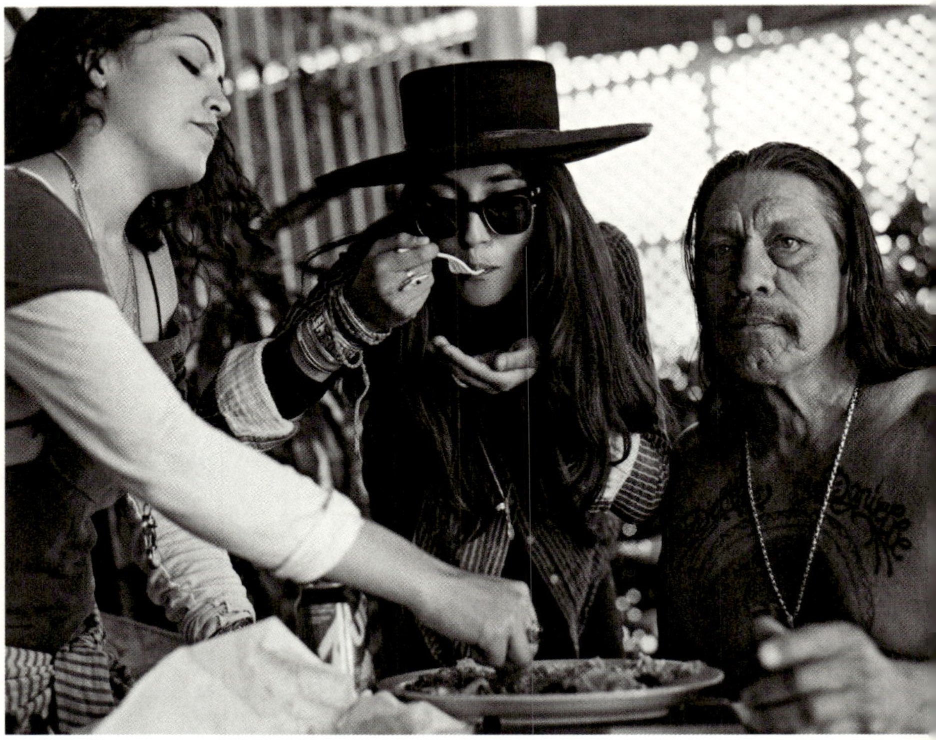
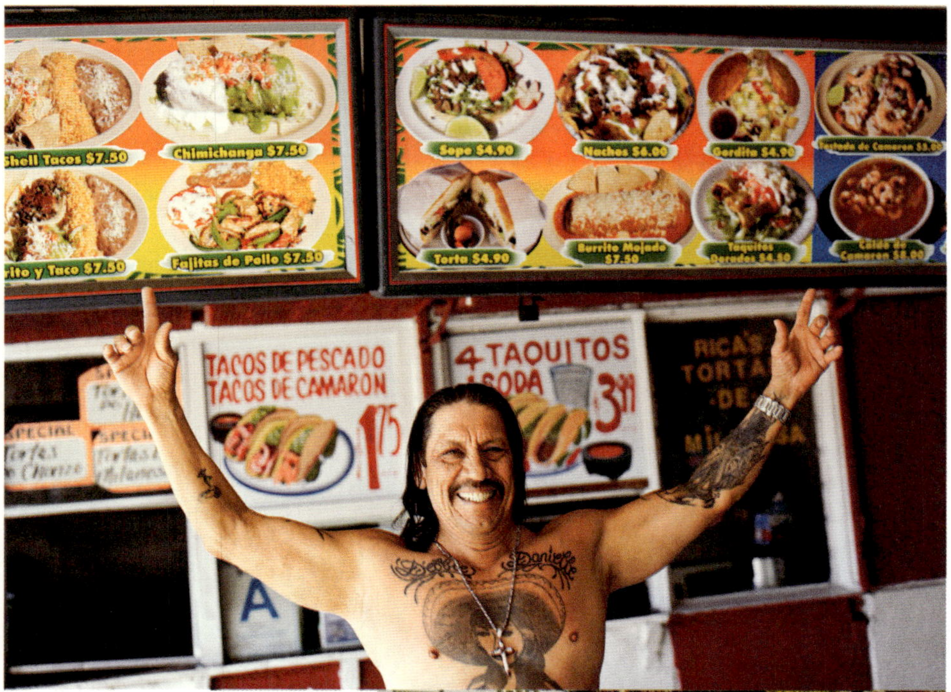
Shell Tacos $7.50
Chimichanga $7.50
Fajitas de Pollo $7.50
Sope $4.90
Nachos $6.00
Gordita $4.90
Torta $4.90
TACOS DE PESCADO
TACOS DE CAMARON
4 TAQUITOS
SODA
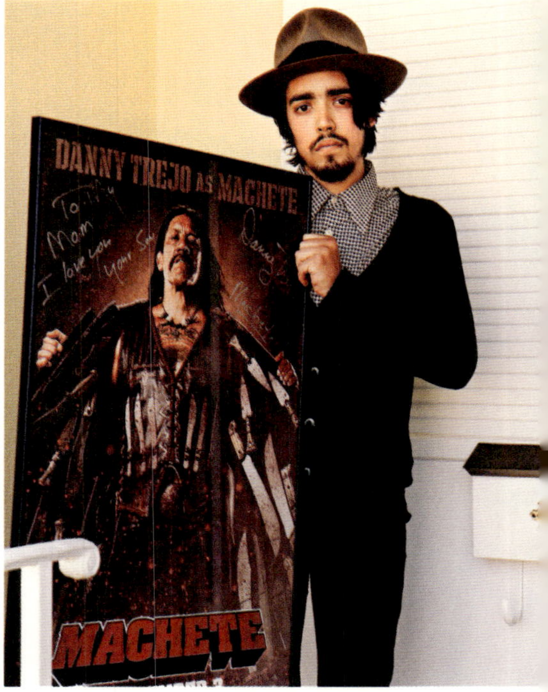
DANNY TREJO AS MACHETE
MACHETE
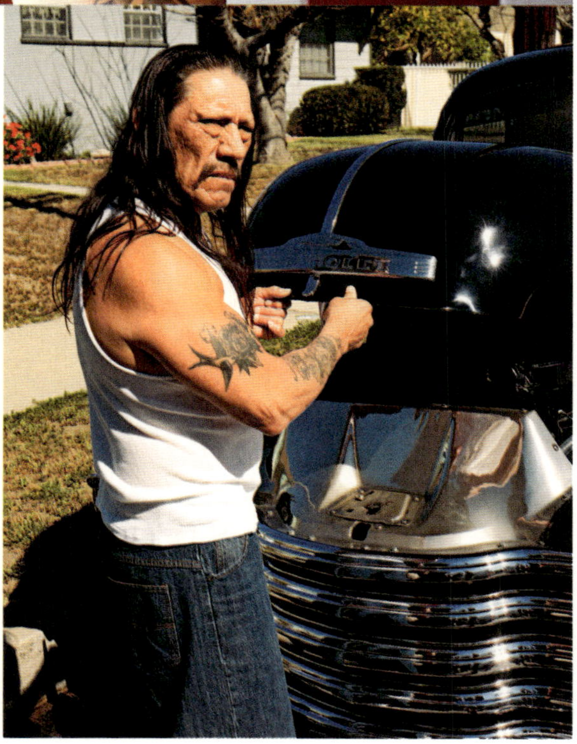
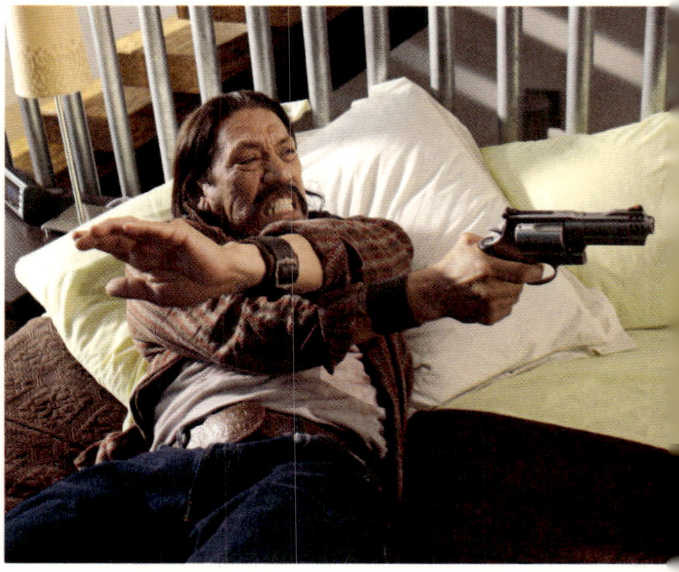

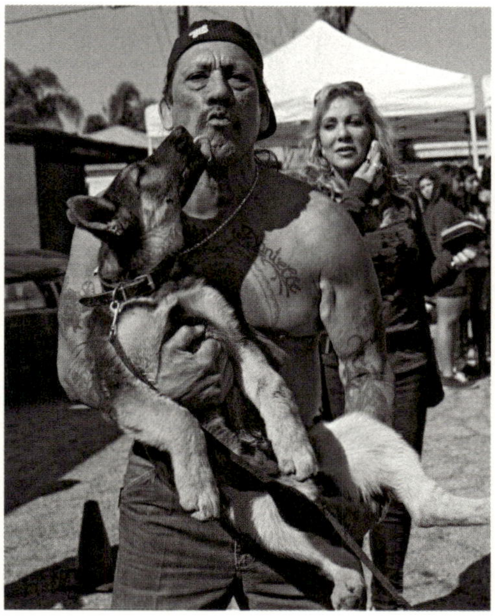
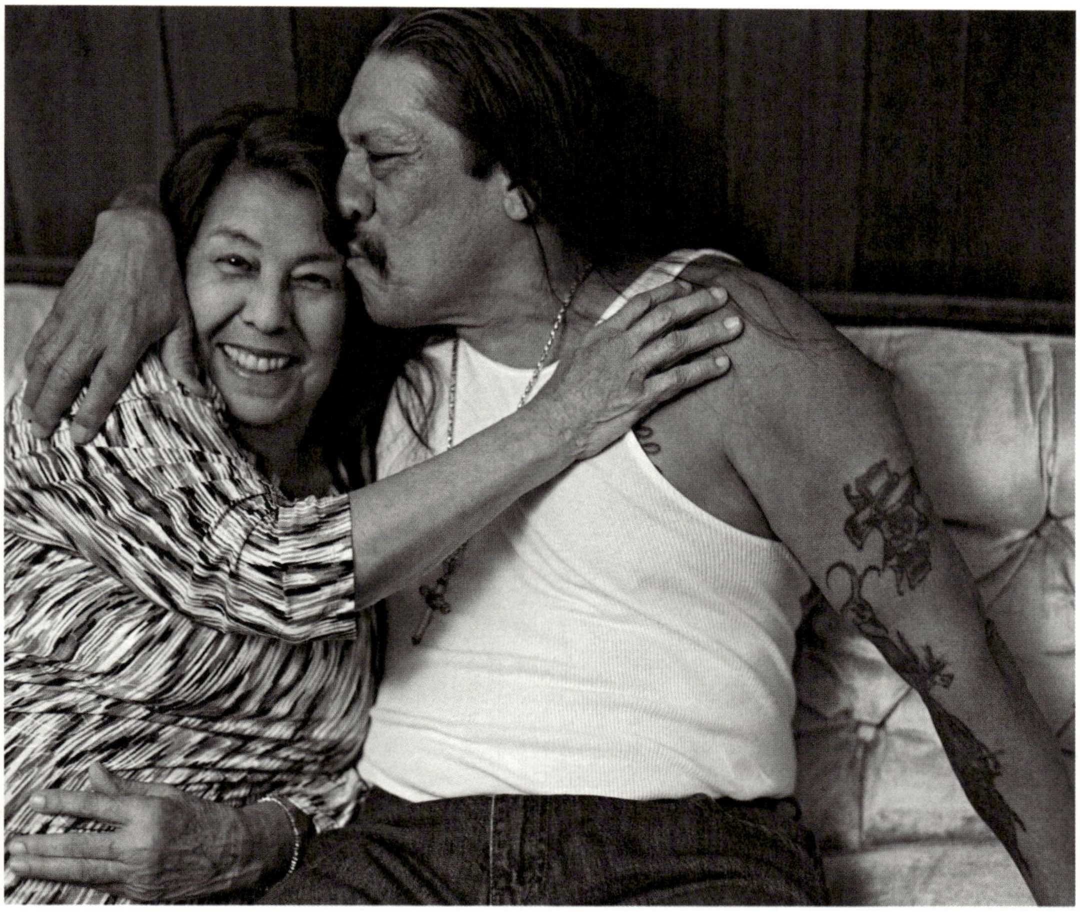
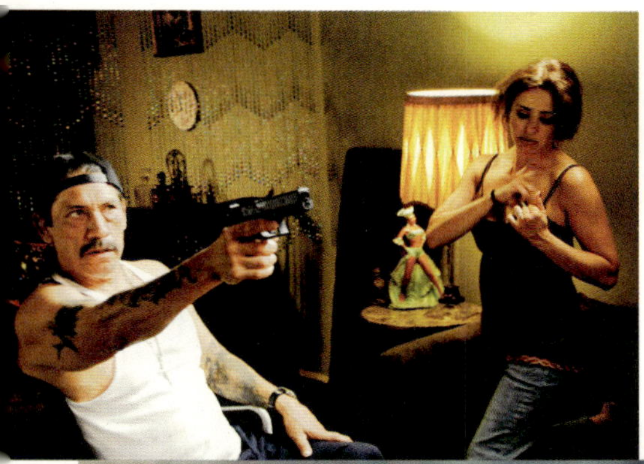
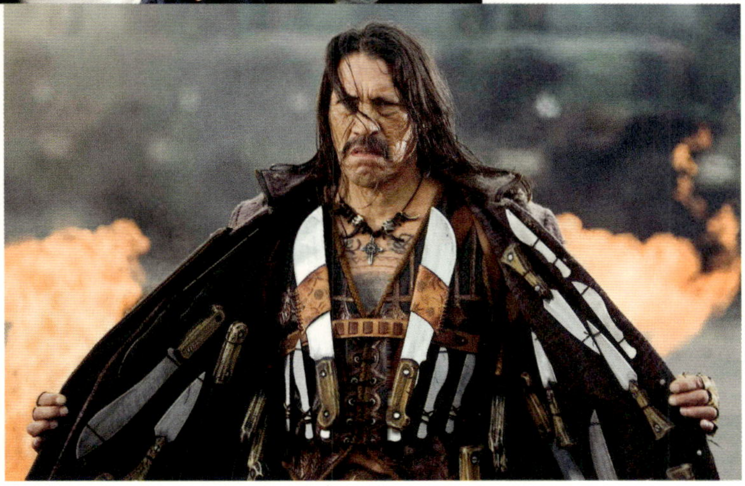
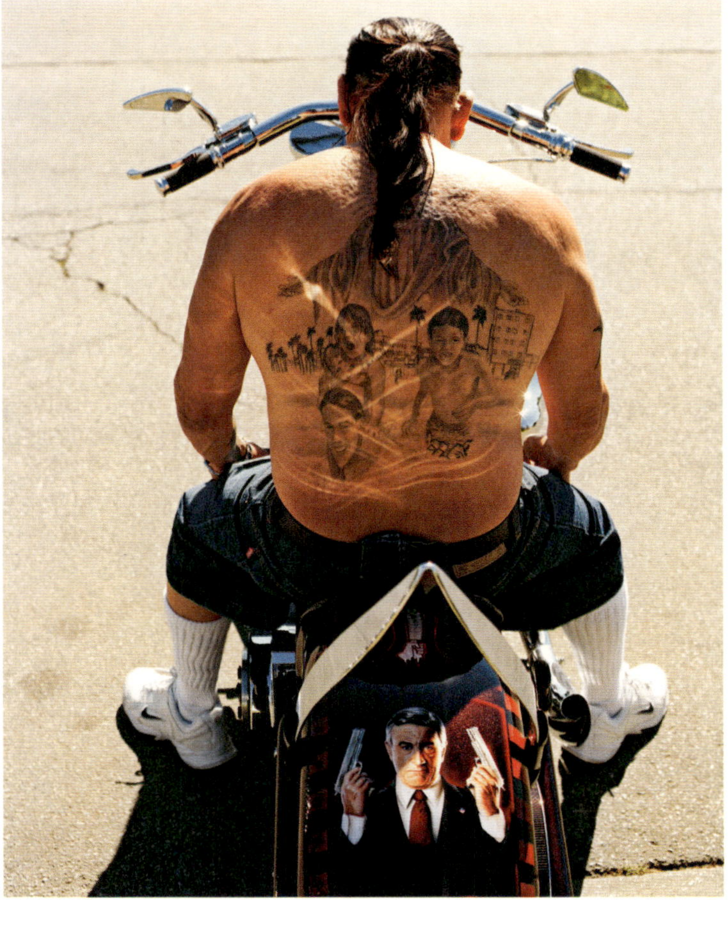
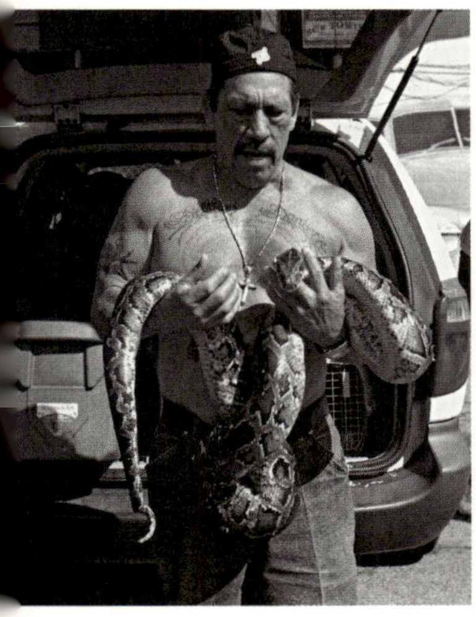
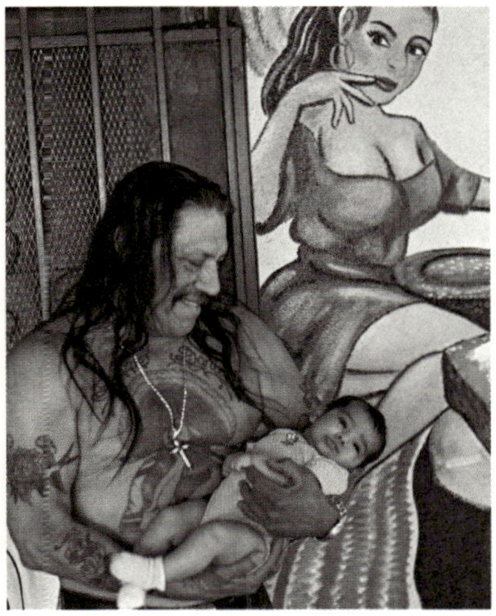

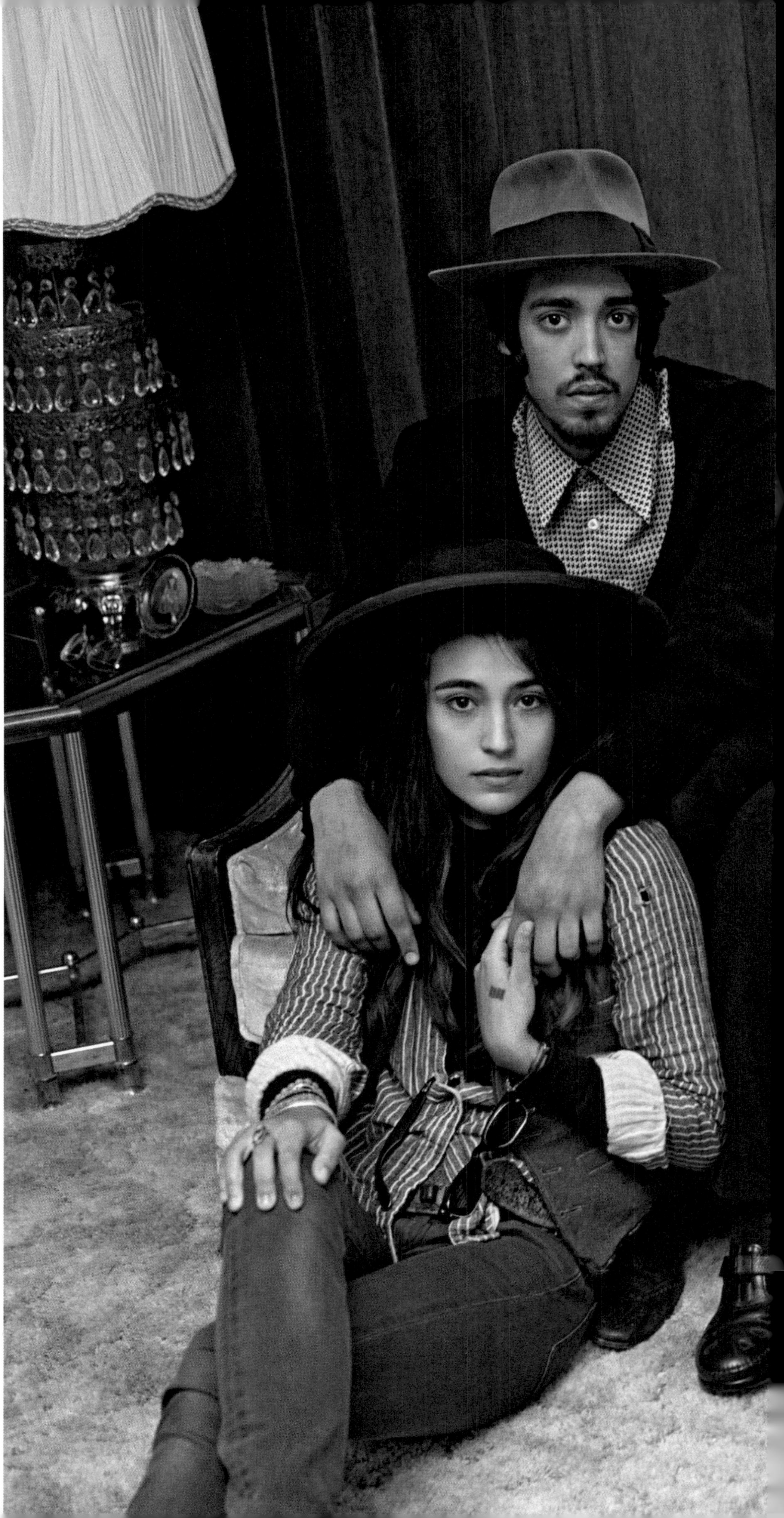

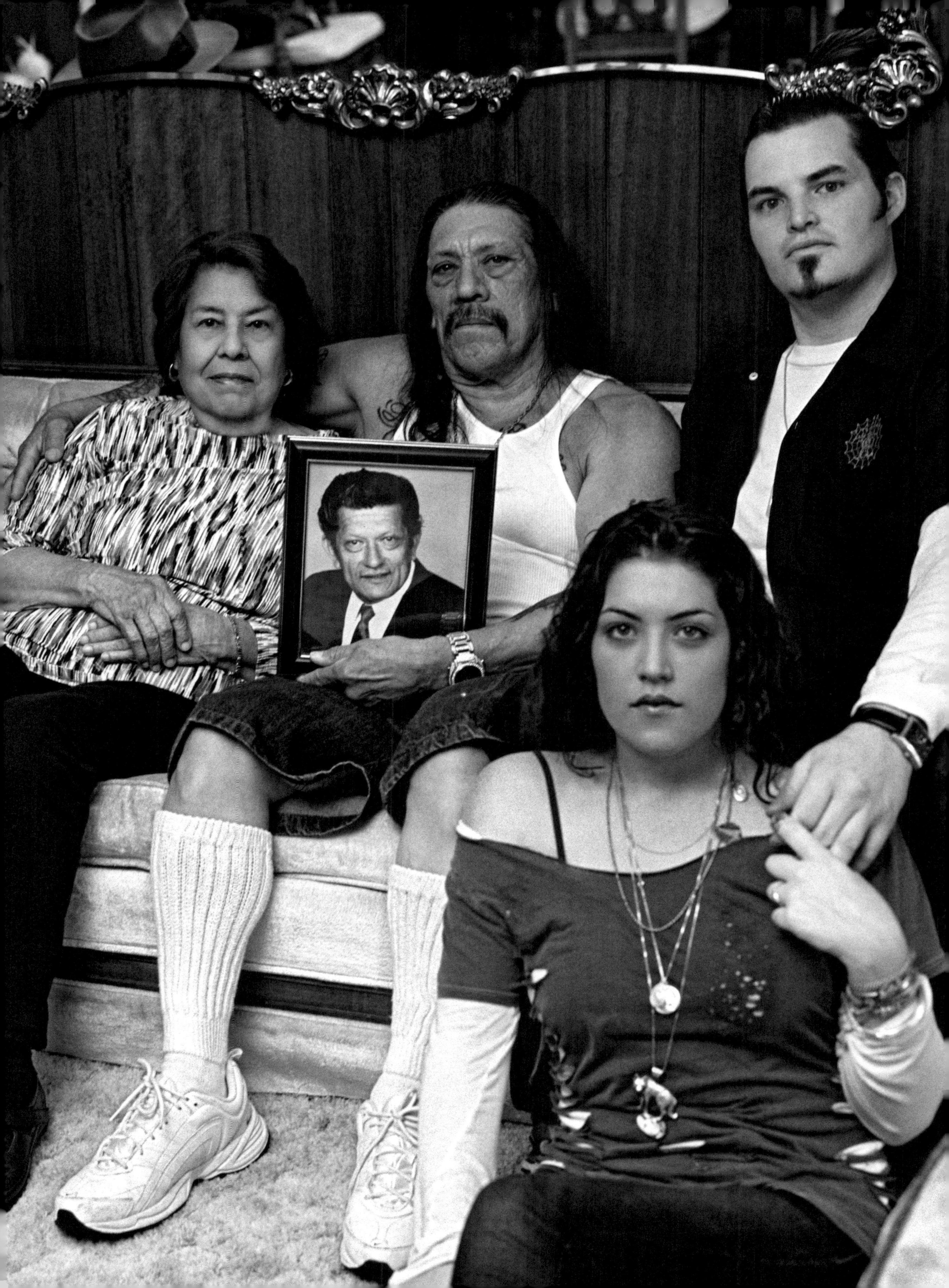

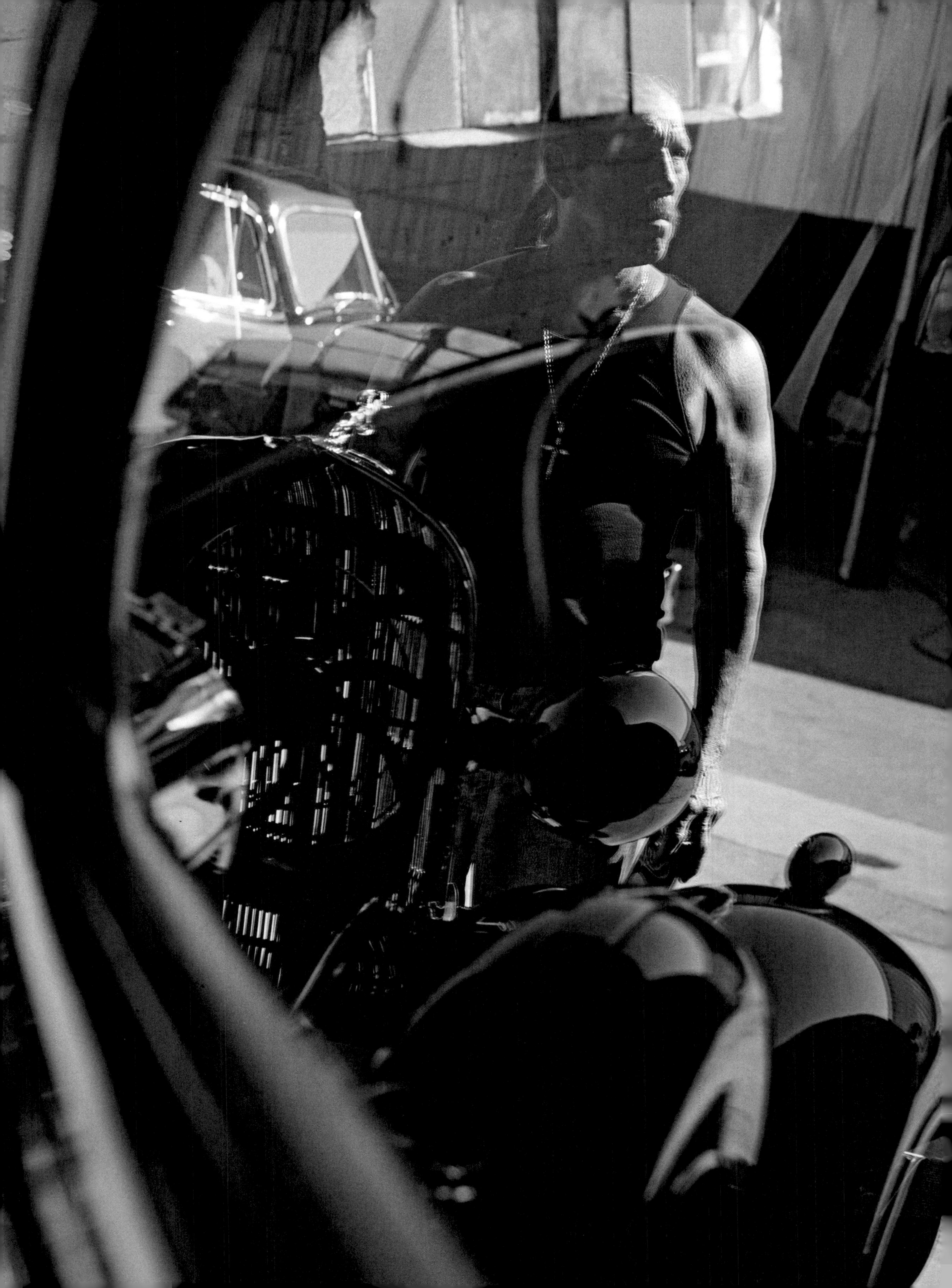

"On the *Desperado* shoot in 1994, Danny asked, 'What's the worst high school they have here in Del Rio? I want to go talk to the students.' That's what impressed me most about Danny. You don't make a mistake by falling down in life—you make a mistake by not getting up and doing something about it, learning from the experience and helping others. That's what Danny does."

—*Robert Rodriguez, director of* Desperado *and* Spy Kids *and* Machete, *all starring Danny Trejo*

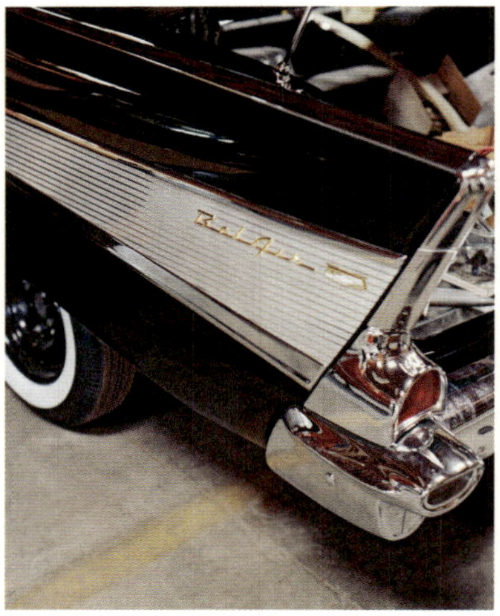

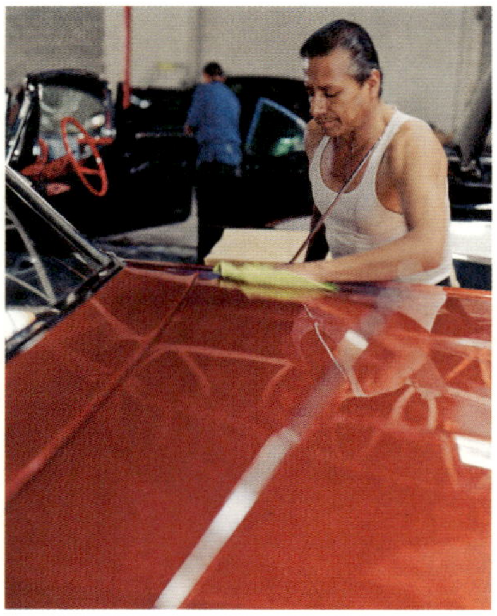

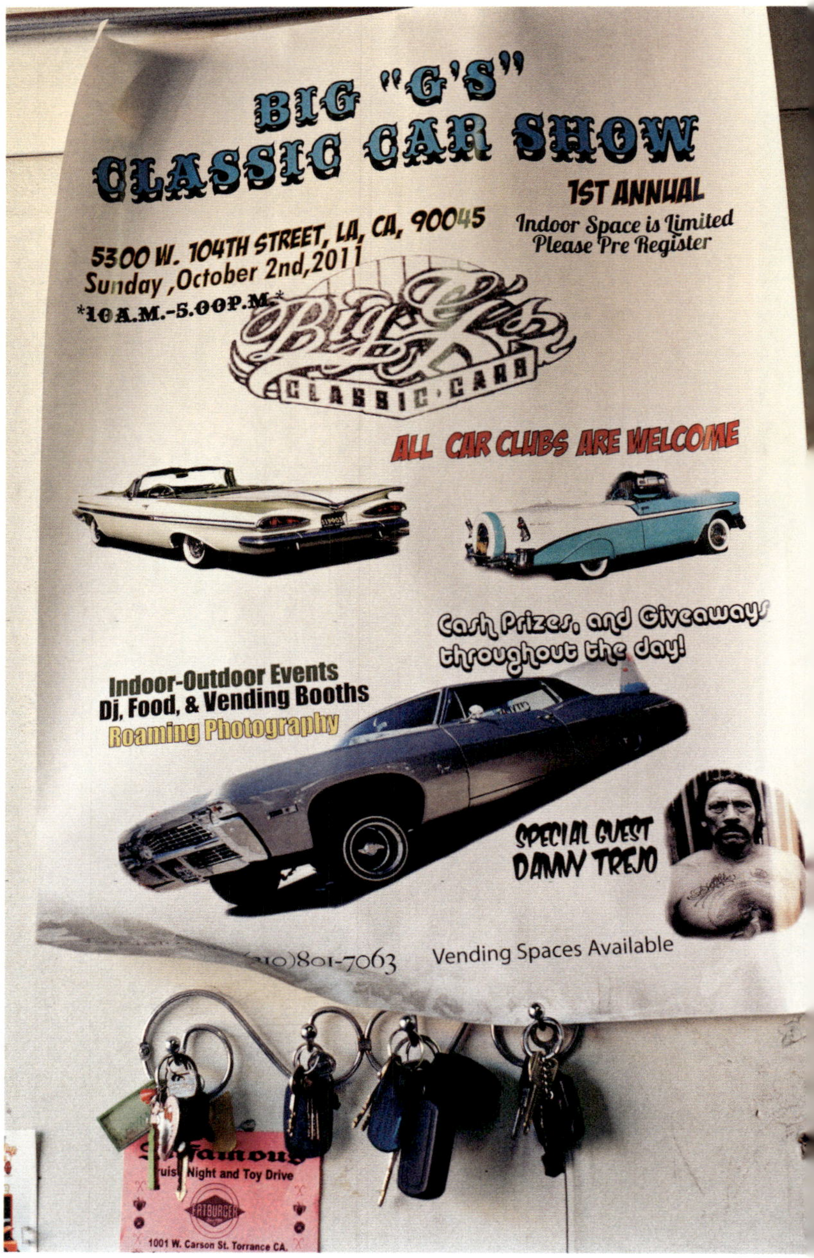
BIG "G'S"
CLASSIC CAR SHOW
1ST ANNUAL
Indoor Space is Limited
Please Pre Register
5300 W. 104TH STREET, LA, CA, 90045
Sunday ,October 2nd,2011
*10A.M.-5.00P.M.*
CLASSIC CARS
ALL CAR CLUBS ARE WELCOME
Cash Prizes, and Giveaways
throughout the day!
Indoor-Outdoor Events
Dj, Food, & Vending Booths
Roaming Photography
SPECIAL GUEST
DANNY TREJO
(310)801-7063
Vending Spaces Available
Cruise Night and Toy Drive
1001 W. Carson St. Torrance CA.

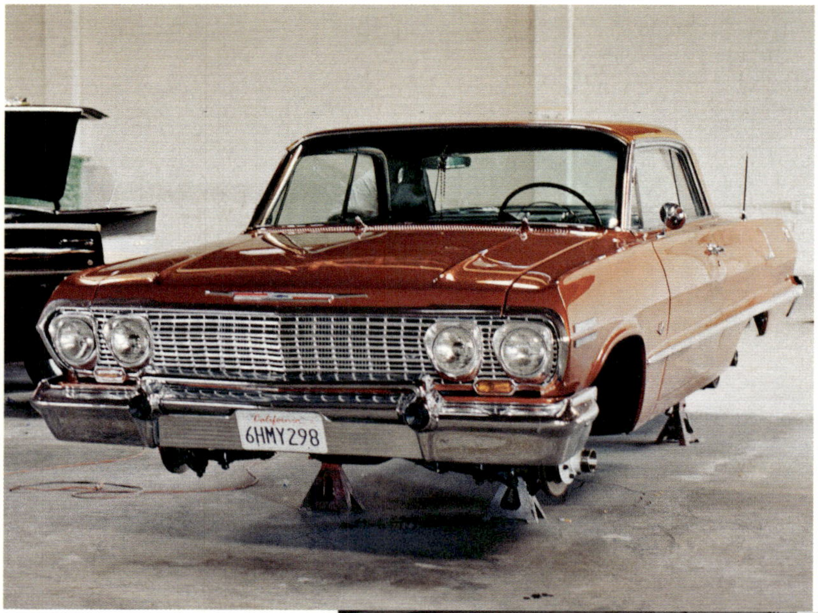
6HMY298

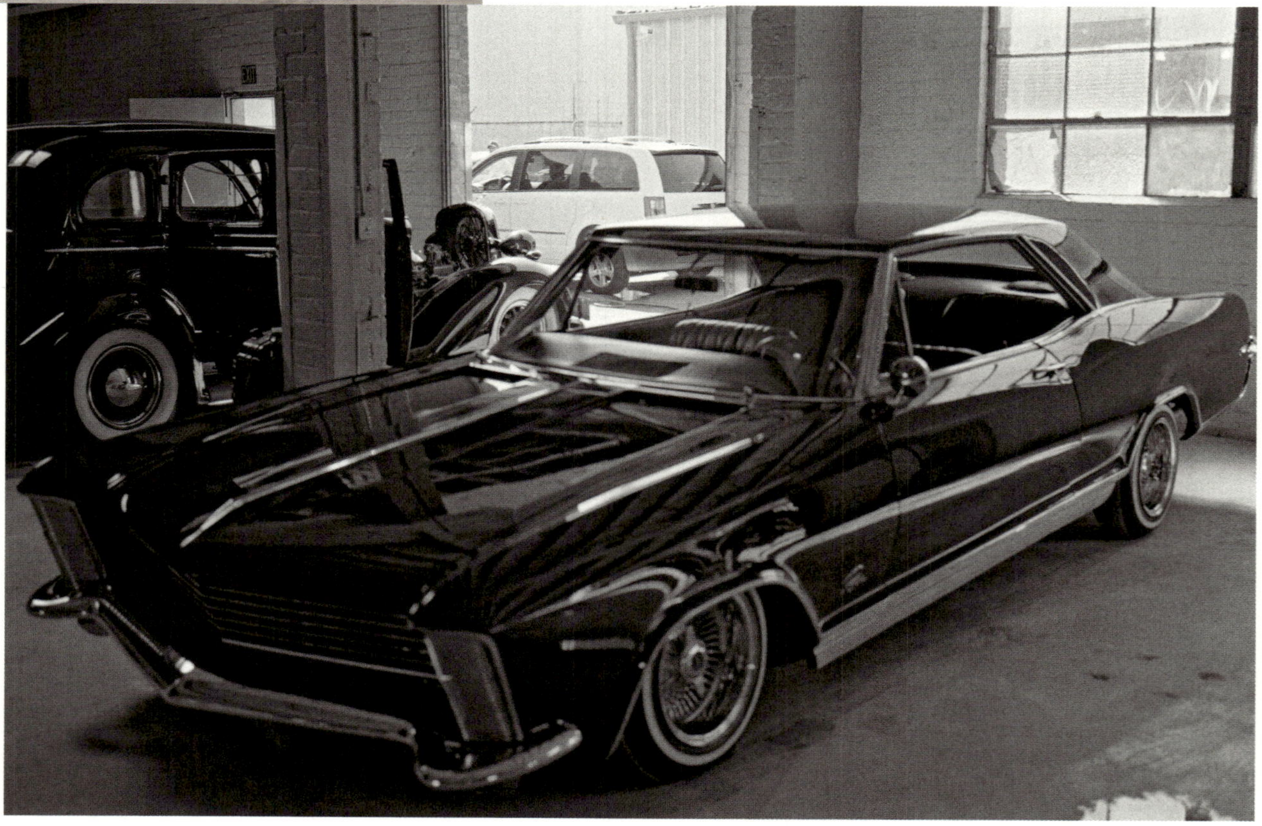

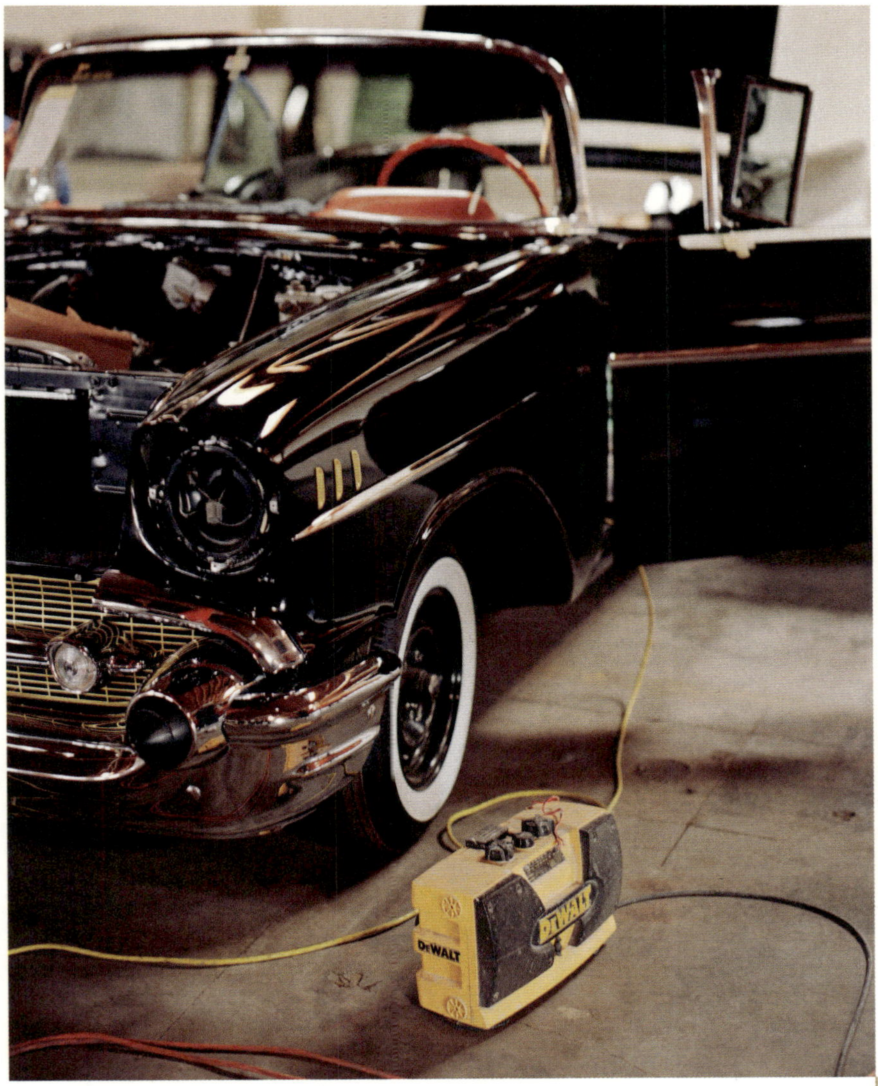
DeWALT
DeWALT

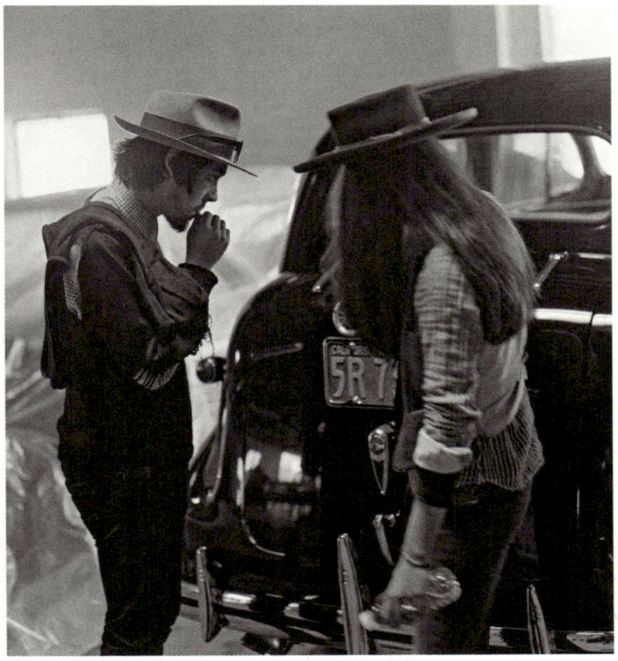

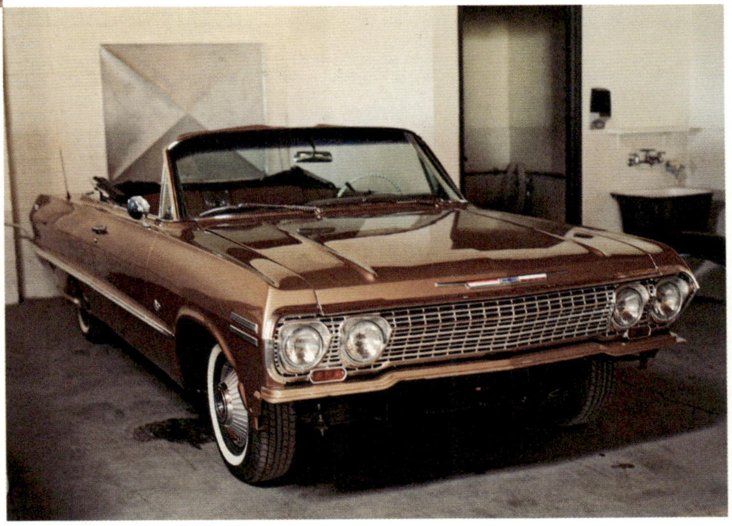

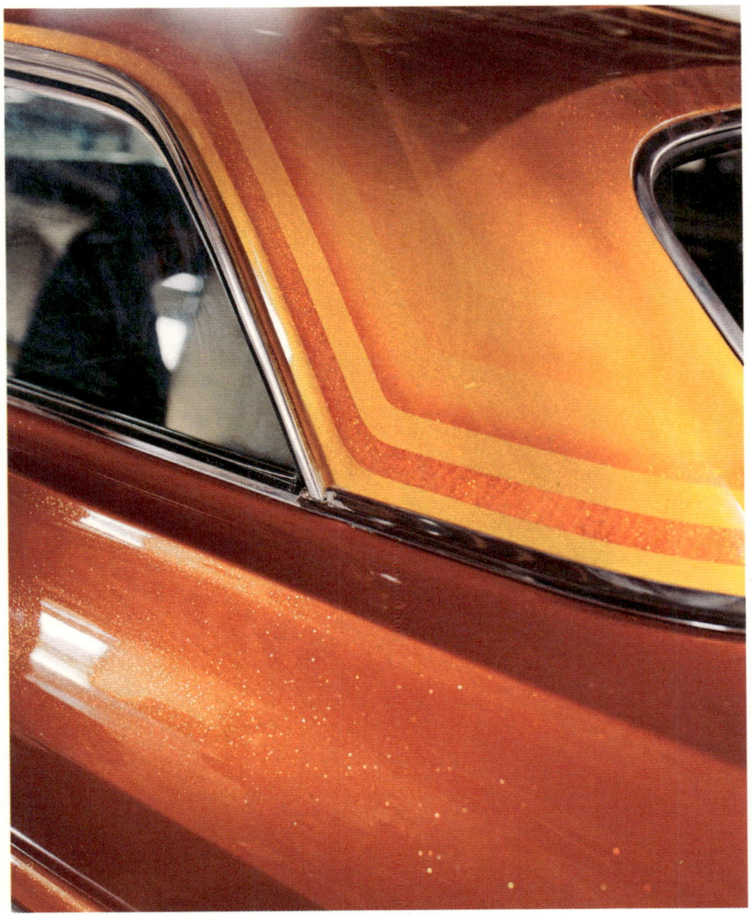

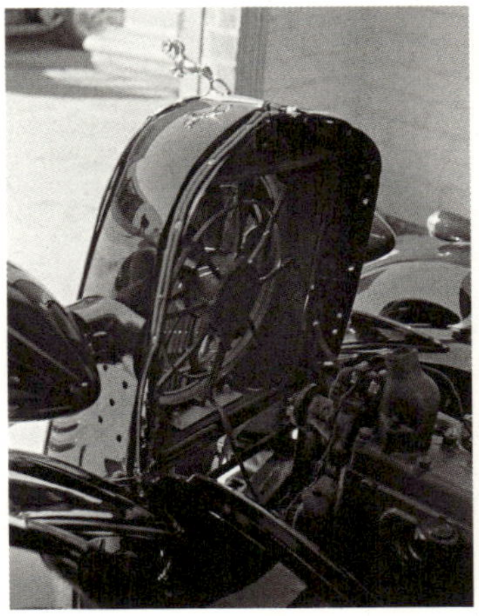

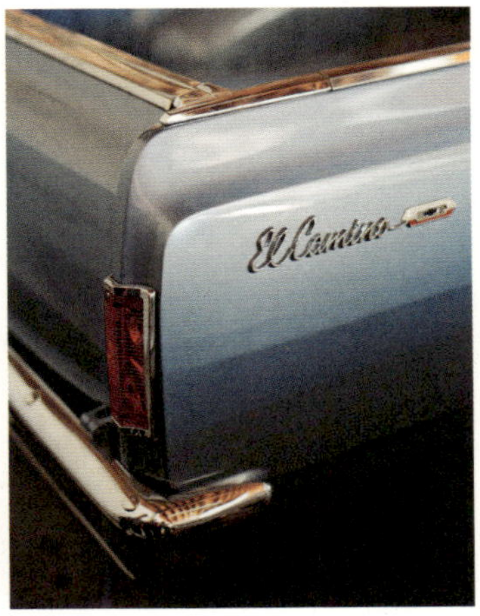
El Camino

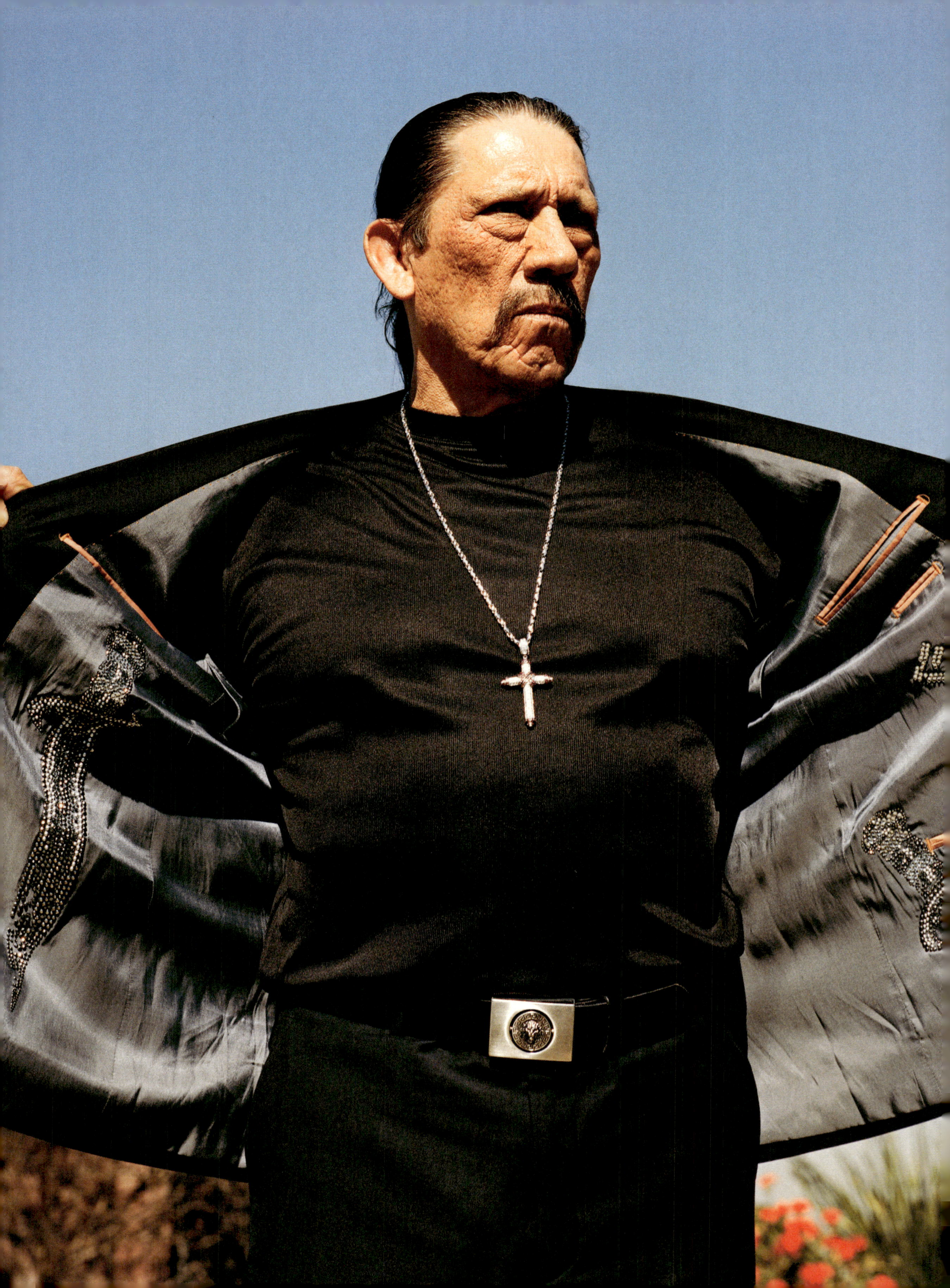

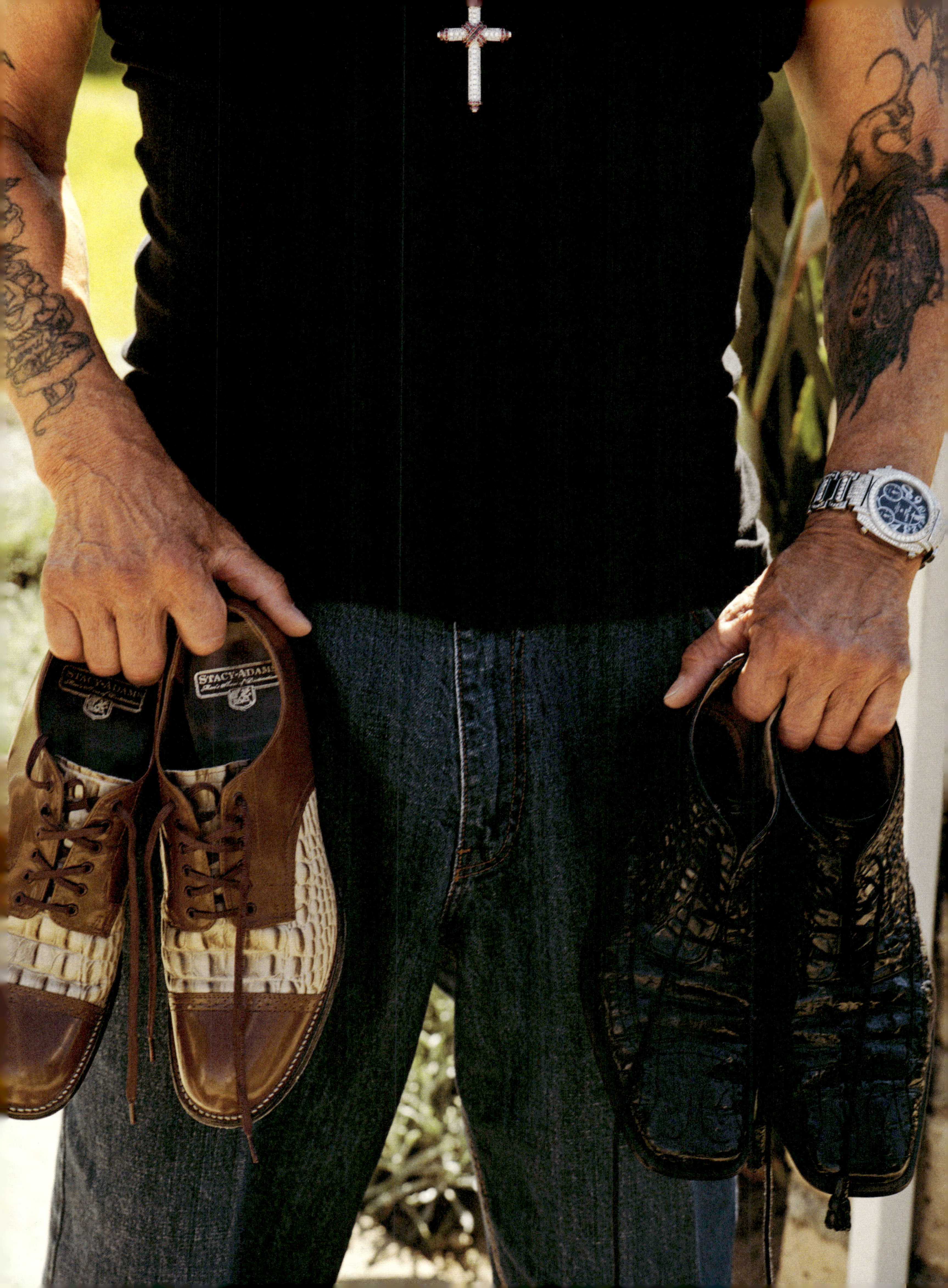

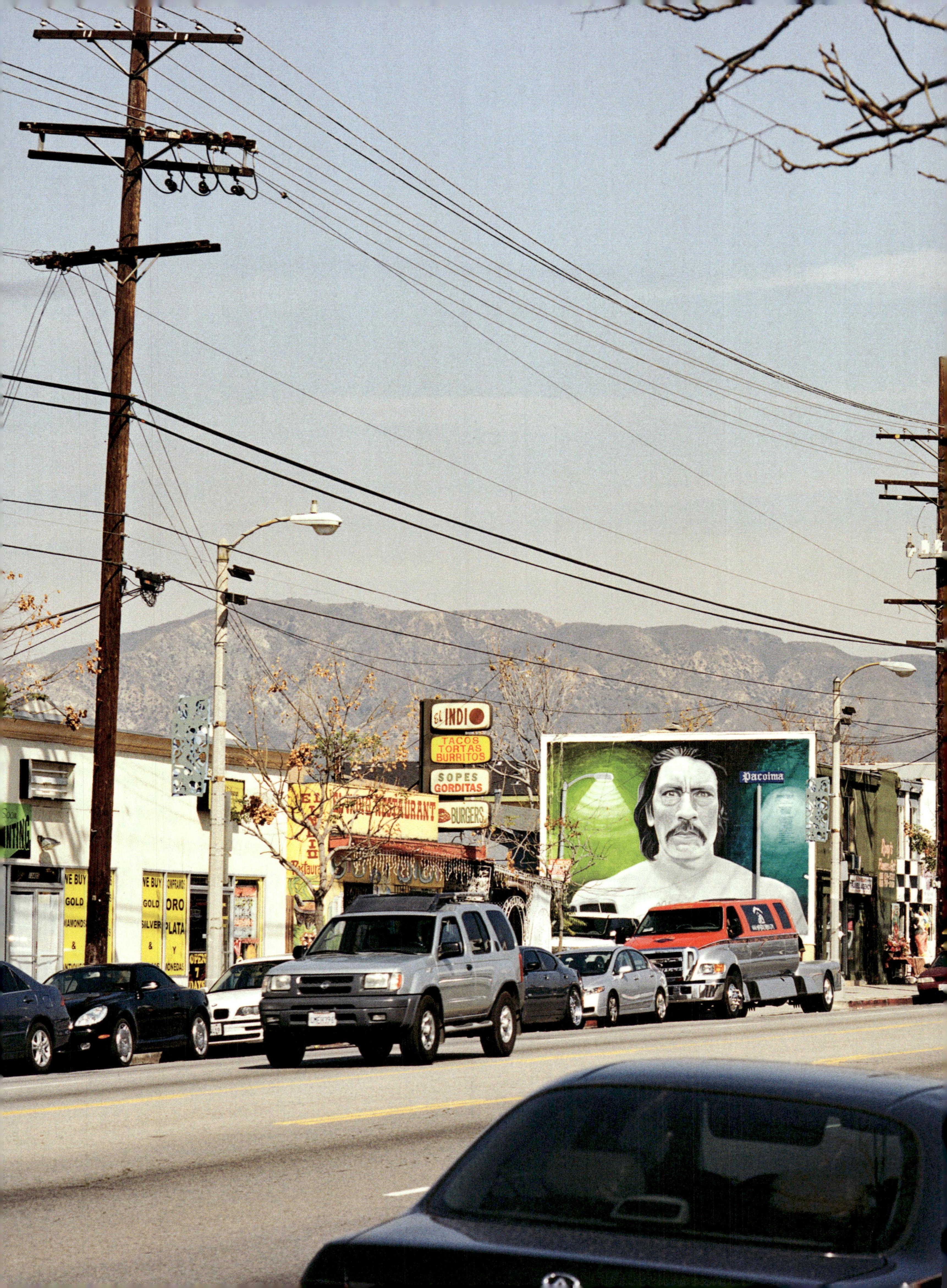
EL INDIO
TACOS
TORTAS
BURRITOS
SOPES
GORDITAS
BURGERS
RESTAURANT
Pacoima
WE BUY
GOLD
ORO
PLATA
Y

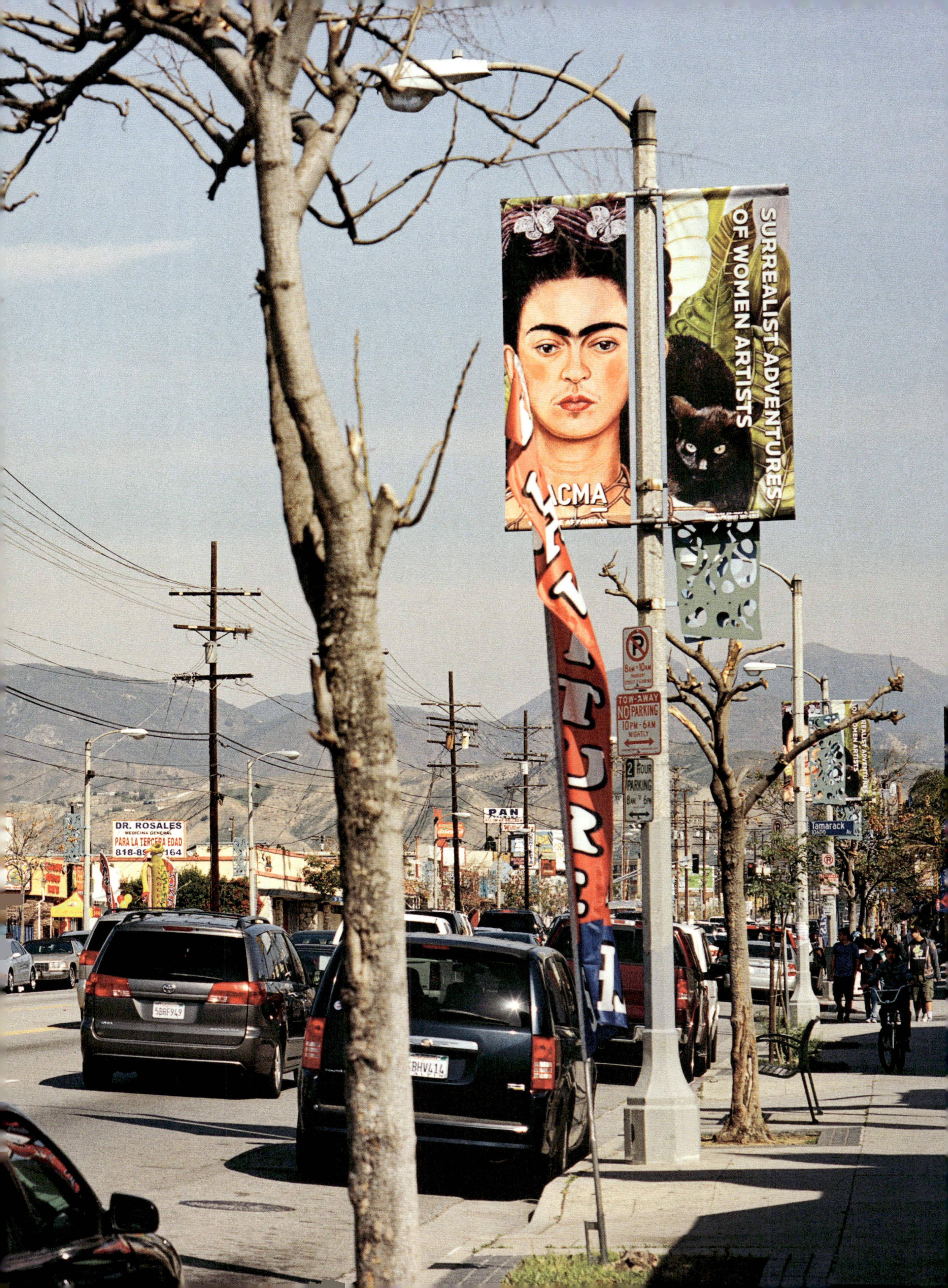
SURREALIST ADVENTURES OF WOMEN ARTISTS
DR. ROSALES
MEDICINA GENERAL
PARA LA TERCERA EDAD
TOW-AWAY
NO PARKING
10PM-6AM
2 HOUR
PARKING
PAN
Tamarack

# A TRUE ACCOUNT OF TALKING TO THE SUN AT FIRE ISLAND

BY FRANK O'HARA

The Sun woke me this morning loud
and clear, saying "Hey! I've been
trying to wake you up for fifteen
minutes. Don't be so rude, you are
only the second poet I've ever chosen
to speak to personally
                                        so why
aren't you more attentive? If I could
burn you through the window I would
to wake you up. I can't hang around
here all day."
                    "Sorry, Sun, I stayed
up late last night talking to Hal."

"When I woke up Mayakovsky he was
a lot more prompt" the Sun said
petulantly. "Most people are up
already waiting to see if I'm going
to put in an appearance."
                                        I tried
to apologize "I missed you yesterday."
"That's better" he said. "I didn't
know you'd come out." "You may be
wondering why I've come so close?"
"Yes" I said beginning to feel hot
wondering if maybe he wasn't burning me
anyway.
            "Frankly I wanted to tell you
I like your poetry. I see a lot
on my rounds and you're okay. You may
not be the greatest thing on earth, but
you're different. Now, I've heard some
say you're crazy, they being excessively
calm themselves to my mind, and other
crazy poets think that you're a boring
reactionary. Not me.
                                Just keep on
like I do and pay no attention. You'll
find that people always will complain
about the atmosphere, either too hot
or too cold too bright or too dark, days
too short or too long.
                                If you don't appear
at all one day they think you're lazy
or dead. Just keep right on, I like it.

And don't worry about your lineage
poetic or natural. The Sun shines on
the jungle, you know, on the tundra
the sea, the ghetto. Wherever you were
I knew it and saw you moving. I was waiting
for you to get to work.

And now that you
are making your own days, so to speak,
even if no one reads you but me
you won't be depressed. Not
everyone can look up, even at me. It
hurts their eyes."
"Oh Sun, I'm so grateful to you!"

"Thanks and remember I'm watching. It's
easier for me to speak to you out
here. I don't have to slide down
between buildings to get your ear.
I know you love Manhattan, but
you ought to look up more often.
And
always embrace things, people earth
sky stars, as I do, freely and with
the appropriate sense of space. That
is your inclination, known in the heavens
and you should follow it to hell, if
necessary, which I doubt.
Maybe we'll
speak again in Africa, of which I too
am specially fond. Go back to sleep now
Frank, and I may leave a tiny poem
in that brain of yours as my farewell."

"Sun, don't go!" I was awake
at last. "No, go I must, they're calling
me."
"Who are they?"
Rising he said "Some
day you'll know. They're calling to you
too." Darkly he rose, and then I slept.

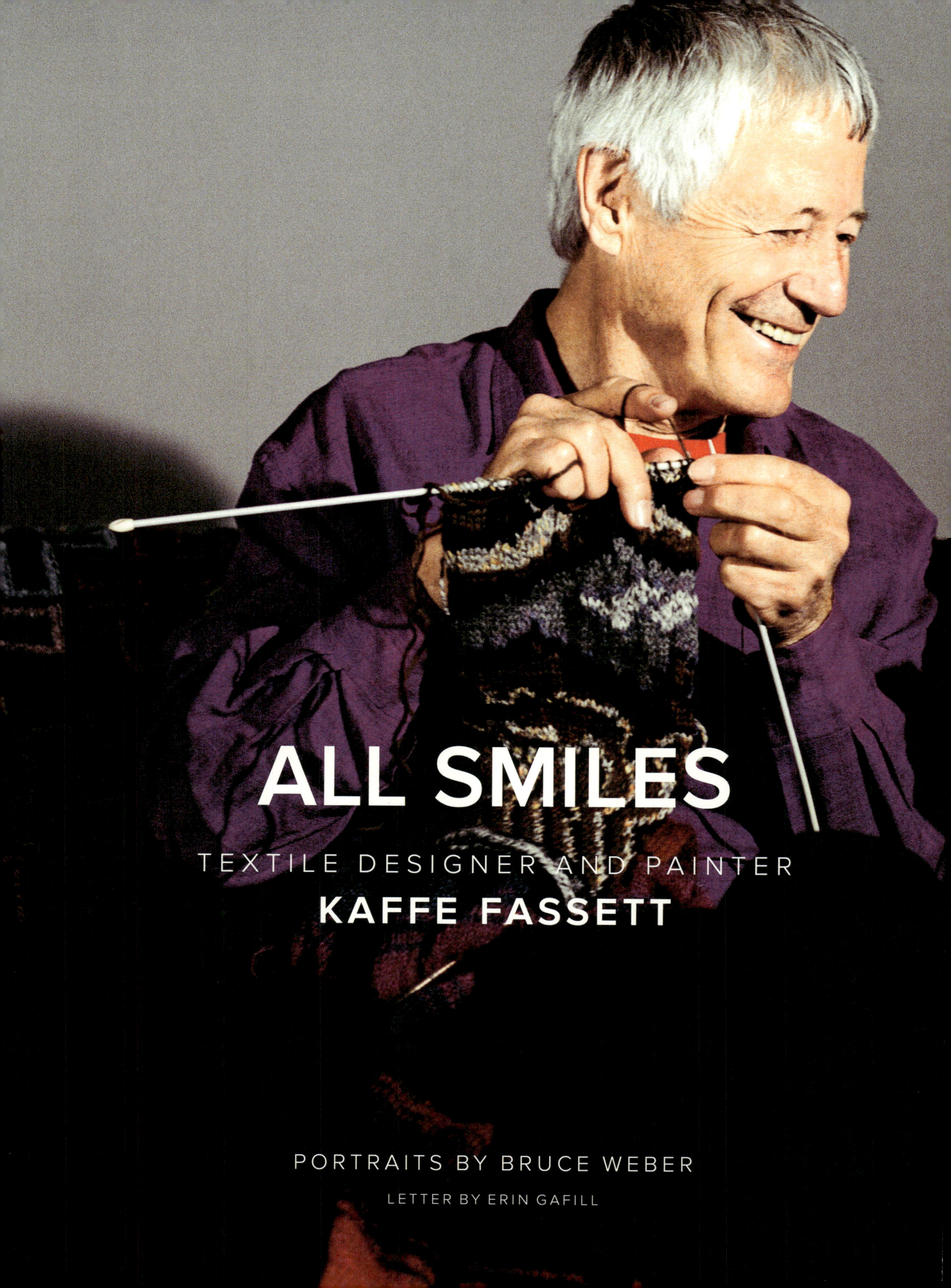

# ALL SMILES

TEXTILE DESIGNER AND PAINTER

## KAFFE FASSETT

PORTRAITS BY BRUCE WEBER

LETTER BY ERIN GAFILL

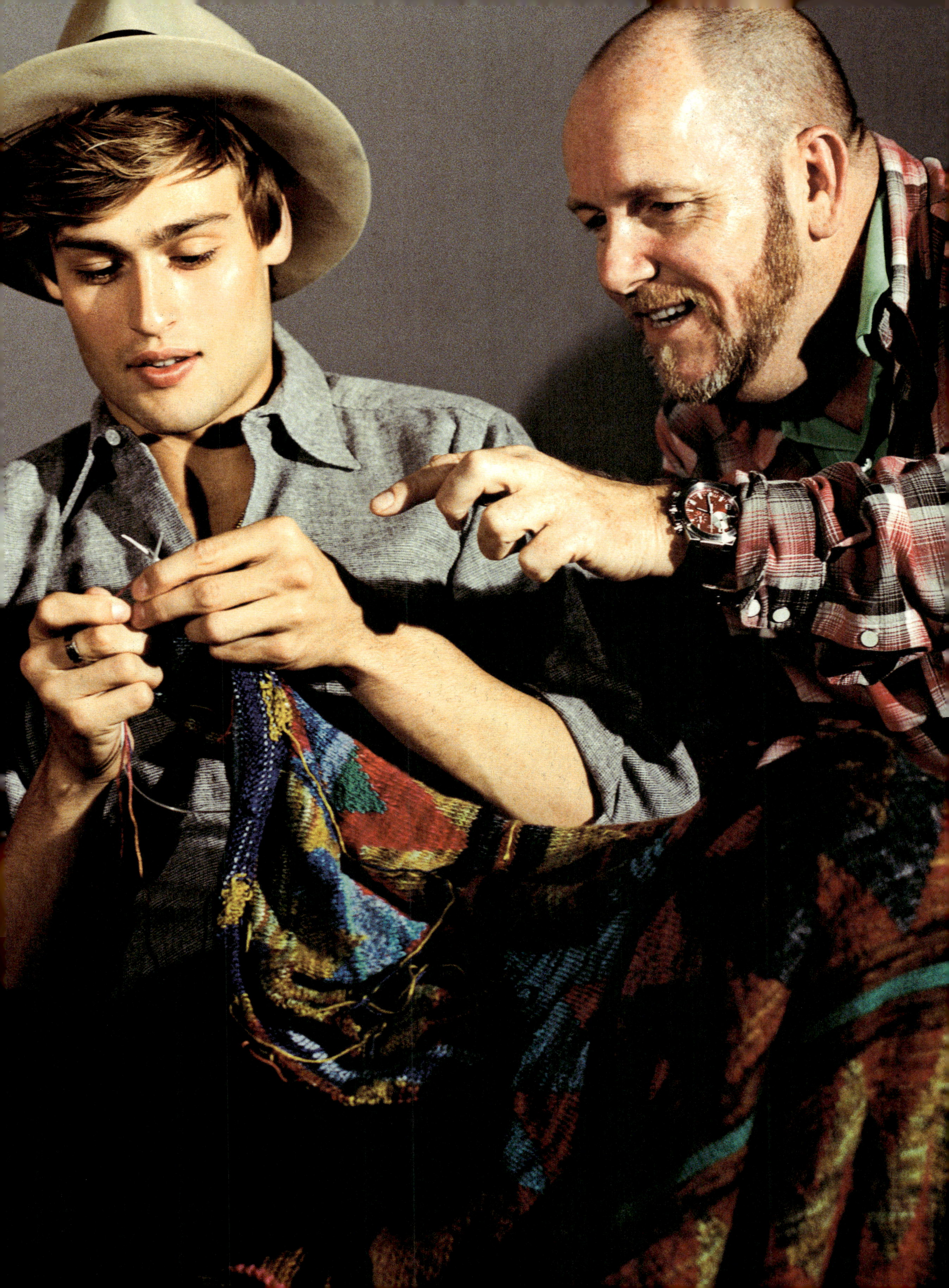

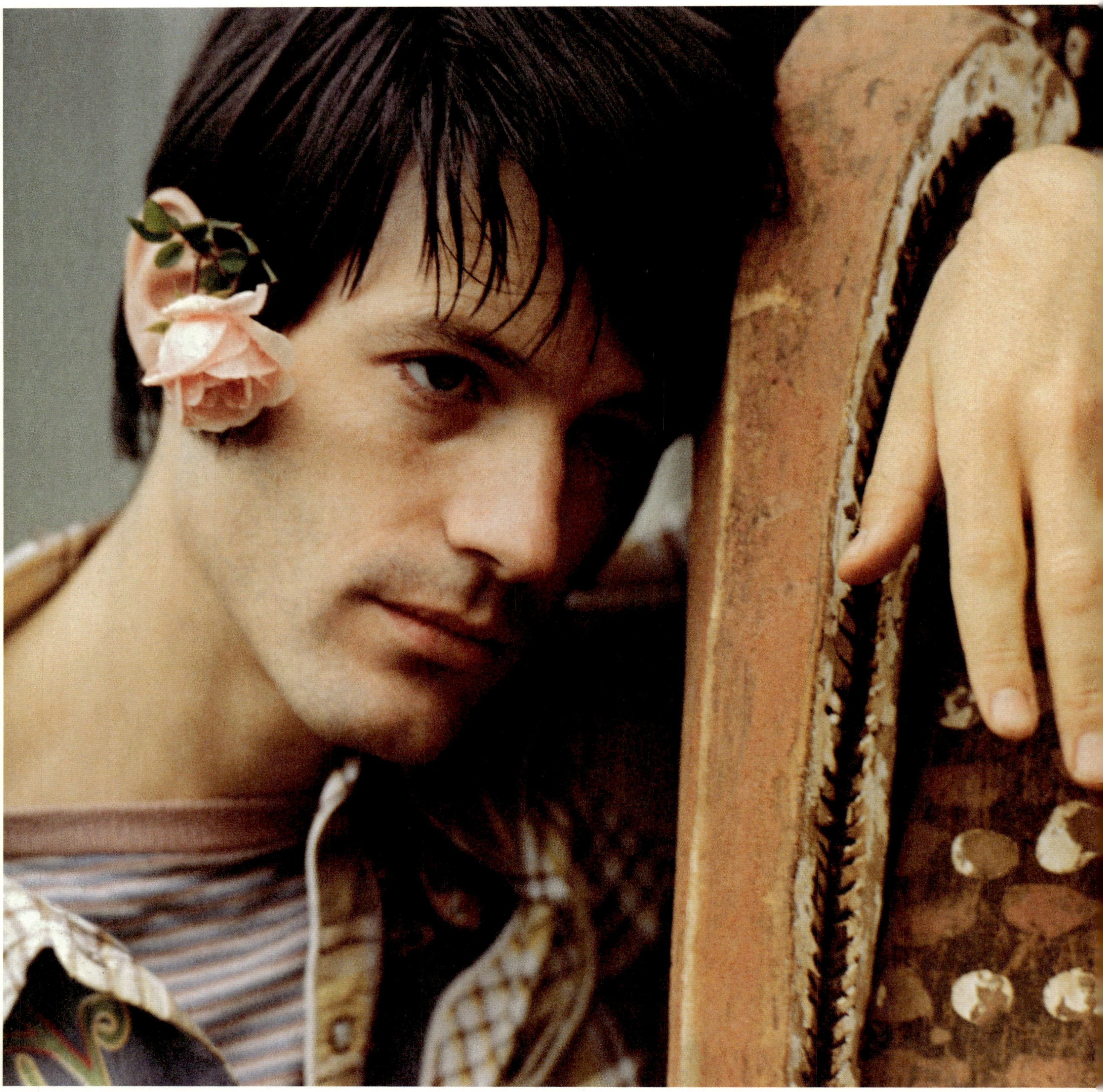

The multitalented Kaffe Fassett—painter, textile designer, knitter, ceramicist—was born in 1937 in Big Sur. His parents built Nepenthe, the famous restaurant, and he credits the beauty and isolation of that landscape as the early inspiration for his art. Kaffe started painting seriously as a teenager, then briefly attended art school in Boston before moving to England. He met Bill Gibb, the influential fashion designer, and began to knit pieces for Gibb's line. This eventually led to commissions for Missoni and Rowan, as well as an eponymous collection for Neiman Marcus. Kaffe has written many best-selling books about knitting and needlepoint and has hosted a number of craft-related television programs. In 1988, the Victoria and Albert Museum presented a one-man show of his designs, a first for a living textile artist. His personal commissions are highly sought after by collectors and fashion enthusiasts to this day. Kaffe continues to travel extensively, often visiting his family in California, including his niece Erin, who celebrates this colorful character in the following letter.

PREVIOUS: KAFFE FASSETT, DOUGLAS BOOTH AND BRANDON MABLY, KAFFE'S ASSISTANT • ABOVE: KAFFE IN LONDON, PHOTOGRAPHED BY STEVE LOVI

Erin Gafill
The Log House
Nepenthe
Big Sur, CA
93920

Dear Bruce,

You asked me about my earliest inspirations in art and I told you – it was Kaffe – my uncle, artist, story-teller – visionary dreamer. I hope that you shall know him one day, you will love him and his magical world of color, pattern, and passion I have no doubt.

He was born in San Francisco, raised up in Big Sur (Lolly and Bill were building Nepenthe then and it was a crazy madhouse of artists, poets, actors, dancers and retired Berkeley intellectuals) in the old log house Orson Welles bought for

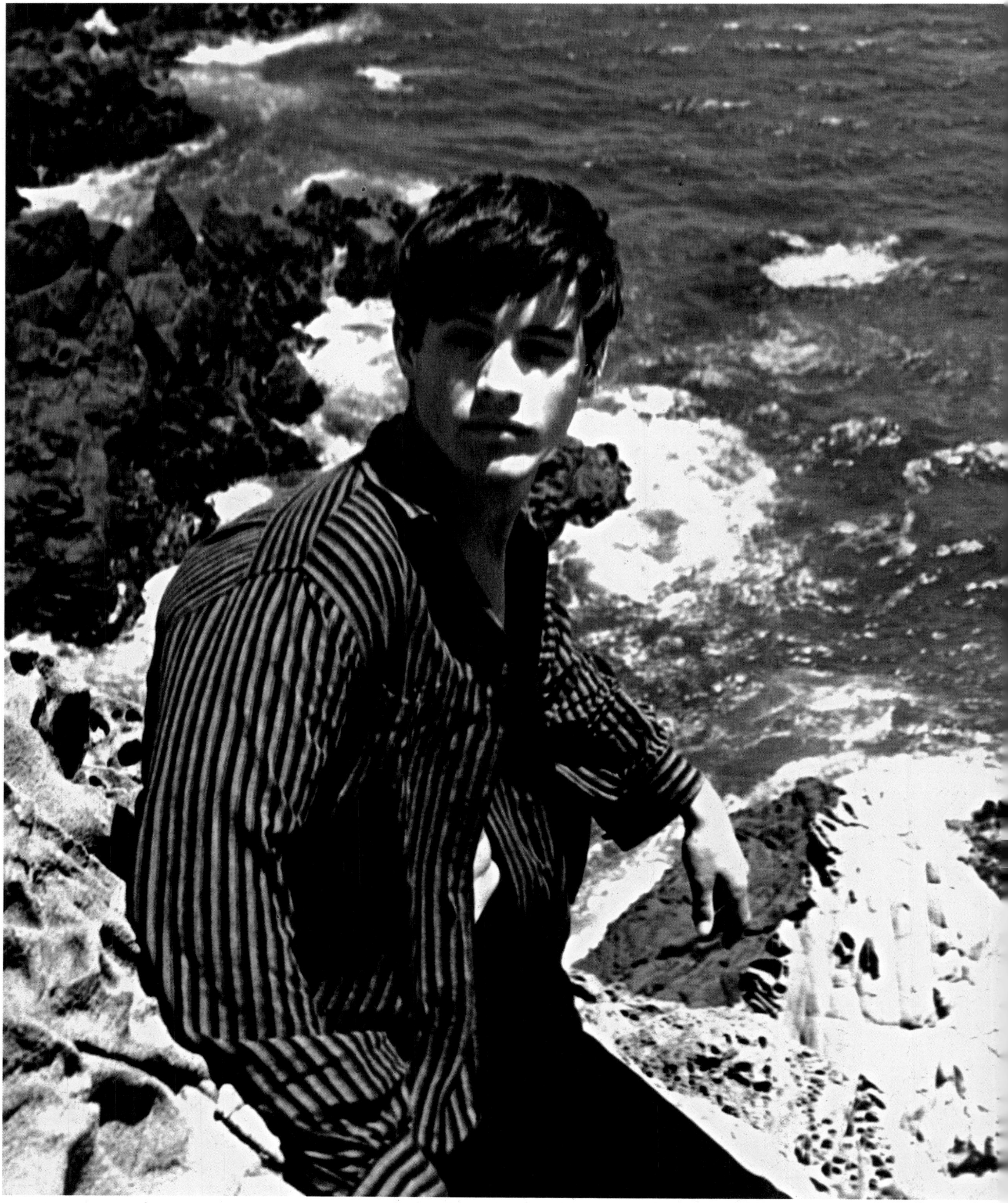

ABOVE: KAFFE NEAR HIS HOME IN BIG SUR, C. 1957  OPPOSITE: DOUGLAS BOOTH WEARS A SHAWL KNITTED BY KAFFE

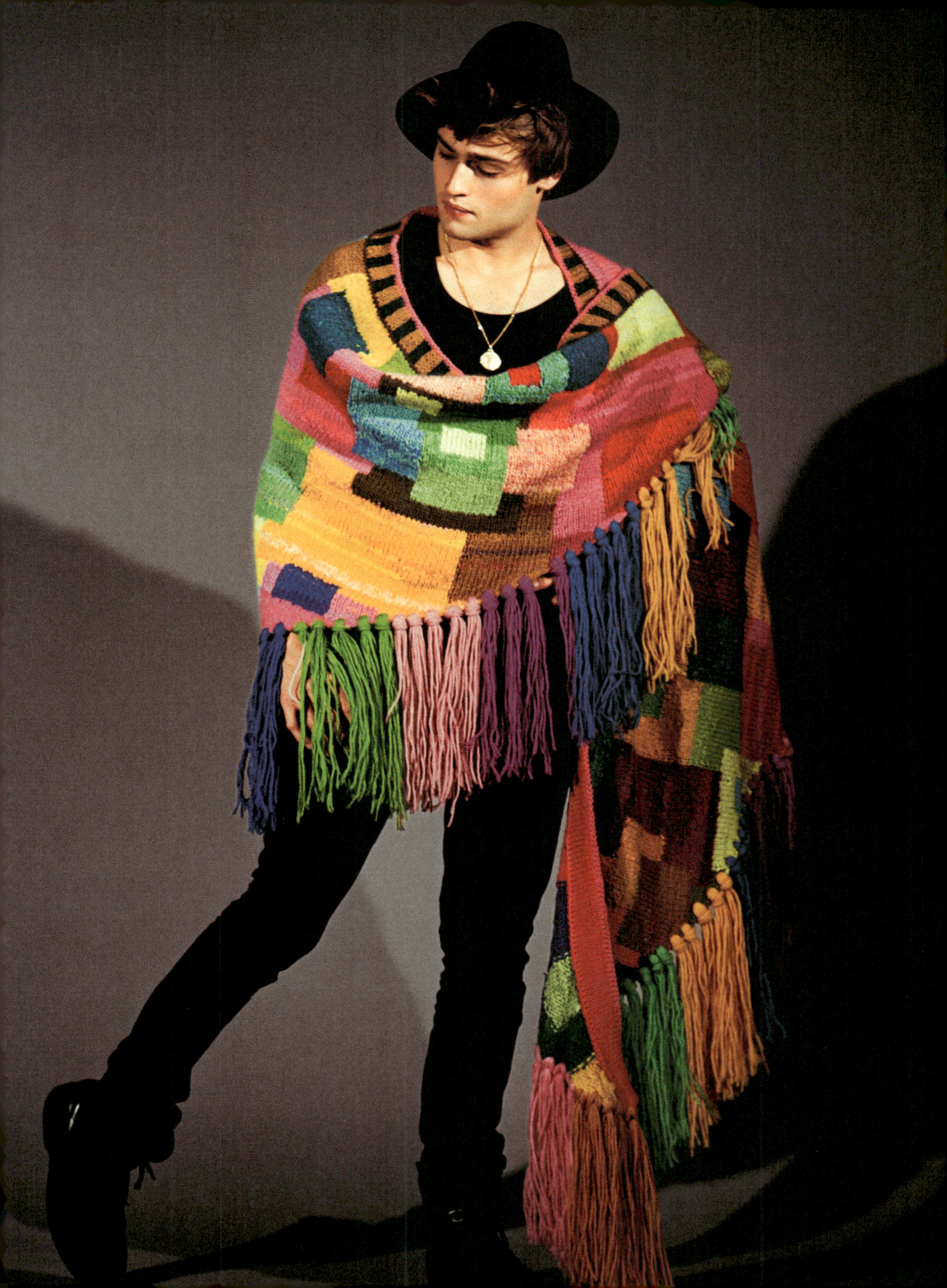

Rita Hayworth, a romantic cabin those two never returned to but ended up our family home these past six decades or so!

Kaffe was a painter - won prizes, a scholarship to art school in Boston in the 60's - but textiles stole his heart, he learned to knit on a train from Edinburgh to London and was hooked from then on - his first design featured in VOGUE!

He designed for the great Scottish designer Billy Gibbs, and the great Italian fashion house, The Missonis, but Kaffe's voice is all his own - in all his books (there are 29 now I think) on knitting, needlepoint, mosaics quiltmaking - soon to be an autobiography too that will explore his childhood beachcombing in Big Sur, how nature was his playground and muse.

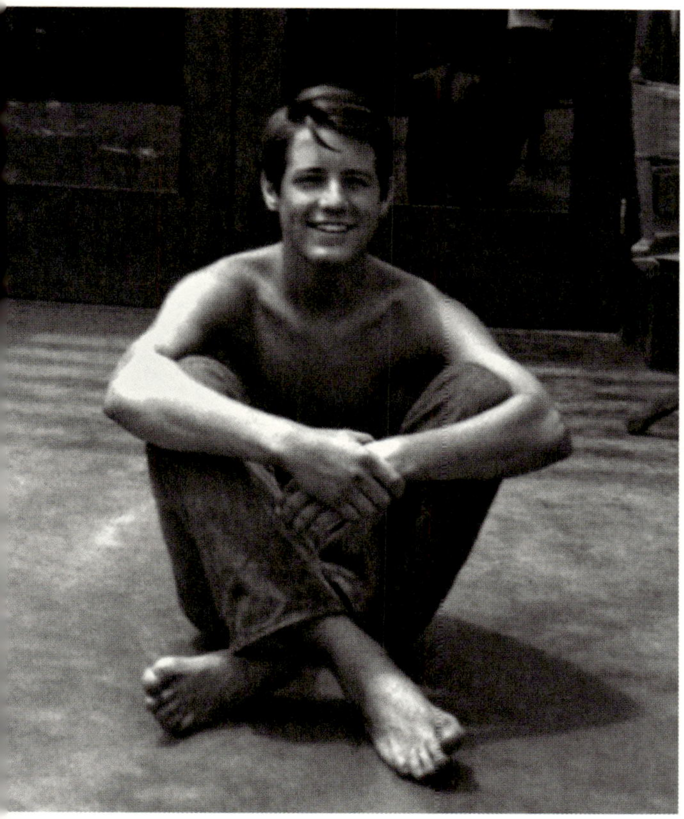

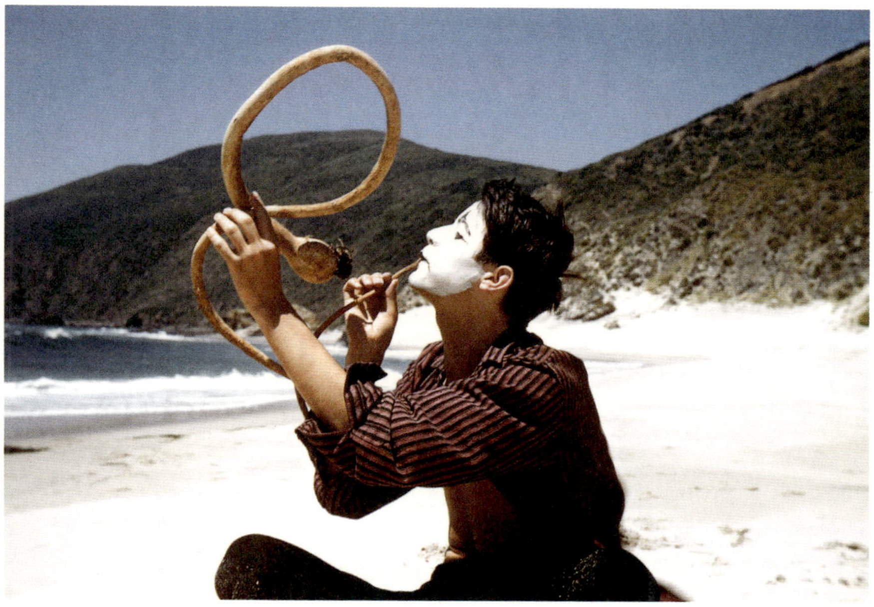

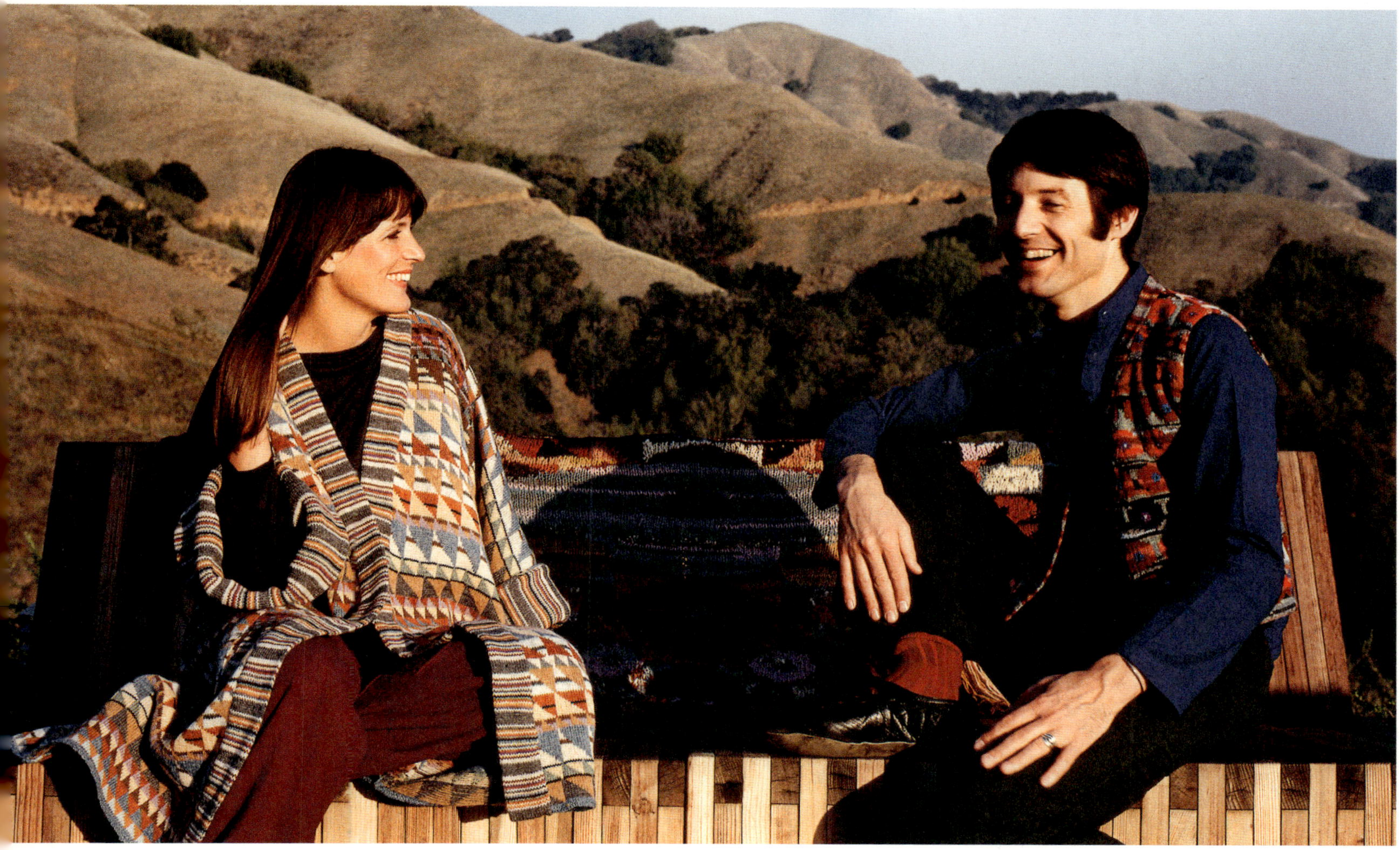

CLOCKWISE FROM TOP LEFT: KAFFE ON THE DECK AT NEPENTHE • KAFFE ON PFEIFFER BEACH IN BIG SUR
KAFFE WITH HIS SISTER HOLLY ON THE CAFÉ KEVAH DECK AT NEPENTHE, C. 1972

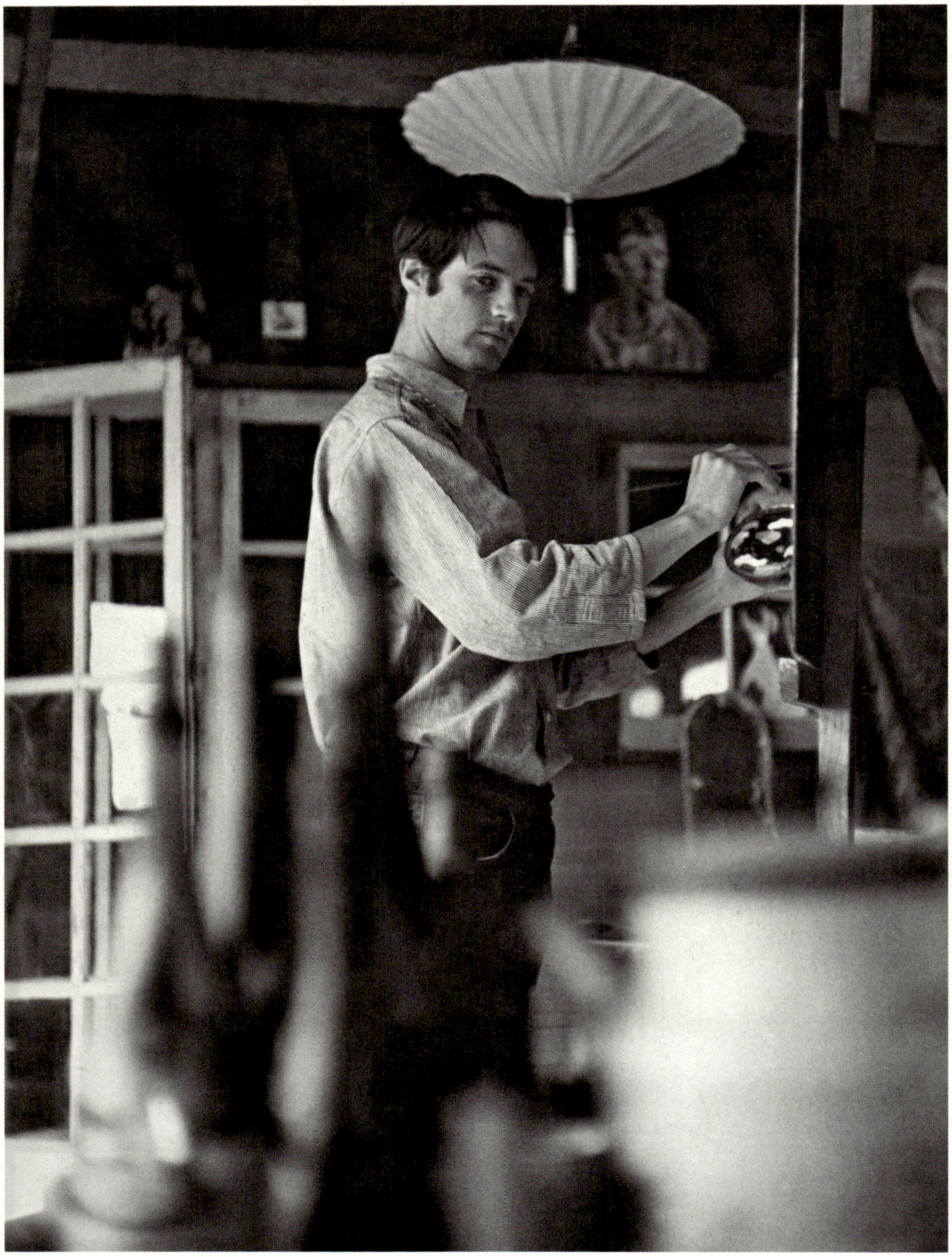

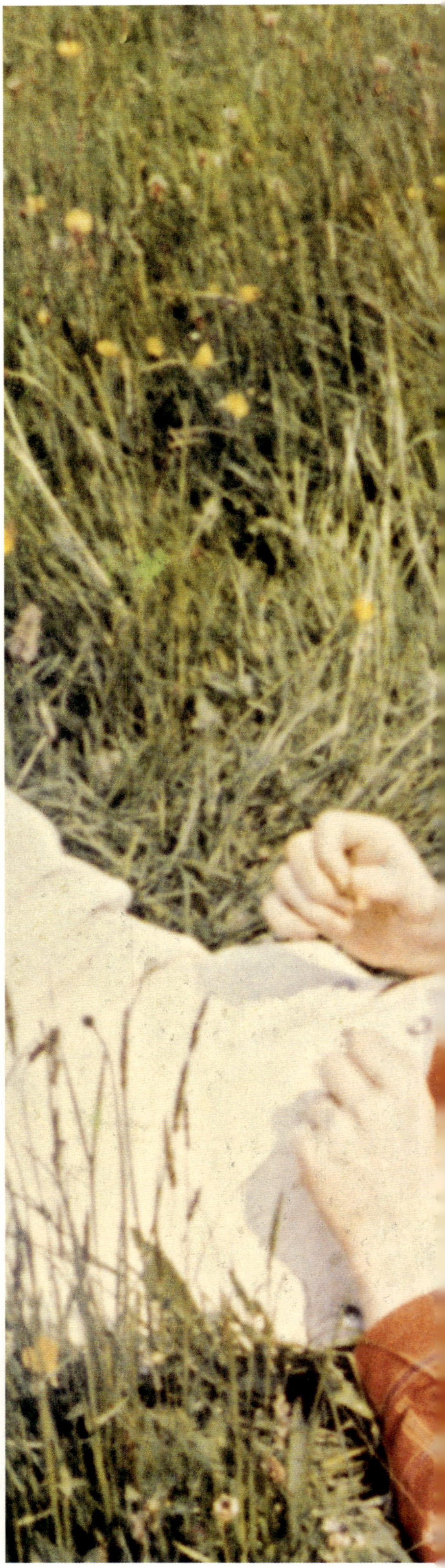

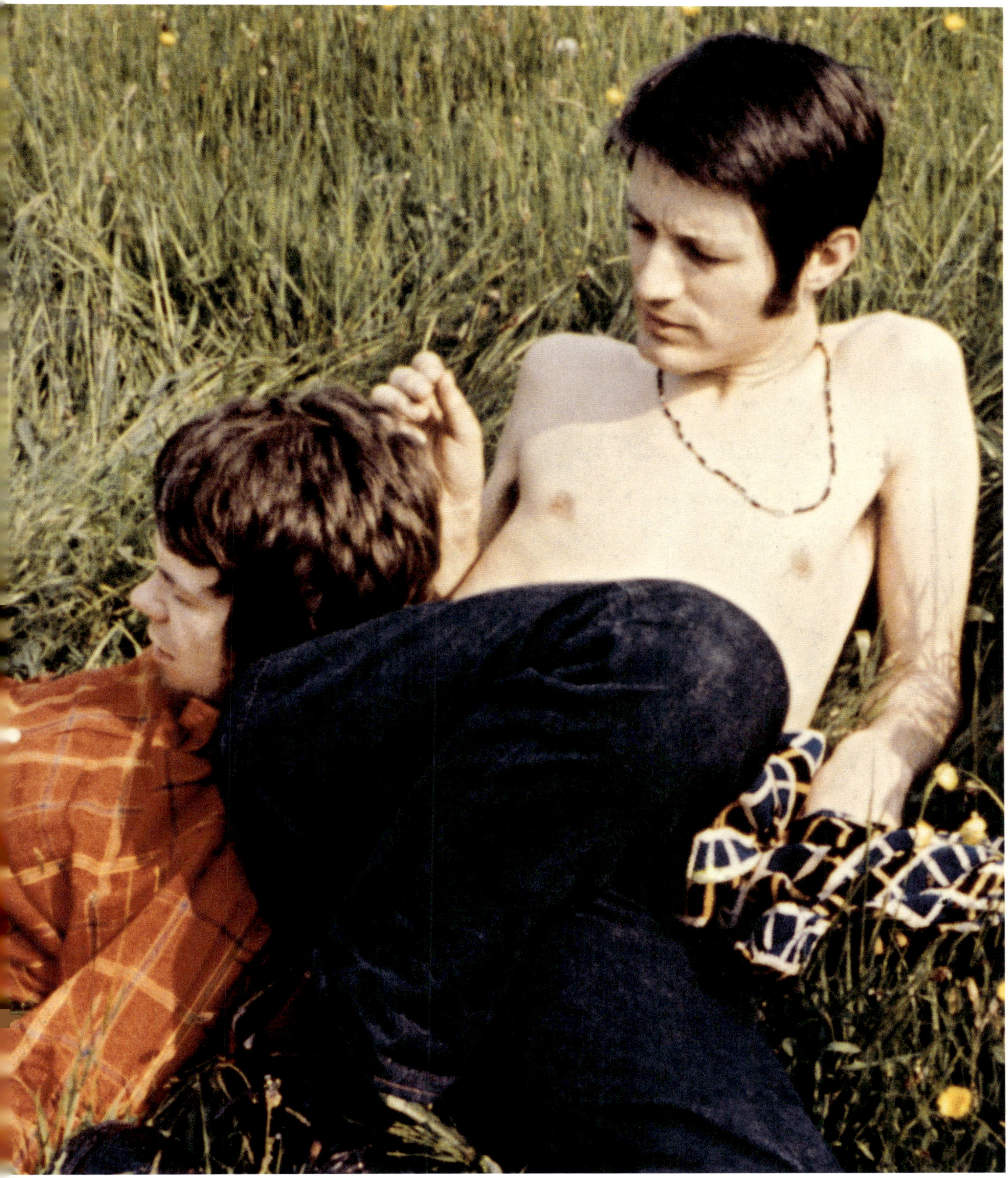

LEFT: KAFFE PAINTING IN HIS BIG SUR STUDIO, WHICH WAS BUILT IN THE 1930S BY THE SAME PRISONERS WHO CONSTRUCTED CALIFORNIA HIGHWAY 1 • ABOVE: KAFFE ENJOYS A SUMMER DAY IN ENGLAND WITH BILL GIBB

There is too much to tell in this letter, but suffice to say that he has touched my life so deeply, living a life in which there are no boundaries between work and play, life and art, that all is, truly one. I knew, even as a young child, that that's what I wanted.

There were a lot of strong women in my family but Kaffe was the cherished man who always came home bearing gifts, telling tales, opening our eyes to the world beyond.

Bruce - You must go and meet him, see his studio in London and he will adore you, too —

Erin

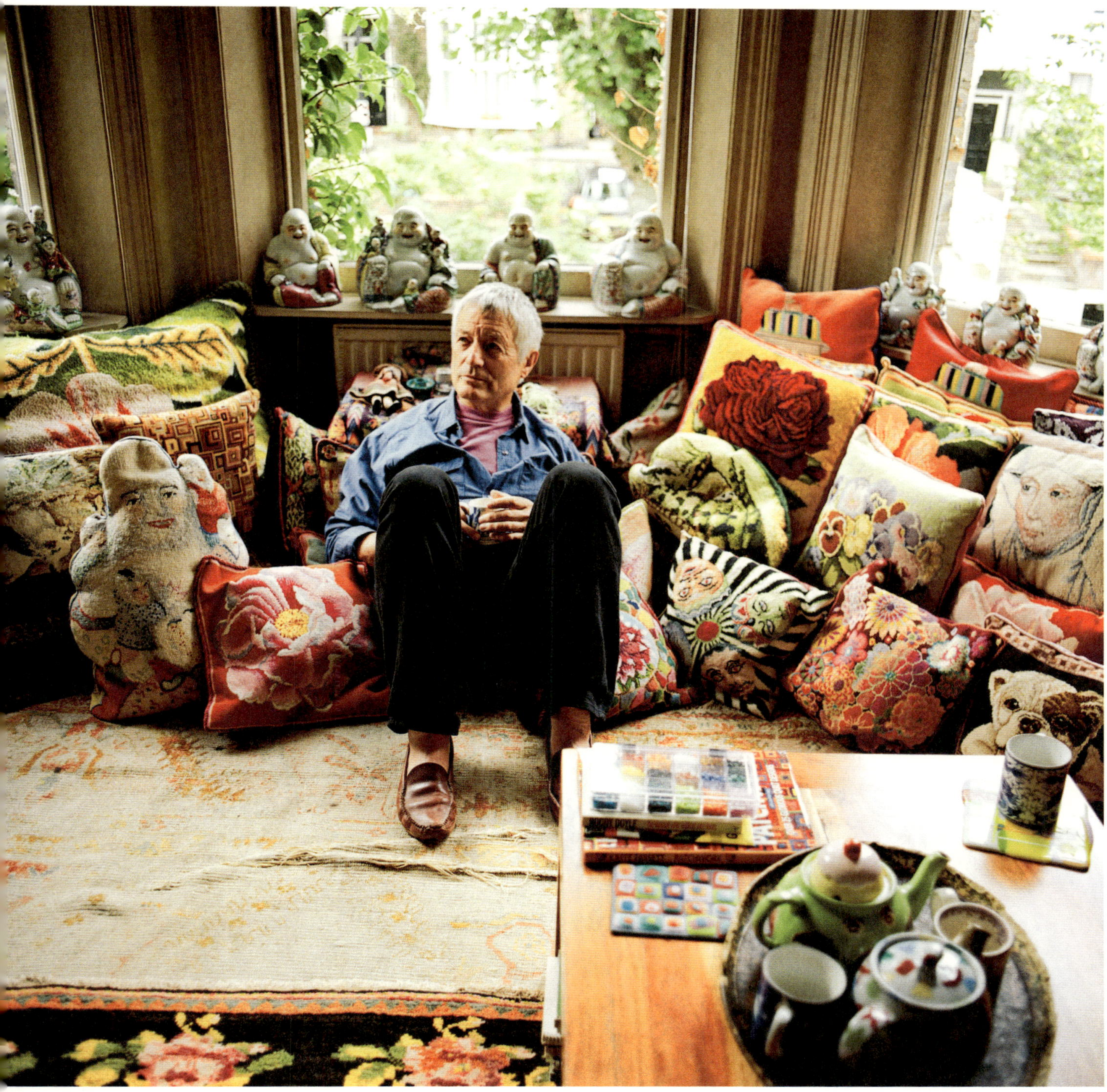

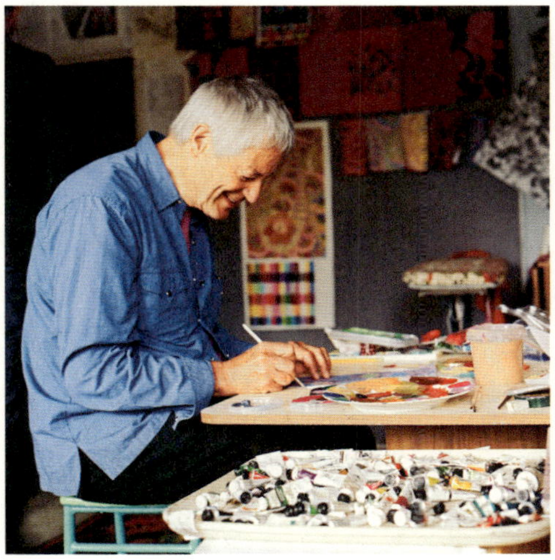

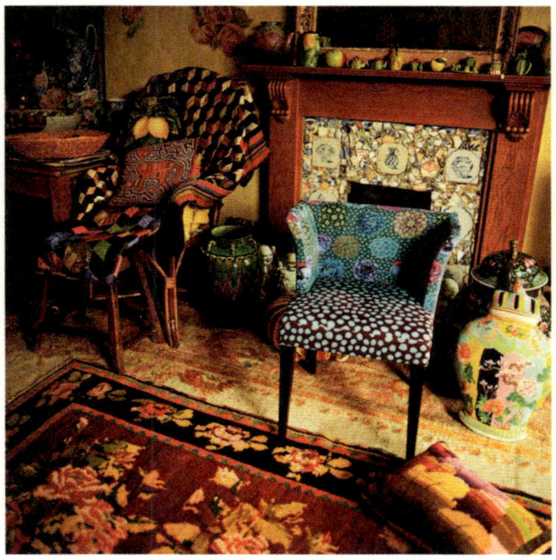

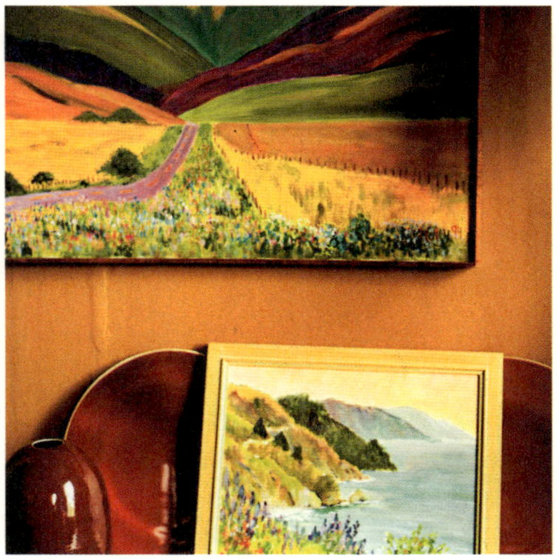

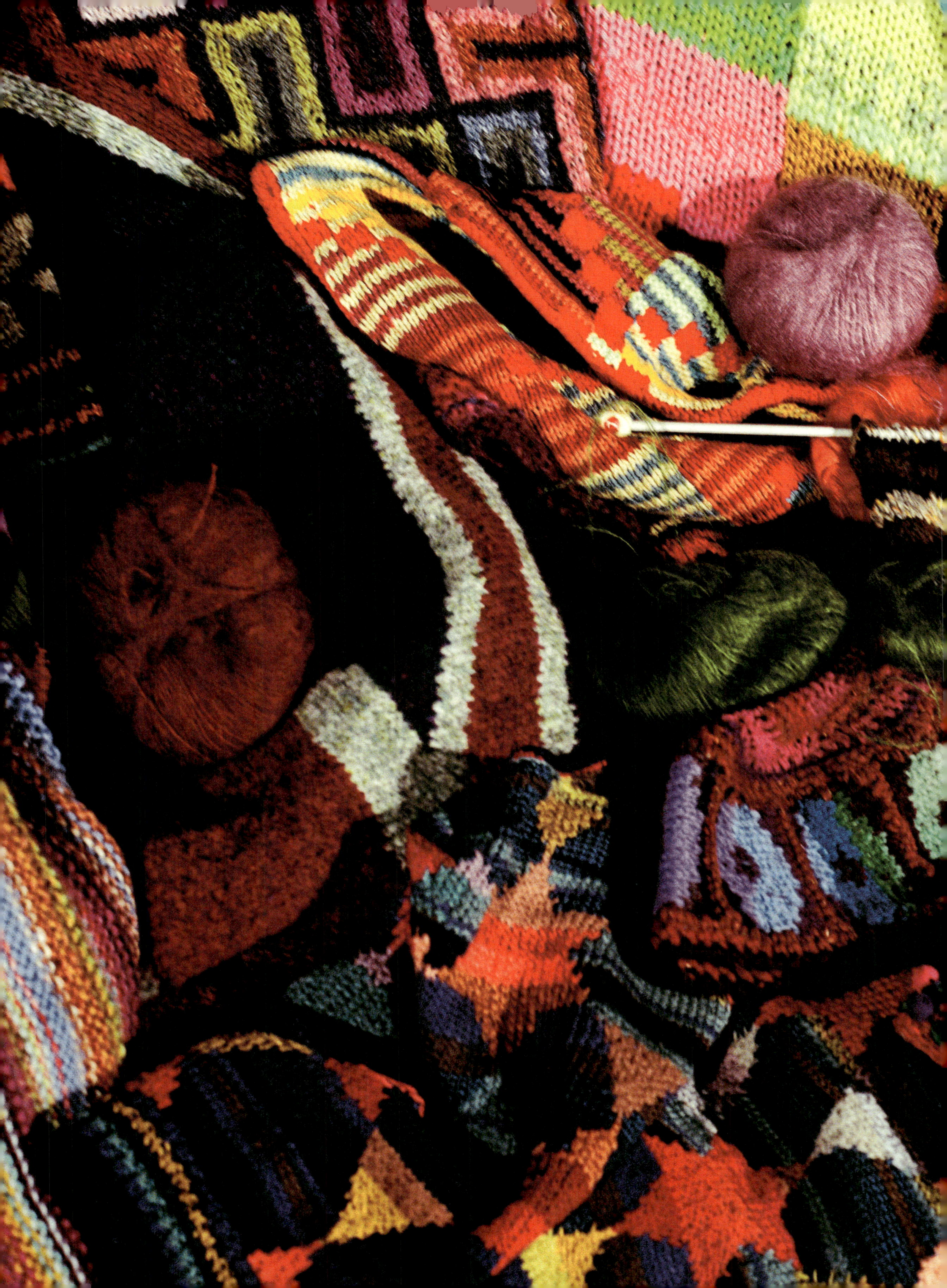

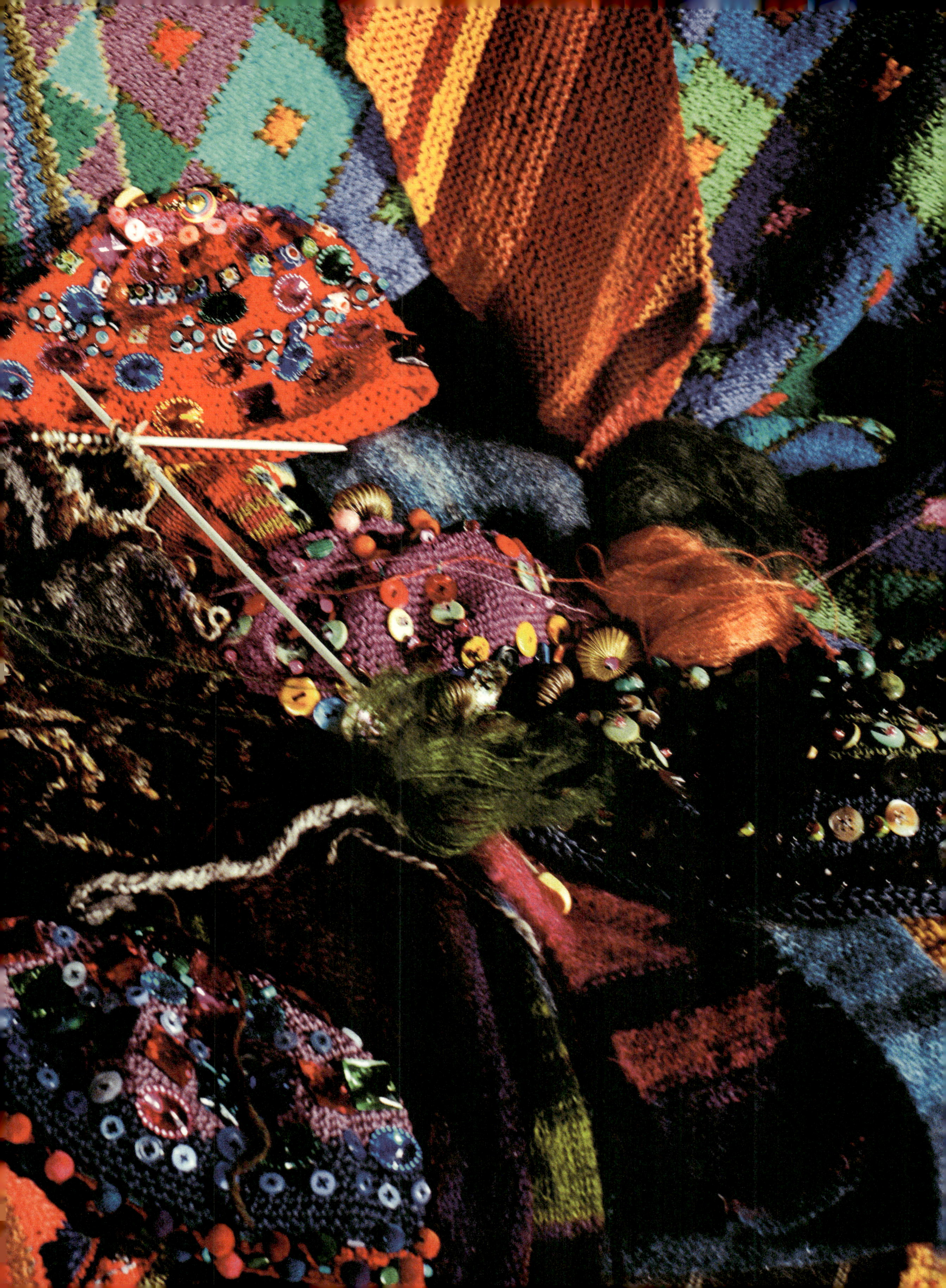

IN PRAISE OF

# STUDS TERKEL

At the dedication of a bridge in Chicago bearing his name, Studs Terkel quipped, "If things go bad, I might have the privilege one day of jumping off a bridge named after me!" This wry sense of humor and geniune modesty were at the heart of his work as a documentarian of everyday American life. Studs started out as a radio and television personality, but ran into trouble during the McCarthy era for his left-leaning politics. Kicked out of broadcasting, he set off on a one-man mission to create an oral history of his time. Armed with only a tape recorder, an attentive ear, a love for debate, and an insatiable curiosity about his fellow man, Studs interviewed hundreds of people in his native city and beyond, asking their thoughts on such grand subjects as work, race, war, and faith. Their conversations became the material of his many best-selling books. Here, in an excerpt from his later volume *Hope Dies Last*, Studs recounts how his sympathies for the left landed him in hot water, and how Mahalia Jackson of all people came to his rescue.

During the witch-hunt days of the late '40s and early '50s, I encountered some slight difficulties...The political influences in my life were not the associations that made the attorney general's subversives list nor caught the gimlet eye of the director of the FBI, though my name was associated with a fair number of them. No, what most affected me during my formative years in high school and college during the boom before the Wall Street crash and the Great Depression that followed was the lobby of the men's hotel my mother ran after my father died. They were a motley, lively lot: skilled, semiskilled, and unskilled workmen.

There were autodidacts who'd call upon Shakespeare, scripture, and Mark Twain, with added expletives. A number of them were old-time Wobblies, the idiomatic name for the Industrial Workers of the World (IWW). There were journeymen carpenters, boomer firemen, and seafarers, restless and transient in nature. Their dream was one big union. Their *bêtes noires* were equally voluble guests who believed that the boss, the man behind the mahogany desk, deserved to be there, deserved his privileges, because he'd *earned* them, and that the IWW was an acronym for "I won't work."

Oh, the debates, if you call them that, were wondrous to hear (their perorations were seldom *sotto voce*). The Wobblies referred to their antagonists as scissorbills, "capitalists with holes in their pockets."

Most of the other guests didn't give a hoot one way or the other. Earning their daily bread wearied them enough, though, that I'm certain they looked forward to the entertaining nature of these lobby disputes, aside from a shot or two of sour mash and Sunday visits to the girls in the cribs a block away.

There were three bleak years at the University of Chicago Law School, where I was singularly silent, dreaming of Clarence Darrow and Wobblies and scissorbills, while hearing academic dissertations on real property, corporations, and partnership.

To escape the fate of becoming a lawyer, I became an actor in radio soap operas. I was always typecast as a Chicago gangster. Subsequently, I became a disc jockey with an eclectic repertoire: classical, jazz, and folk music. Among the artists I favored was a spiritual and gospel singer, Mahlia Jackson. She and I had become friends.

With the advent of a new medium, television, in 1949 or 1950, I joined that world. TV, heard from six in the evening till ten at night, was not the commercial and political force it is today, and the free-marketeers had not yet taken over. There were a few Chicago-originated programs that John Crosby, the preeminent TV critic, called "TV, Chicago style"; they were improvised in nature and live, of course.

One of them was *Stud's Place*, with which I was involved. There was no script, merely a plot. The dialogue was by the cast. I was considered a "hot property" by the New York agents. Parenthetically, my political leanings had become common knowledge in the trade. The influence of the Wells-Grand Hotel (that was the impressive name of my mother's place) had never left me. I found myself attending rallies, many sponsored by people of the left.

Some of the speakers were eloquent, some on the dreadfully dull and doctrinaire side. All were impassioned, reminding me of those Wells-Grand lobbyists. I walked picket lines. I signed petitions. I never met a picket line or a petition I didn't like. Eventually, I spoke at some rallies and became the emcee of a good number.

It was during this time that the cold war had taken off, as had Joe McCarthy. My past (and present) had caught up with me.

There were occasional visits from the FBI. They always came in pairs. Always polite. My wife was cool to them, suggesting that they had not been invited and thus were unwelcome. I, on the other hand, was always hospitable. Remember, I was an innkeeper's boy. Unlike the occurrence in

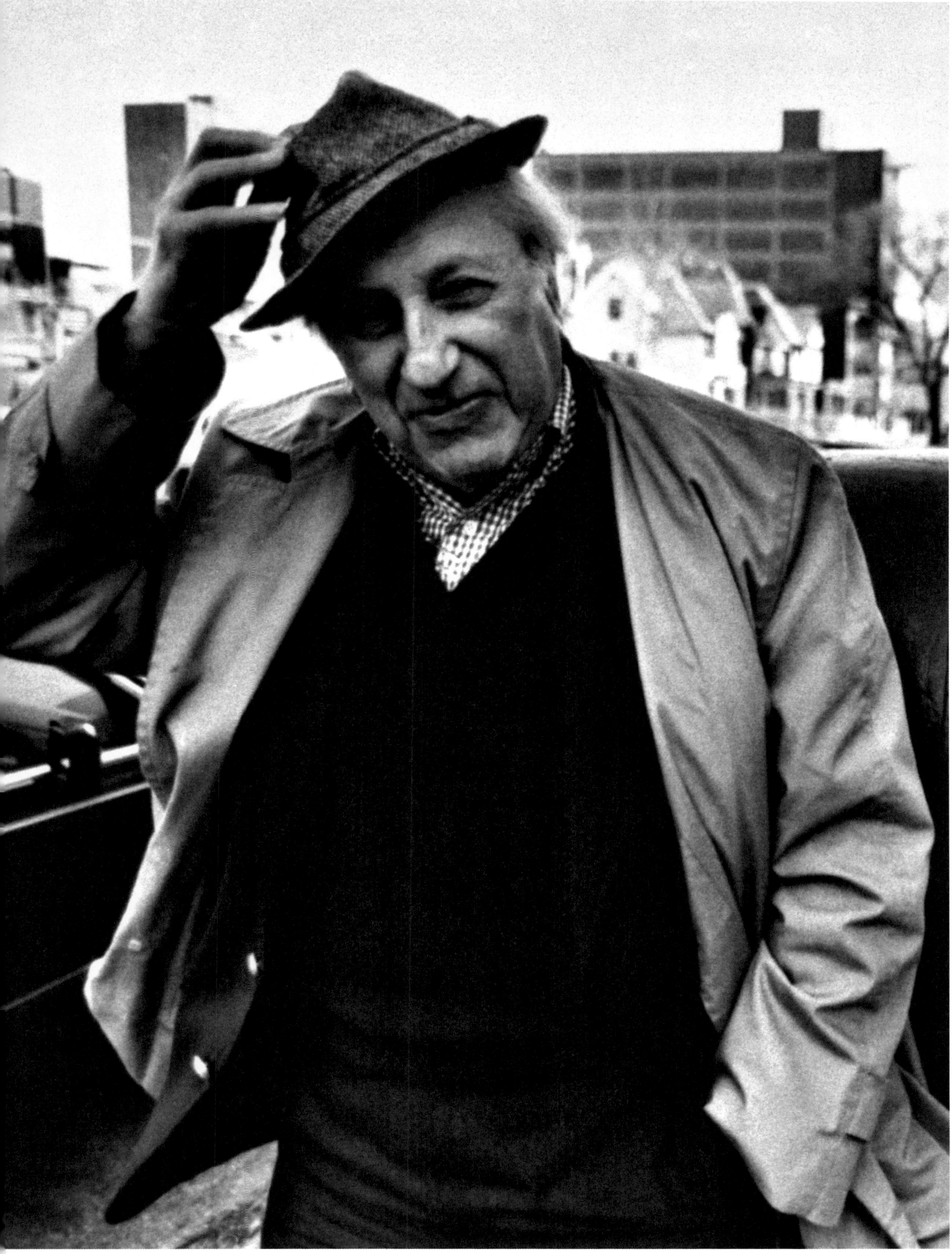

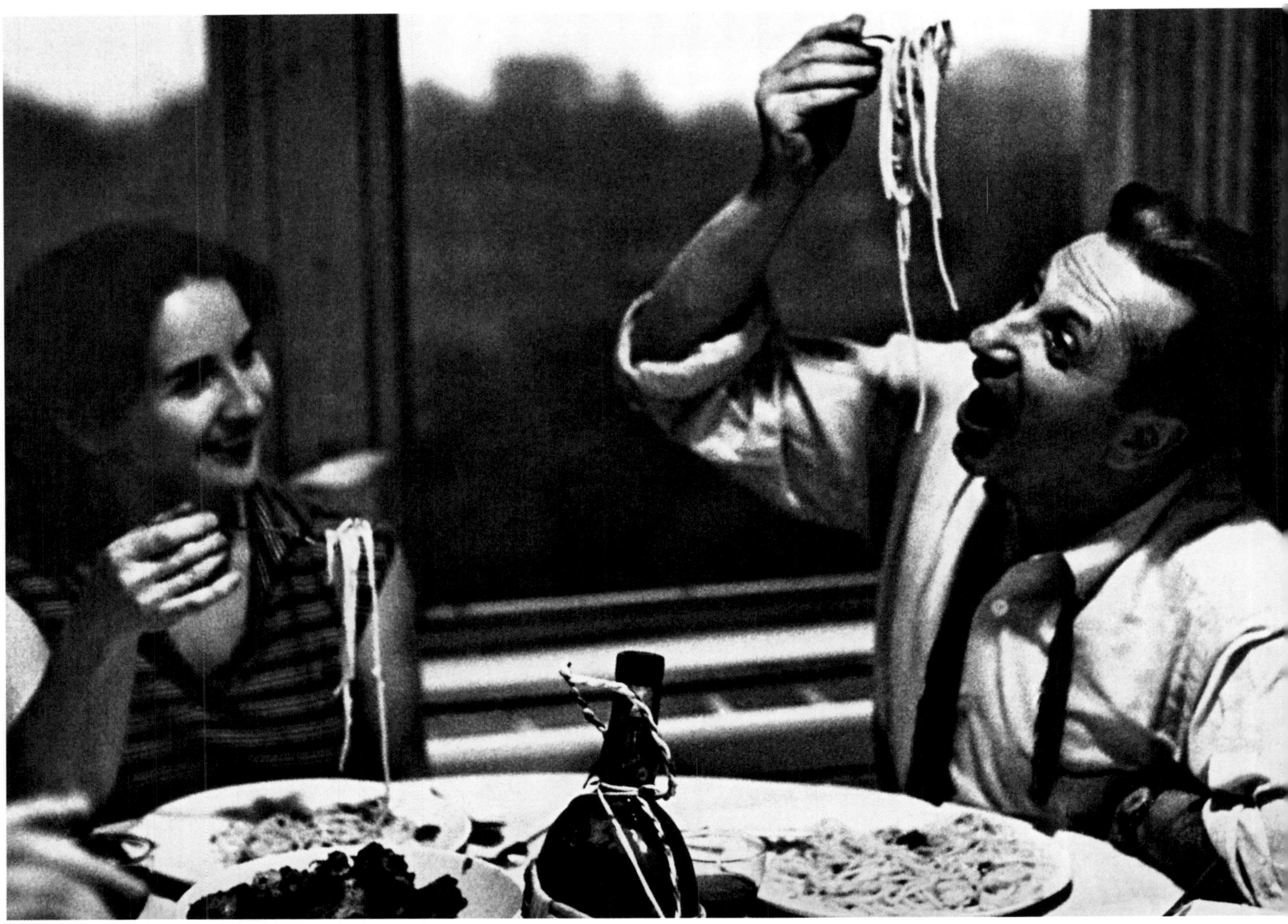

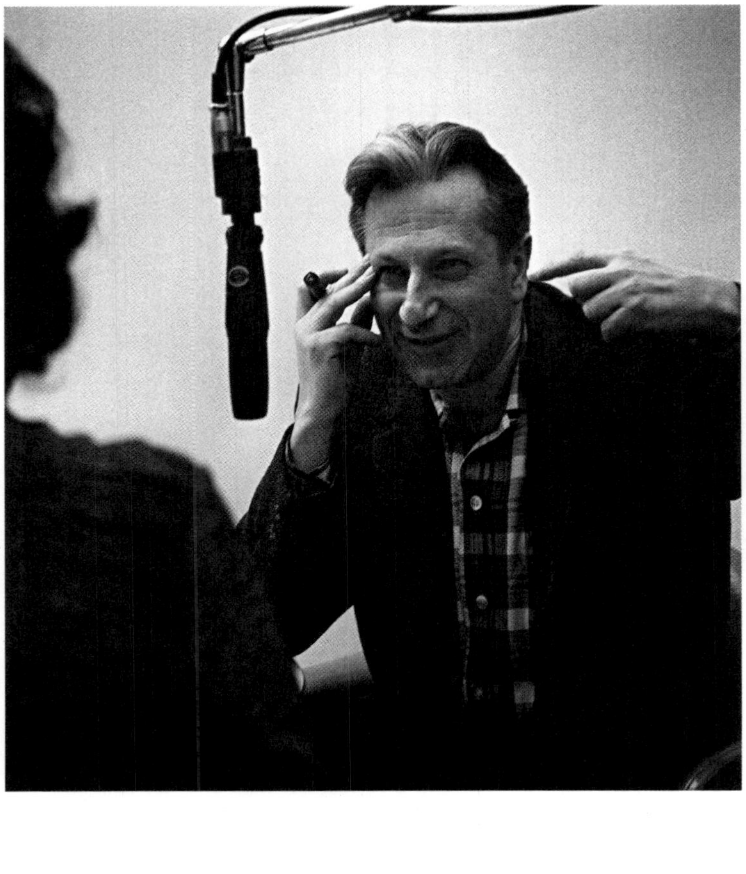

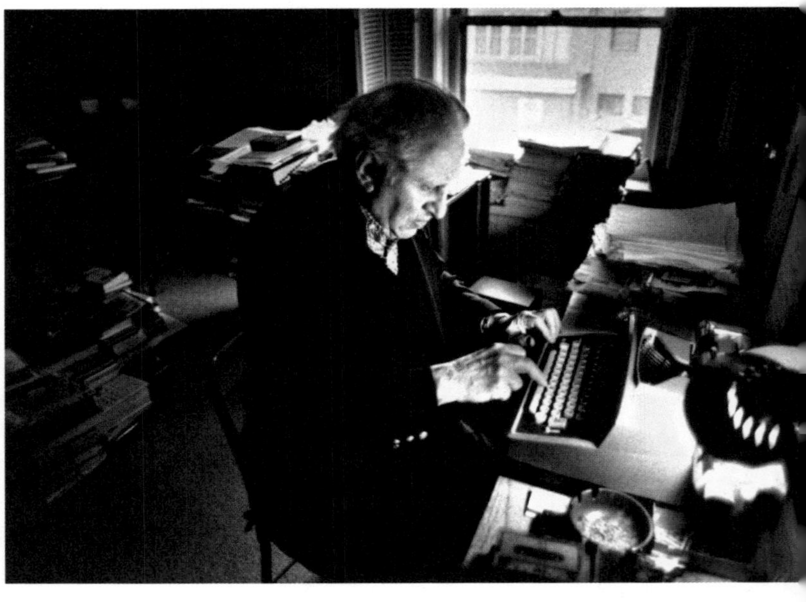

the Book of Luke, there was always room at our inn. Even for couples without baggage. Even for the FBI.

The visits were brief and uneventful. For some reason, our uninvited guests seemed ill at ease, always seated at the edge of their chairs. Whether it was my wife's coolness or my overwhelming hospitality, I don't know. After a time, the visits ceased, but not my troubles.

While *Studs's Place* was still riding high, an emissary from NBC headquarters in New York appeared. We sat down in solemn conference, he, I, and the Chicago station's executives. "We're in big trouble," the visitor said. I was moved by his use of the royal pronoun. "I have a list of petitions that you have presumably signed." He ran off a good number, a dozen or so. "Is that true?"

"Oh, sure."

"Didn't you know that communists are behind all these?"

I remember my reply. It was in the form of a question. "Suppose communists come out against cancer. Do we have to come out *for* cancer?"

"That is *not* very funny." I was facing Queen Victoria. He continued, suddenly assuming the tone of a drill sergeant. "These days, you've got to stand up and be counted."

I stood up.

"That's not very funny either. Sit down!"

I sat down.

"There is an easy way out," he suggested, a hopeful note in his voice. "All you have to say is that you were duped by the communists. You didn't mean it. You take it back. A lot of people have done that, and they're doing fine."

I demurred. NBC decided they could do without my services.

I was blacklisted for several years. I should point out that Chicagoans, by and large, knew little about this. It hardly made the local press. I'm certain that had I been in New York or Hollywood, I'd have suffered another fate. My kind of town, Chicago is.

During my *persona non grata* days in the trade, I'd pick up a few bucks lecturing at women's clubs on jazz, folk music, and such. After word got out that I'd been invited, each club would then receive, with railroad-watch regularity, a note from Ed Clamage warning them to desist. He was the Chicago Legionnaire who proclaimed himself a one-man Americanism committee. To their everlasting credit and my gratitude, not one club canceled.

One chairwoman, elderly and elegant, whose memory I shall always cherish, was offended by the note from "that vulgar bully." She insisted on doubling my fee from $100 to $200. Naturally, I sent Clamage a $10 check, explaining to him that it was his 10 percent agent's fee for making me a hundred dollars richer. He did not acknowledge the note. Nor the check.

One day in the mid-fifties, CBS hired Mahlia Jackson, now internationally celebrated, for a weekly network radio show. She insisted that I be the host. They reluctantly agreed. It had a live audience, about three hundred, in the Wrigley Building CBS studio.

During the third or fourth week of the series, another emissary from New York appeared. He was from CBS headquarters. It was during a dress rehearsal, an hour or so before the audience was let in.

He approached me onstage as I was going over the script (what there was of it; we mostly ad-libbed between her songs). He was quite polite.

"Would you mind signing this? It's *pro forma*."

It was a loyalty oath. I demurred. He insisted. Voices were raised.

Mahlia was passing by on her way toward Mildred Falls, her accompanist. She, of course, had known all about me. "Studs," she often said, "you have such a big mouth, you should have been a preacher."

Now she asked me, "Is that what I think it is, baby?"

"Yeah." I was worried about the audience impatiently waiting in the lobby. It was getting close to broadcast time.

"Are you gonna sign it?"

"Of course not."

"Okay, let's rehearse."

"Pardon me, Miss Jackson," said the emissary. "Mr. Terkel has to sign it." Orders from headquarters in New York, he explained.

Mahalia stared at him as though he were from Mars. "Studs just said no." But he simply didn't know when to quit. Finally, the now-weary singer said, "Look, you tell Mr. Whatshisname in New York, if they fire Studs to go find another Mahalia."

Our visitor disappeared and was never heard from again. Moral: Mahlia Jackson, in saying no, revealed more self-esteem, let alone what our country is all about, than William Paley, David Sarnoff, and all the sponsors and agencies rolled into one. In the *beau geste* of Mahlia Jackson, I saw the radiant vision once more of Clifford and Virginia Durr, affirming themselves, saying no to the official word. They may have always been in the minority, but it has been a prophetic one.

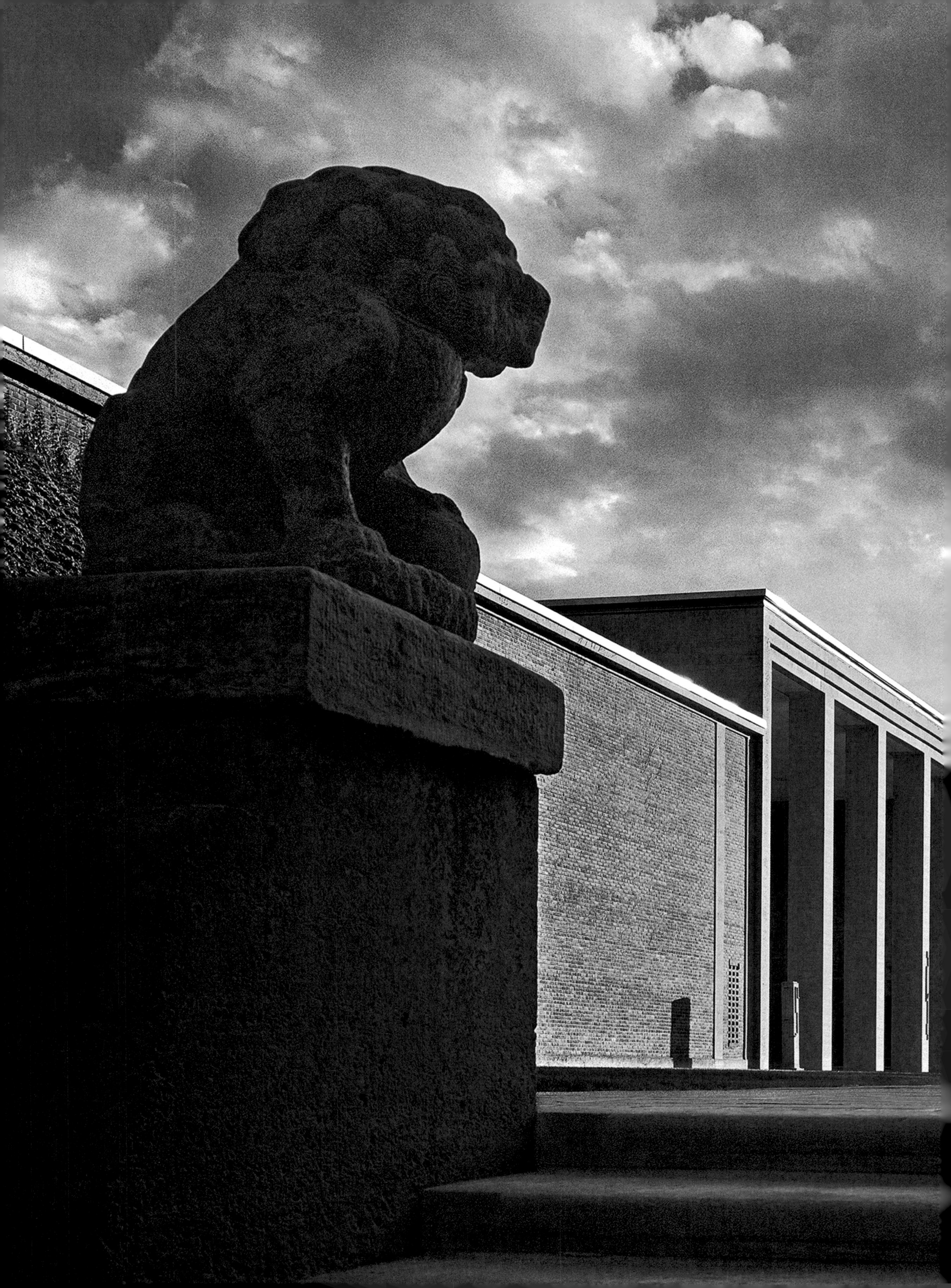

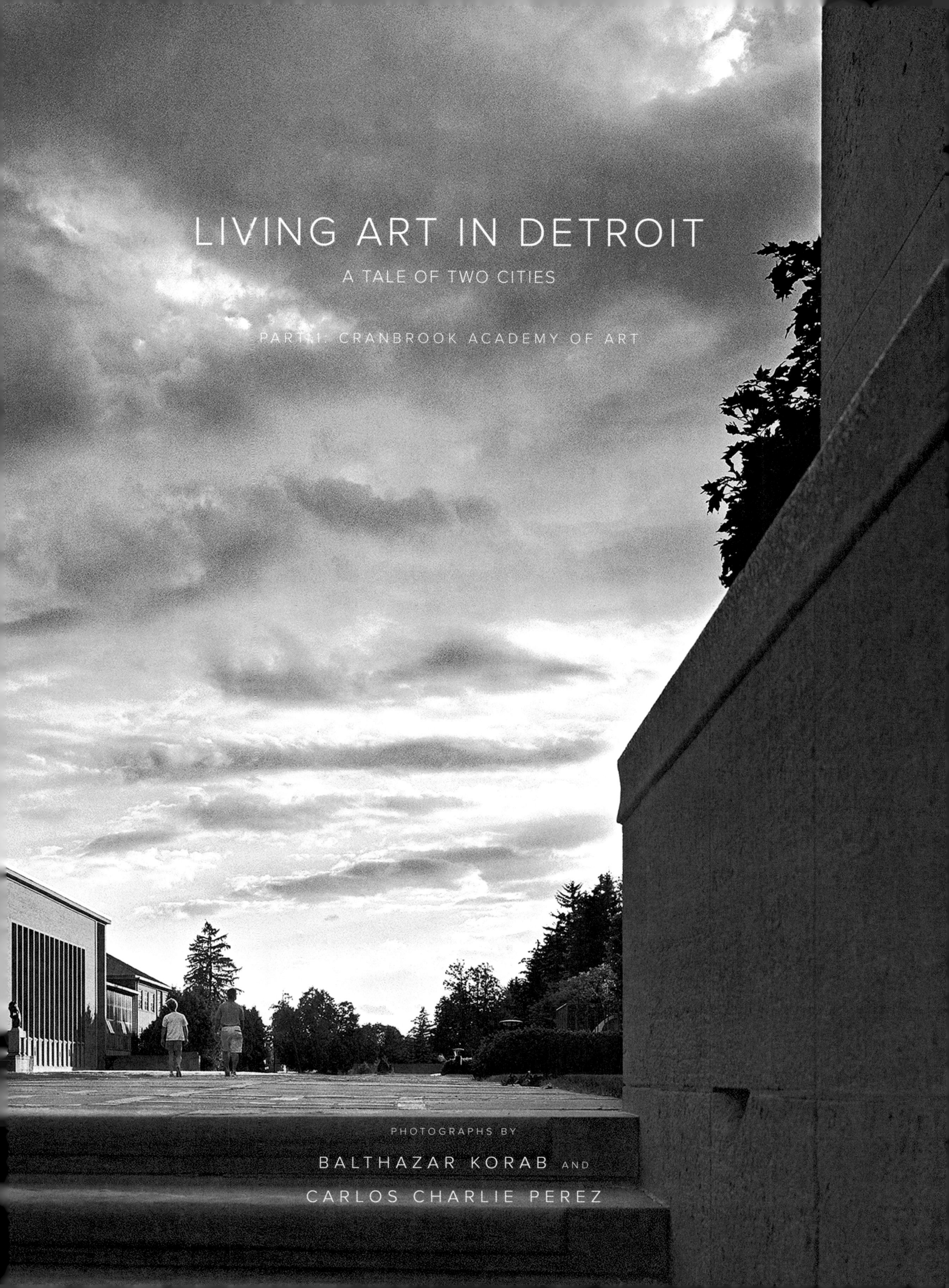

# LIVING ART IN DETROIT

## A TALE OF TWO CITIES

PART 1: CRANBROOK ACADEMY OF ART

PHOTOGRAPHS BY

BALTHAZAR KORAB AND

CARLOS CHARLIE PEREZ

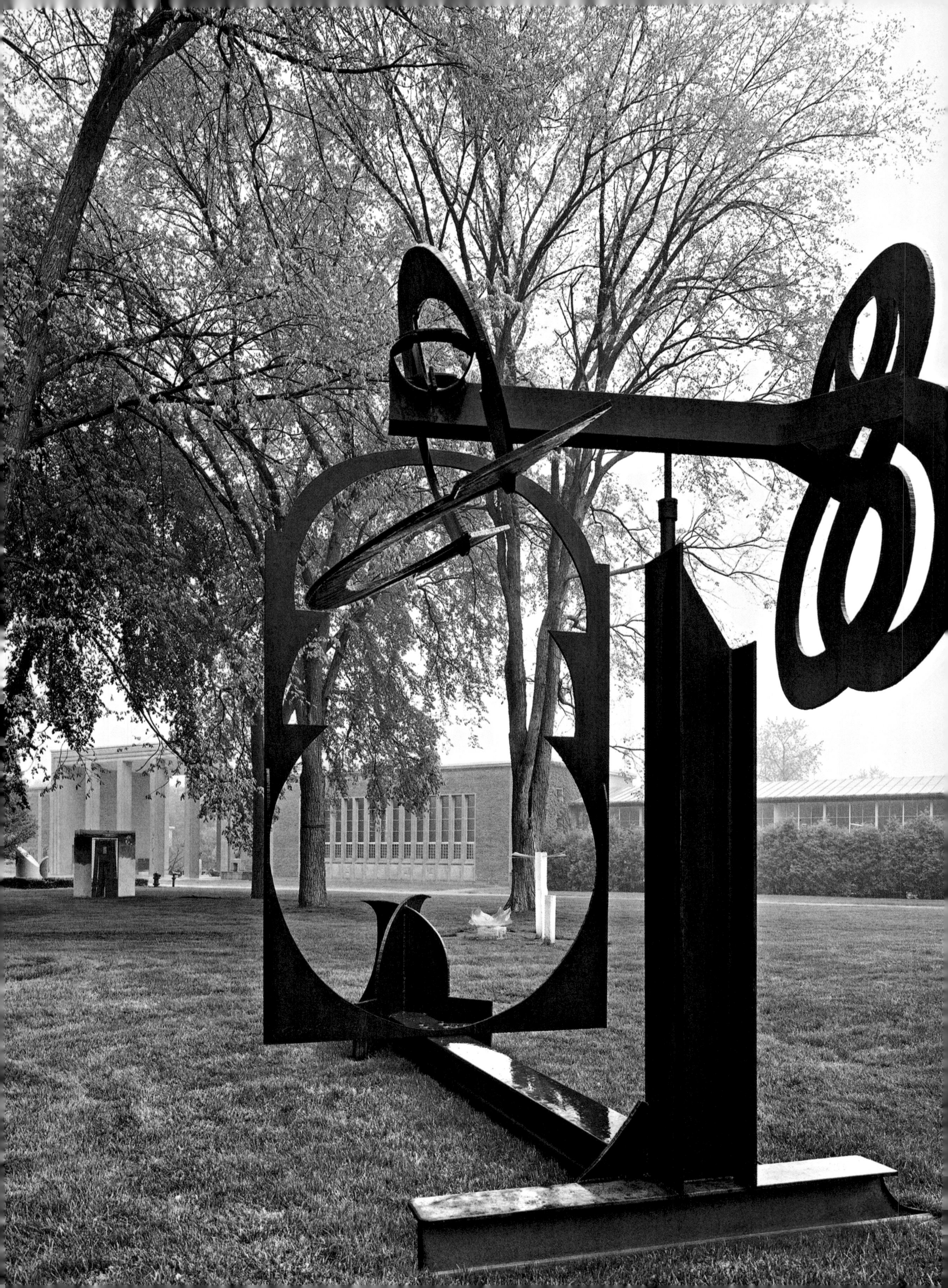

The creation of the Cranbrook Academy of Art was motivated by the altruism and patriotism of its founder, George Booth. He was a rare type of media baron, one who felt a deep obligation to those who had made him wealthy Booth's fortune came primarily from the ownership of *The Detroit News*, a position he enjoyed by virtue of his marriage to Ellen Warren Scripps, the daughter of the paper's founder. But he also held a grand passion for the emergent Arts and Crafts movement of the time, which emphasized hand fabrication, guild-like organization, and the application of beautiful design to everyday life as a counterpoint to darker aspects of industrialization, technology, and urbanization. Booth dreamed of creating a school like the American Academy in Rome or the Bauhaus in his own backyard—a gift to the people of Detroit—where young Americans could learn and create in the type of free, open, collaborative environment that was common in European art schools of the time. He hoped that the artists who trained there would in turn advance American design to a place where it rivaled its European counterparts. Thus the plan for the Cranbrook Academy of Art was born.

It's fitting that Booth's ambitious vision really took form through a creative partnership. In 1923, he was introduced to the star Finnish architect Eliel Saarinen, a man at the forefront of the Arts and Crafts movement who had already made a name for himself with ambitious civic designs, including the breathtaking Helsinki train station. Together Booth and Saarinen conceived of the Cranbrook Academy of Art as it exists today on the property of Booth's Bloomfield Hills estate. The campus would eventually feature many structures, including a library, a museum, a chapel, an institute of science, and several lower schools with the aim of preparing students for future enrollment in the Academy. Saarinen shared Booth's vision of a fully integrated education. He believed that "art education must grow from personal experience with the life problems of today and under the good guidance of a creatively alert mind." Their idea was to favor work, interaction among artists, and interdisciplinary exchange over formal instruction and rigid disciplines. They wanted the Cranbrook Academy to be a vibrant, productive community, with master artists-in-residence serving as *de-facto* mentors to students wishing to freely explore their creativity.

Perhaps even more than the magnificent grounds, Saarinen and Booth's legacy of freedom is the most enduring feature of the Cranbrook experience today. Graduate students from all over the world come to this orderly campus a short distance from downtown Detroit. They participate in symposia and critiques but immersion in one's process remains the primary focus, with prominent working artists serving as the guides. The program at Cranbrook has expanded since its founding. It is now composed of 10 loosely structured disciplines: 2-D design, 3-D design, architecture, ceramics, fiber, metalsmithing, painting, photography, print media, and sculpture. The school boasts an impressive roster of alumni, including painter Carol Wald, ceramicist Toshiko Takaezu, and designer Ray Eames. The students who follow their footsteps today consistently express gratitude for their time at the school and the space—both physical and mental—that it provides them. The tradition set forth by George Booth and Eliel Saarinen lives on in students like Jackie Laurita, who explained the unique journey of self-discovery that unfolds at Cranbrook: "I have been surrounded by so many amazing artists here that I now understand what the life of an artist can be, what it looks like." It is voices like hers that will continue to shape the world of art for years to come.

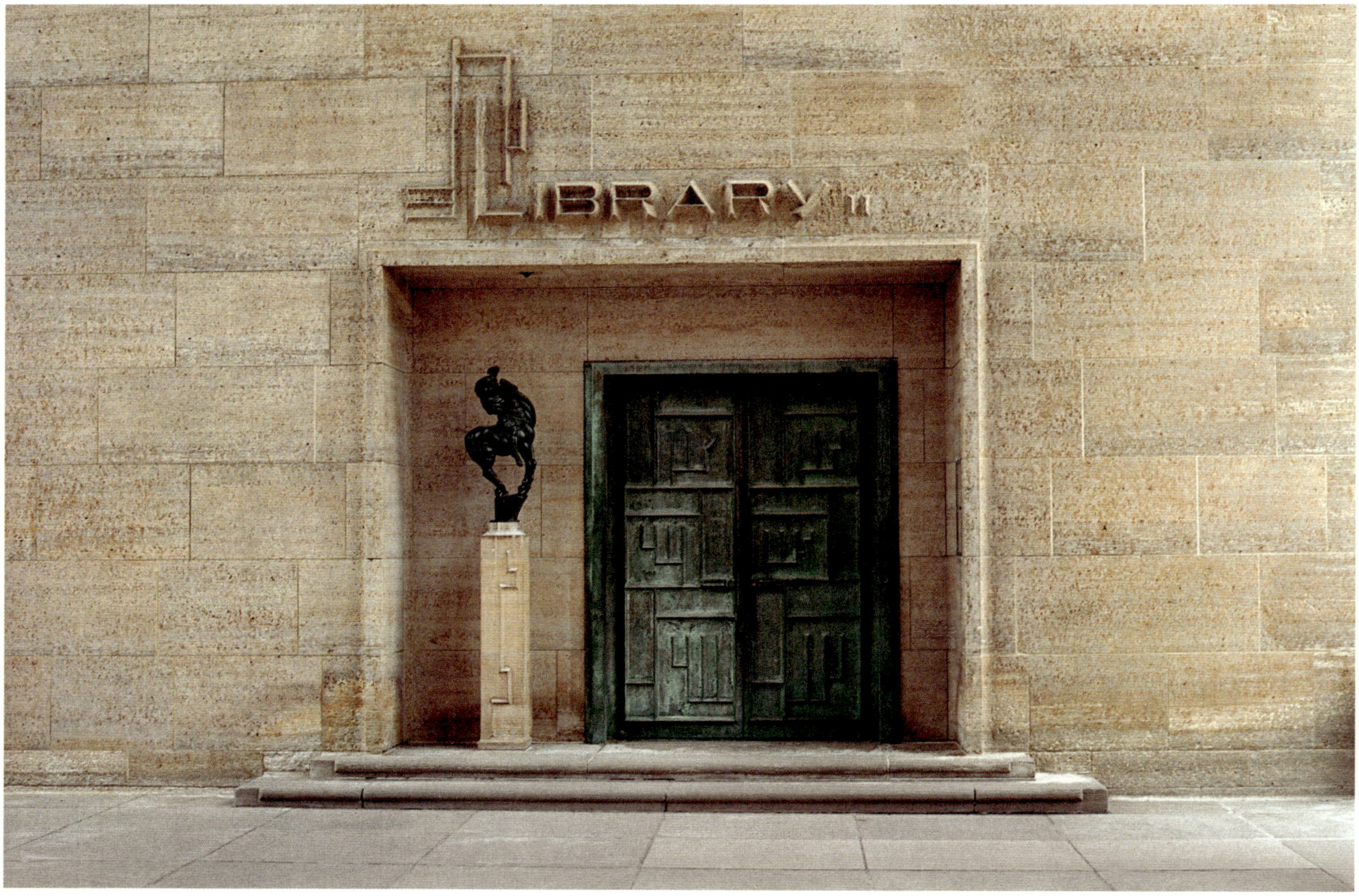


CRANBROOK LIBRARY DESIGNED BY ELIEL SAARINEN

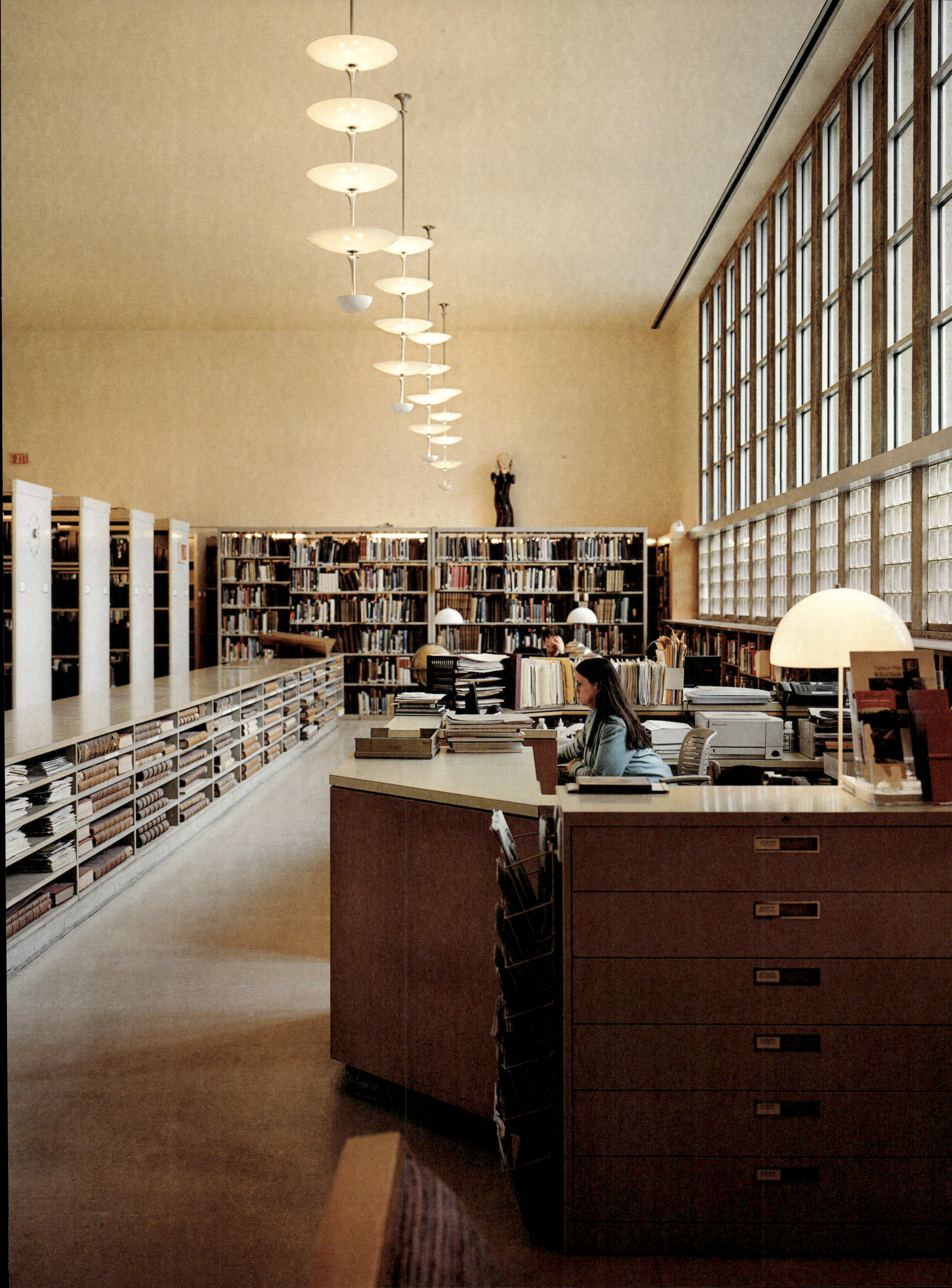

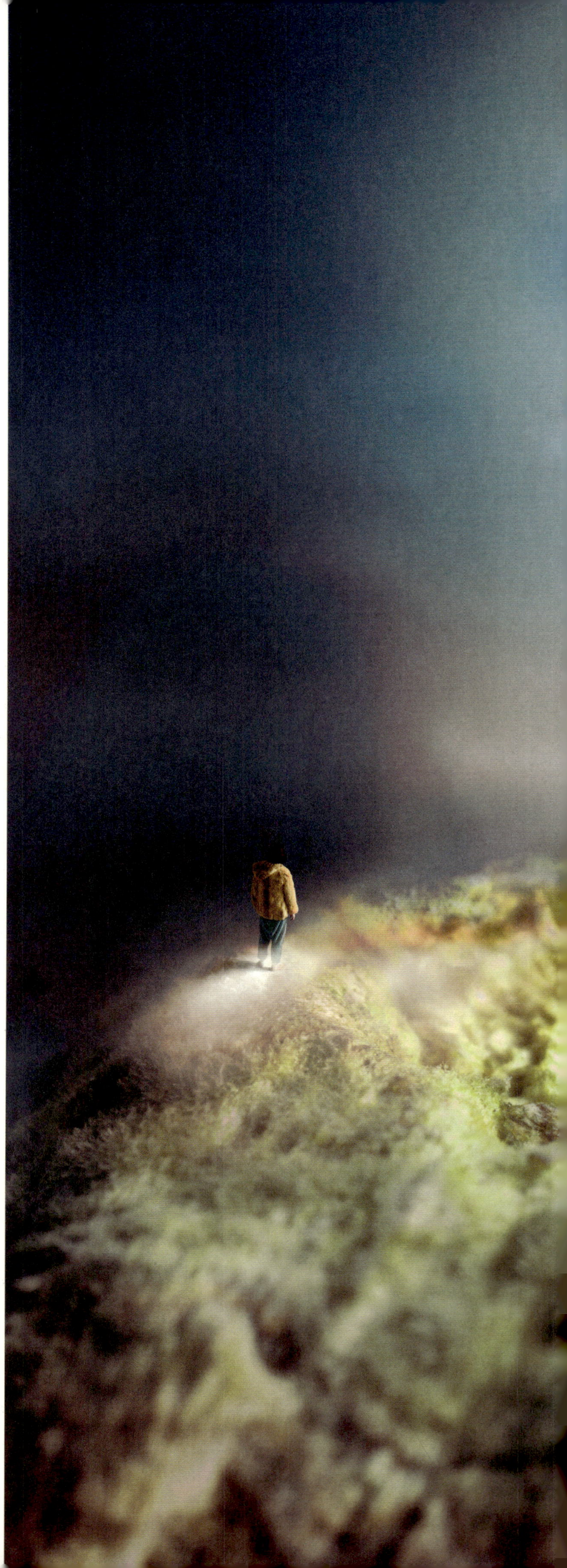

PHOTOGRAPH BY ALEX SOLOMON, PRINT MEDIA DEPARTMENT, CLASS OF 2012

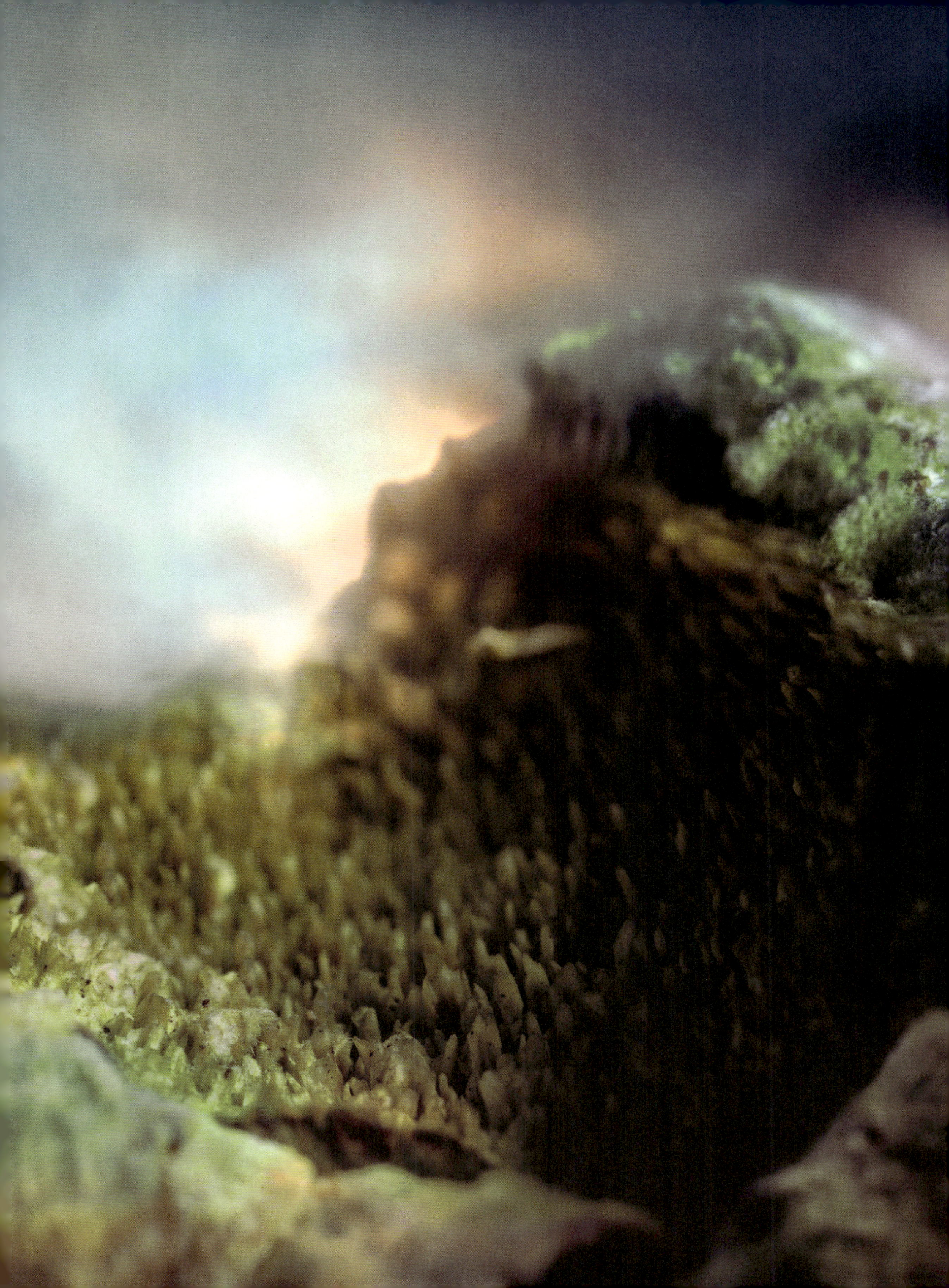

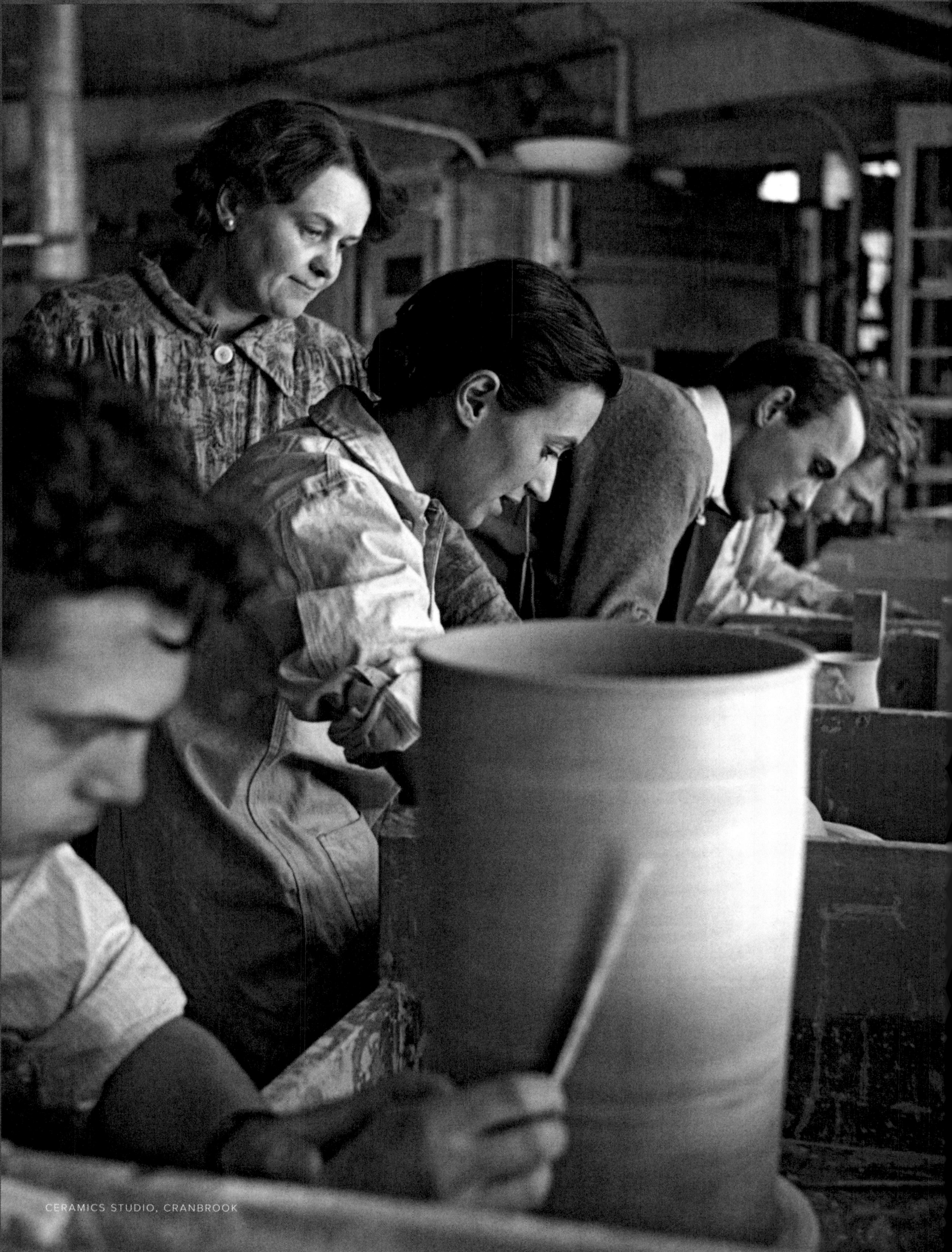

CERAMICS STUDIO, CRANBROOK

**SHARAN ELRAN** I've been studying the use of digital fabrication within ceramic design. I often work with bricks as a design strategy, so I started messing around to see what the possibilities were. At some point, I realized that if I made a set of bricks that were unique but interlocking, I could rearrange them and make slightly different works again and again from the same mold. Each time I cast, I would get something new. That lucky breakthrough moment was the start of my final project, *Unlimited Edition—1 of 6,227,020,800.* By using a 14-piece mold, I can create a unique vase for every person on earth. I found a way to interweave traditional mass production with mass customization. The vase is a strong symbol in many cultures—something everyone can relate to—so the project works on many levels. I also relate strongly to the Cranbrook idea that there's a connection between fine art, architecture, and craft. The disciplines all communicate at the school, and I feel that in *Unlimited Edition* as well.

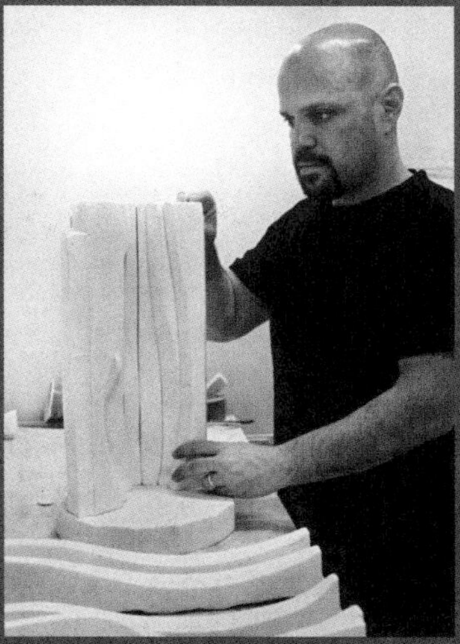

There's a tension in the project—on one hand, there are only 14 pieces to my mold, so it seems kind of reasonable. But then there's this huge number of permutations available. *Unlimited Edition* maps how big humanity is, but at the same time it implies how little one person can do. That's the main interest of the project for me—I really feel how limited I am. Even if I only made these vases for the rest of my life, I would never finish. It's a very visceral experience. I can be in the studio on my legs working for 12 to 15 hours a day. But I definitely want to give the project more time to see how it develops and how the meaning changes after 200, 300, or 1,000 pieces.

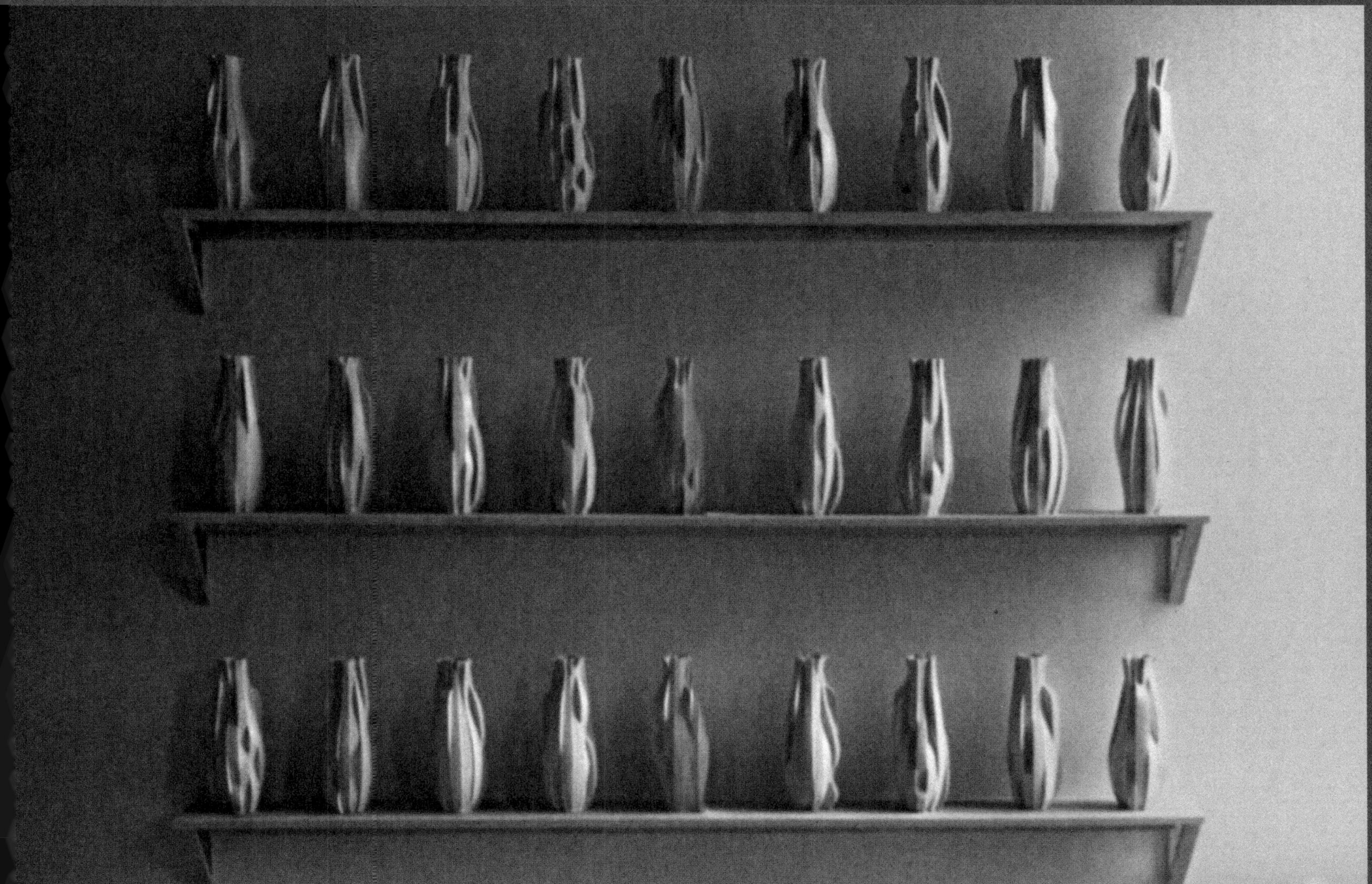

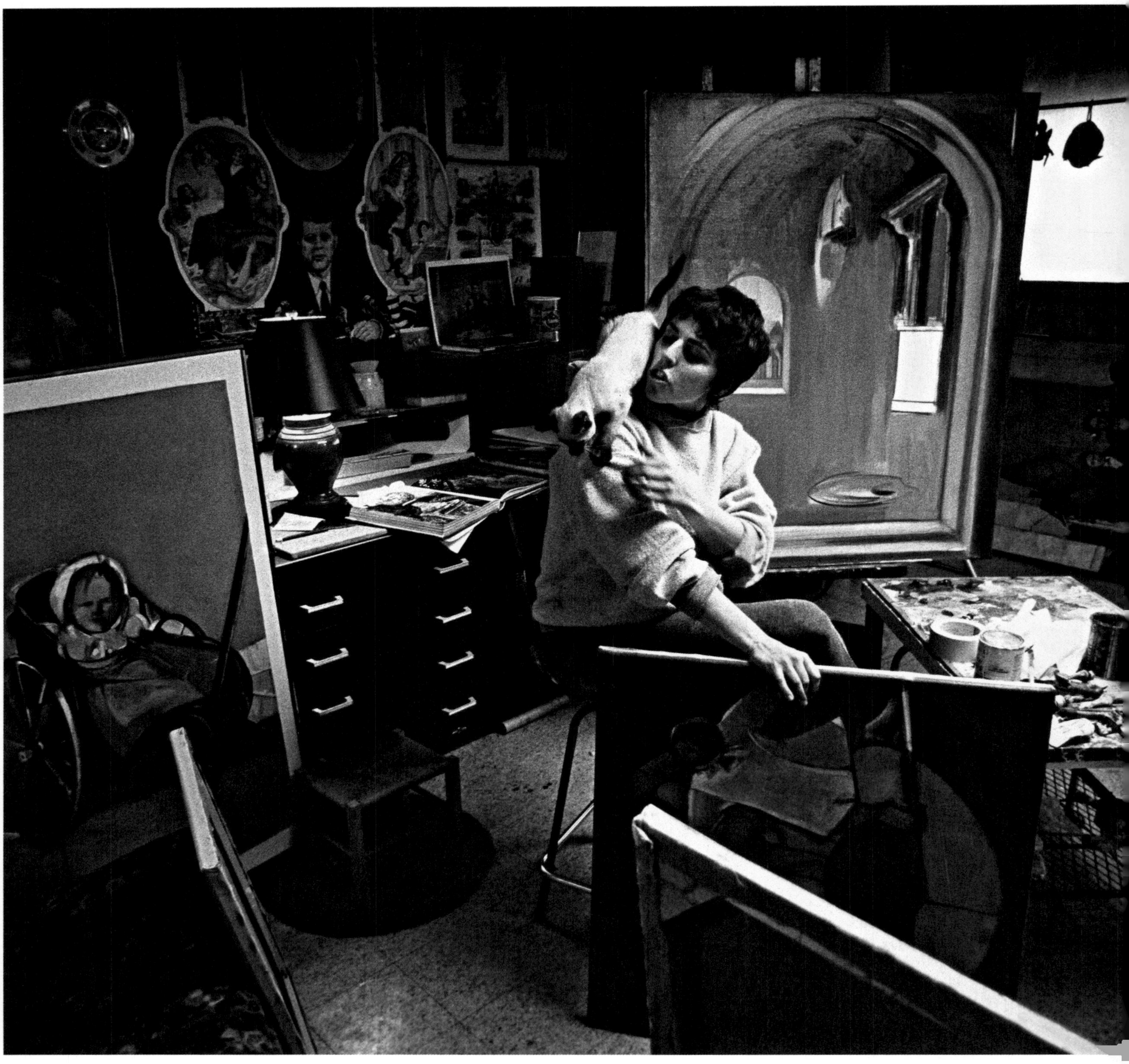

CAROL WALD, CLASS OF 1967

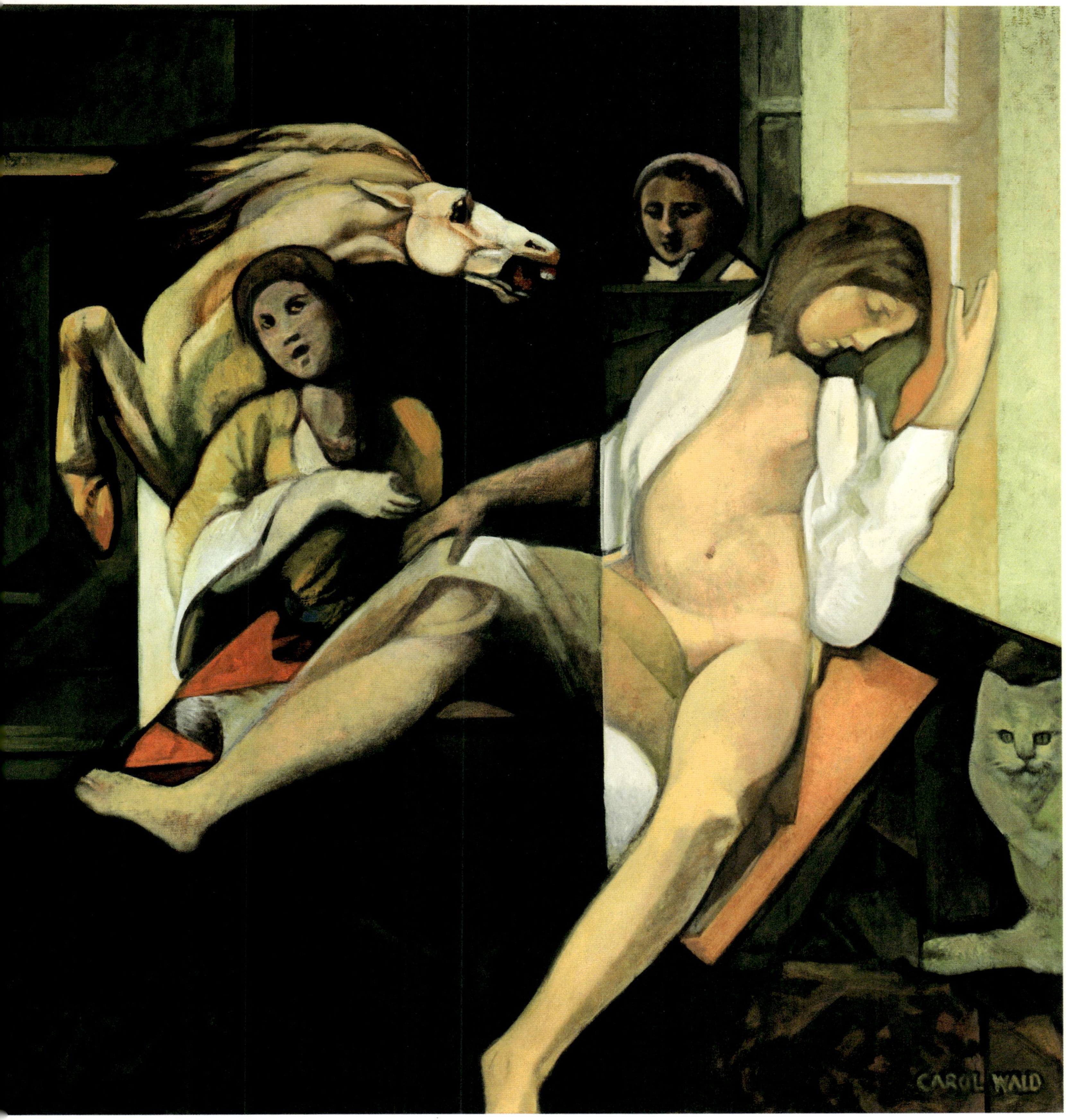
CAROL WALD

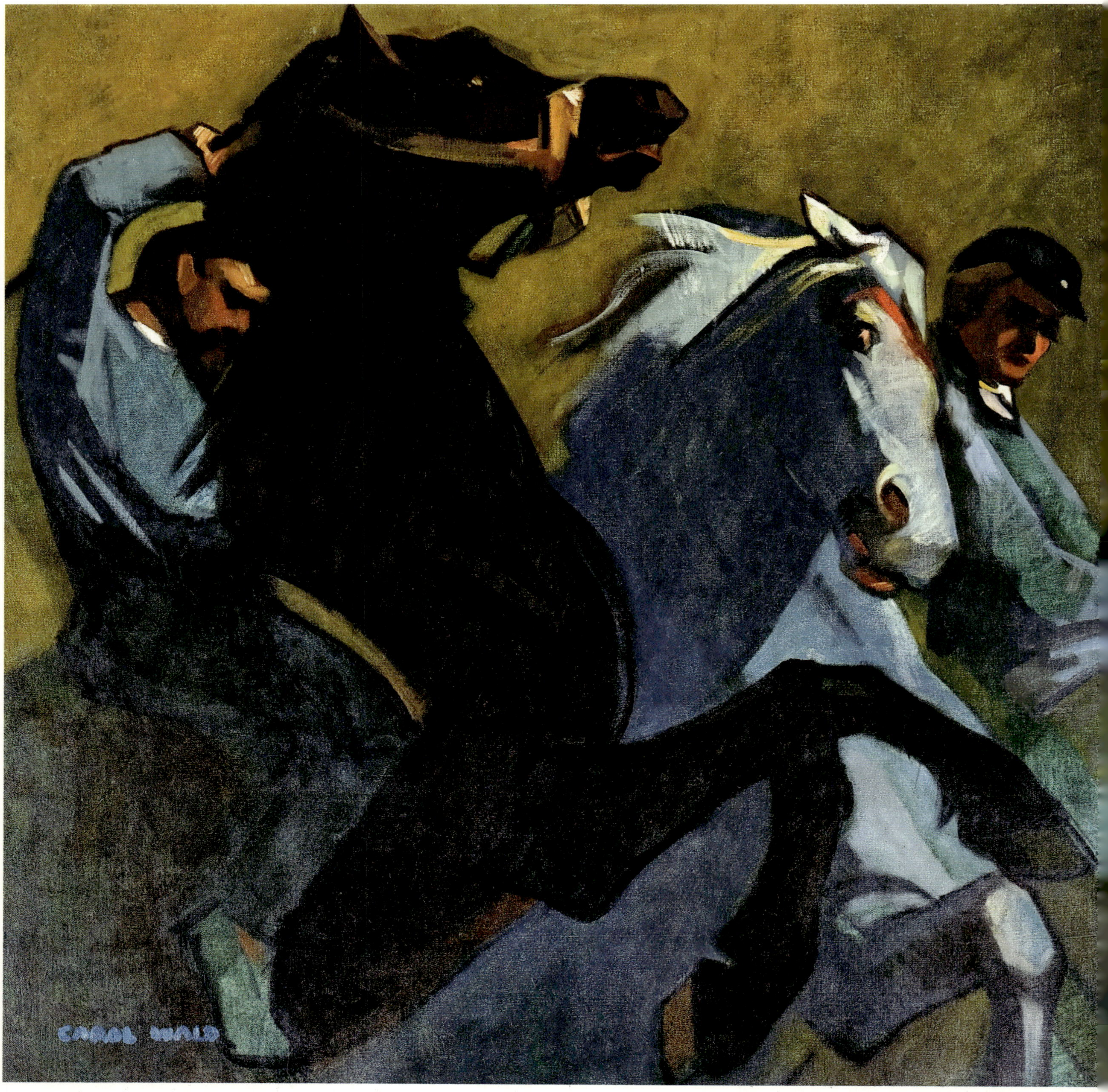
CAROL WALD

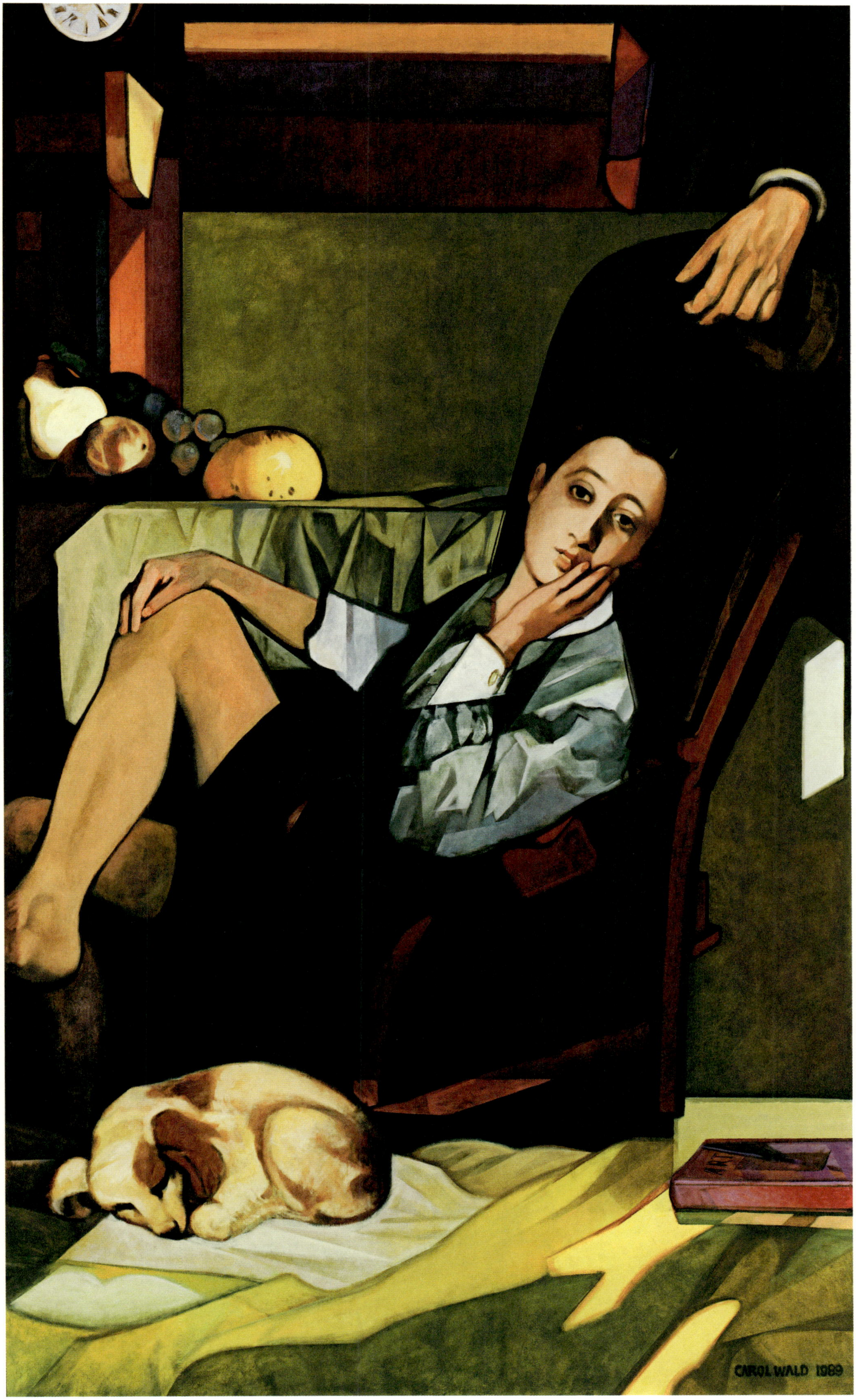
CAROL WALD 1989

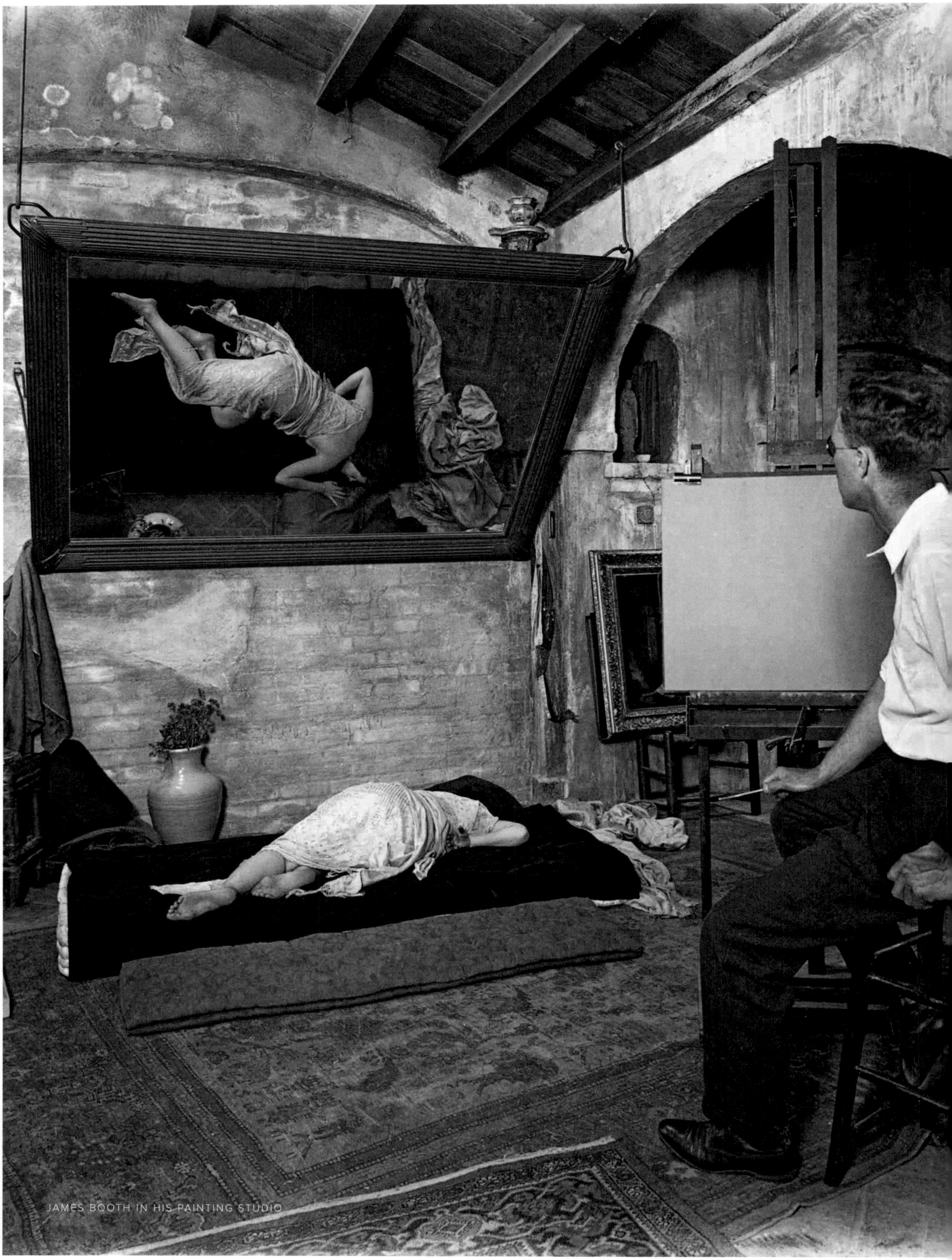

JAMES BOOTH IN HIS PAINTING STUDIO

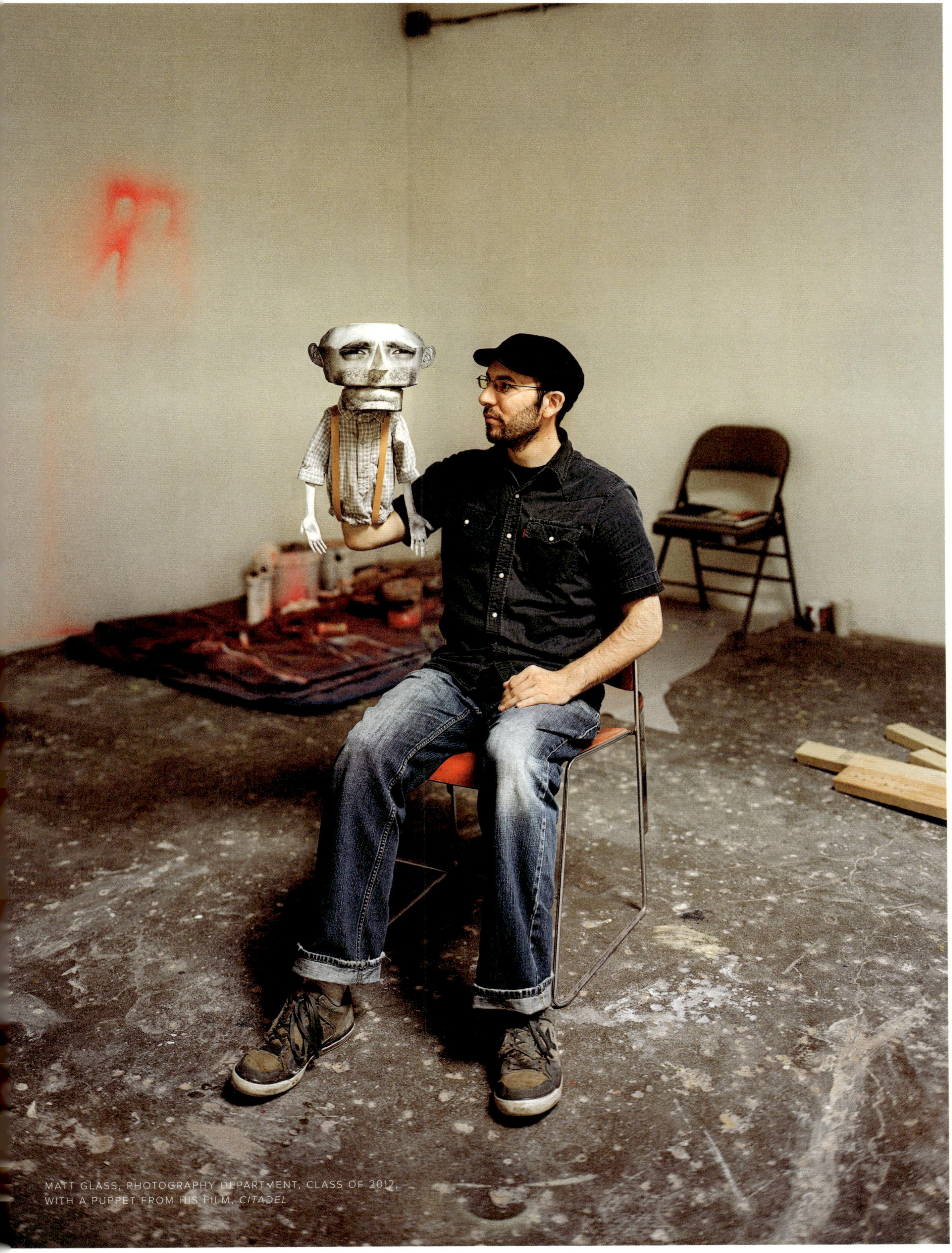

MATT GLASS, PHOTOGRAPHY DEPARTMENT, CLASS OF 2012,
WITH A PUPPET FROM HIS FILM, *CITADEL*

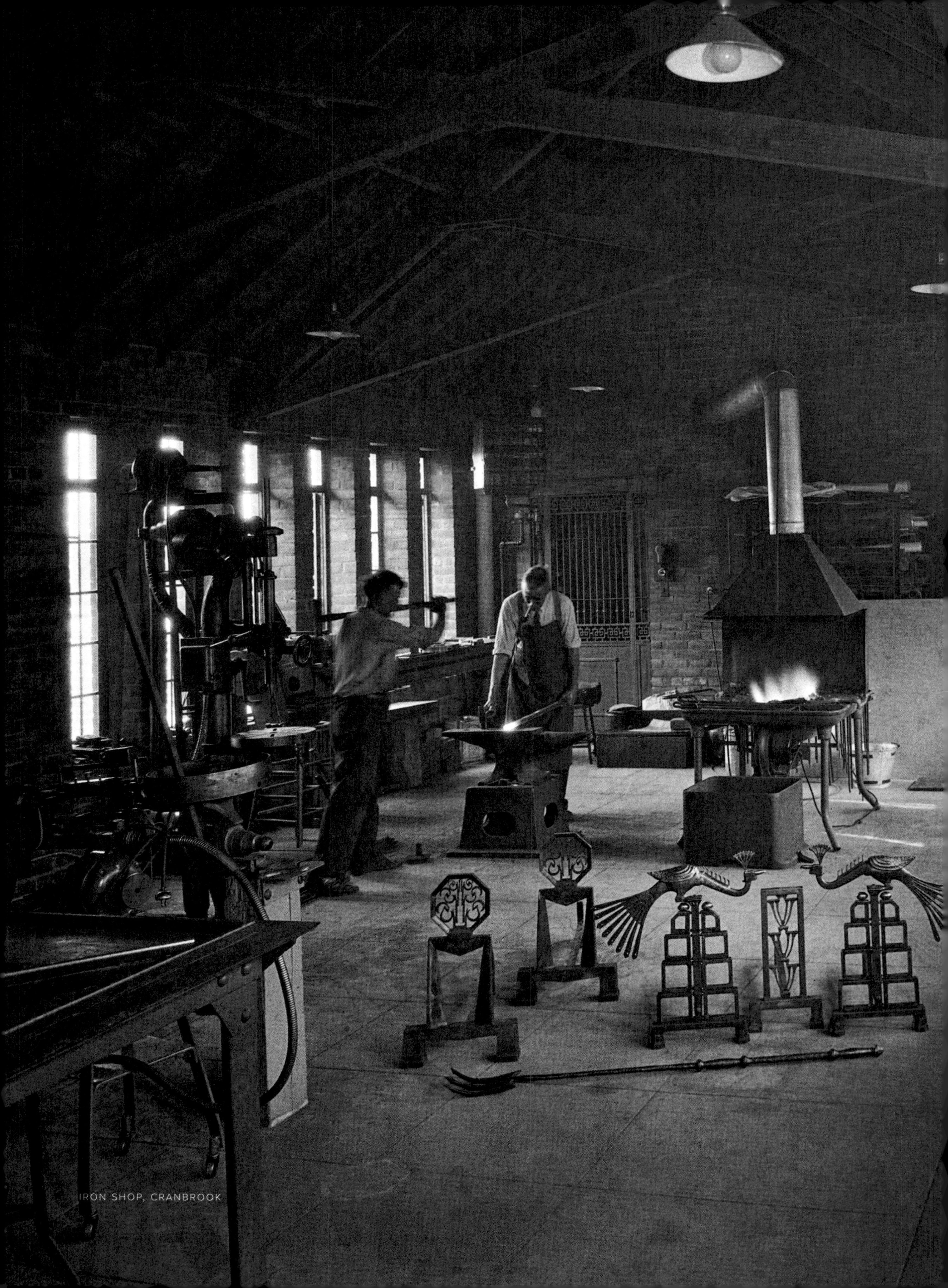

IRON SHOP, CRANBROOK

MOHAMED THIAM You have the freedom to do your own thing here at Cranbrook, but you quickly figure out that most of the people you're surrounded by share your ambition and have the ability to think outside the box. You get here the first week and have all this free space, so you start asking questions that you didn't ask yourself before. You can't really trick anyone—people will call you out if your work is vague or cliché. You have to be clear about what you're saying. I find sometimes I push my work too far, and it either becomes way too abstract or I lose control over it. But by doing that, I start to discover new territories and bring it back to my strengths. That's when I realize that there's no end to artistic progress. All these questions of doubt and self-awareness that I've never had to address start kicking in, and the results are pretty interesting creatively.

Lately my work has dealt with perception, how people see themselves and others or are perceived depending on the context. I'm from Senegal originally, but when I'm walking in the street here, most people assume I'm an African-American from the States. This phase of my work explores race in relation to my personal experience. I'm curious about how certain objects come to be labeled and associated with certain ideas, whether it's race or religion. I happen to be black and Muslim, so I guess I'm trying to see how objects can be a source of empowerment, but at the same time in the hands of the wrong people they can become a source of oppression. I'm curious about that double effect—the two sides of stereotypes and prejudices—and want to expand the visual vocabulary for those ideas.

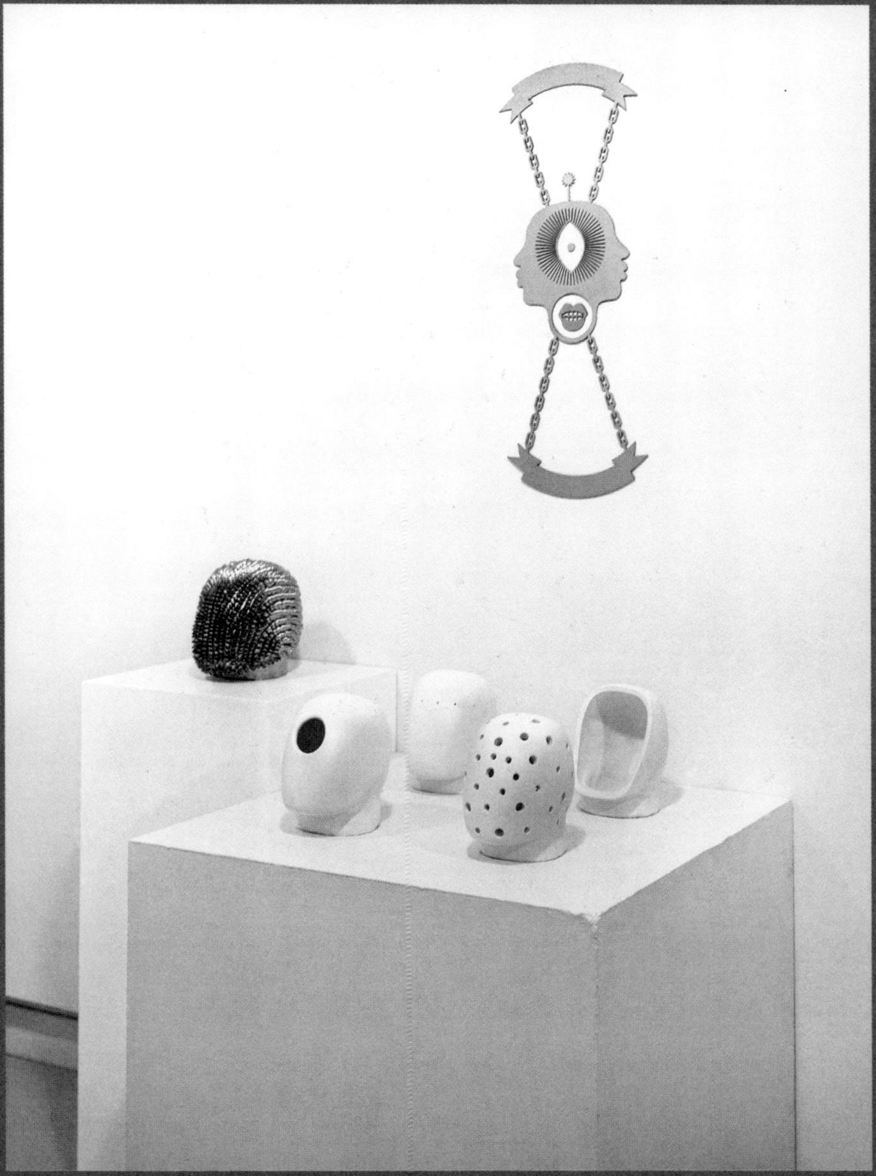

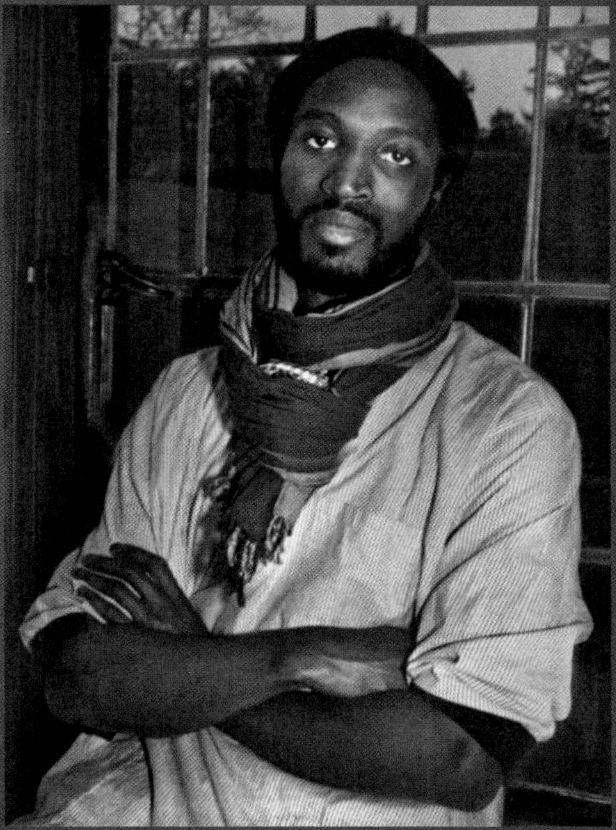

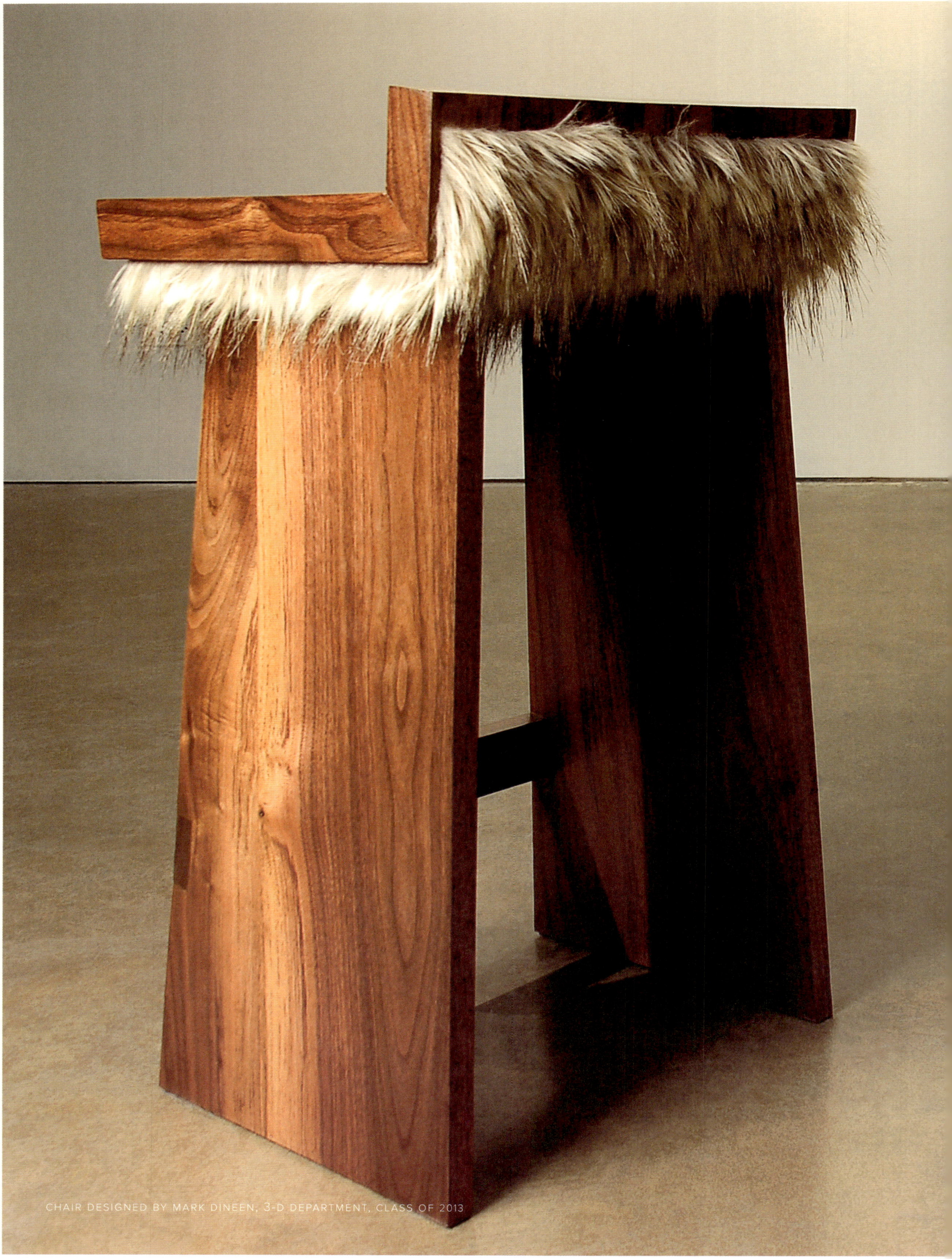

CHAIR DESIGNED BY MARK DINEEN, 3-D DEPARTMENT, CLASS OF 2013

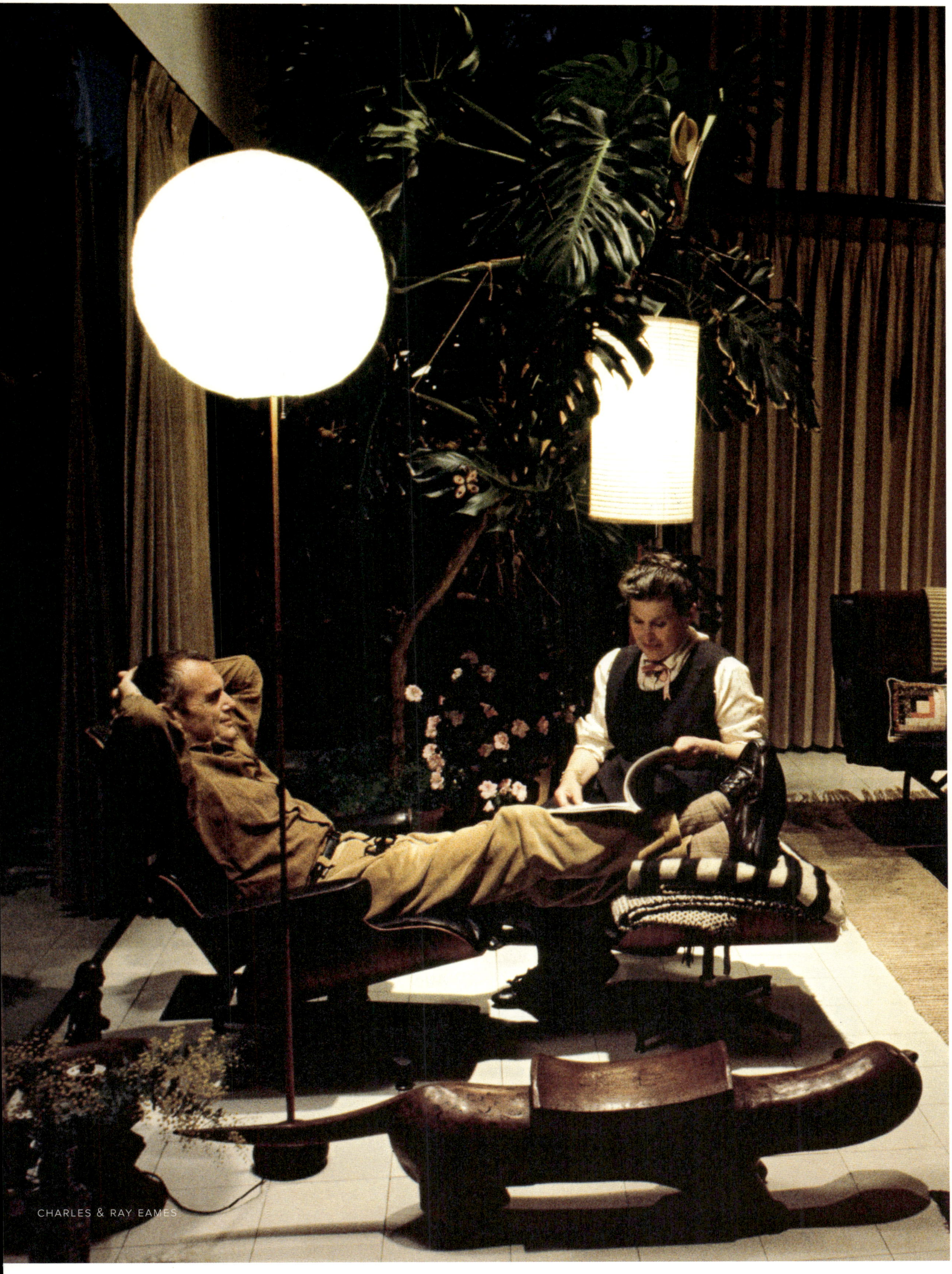

TOSHIKO TAKAEZU, CERAMICS DEPARTMENT, CLASS OF 1954

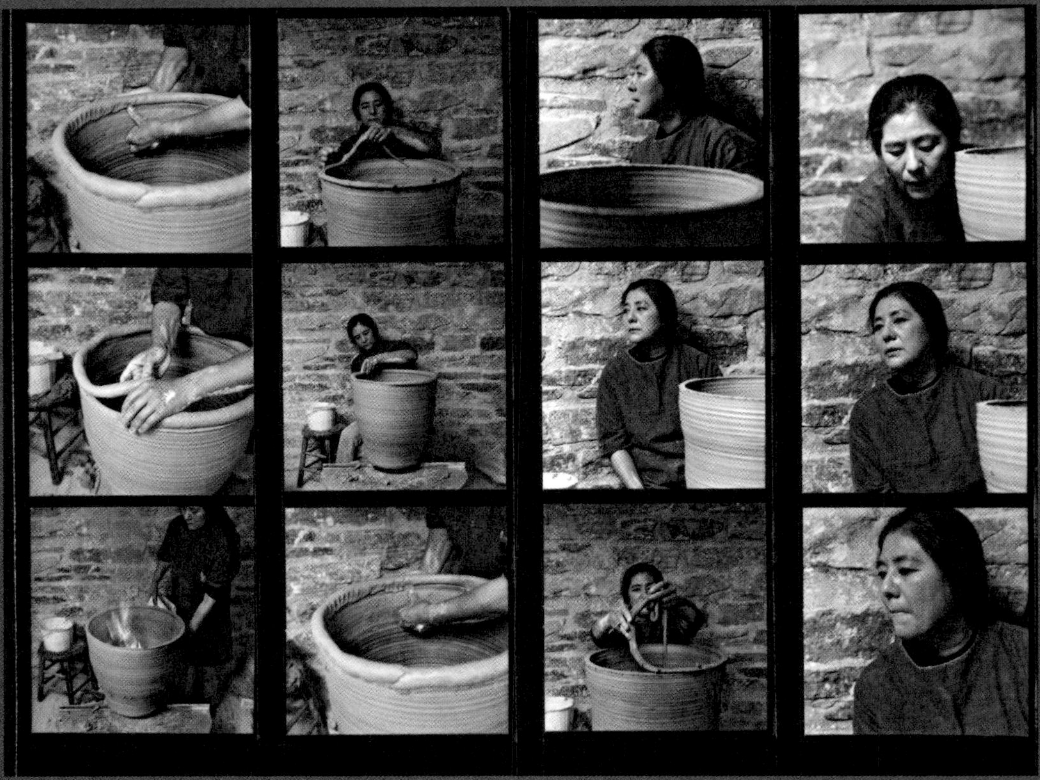

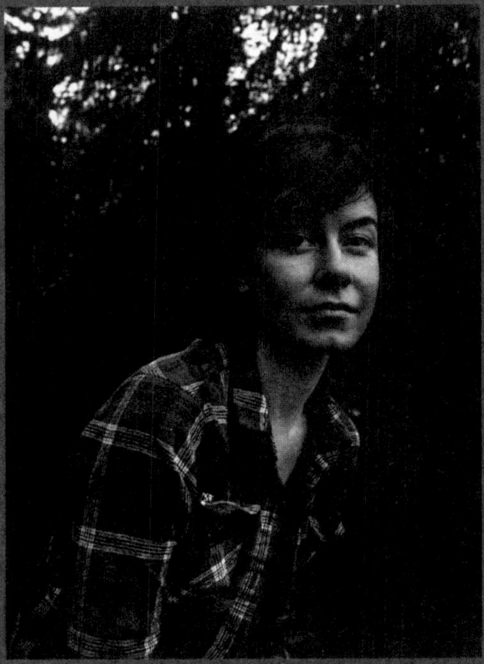

"THE ARTISTS IN RESIDENCE DON'T REALLY HAVE AN AGENDA. WE ARE RESPONSIBLE FOR MAKING THE DEPARTMENT WHATEVER IT IS, SO WE HAVE TO STEP UP AND BE PRESENT. WE AREN'T IN A DEPARTMENT, WE *ARE* THE DEPARTMENT."

KATIE WOOD, FIBER DEPARTMENT, CLASS OF 2013

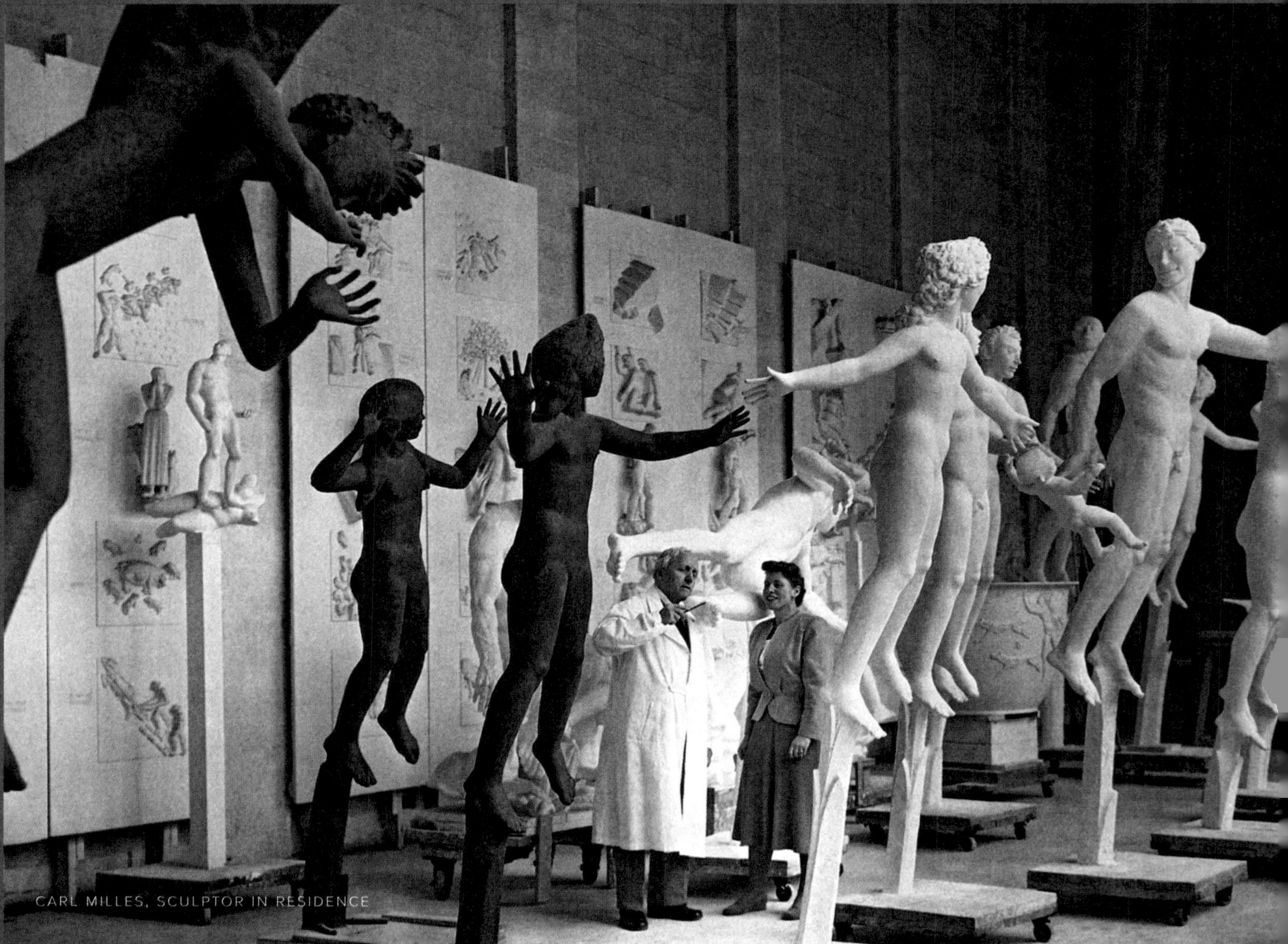

CARL MILLES, SCULPTOR IN RESIDENCE

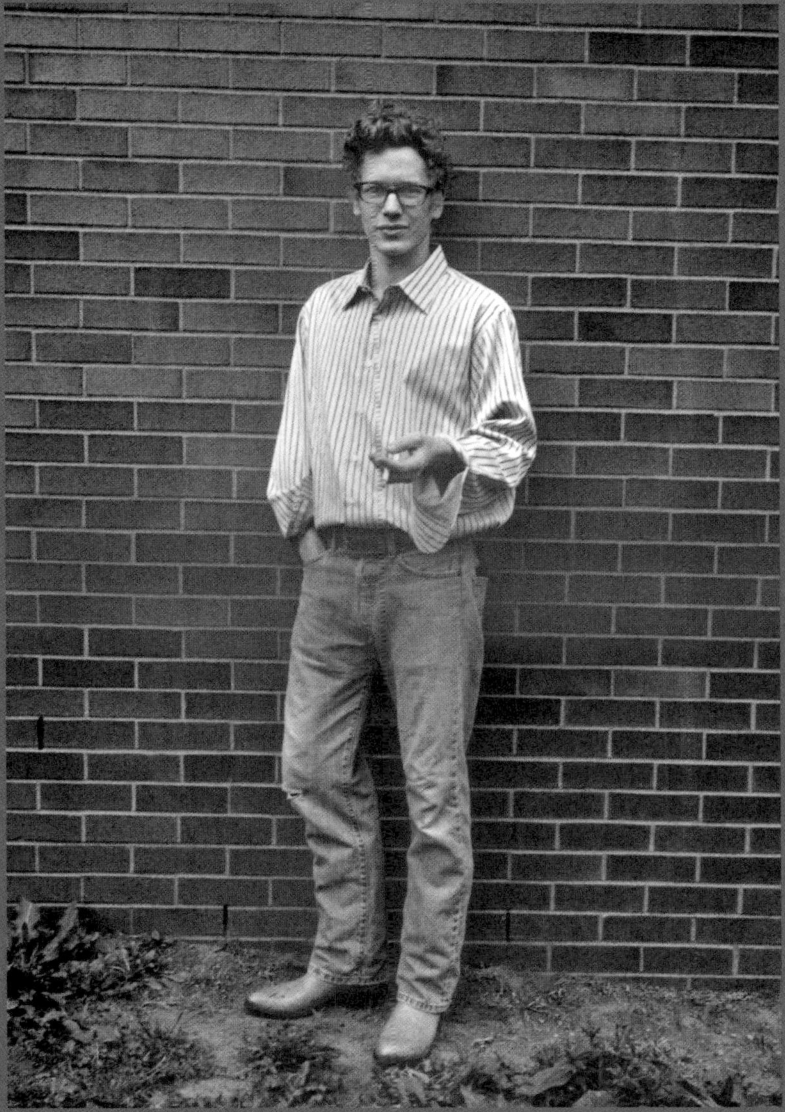

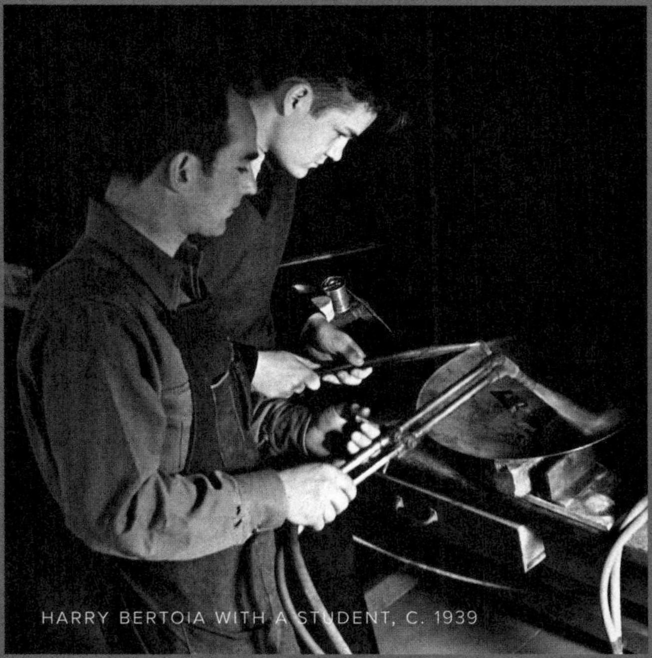

HARRY BERTOIA WITH A STUDENT, C. 1939

"I THINK OF THE CRANBROOK EXPERIENCE METAPHORICALLY AS A FIELD OF CONVERSATION THAT YOU EXIST WITHIN. WHEN I'M WORKING OR THINKING ABOUT MY OWN PRACTICE, THAT GROUP OF VOICES IS VERY PRESENT. IT'S ALMOST LIKE THE COMMUNITY ENDS UP TAKING THE ROLE OF THE TEACHER."

CHARLIE TALBOT, CERAMICS DEPARTMENT, CLASS OF 2013

WORKSPACE OF AMY WEIKS, METALSMITHING DEPARTMENT CLASS OF 2012

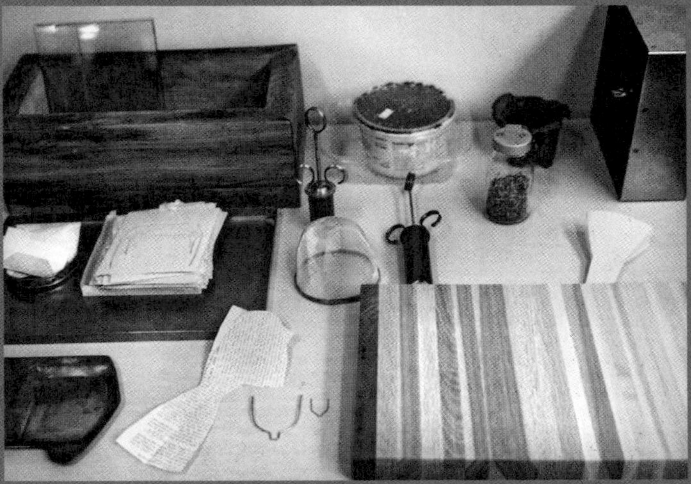

"IN OUR CRITIQUES, WE PULL EVERYTHING APART AND DIG THROUGH ALL THESE LAYERS, SO WE REALLY BECOME SELF-AWARE OF HOW WE MAKE THINGS AND LOOK AT THE WORLD. BEING AT CRANBROOK HAS HELPED ME TO STEP BACK AND SEE."—AMY WEIKS

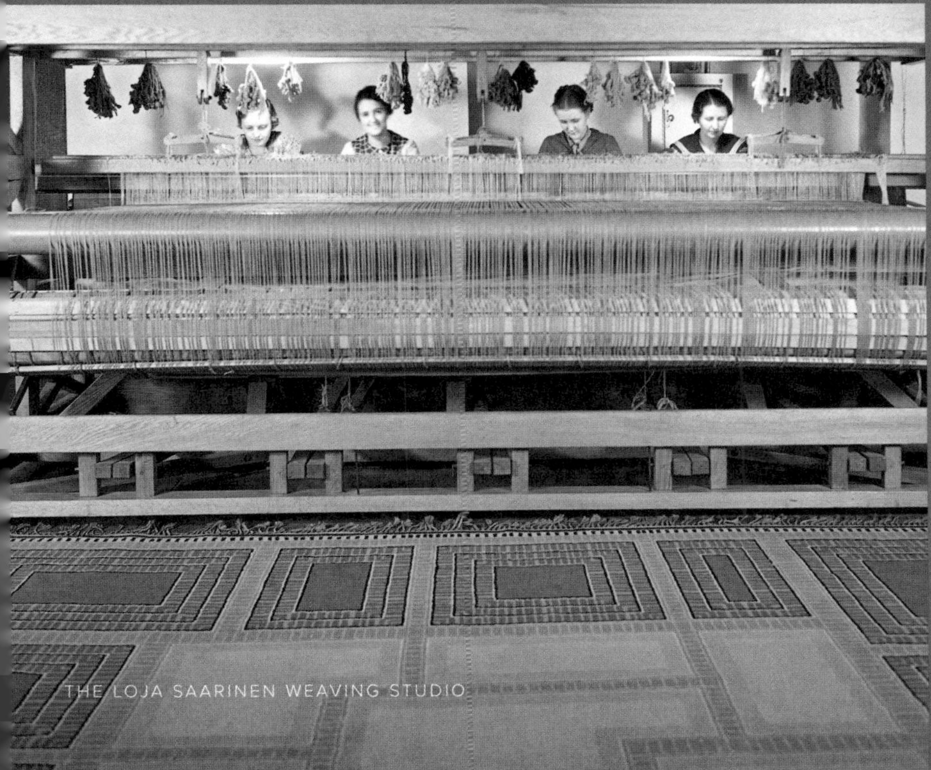

THE LOJA SAARINEN WEAVING STUDIO

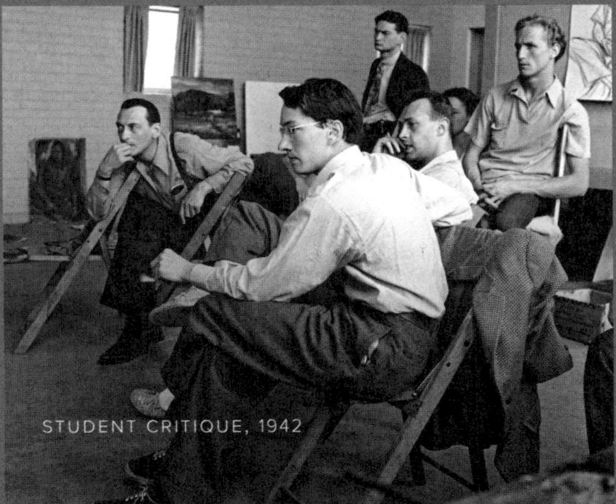

STUDENT CRITIQUE, 1942

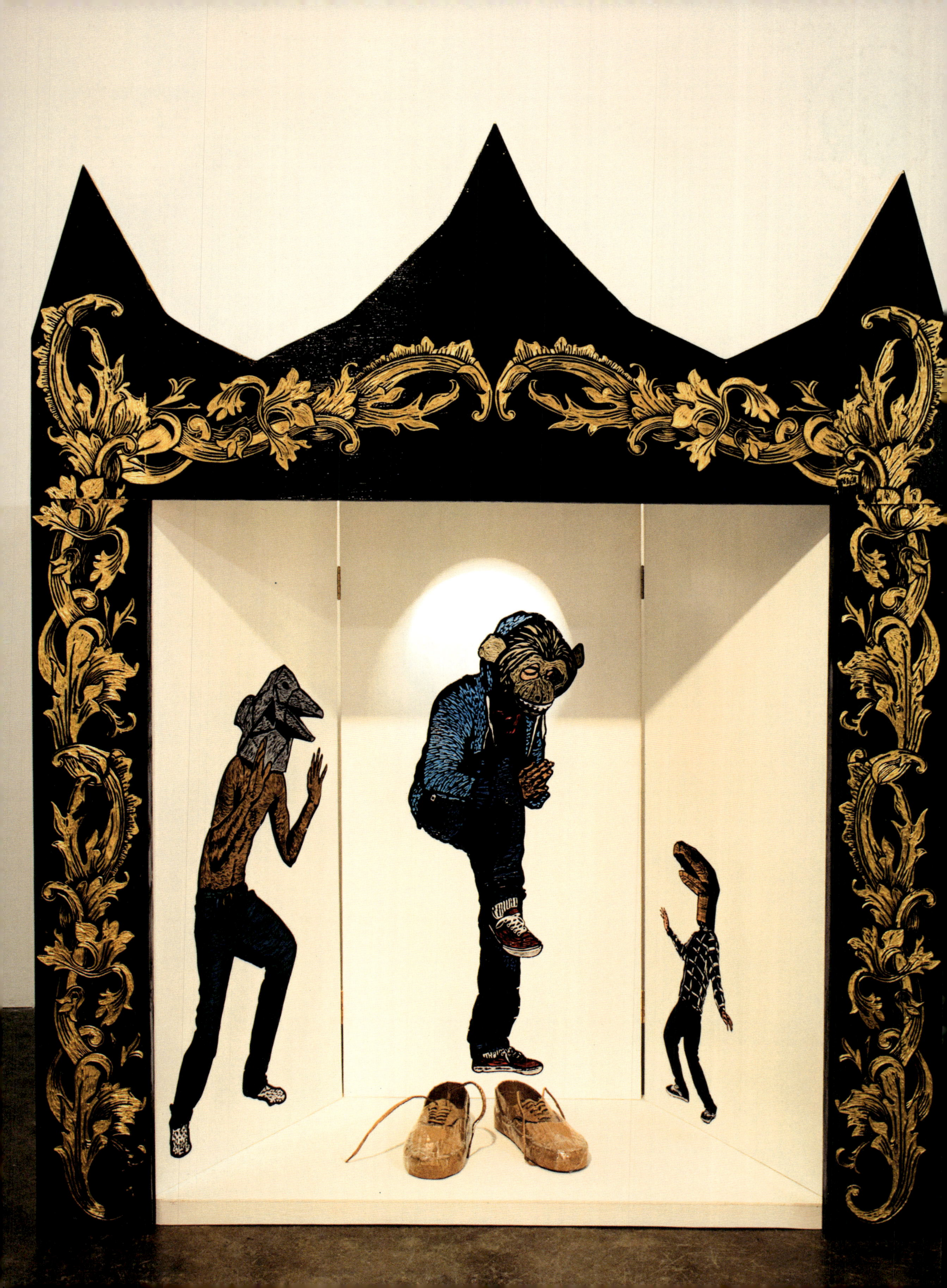

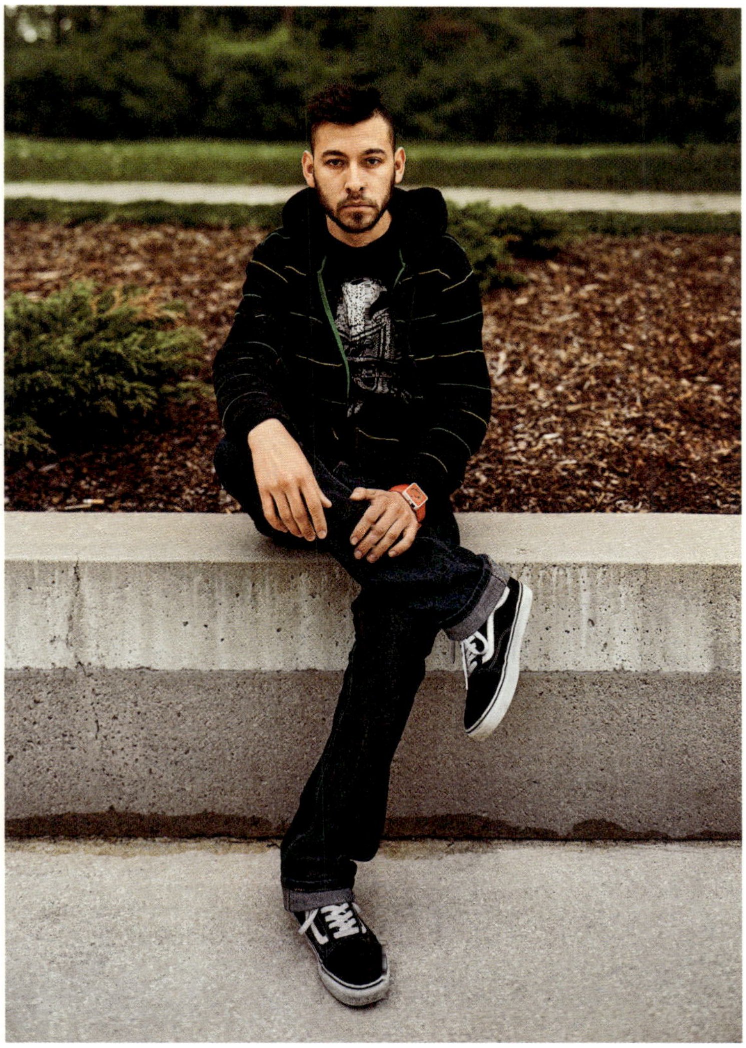

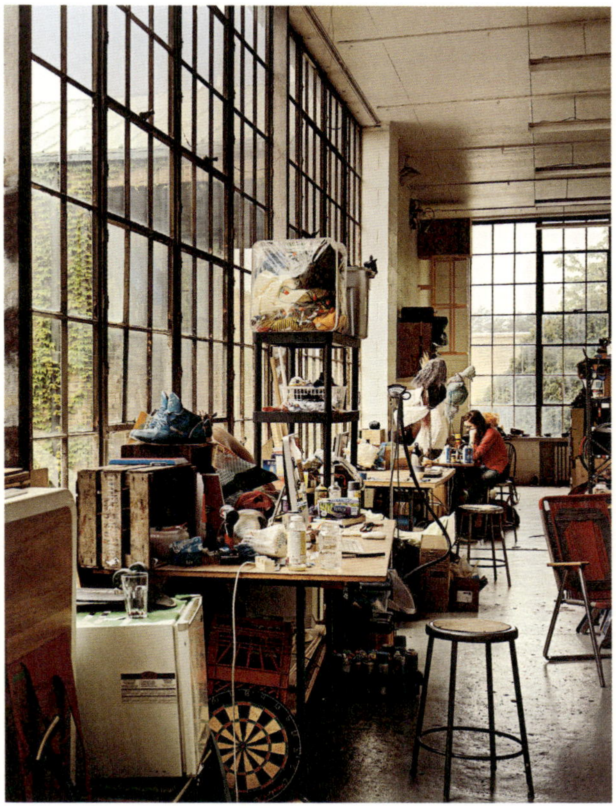

CRANBROOK SCULPTURE STUDIO

FRANCISCO ALONZO This is my first year at Cranbrook in the Print Media Department. I'm an immigrant from Mexico who spent pretty much my whole life in California. When I work, those two places and the experience of never being able to fit in are always in the back of my mind. I reference a lot of pop culture, icons, images, and symbols that I hope will relate to peoples' lives, including their culture, subculture, and different kinds of families. I always want my work to be aesthetically pleasing—it's important to me that people want to look at it. My mom was incredibly supportive of anything I did when I was growing up, but my dad wasn't as much because he didn't understand what I was trying to do. I want my work to be able to grab on to that audience as well, people who are less trained in the art world. And because I grew up in poverty, I always try to use really affordable materials, stuff that's just around.

I work with subjects that people are sensitive to. Nobody likes to talk about race or stereotypes. I bring humor into my work, so that the audience doesn't immediately recognize the stereotypes I'm confronting them with. The community at Cranbrook is actually the opposite of the audience I'm most hoping to reach with my art. Many of the symbols I use from the history of Mexican art that might be really obvious back home in California are often lost out here in the Midwest. So I've had to learn how to take comments from my peers at Cranbrook. I want to be challenged and grow, but I also need to pick and choose what will actually move my work forward without changing what I want to say. That has been a struggle for sure.

Right now, I'm trying to play with this idea that while I'm Mexican-American and belong to that community, I'm also exploiting it. I've separated myself from being a "Mexican-Mexican," which feels shameful to my culture. But at the same time I'm grabbing onto a culture that's new, so there's really nothing to be ashamed of. It's actually a lot of fun. I take inspiration from all aspects of my life: the clothes I wear, the music I listen to, the political history of printmaking. I'm always changing. I can never completely know myself, so I'm always trying to learn more.

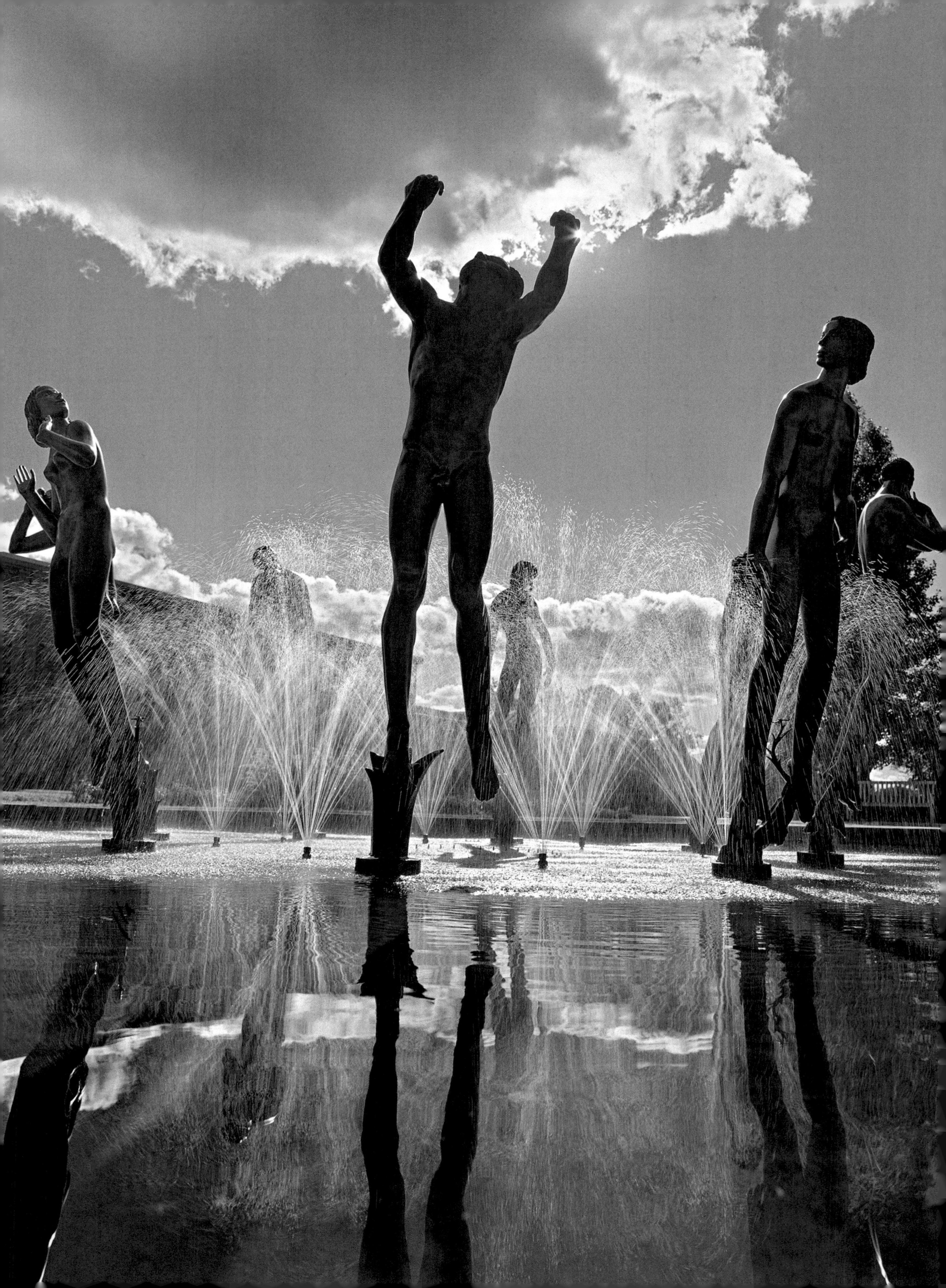

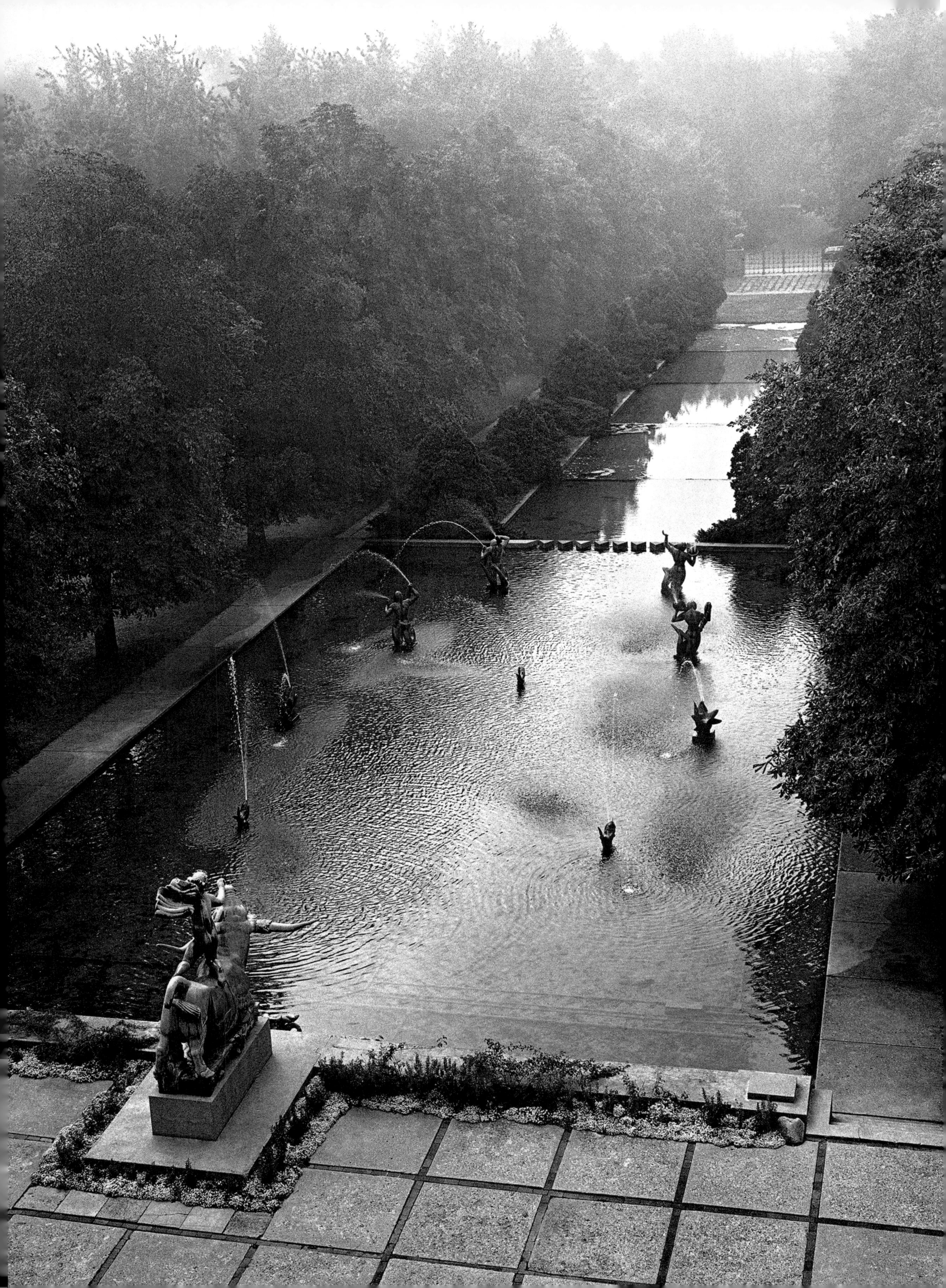

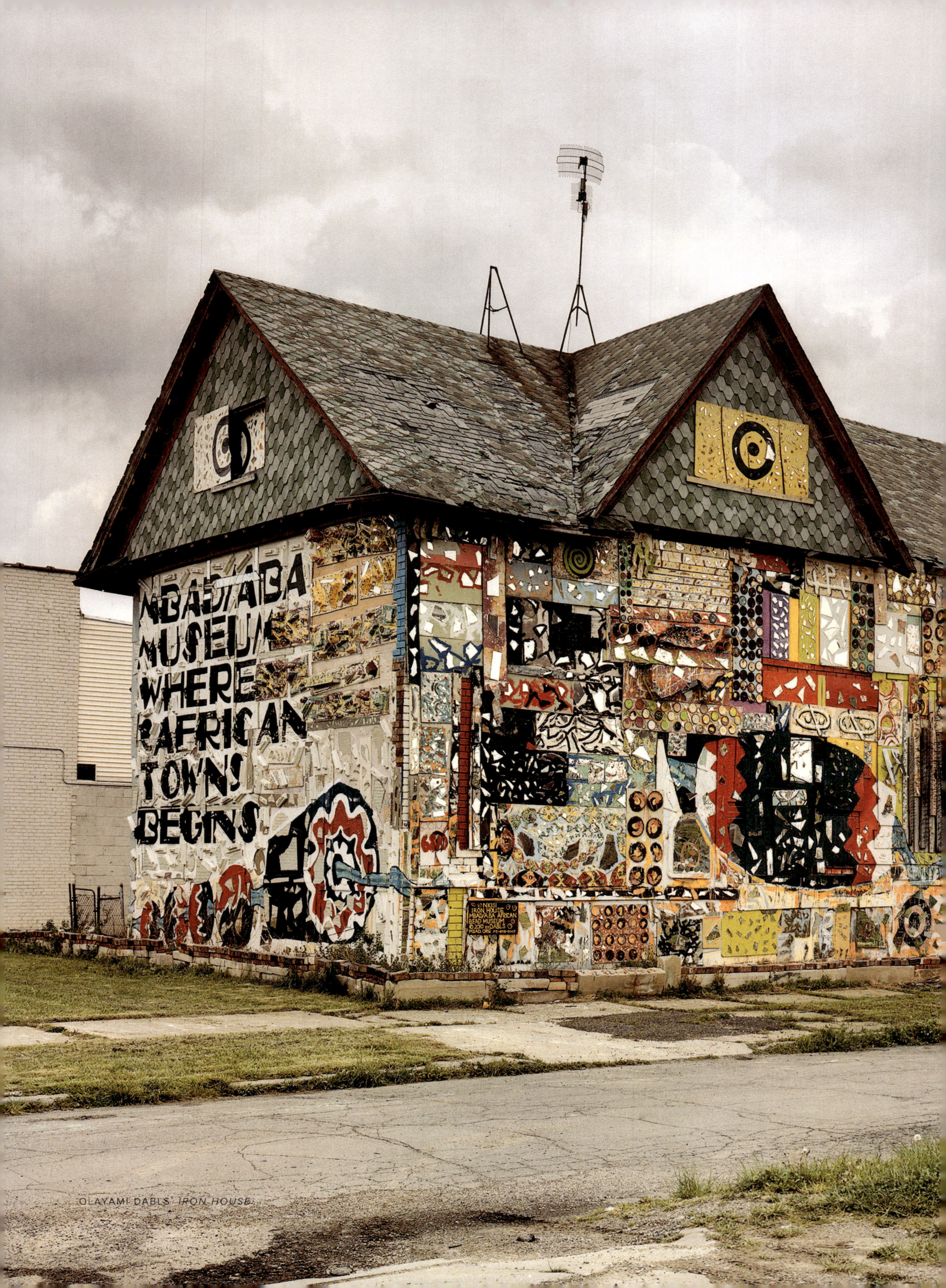

OLAYAMI DABLS' *IRON HOUSE*

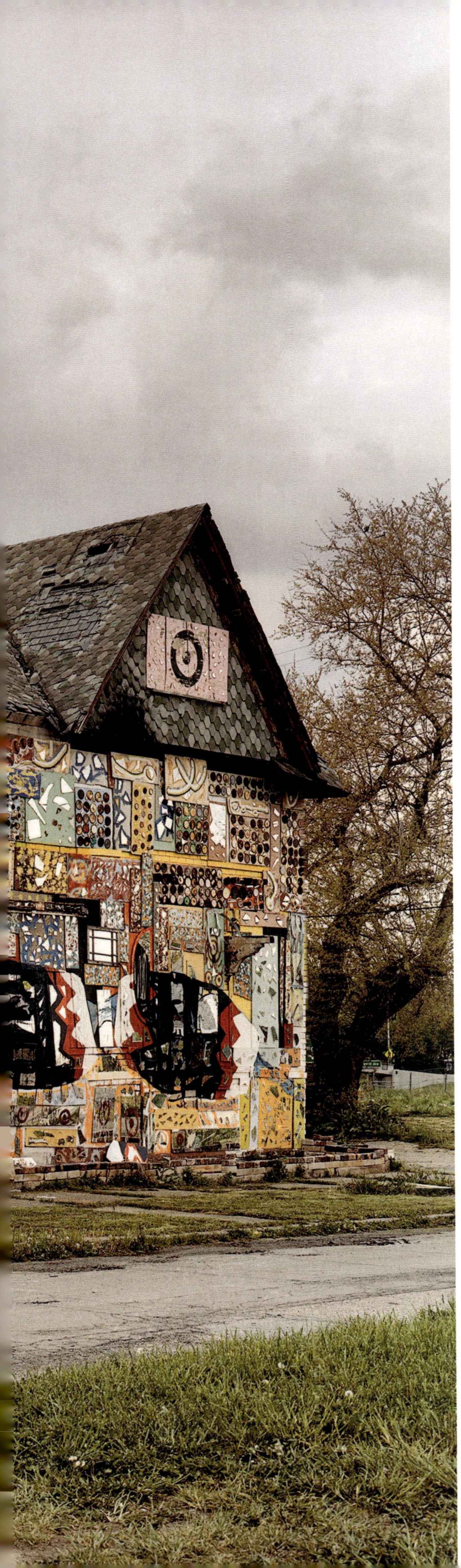

# LIVING ART IN DETROIT

## A TALE OF TWO CITIES

### PART 2: DOWNTOWN CONVERSATIONS

For all its ups and downs, Detroit holds a unique place in the American psyche. This sprawling metropolis proudly claims everyone from Aretha Franklin and Elmore Leonard to Motown and Chrysler as its own. But to outsiders, Detroit rests uncomfortably at the convergence of three potent myths. The first is a tale of mourning, for the decline in American manufacturing, the vanishing of steady factory work, and the loss of pride in products "made here." Then there's the myth of urban collapse—the abandoned Michigan Central train station photographed over and over, wide quiet streets echoing the riots years ago, flight to the suburbs, a beleaguered city government haunted by corruption. And perhaps most powerfully, there is the pioneer myth—a recent flurry of media attention pointing to young artists and entrepreneurs who have found in Detroit a land of opportunity—warehouses converted to working studios, community gardens springing up in vacant lots. Is Detroit on the brink of a renaissance, the comeback kid of the Midwest, a new story of American optimism?

Like all myths, these visions of Detroit are incomplete, the stories overly simplified. The reality of the city today is much more ambiguous and best articulated by those who know—the people who love the place and call it home. Detroit is definitely undergoing some kind of evolution, and as is often the case, artists and creative people are playing a central role. We asked a handful of these characters to explain what they see happening in their backyard. Through their stories, told from the heart, we begin to understand.

PHOTOGRAPHS BY

CARLOS CHARLIE PEREZ

## A CONVERSATION WITH OLAYAMI DABLS

CREATOR OF IRON HOUSE

*An afternoon spent with Olayami Dabls is unforgettable. Over the past decade, this long-time Detroit resident has gradually transformed his home and abandoned properties nearby into a visual spectacle evoking African folklore, language and custom. Dabls' insights into matters of race and politics—and his take on Detroit's misrepresentation in the media—are invaluable to anyone seeking out the "real deal" in Motor City.*

Iron House and the surrounding installations started out as a beautification project. When we first moved to this area in

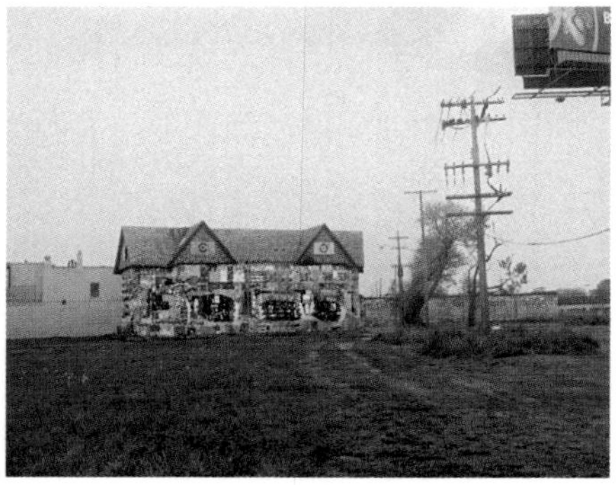

1994, I had intended to create a museum of African beads. But we didn't have the money at the time, so instead of wallowing in our disappointment, we decided to create something that would say, *We are proud to be here.* I had been a curator and lecturer with the Museum of African American History and had trained as an artist at Wayne State. But I had never worked on such a large scale. Coming here opened up a whole new approach to making art. The first mural we did just made everything to the right and the left of it look really bad. So the next summer we began work on the other side and each summer after that for 10 years. People kept coming by saying they liked it, but we had no idea that it would make such an impact on the community. Our goal had just been to make our place of work appealing.

In Detroit, there's a Greektown, a Poletown, a Mexicantown. At some point, it occurred to me that in a city which has over 800,000 African people, there was nothing to remind us of Africa in any form or fashion. So in addition to beautifying the area, these works attempt to remind people of Africa in a genuine way. We accomplished this by tapping into the essence of African symbolism. The materials I used were straight from African material culture—iron, rocks, and wood.

Iron House was originally a four-family unit. There were some folks who squatted there for about 10 years. When they left, they told their friends, who came and took everything of value from the inside—the molding, wiring, fixtures, bricks, etc. When the city inspectors came out one day, we asked, "Can we board this building up?" They said sure, but they didn't know we were going to board it up the way you see it now! We created the building as an N'Kisi—an African totem, often made out of a tree trunk, which guarantees that folks will not bother the community. We asked the N'Kisi for three things—that the city officials not see the property, that vandals not destroy it, and that graffiti artists not tag it. The Iron House has been there 10 years now, out in the open, and no one has done anything to it. There are also 11 installations on the property. All are made from iron, rocks, and wood and deal with the political differences between Africans and Europeans in this country.

One of the greatest things about this installation is how the community has participated. When someone asks, "How can I help?" I suggest they donate materials or paint. I can't use a regular crew, because I don't have any idea where I'm going when I work—it all just comes out of the process. But people will come by to lend a hand or to donate materials, some from as far away as Lansing, Michigan. I had the idea to include mirrors in the installation because so many cultures have special stories about them, particularly in Africa, where they were used to communicate with ancestors. Mirrors are actually quite expensive.

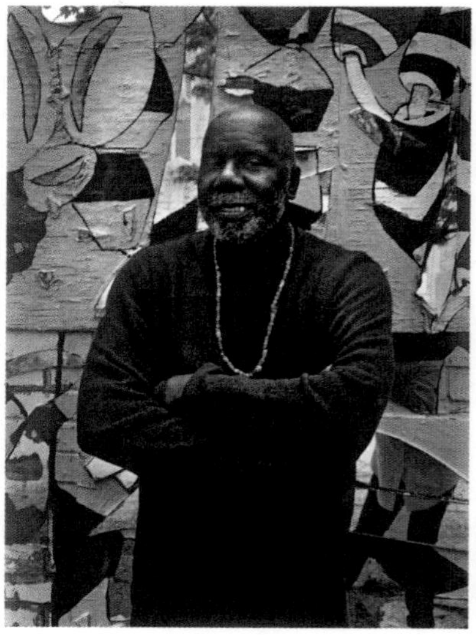

But since broken or cracked mirrors have a negative connotation in this country, people have been happy to donate them. Last year, a woman donated paint cans left behind in a building she had purchased. One of the cans was industrial enamel sign paint, so we've been redoing the whole house using these vibrant colors designed to withstand the sun. So there's a lot of people's energy in this installation. It's wonderful that a project we started to make our lives meaningful has reached out to the world in this way.

I first came to Detroit 50 years ago with my family, seeking work and a better life. And I feel very strongly about the

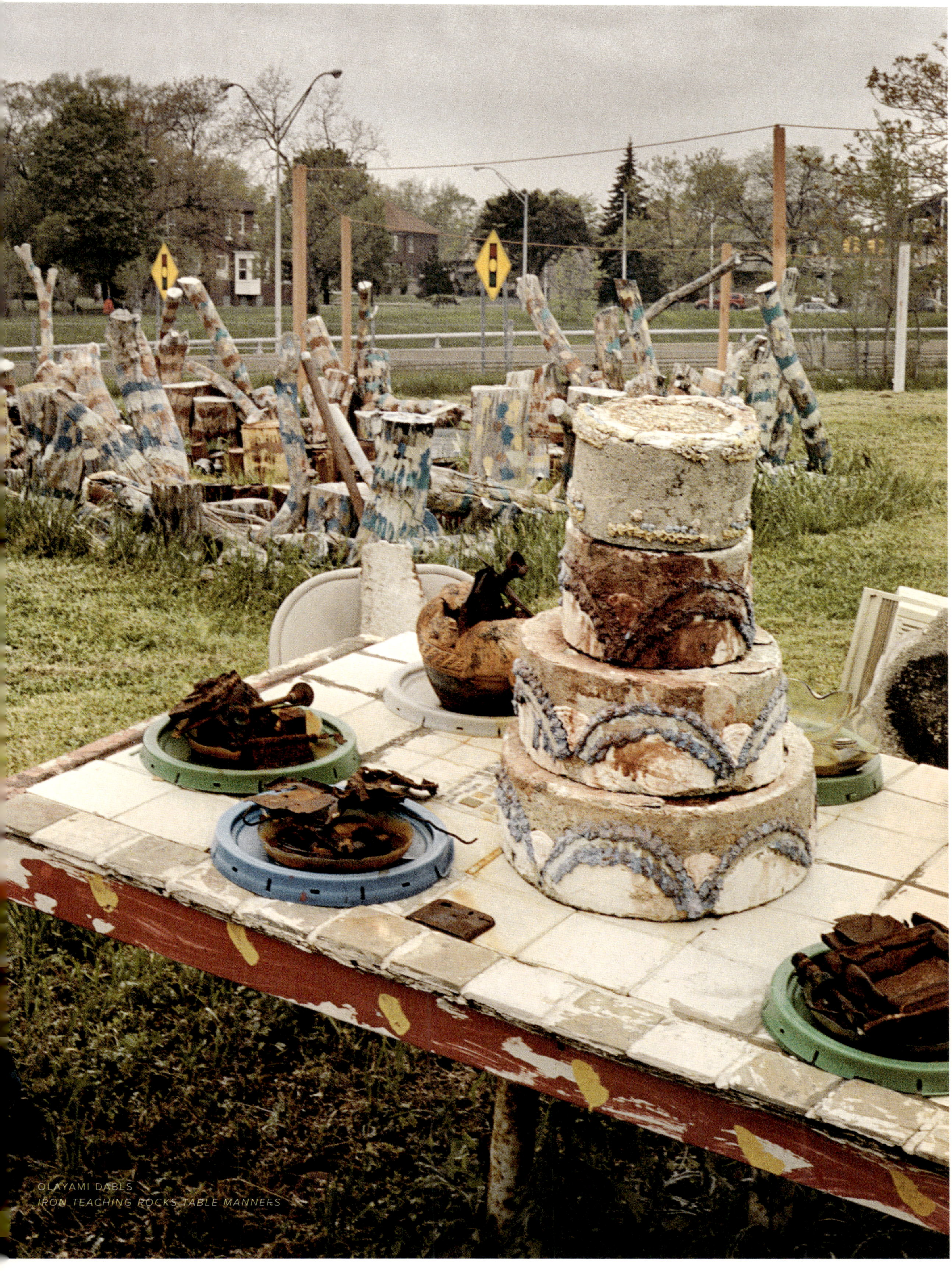

OLAYAMI DABLS
*IRON TEACHING ROCKS TABLE MANNERS*

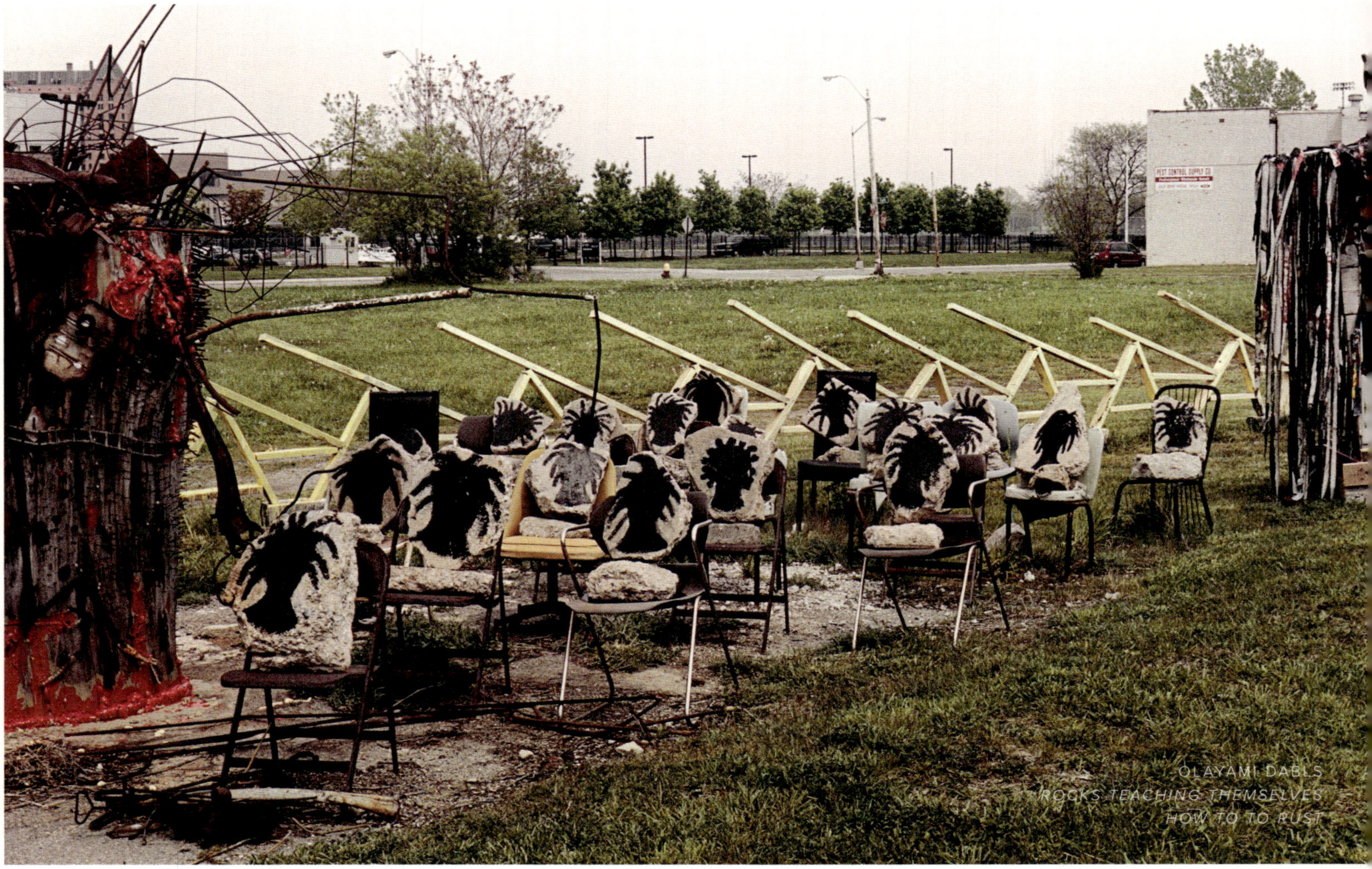
OLAYAMI DABLS
*ROCKS TEACHING THEMSELVES HOW TO TO RUST*

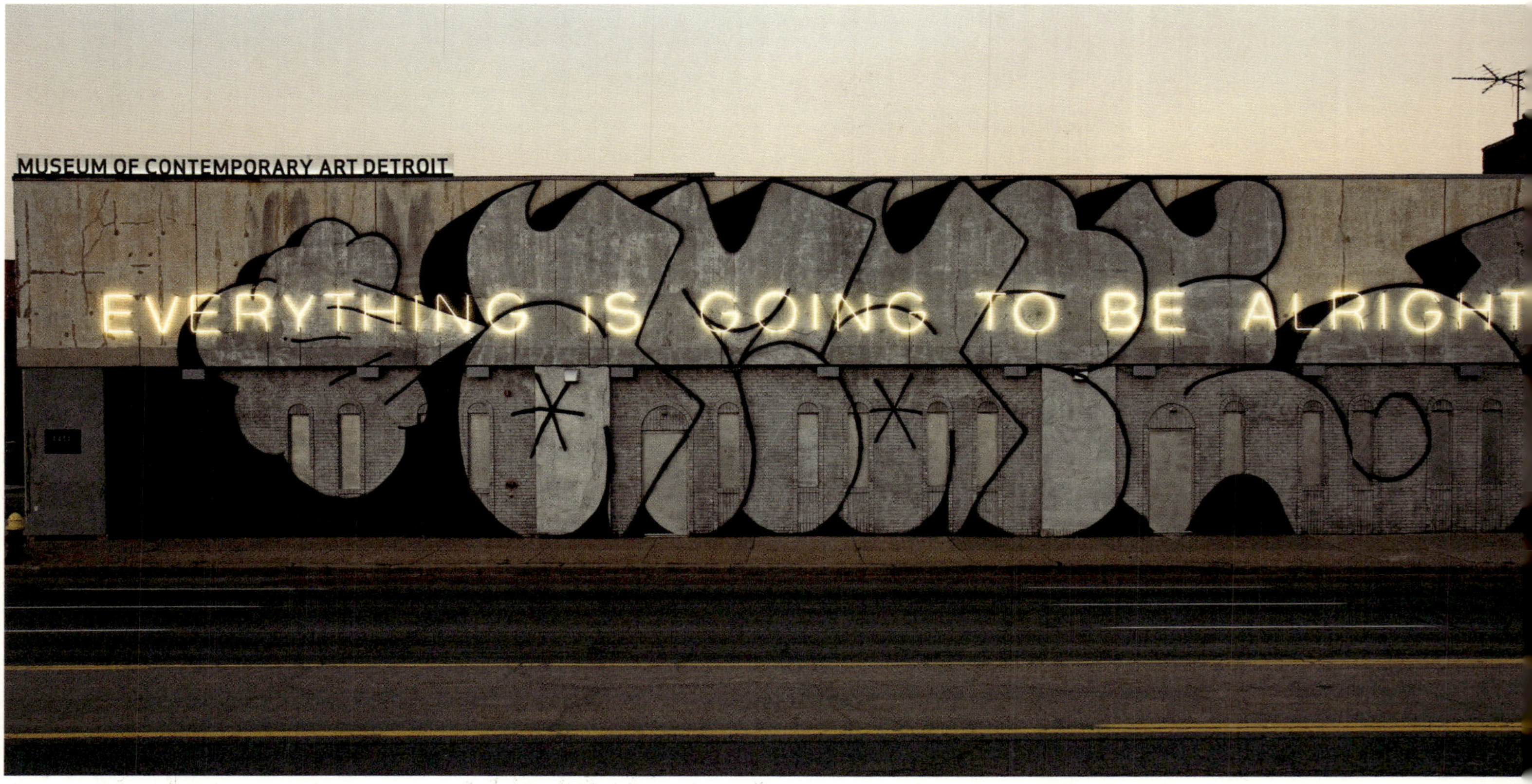

suggestion that Detroit is a dying city. I see it as part of a living organism and think of it this way—if a mosquito bites me, I'm going to hit that spot. But nothing else occurs to the rest of my body. That's how I see Detroit. Certain areas will heal themselves, some will thrive, others will diminish. What we have is an abundance of materials here for artists to use. I don't see Detroit as being sick—I just see Detroit as suffering from a bunch of overzealous reporters who about 20 years ago started writing stories about how the city was dead, overrun by hoodlums. This so-called death of Detroit has brought some of the most individual thinkers on the planet here, and those are artists. This city has been quite good to me.

## A CONVERSATION WITH REBECCA MAZZEI

DEPUTY DIRECTOR - MUSEUM OF CONTEMPORARY ART, DETROIT (MOCAD)

*It's a rare museum that balances its academic influence and art world cred with a radical social message and punk-rock attitude towards the finery of institutional structures. Perhaps it's no surprise that the same town that brought us Iggy Pop and MC5 would also be home to a place like MOCAD. Here, the deputy director presents her vision of how to keep the museum relevant through Detroit's latest evolution.*

MOCAD was established as a space to bring contemporary art to Detroit from all over the world. The building was originally a car showroom designed by Albert Kahn, an architect who was known primarily for industrial work—he did the big Ford plant, GM's design studio. Eventually the building was purchased by the Manoogian Foundation, who first rented and recently gifted it to the museum. This was a huge moment for us.

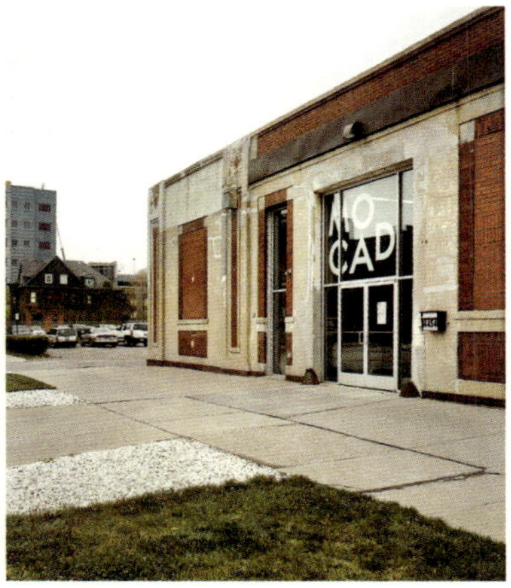

From the very beginning, we wanted the museum to be a place where people could gather and share ideas, because there are so few spaces for that in the city. With that in mind, the museum set out to be as open and adaptable as possible. Because MOCAD doesn't have the baggage of legacy like many other contemporary institutions, we had the freedom to question what a museum really means for a city like Detroit. It has always been important that MOCAD look and feel accessible, because we want it to be relevant to the whole community. In addition to a curator of education, we have a curator of public engagement and a curator of public programs, two of only a few positions like them in the United States. They all do more than provide programming for the exhibitions—they really investigate, challenge, and experiment with the entire infrastructure of the museum. MOCAD is actually in a position to establish new modes of working for our artists and also new ways of being for art institutions. I believe we can become a model for other art museums that are still very traditional. In the beginning, people asked, "Do we even have enough money in this town to support another institution?" Now they can't imagine what Detroit was like before it.

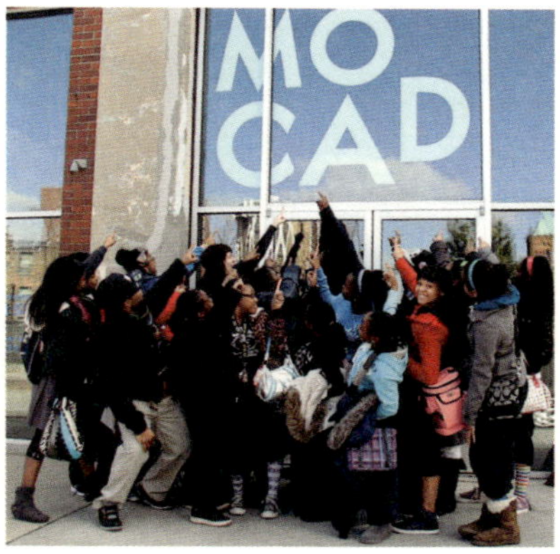


There's a genuine interest on the part of most artists and creative people here to connect with their neighbors and to make the community a better place for everyone. There are the artists who have lived here for a long time, and then a growing group of new arrivals who have fit into the community really gracefully. In addition to their work, many create or participate in projects that make a difference in their neighborhoods on a day-to-day basis. The real challenge for any grassroots organization in Detroit is to maintain the thoughtful pace that is necessary for change to be sustainable. The people who have done exceedingly well in the community are the ones who made it through the most difficult periods. Those people never get much credit, but their endurance and business sense deserves consideration.

People in Detroit are constantly thinking about the big issues and discussing their city in a very honest way. Everyone confronts the challenges and the beauty of the city on a daily basis—both are so present that we can't escape them. On one level, there's a general optimism about Detroit. But there are still vast parts of the city where either the schooling is poor or the city services are lacking. The infrastructure issues in the city are considerable, so it sounds naïve or privileged to have a simple optimism. It's better to think of it as a survivalist mentality—no matter who you are, anyone who lives in the city has to deal with some nonsense that people in other cities don't have to bother with. But as a result, the nicer things in life seem that much nicer because everyone experiences both the highs and lows. I would rather live and work here than move away and know those problems still exist. No one in Detroit lives in a bubble, which I appreciate.

## A CONVERSATION WITH BRITTNY ANDREWS, JEFF NOLAN, IVAN GAMBOA & ASHLEY COOK

MEMBERS OF NORTH END STUDIOS

*Driving down East Grand Boulevard in downtown Detroit, a gorgeous waterfall of color suddenly appears and overruns the entire facade of an abandoned former insurance building. The mural is the handiwork of North End Studios, a collective of artists and musicians who called the building home for three years. Their story reveals the challenges faced by young people making a go of it in Motor City.*

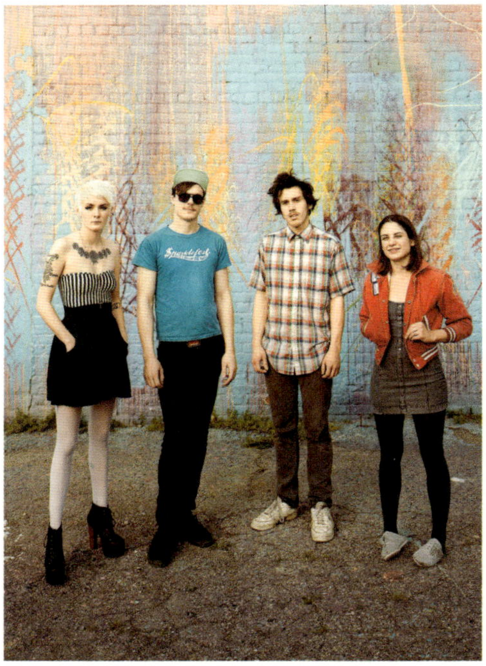

North End Studios developed in a really organic, haphazard way. Katie [Craig, another member] received a grant to do a large work of public art and worked with the landlord to use the building for the mural. She involved all these kids from the neighborhood in the painting of the piece. She finished around the time we graduated from art school, so a bunch of us moved in and set up studios. We turned the entire third floor into an art gallery. But after about six months, the expenses started to add up. Because some of us worked in the music scene, we decided to start throwing shows in the first floor space to pay our bills. It got kind of crazy, but the building had a history of that sort of thing. Before it was abandoned, it had been a rave spot called The Vault in the '90s.

We had a really successful three years in this space, up to 20 members at one point. North End Studios started out as a fun project and evolved into something unique that benefited the whole community. When we first moved in, the street was mostly abandoned buildings. But we got the city to plant trees and fix the streetlights, then cleaned up the lot and put in a garden. After us, a theater group moved in, a kiln-firing ceramics studio opened, and a movie was filmed on this street. The area just generally got nicer.

We don't have business degrees, so we didn't anticipate the consequences of these changes. And once we understood what was happening, it was too late. We recently lost our lease to some entrepreneurs who are turning the building into a paintball arena. People get kicked out of spaces all the time in Detroit, but usually because of malfeasance. When the building went on the market, it cost too much for us to buy, which was *so* frustrating. We had invested all this time, energy, and resources into getting the building up to code, only to have it sold off.

This kind of thing is common in Detroit—many organizations spring up that don't last very long. But we're not giving up. We have a team of people and are in the process of relocating. The new space has heat, hot water, and—the best part—a freight elevator. We had so many art shows in our original space and always had to haul everything up all those stairs by hand.

Detroit continually inspires us and influences what we create. Many people come to Detroit from around the world thinking they can just do anything they want here. What they don't realize is that although there is real freedom here, they have to be that much more committed, because no one in government is going to help. Everything here is very DIY and comparatively underground. It's much less expensive to start something here, and the lack of oversight means people can do much crazier things—have a huge rave, install a massive sculpture in a park. But if you want to grow to the next level and be more professional, the lack of organization in the city is very difficult. You just get transferred from one city department to another. It takes months to even get the simplest information. The trick is to use the lack of organization to your advantage.

## A CONVERSATION WITH PHILLIP COOLEY

PONYRIDE EXECUTIVE BOARD MEMBER

*Committed, saavy, and ethical, Phillip Cooley is a hard-working entrepreneur at the forefront of revitalization in Detroit. With a degree in fine arts, a successful restaurant, and a real estate development company under his belt, Cooley sets out with his most ambitious project yet—to transform a Corktown warehouse into affordable workspaces for artists and socially-conscious small-business owners in need of a break.*

I grew up in Marysville, Michigan, a picturesque town of about 9,000 people. There's no arts scene there whatsoever, no real restaurants, so I used to come down to Detroit for food and culture and music. I loved going to the Gold Dollar and The Magic Stick. I found this city both amazing and confusing. As an 18-year-old, I didn't know how I could plug in. I grew up in a town that was basically all white, the eccentric kid with the Fishbone "Fight Racism" T-shirt who got called all kinds of names. But when I came down to Detroit, I'd often find myself as the only white person in certain situations, which didn't necessarily feel natural either. So it took me a while to find my place here—I lived overseas for a while, spent time in Chicago. Eventually returning here seemed like a logical move.

Detroit is one of the most democratic cities in the United States. The barriers of entry are lower, and there's an openness to folks. When I came back here, I was broke. I didn't have any real skill set, but I had a voice and wanted to participate. In other cities, the path was, *You can have an internship here, an internship there,* and eventually join this traditional vertical structure. Detroit is a city that allows you to skip all that and jump right in. The prevailing attitude is, *No one else is going to do this, so we have to.*

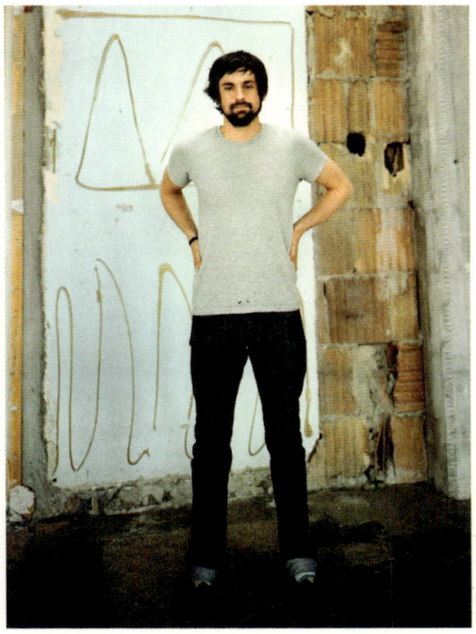

Detroit is a city of tinkerers. There's a deep creative impulse here that people don't often associate with a blue-collar industrial town. In Detroit, people can afford to try things. I always compare it to New York, which is a utopia for so many artists. But can you really steer that ship, can you really change it? It's increasingly expensive to live there, which pushes out all of the culture that made it interesting. I'd tell a young artist to move to Detroit any day. It's not utopia by any means, but most Detroiters have fewer resources, so we collaborate and work together out of necessity.

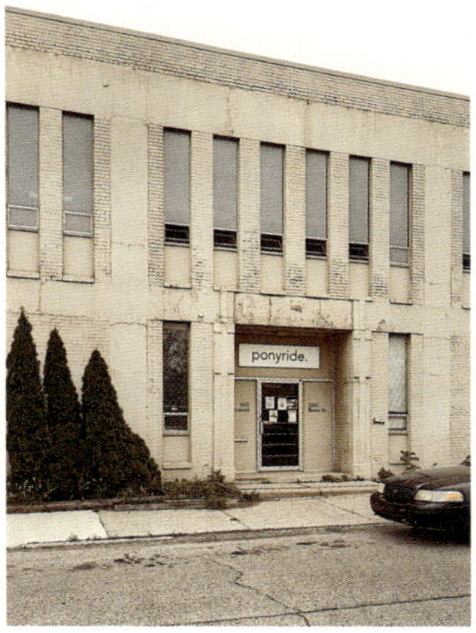


With PonyRide, we learned early on that it's essential to consider the community. Whether you're a volunteer organization or a for-profit business, if you're not inclusive, it's going to be so much harder to succeed. In Detroit, people who buy buildings sometimes don't even develop them—they just sit there for speculation, and the community loses out twice. When we bought this building—all 30,000 square feet—I thought, *How can we include the community so more people benefit?* We studied the costs to find a way to give people access to our resources in an affordable way. The folks who rent space at PonyRide have the freedom to work on their passion rather than always worrying about the bottom line. It has been great to watch everyone come in—hip-hop dancers, African drummers, a modern ballet group. Many of these people found out about PonyRide through word of mouth, which is awesome. We have a waiting list of 40 people right now, so we're trying to find other developers who are interested in participating in this kind of model. I think that we can get a second PonyRide up and running soon. There are so many empty buildings—it would take such minimal development to activate these spaces. The costs are low to these owners—if I can afford to do this, other owners can.

The prevailing story about Detroit used to be about urban blight. Recently there's been a lot of focus on positive grassroots change. I think both certainly exist. Artists are at the forefront of efforts for change in Detroit because they tend to thrive off of adversity. When artists get comfortable, they get complacent, just like most of us. Innovation often comes from people in desperation doing incredible things. That's certainly the case in our city today.

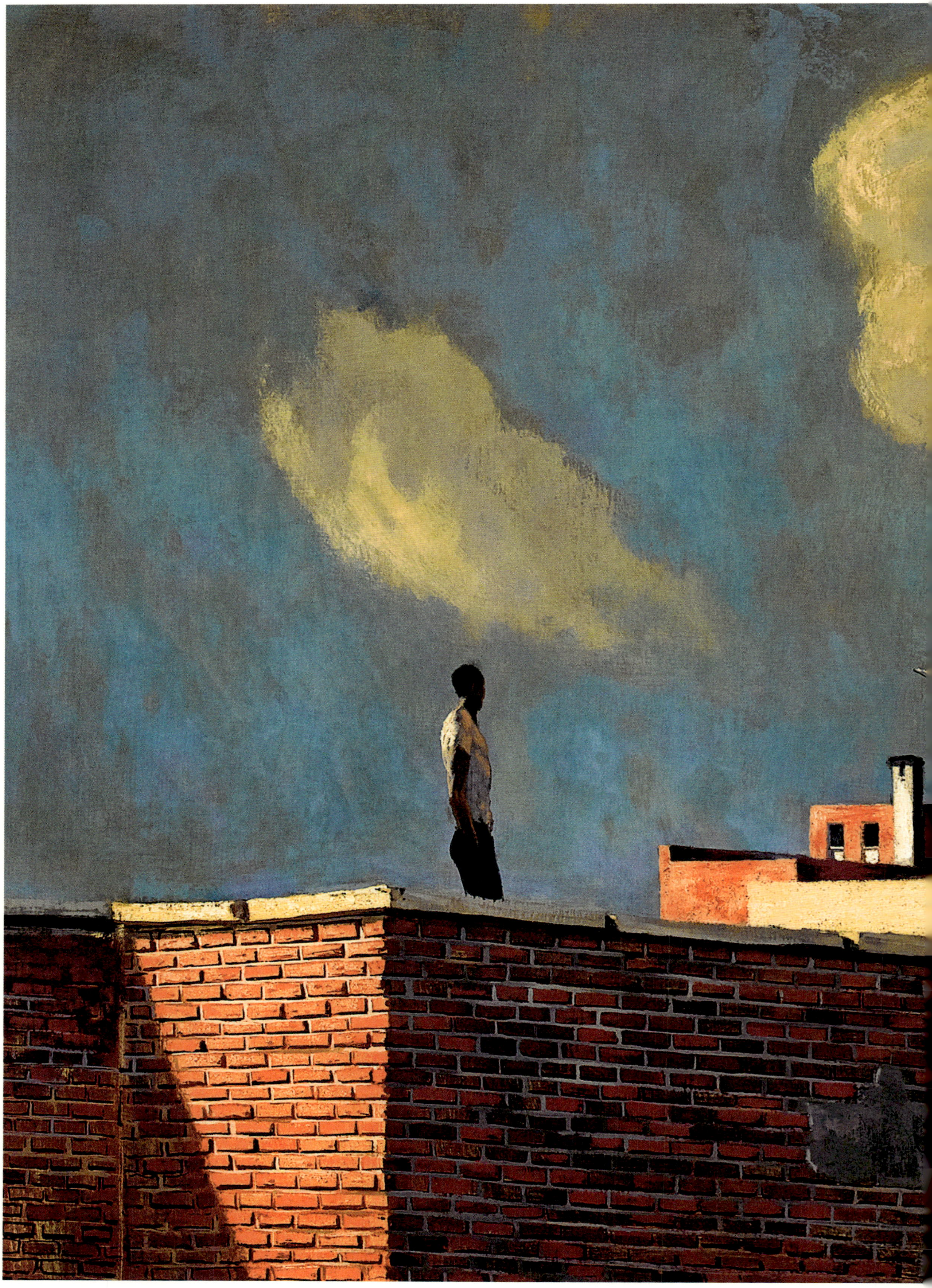

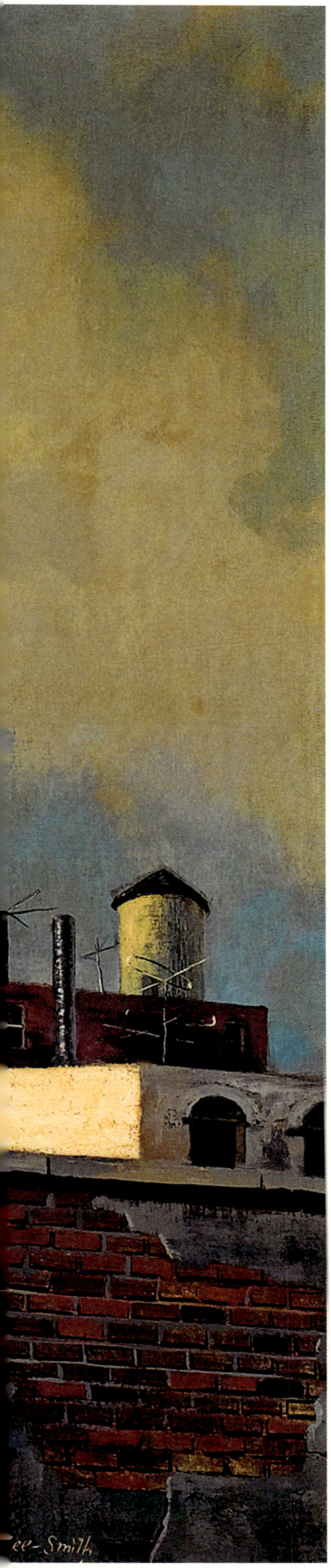

# VISIONS OF "THE D"

## HUGHIE LEE-SMITH, PAINTER

The city of Detroit played a significant role in the creative expression of the African-American painter Hughie Lee-Smith. Born in Florida and raised in Ohio, Lee-Smith studied at the Cleveland School of Art and the Detroit Society of Arts in the early 1930s. He met his wife Mabel Louise Everett in Detroit and started spending more time in the city from 1938 on. Throughout the latter part of the Great Depression and the early years of World War II, Lee-Smith would alternate work as a sand molder and foundry worker for the Ford Motor Company with his artistic practice. After his service as a "morale painter" in the Navy, Lee-Smith studied painting and art education at Wayne State University on the G.I. Bill. Eventually he would move to New York City, where he spent the remainder of his career.

The paintings Hughie Lee-Smith created during his years in Detroit capture the moody expanse and solitude of its urban landscape and evoke the quiet struggle of those living in poverty. His paintings offer a unique insight into the look and feel of Detroit at that time, and remain uncannily relevant to the city as it exists today.

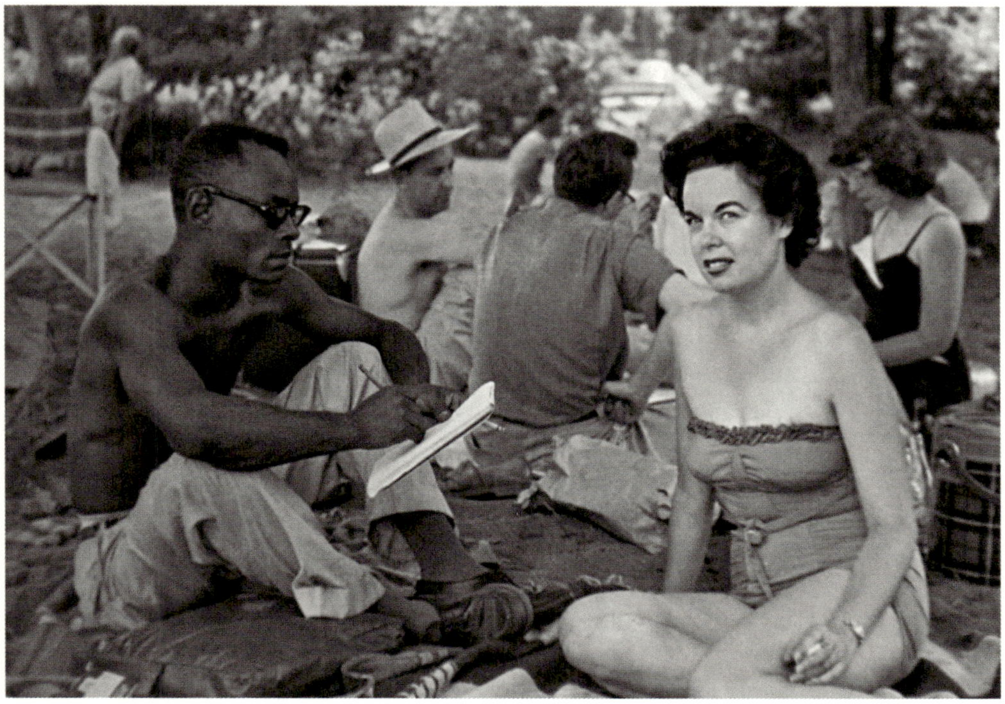

HUGHIE LEE-SMITH
*UNTITLED (ROOFTOP VIEW)*, 1957

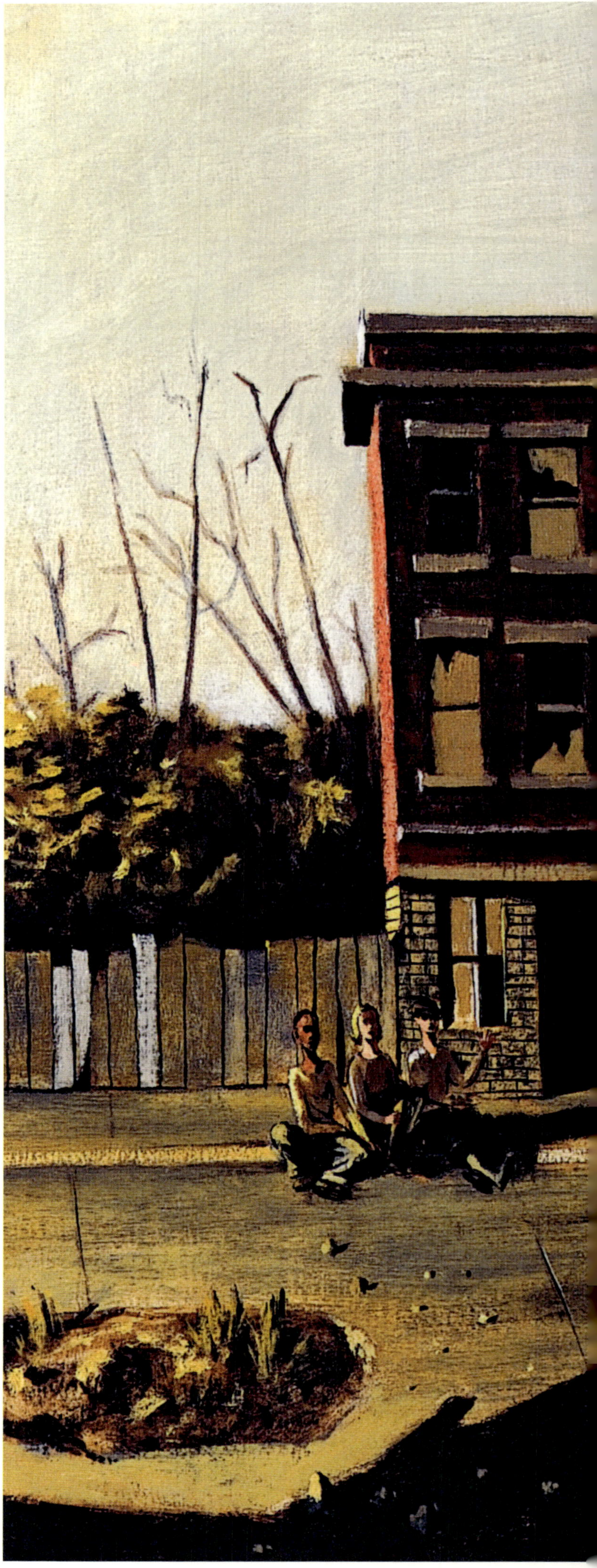

HUGHIE LEE-SMITH
*STREET SCENE*, C. 1951

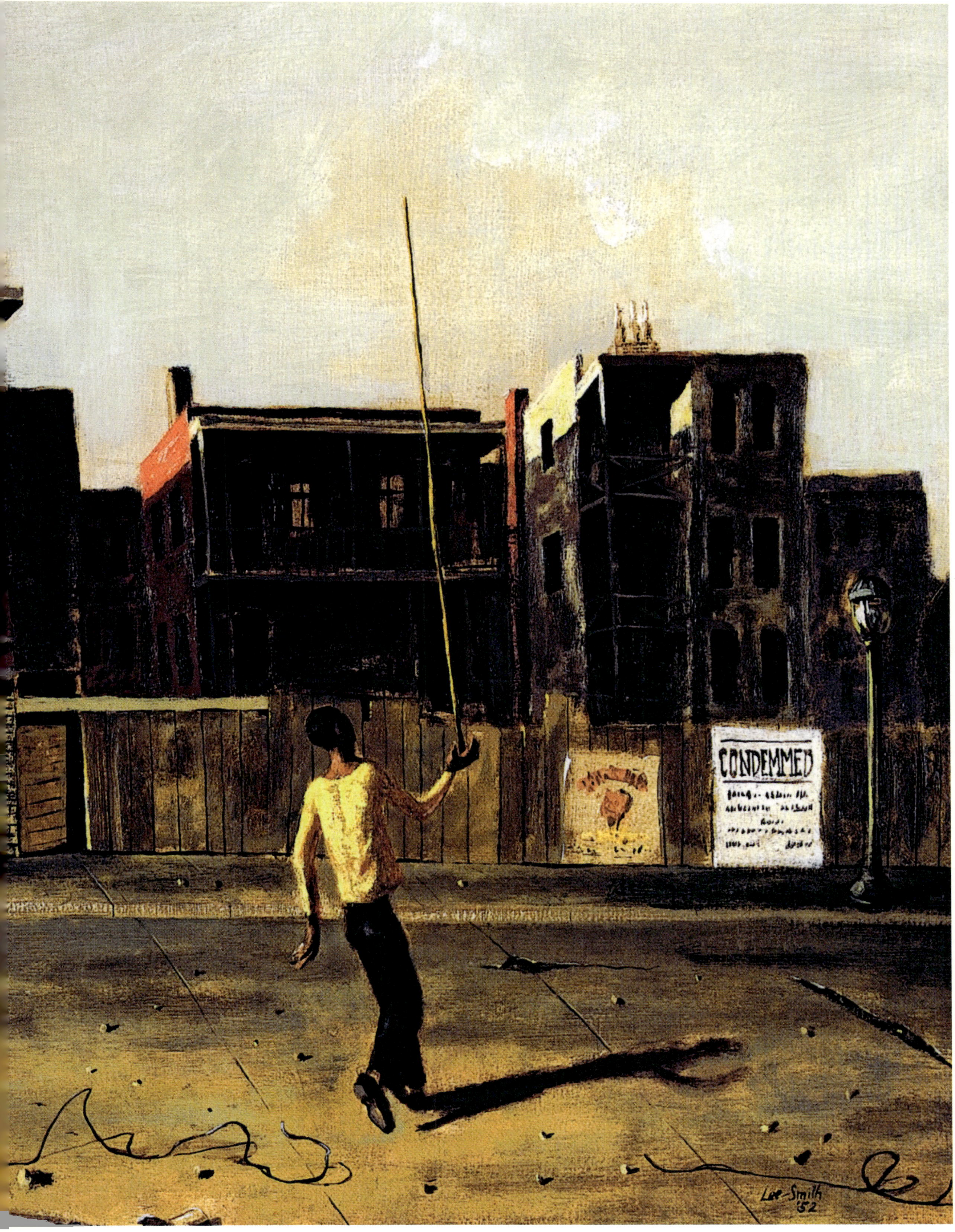
CONDEMMED
Lee-Smith '52

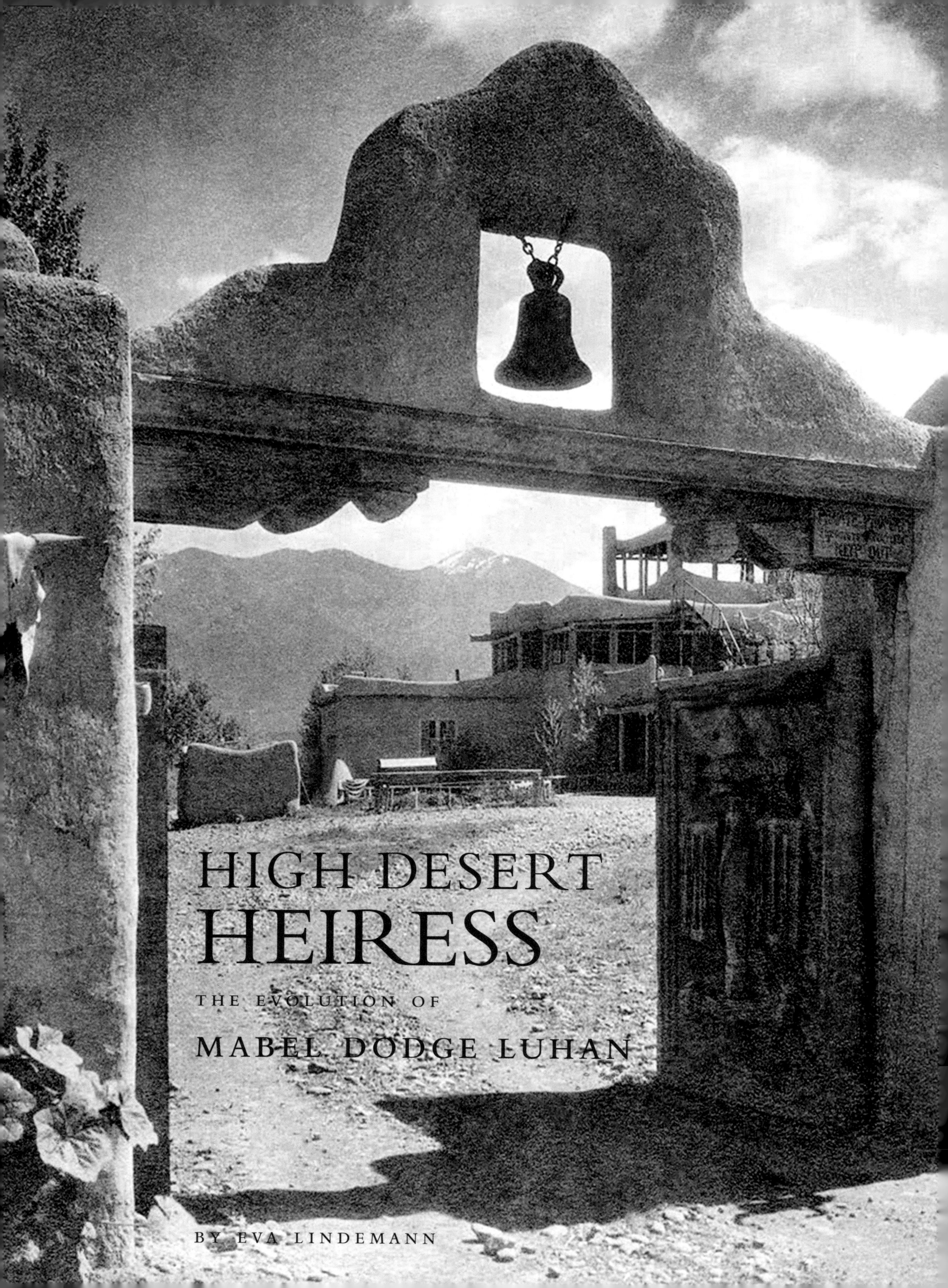

# HIGH DESERT HEIRESS

## THE EVOLUTION OF MABEL DODGE LUHAN

BY EVA LINDEMANN

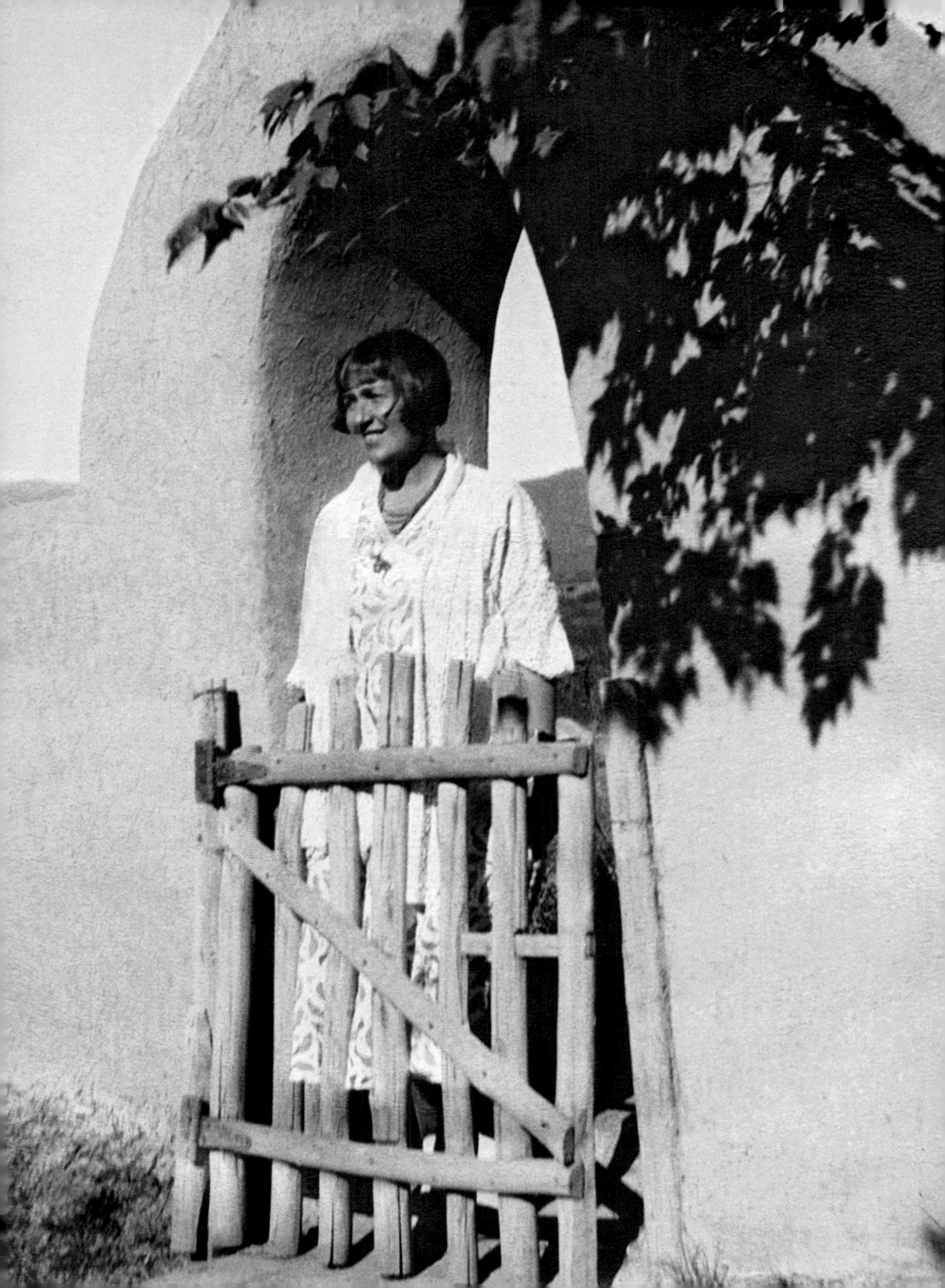

In the sleepy hamlet of Taos, New Mexico, nestled high in the Sangre de Cristo Mountains, the name Mabel Dodge Luhan seems to lilt on the lilac-scented breeze and through the wisteria. Her name sounds like a vague recollection from a dream, an abstract impression that calls from the past and echoes off the town's adobe walls. Standing before the entrance of her estate, Los Gallos, one cannot help but feel a deep appreciation and reverence for the grand adobe sanctuary this woman built. It is a three-story testament to love and creativity, a beautiful convergence of materials and gumption. But Los Gallos also raises questions and conceals mysteries. Who was this infamous East Coast hostess, muse, patron, and writer? Why did she create this retreat, this experiment in communal living for artists she modestly called "the cosmos?" The search for answers reveals a woman of deep conviction who created a world of her own imagining out of the stark northern New Mexico landscape and blazed a trail for the counterculture that took root there.

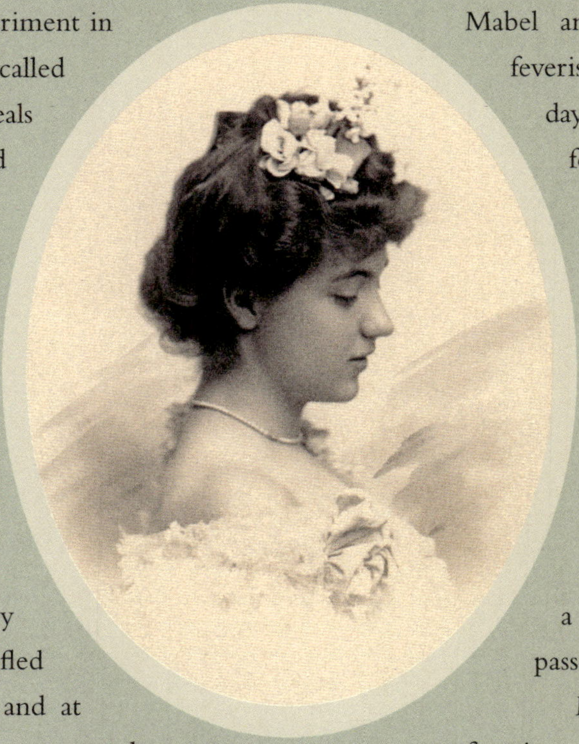

The Mabel Dodge Luhan who became doyenne of the Southwestern culturati was a far cry from the society girl born to a wealthy banking family in Buffalo, New York, in 1879. She was schooled in charm and groomed to marry like the Victorian women of her class. Stifled emotionally and intellectually at home and at school, Mabel longed for a life of beauty, poetry, and grand sweeping passions. At age 21, she ran away to secretly marry Karl Evans, the son of a wealthy steamship owner. Her only child, John Evans, was born the following year. Karl Evans died in a tragic hunting accident, leaving Mabel a widow at 23. Encouraged by her family, Mabel took John on a trip to Paris where she met the architect Edwin Dodge. They married quickly, moved to Florence and lived in a Medici villa named Villa Curonia. It was here that Mabel first tried her hand at curating a home that reflected her personality, whims, and "the evolution of a soul." In addition to art and decorative objects, Mabel began "collecting" personalities and minds to populate her drawing rooms. Gertrude Stein, Alice Toklas, and Leo Stein were frequent visitors, as were the Queen of Saxony and the infamous Socialist exiles George Herron and Carrie Rand. Mabel poured an extraordinary amount of energy into creating a world that would feed her appetite for people, poetry, ideas, and love. But in the end, she was emotionally unfulfilled and restless. She abandoned Florence—the endless conversations, the love affairs with her chauffeur and her son's tutor—and returned to America to enroll John in school.

Back in the pulse of New York City, Mabel hit her stride. She quickly assimilated into *fin de siècle* America and dove headlong into creating a new salon. Every Wednesday night her home at 23 5th Avenue would be buzzing as Mabel and her panoply of friends argued feverishly over the social movements of the day. Margaret Sanger would advocate for the emerging reproductive rights movement, while writer Hutchins Hapgood promoted his ideology of free love and Emma Goldman argued for the proletariat's rights. Many people first learned about the psychoanalysis of Jung and Freud in Mabel's salon. Big Bill Haywood, Georgia O'Keeffe, Alfred Stieglitz, and Max Eastman were just a few of the activists and artists who passed through her lively home.

Mabel immersed herself in the reformist spirit of the times—supporting, writing, and speaking about causes that sought to free humanity from the shackles of spiritual and intellectual oppression. She relished this new feeling of purpose. Using her Freudian studies as a springboard, Mabel began the first-ever syndicated advice column for Hearst Publications. She participated in the early suffragist movement. She became vice president of the Association of American Painters and Sculptors, the group that sponsored the Armory Show. Mabel contributed to *The Masses*, a leading left-wing journal, and supported the Woman's Peace Party. The historian Frederick Hoffman suggested that Mabel "all but established the pattern of the 'freelance intellectual' of the early twentieth century."

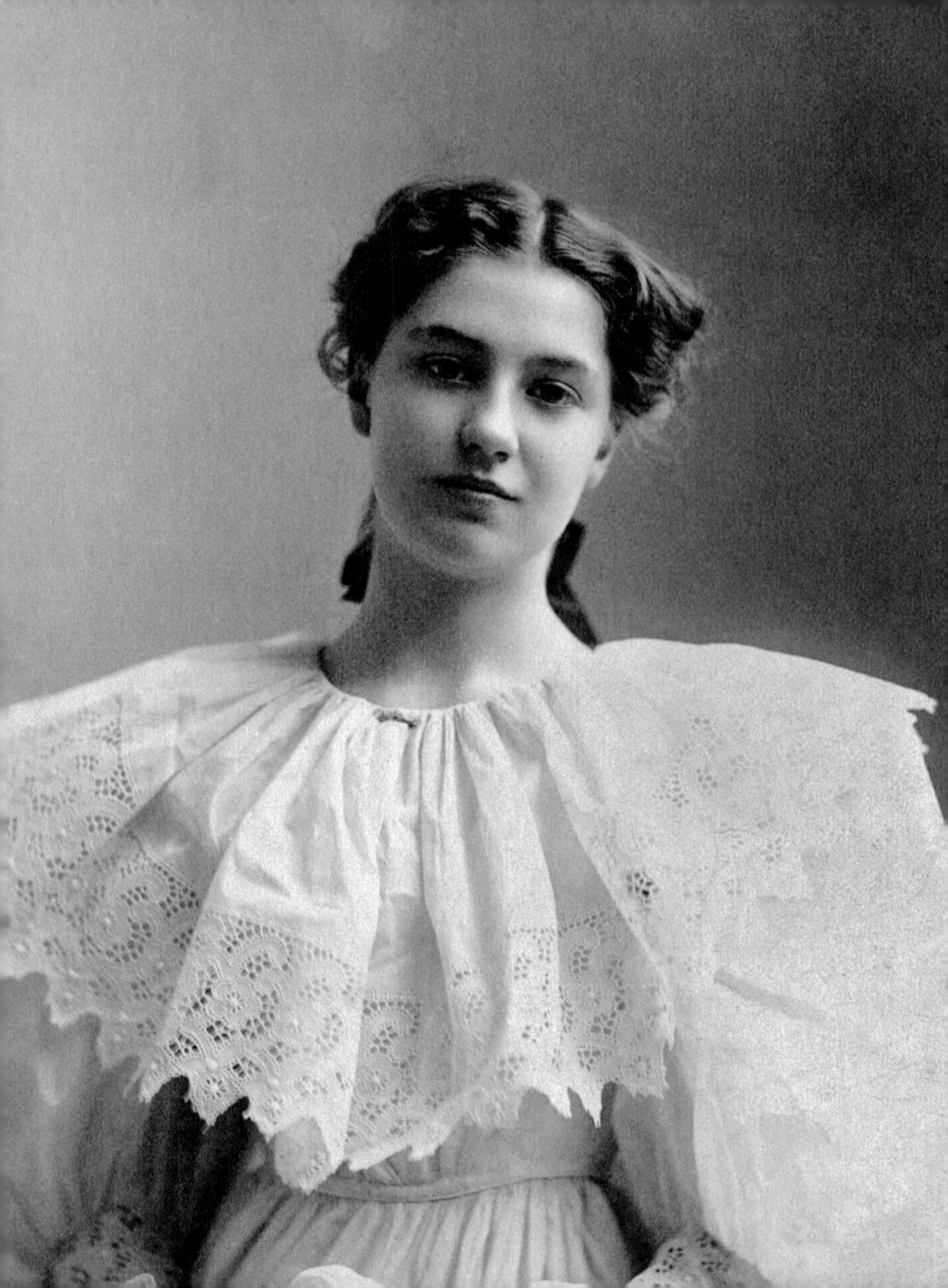

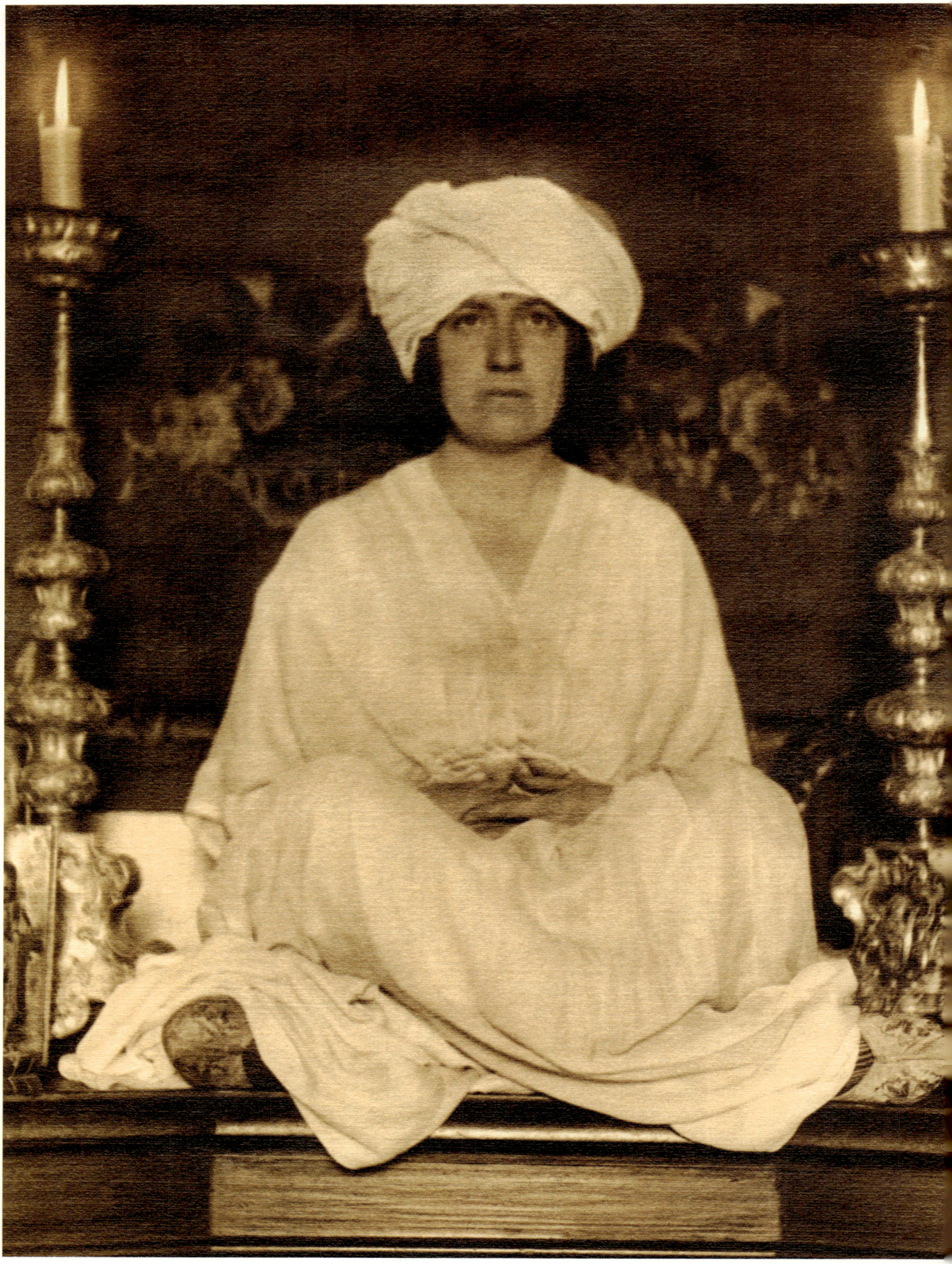

Mabel delighted in the company of great men. She became a muse for writers Carl Van Vechten, Max Eastman and later D.H. Lawrence, all of whom based characters on her voluminous personality. Even the wives of Mabel's friends were fond of her—Fania Marinoff, the actress wife of Van Vechten, was a great admirer, as were Frieda Lawrence and Una Jeffers, wives of D.H. and Robinson, respectively. These women all applauded Mabel's imaginative daring.

But it wasn't all political fervor and salon chatter during Mabel's time in New York. As her marriage to Edwin Dodge faded, Mabel pursued her passions elsewhere. John Reed, a handsome war journalist and poet six years her junior, became her lover. In a fit of passion, Mabel whisked him away to Villa Curonia. The young poet was inspired by Mabel's liberated sexuality and dynamic social life. He dedicated countless poems and love letters to her. As in a scene from a harlequin romance, John would descend into Mabel's bedroom each night on a silk ladder that her husband Edwin Dodge made (but never used) to initiate their nights of abandon. Unfortunately for Mabel, politics interrupted the fun. John was a revolutionary at heart, and he eventually became dismayed by Mabel's flamboyant displays of wealth. He left her in Florence and ran off to report on the Mexican Revolution.

**MABEL LUJAN WAS ROUND AND SQUARE**

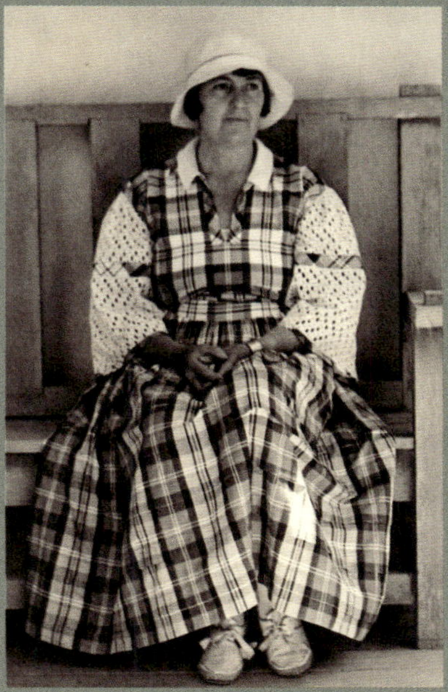

Distraught over the breakup, disillusioned with the Great War and tired of city life, Mabel again sought refuge in reinvention. She purchased a small farm on Croton-On-Hudson, New York, and named it Finney Farm. Still fresh from the glow of her affair with the young revolutionary, Mabel envisioned the farm as a respite for young radicals, a place they could find the emotional and financial support needed to fulfill their dreams. She invited many of her salon attendees from New York to stay, enrolled her son, John, in Elizabeth Duncan's new alternative school and took on boarders. Among them was a brilliant, wistful artist named Maurice Sterne, who soon became her third husband. Theirs was the most cataclysmic of relationships, a union which made her affair with John Reed seem like a petty teenage dalliance. Sterne's biographer, George Biddle, describes their marriage:

"It was one of the most incongruous, incompatible, and tempestuous adventures in the annals of love. From beginning to end it transcends reality. It transcends fiction. It is pure burlesque, Italian comic opera…It is a five-year-long ring fight." [1]

While madly in love with Maurice, Mabel also took the role of patron and manager for his artistic career very seriously. She controlled his destiny, which gave her a sense of purpose. Not unlike John Reed, Maurice saw Mabel as a muse, the undercurrent of his inspiration. Such an intense connection eventually brought discord, and the two were soon locked in an perpetual battle of wills. Mabel sent Maurice on a trip to the Southwest with the hopes of helping him find fresh inspiration. In a fateful turn, she consulted a medium while Maurice was away, who predicted she would soon be surrounded by American Indians. Several days later, while lying in bed, Mabel imagined the face of Maurice floating above her. In this vision, his face was suddently replaced with that of an dark-skinned Native American. Mabel said the experience affected her "like a medicine." Sterne wrote a prophetic letter to her from Santa Fe, New Mexico, on November 28, 1917:

"Dearest Girl,
Do you want an object in life? Save the Indians, their art, culture—reveal it to the world!…There is somehow a strange relationship between yourself and the Indians." [2]

# WORKING FOR A LIVING

BY MABEL DODGE

Do you know what that phrase means?

The factory girl is earning nine dollars a week, but she is not working for a living.

It is not a question of the nine dollars either.

If she got ninety dollars a week—and remained in those close rooms, deadened by the relentless machinery that grinds her soul out of her—she would not be earning her living.

The negroes are remaking the Albany post road.

They dig, and shovel, and carry bricks to and fro and lay them down again, and the road grows.

They, however, are not working for their living.

Even that rich man riding down in his motor to the office where he stays all day trying to make more money—he is not earning a living!

A living is something subtle and mysterious, and yet the simplest thing in the world.

Money doesn't give it to you, though, of course, money is necessary to do it, because one must eat to live.

But just eating doesn't give it to you!

I will tell you who is working for a living and earning a living.

The birds do it. They fly around in the exercise of their instinct to preserve themselves; they search here and they search there. They find food for themselves and they take food home to their young.

They work hard, but their work is the exercise of their instincts. They love to do it!

And flying makes them sing!

Do you sing in the factory, you factory worker?

Do you sing downtown in you office, you rich man?

If anyone sings at work his work is giving him a living.

It doesn't matter what the work is, if you enjoy it you are earning your living, for you are expressing yourself in a kind of song that is true to nature and life.

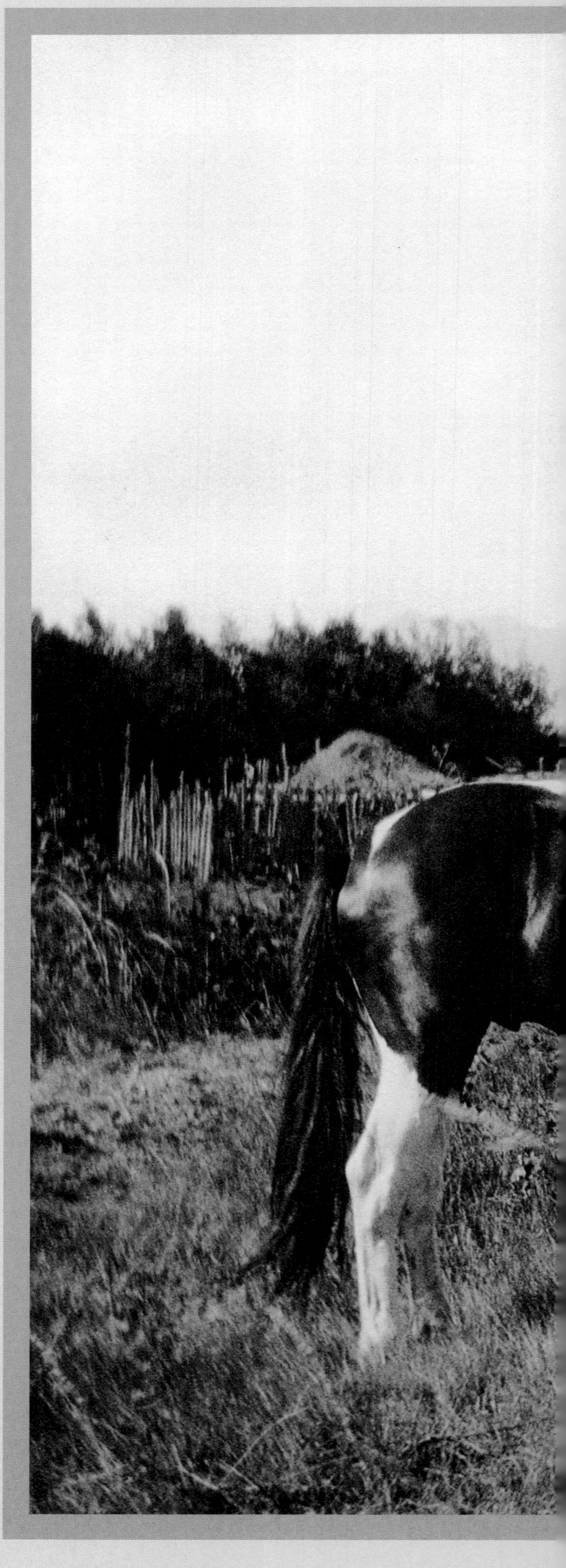

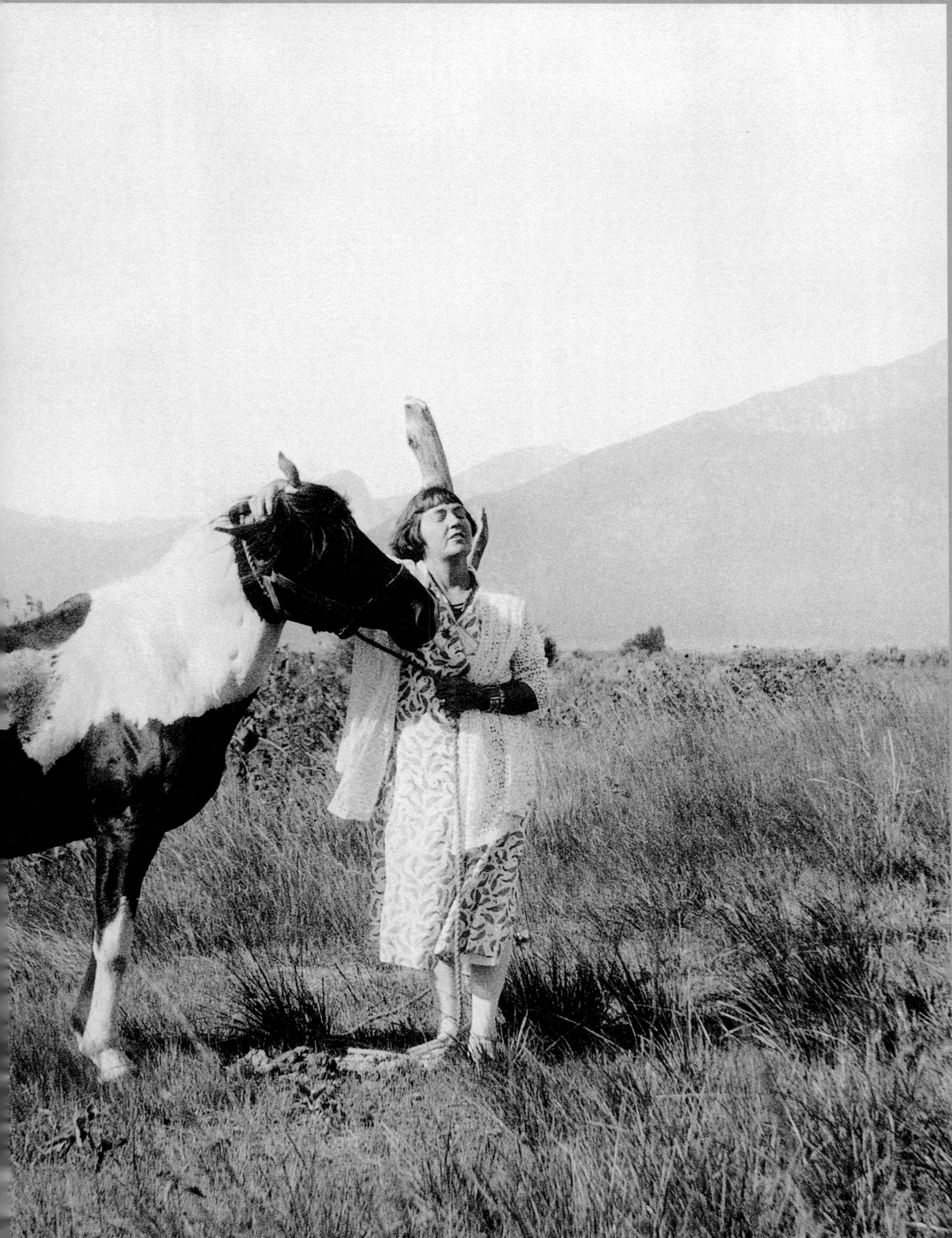

*"My life broke in two right then, and I entered into the second half, a new world that replaced all the ways I had known with others, more strange and terrible and sweet than any I had ever been able to imagine."*

—MABEL DODGE, WRITING ABOUT HER ARRIVAL TO NEW MEXICO

After an initial visit in 1917 to Santa Fe and Taos, New Mexico, Mabel and Maurice decided to settle there permanently. She bought a small adobe house on the edge of town on the advice of Antonio (Tony) Luhan, a local Taos Pueblo Indian who would become her foreman. Mabel and Maurice had met Tony on their first visit to the Tiwa Indian Pueblo in Taos. While wandering the pueblo grounds, Mabel had been called inside by Tony's beautiful wife, Candelaria. There she saw a tall man bent over his drum, singing in a low murmur. When he finally looked up from his drum, Mabel recognized his face as the one from her dream. Mabel and Maurice and the Luhans became friends, and Mabel invited Tony to come and drum at her home from time to time.

Mabel planned her dream home, and Tony oversaw the whole project. During the four years it took to complete, he would camp out in a teepee on her property. Tony took to singing and beating his drum in a love call to Mabel. Before long, Maurice Sterne realized Tony Luhan was his rival. Inevitably, Tony and Mabel fell in love during the construction of Los Gallos. They had developed an otherworldly bond so deep that they would remain together for the rest of their lives.

Mabel felt Tony "saw her into being." He became her spiritual guide and closest friend. Tony was magnanimous, gentle, and respectful of all, a paragon of the values held high by his tribe. His kindness did for her what no man had been able to do: "...facing Tony when he spoke to me...I was by grace *born*...as I should have been years and years ago..." The night Tony and

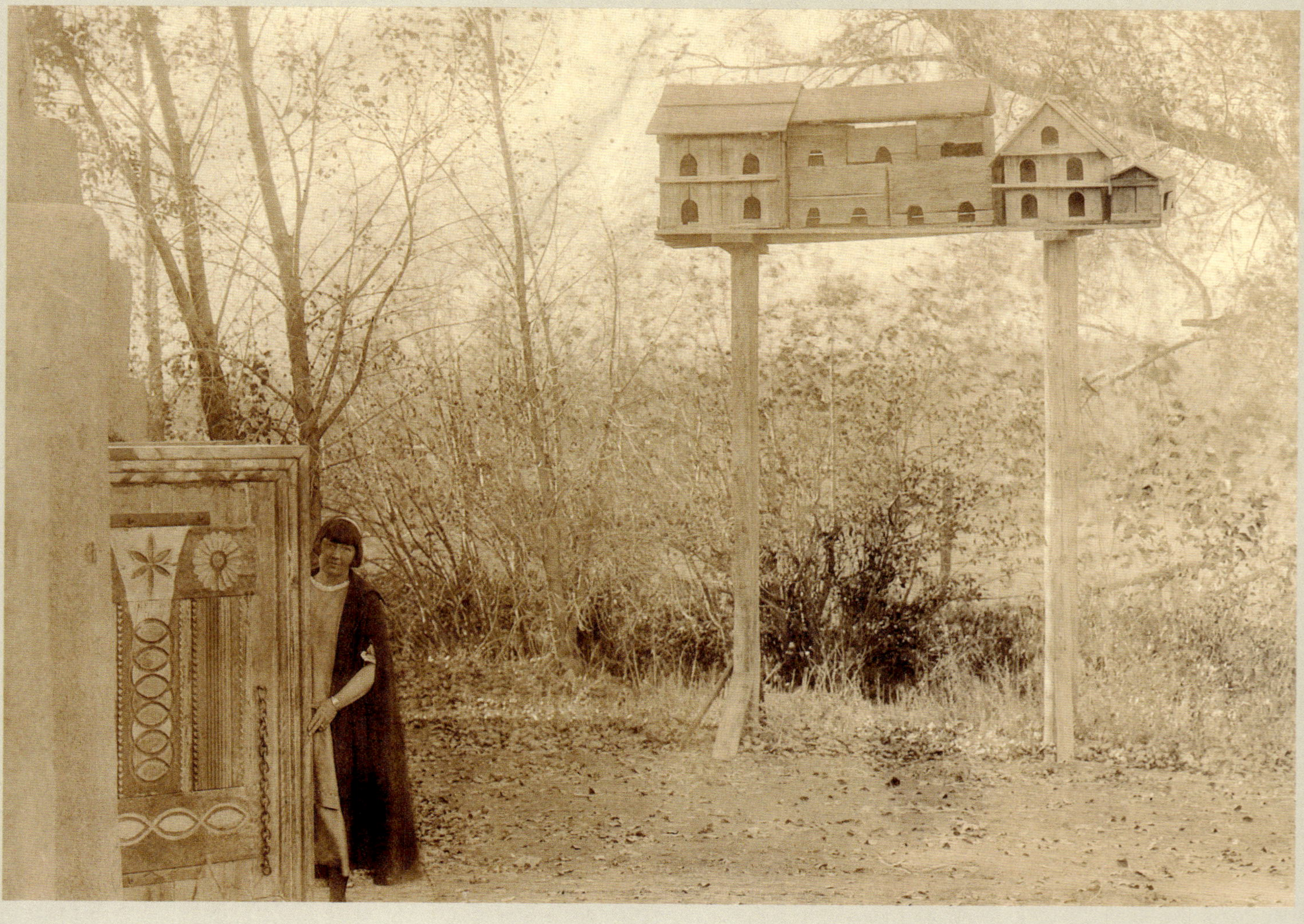

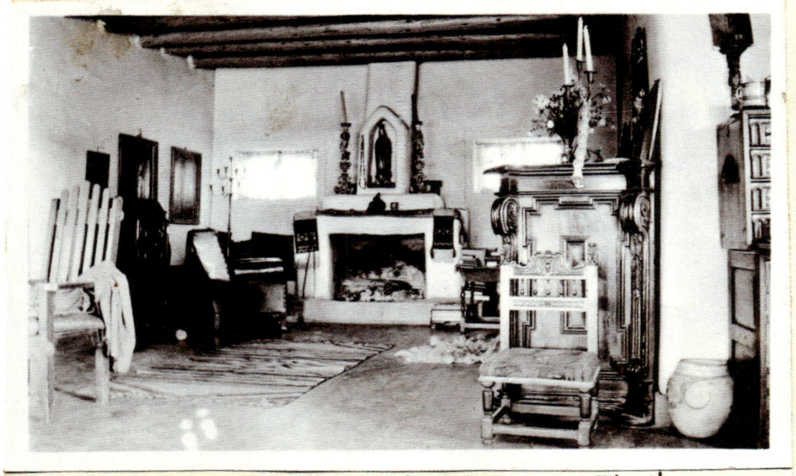

Living Room - Big House

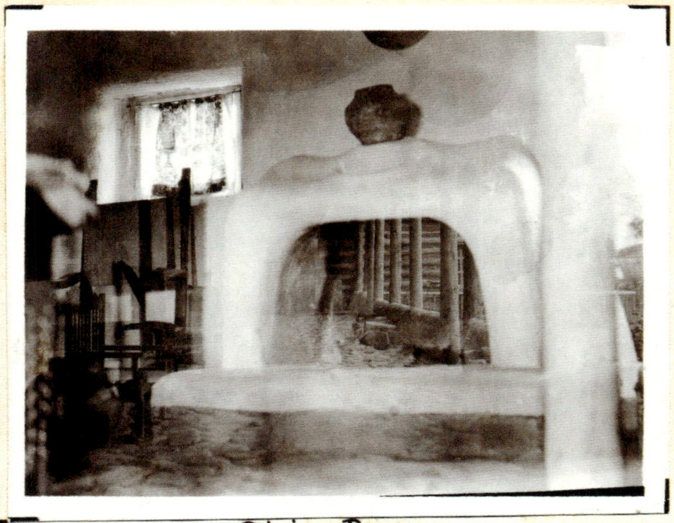

Dining Room

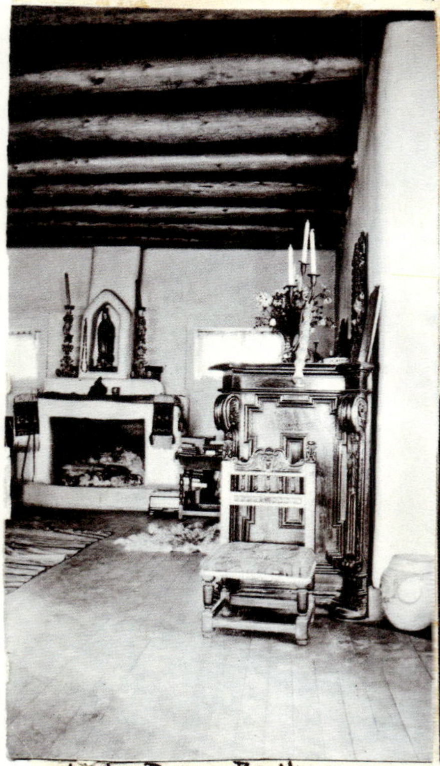

Living Room - Big House

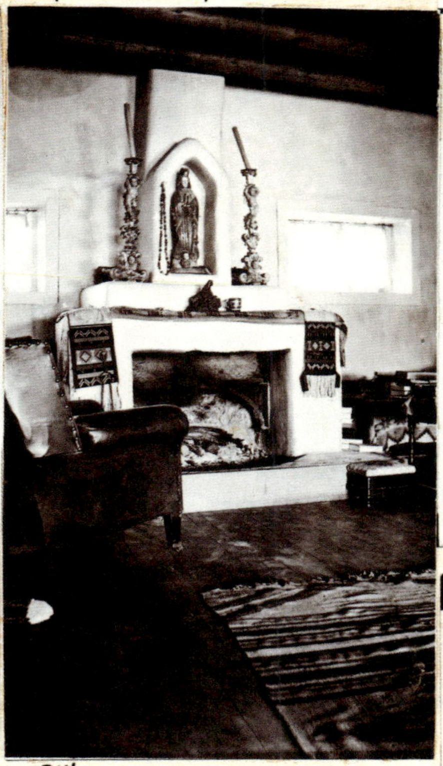

— Ditto

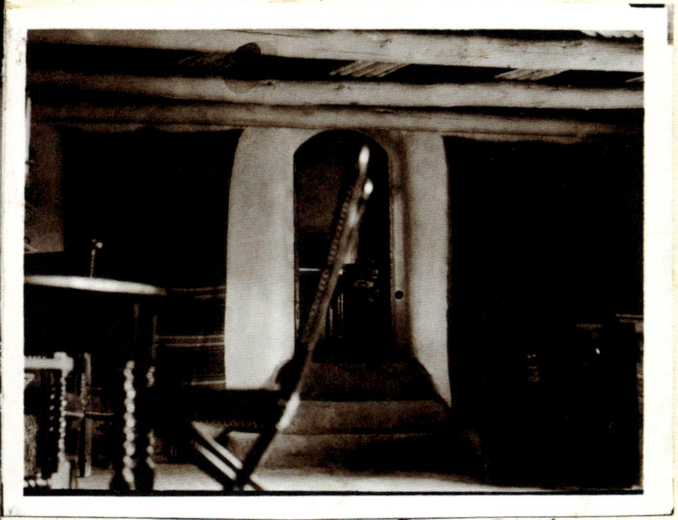

Dining Room - Big House

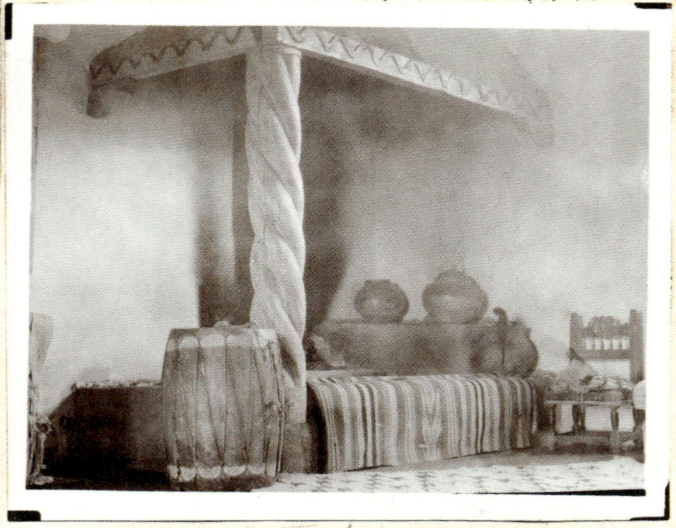

Studio

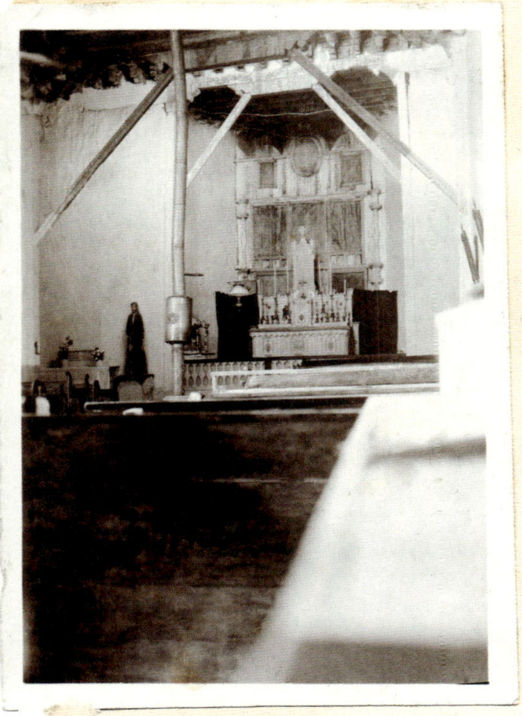

Ranchos church

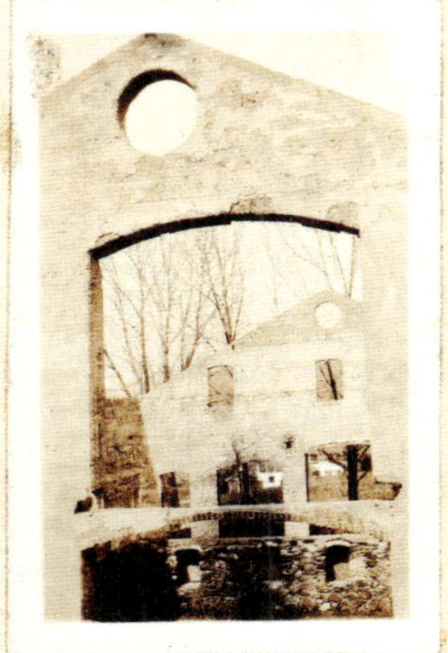

Finney Farm - Croton

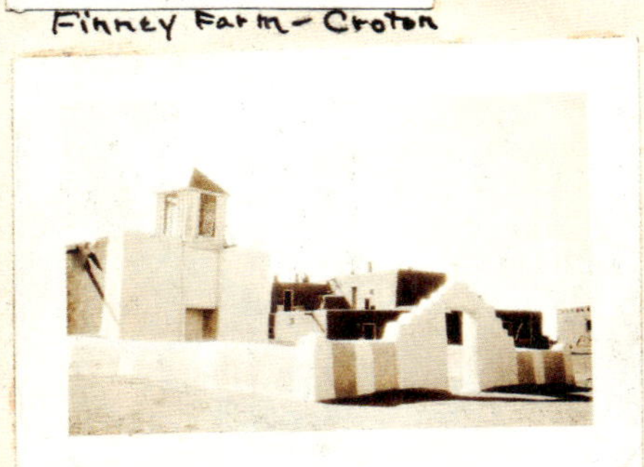

Taos Pueblo Church

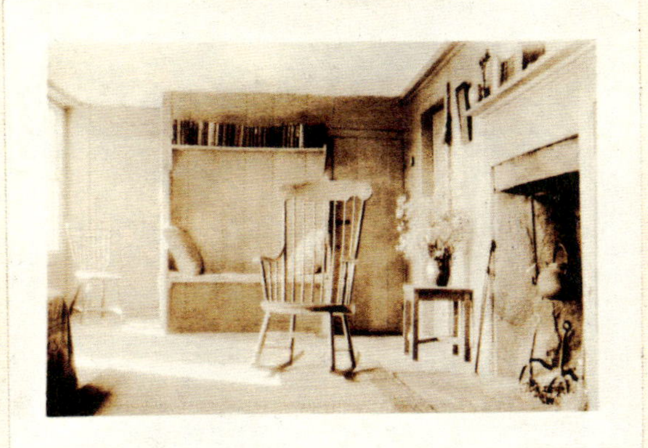

*"He who loves with passion lives on the edge of the desert."*

—EAST INDIAN PROVERB, QUOTED BY MABEL DODGE IN HER BOOK *EDGE OF TAOS DESERT*

Mabel's spiritual relationship finally became a physical one, he promised to give her "a new life, a new world—a true one." [3]

Their union was an absolute scandal. Tony was an imposing figure, with broad shoulders and the striking looks of an ancient pharaoh, the antithesis of the world-weary, materialistic intelligentsia who had crowded Mabel's New York salon. The press back East had a field day with the story of Mabel's latest relationship, citing it as yet another exotic whim, her latest exploration of primitivism. Mable's social circles remained skeptical, suggesting that Tony Luhan was but another sexual pawn for Mabel. Their affair also strained Tony's relationship within the pueblo community. He was married, and as a Taos Pueblo Indian, he was strictly forbidden to mix with people outside of his race. In spite of the prejudices of their respective cultures, Tony and Mabel divorced their spouses and married in 1923. Tony had to give up his participation in tribal ceremonies, but he managed to retain a position on the Tribal Council. He continued to be influential in tribal matters, taking advantage of his new access to influential politicians through Mabel.

Their passionate relationship was not without its contradictions, and in this way, it was very modern. As much as she admired the Pueblo culture, Mabel was equally determined to keep Tony close, going so far as to offer a lifetime bribe to his former wife, Candelaria, to stay out of their affairs. For all of his gentleness and generosity, Tony was also very independent. Early in their marriage, he would return to the pueblo to sleep with Candelaria, and he continued to have affairs with numerous other women throughout his life. Tony also developed a taste for the finer things Mabel's wealth afforded him: expensive boots, tailored clothes, and fancy cars. Theirs was a game of give and take, the complicated psychology of two strong-willed, fiercely independent people inexorably drawn together. But it remains without question that Tony and Mabel loved each other uniquely and unreservedly to the end.

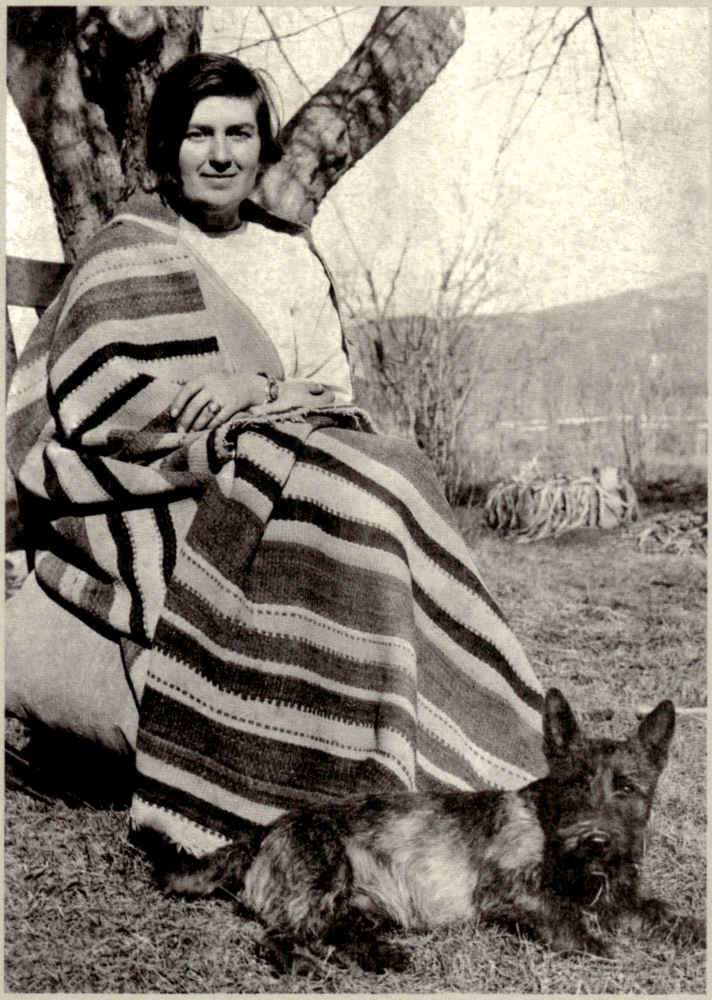

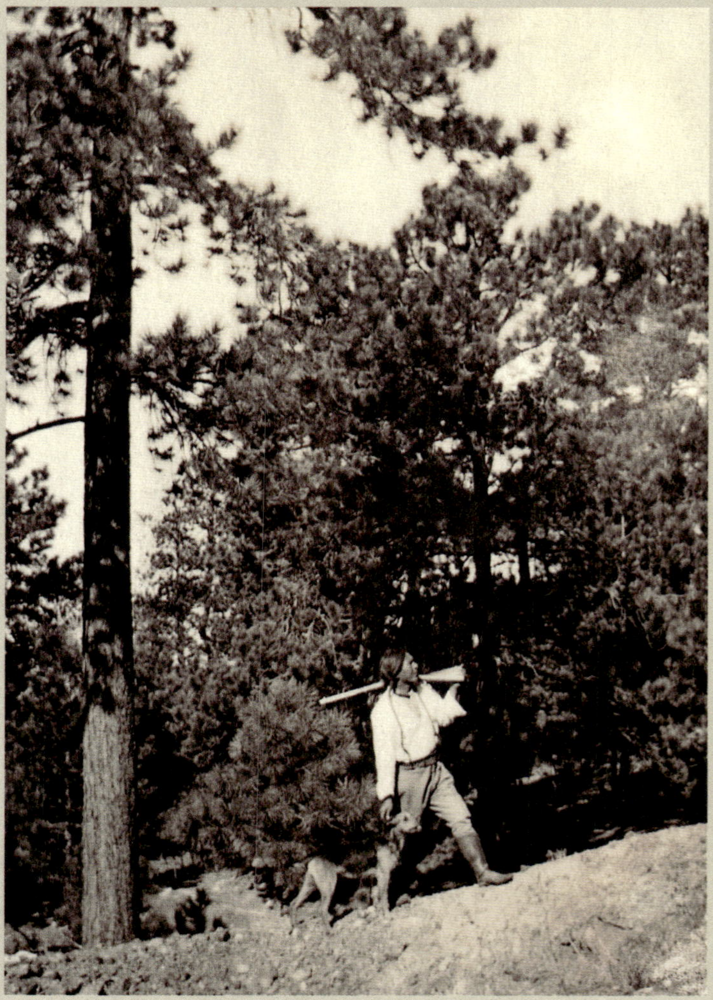

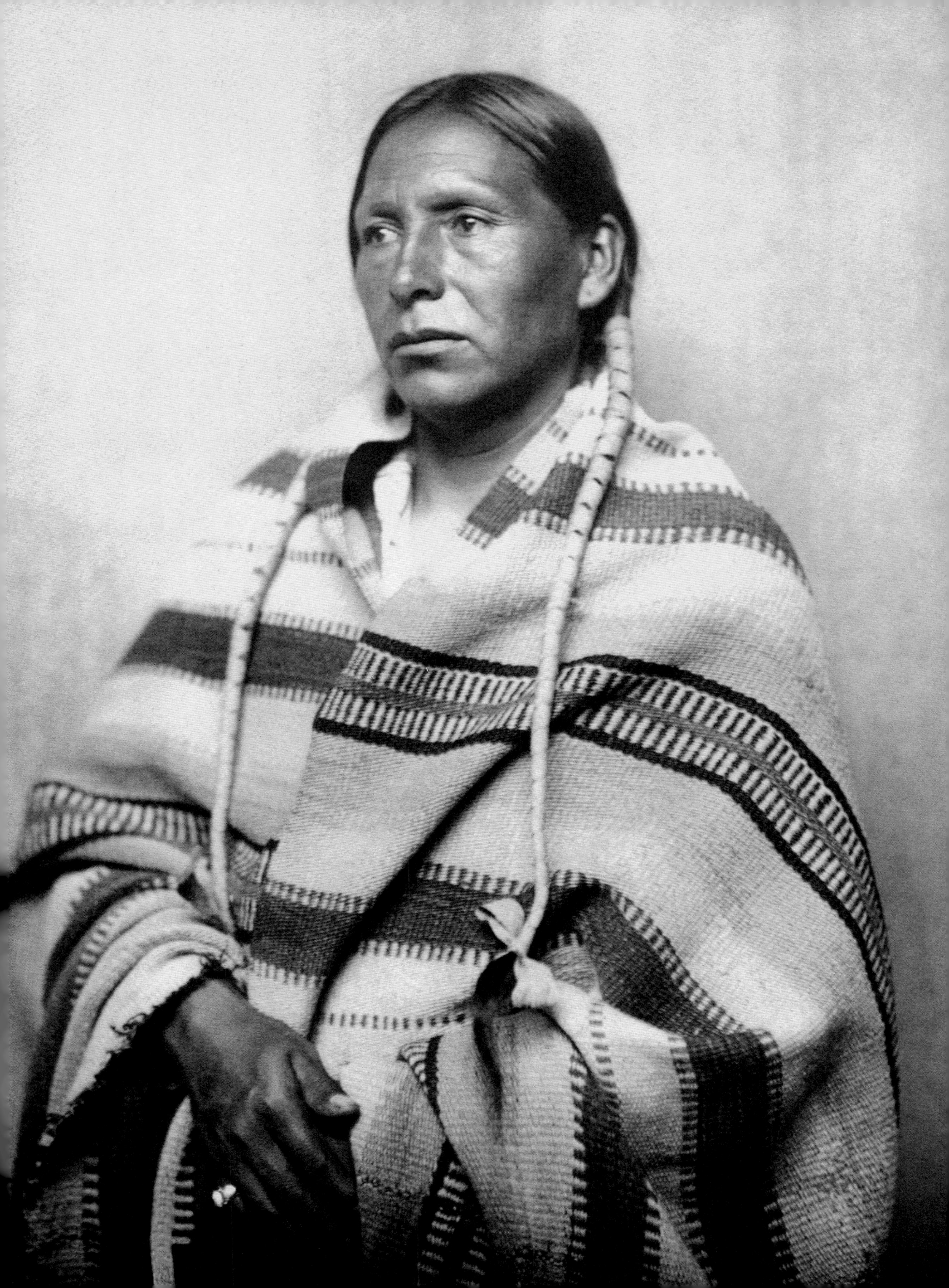

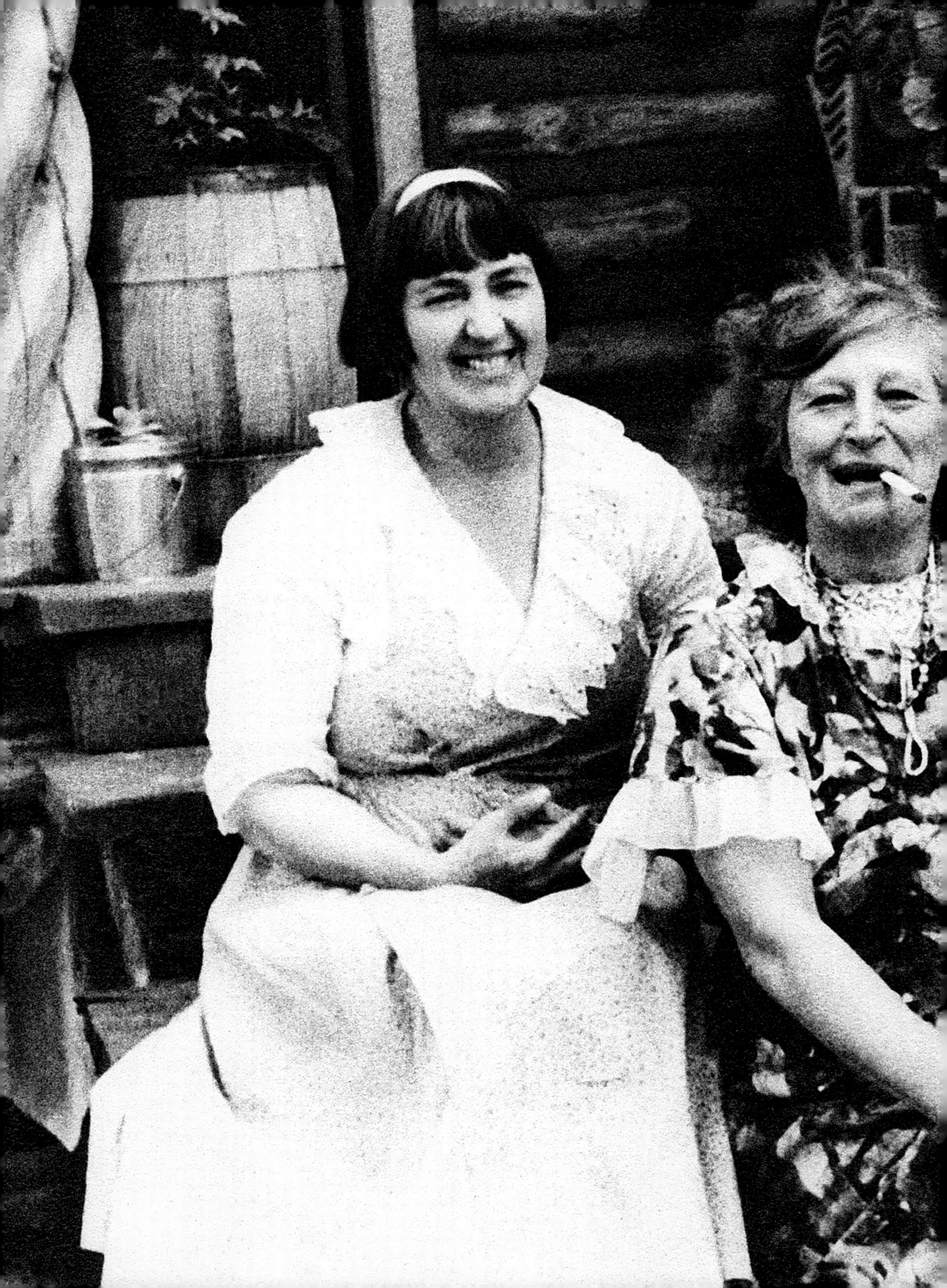

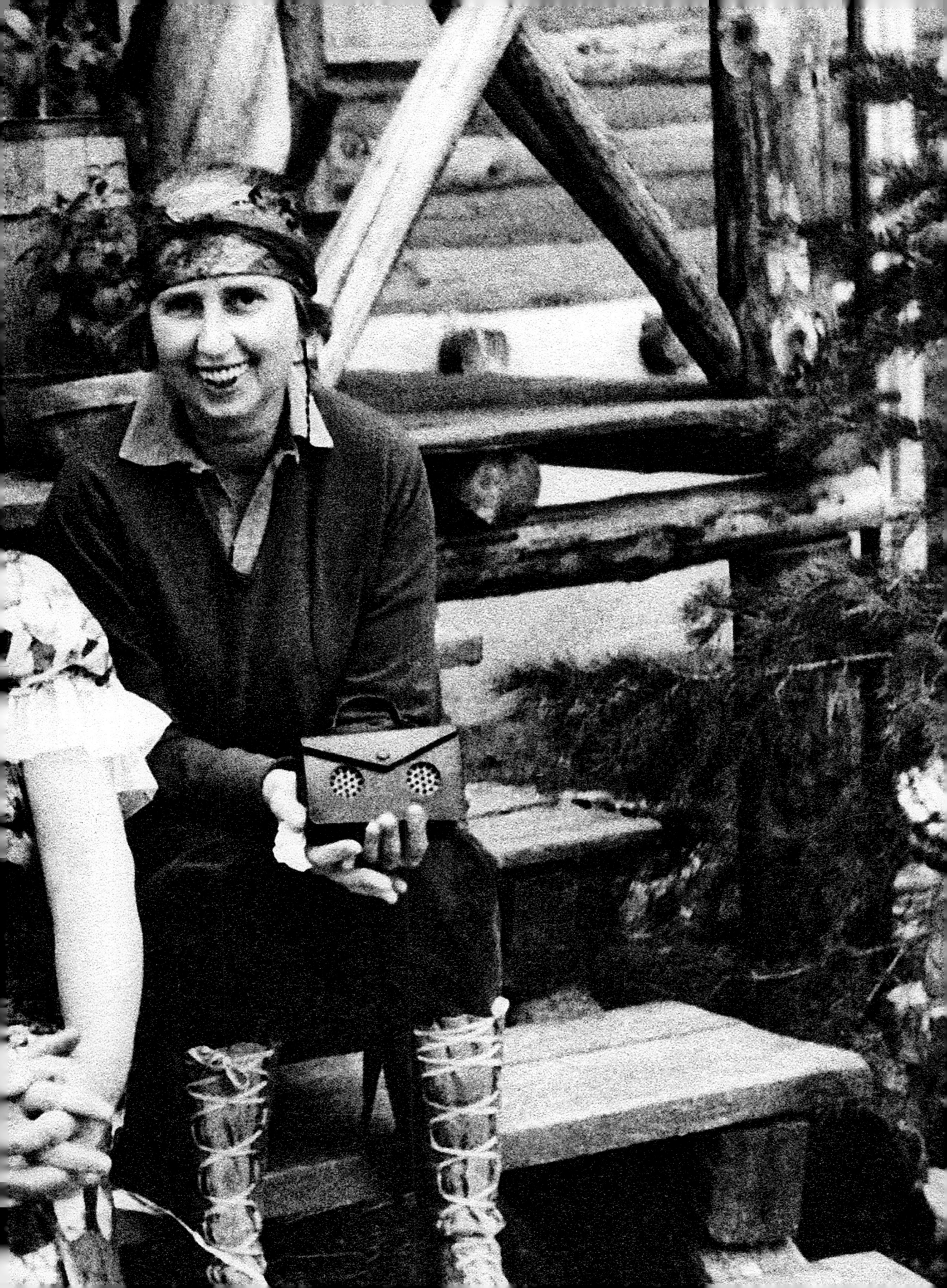

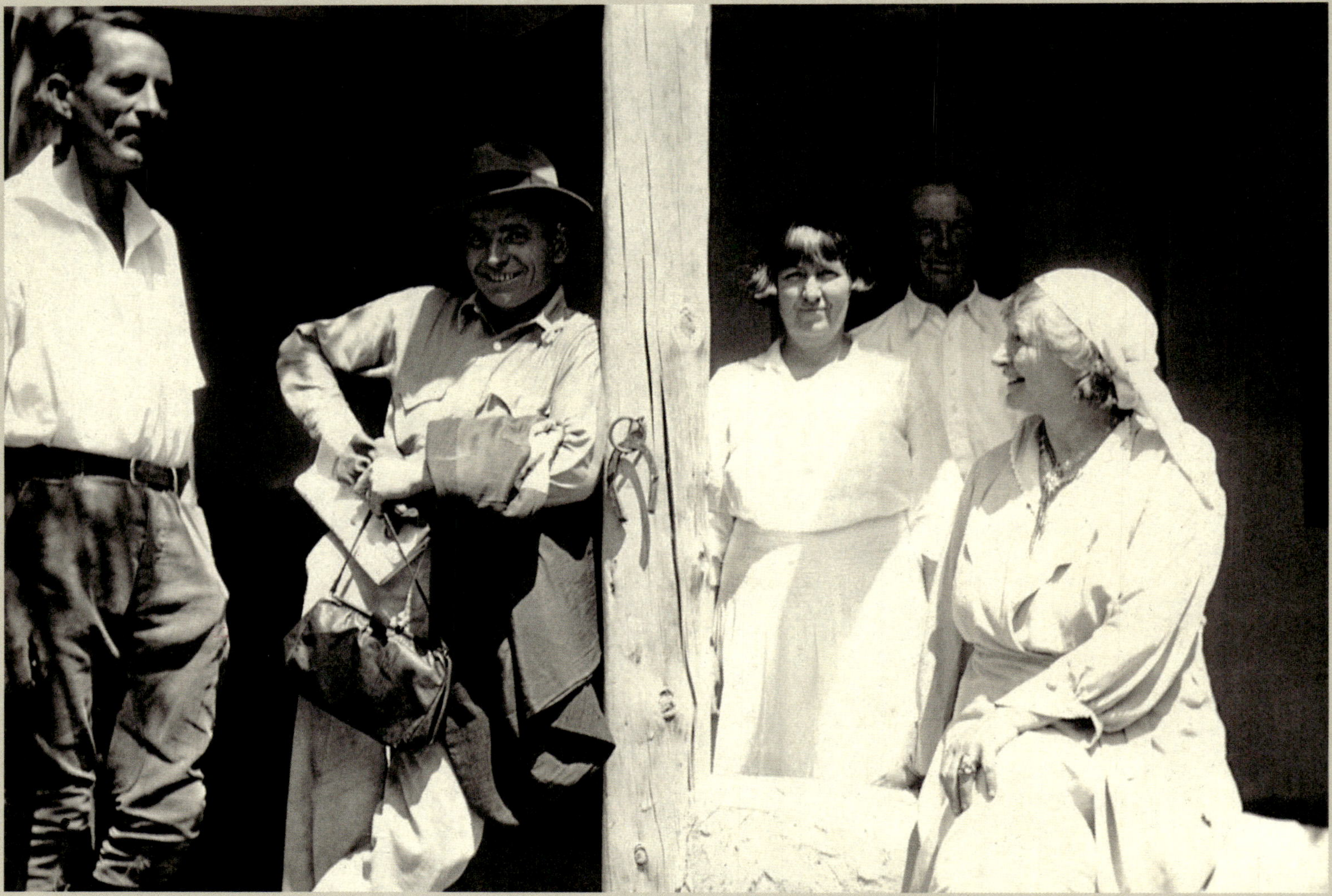

Mabel earned the nickname "regent of New Mexico" and "first lady of Taos" by building Los Gallos. She aimed to create a utopia in the desert, where consciousness and creativity would evolve through a community based in her home. She welcomed prominent artists, writers and thinkers to participate, including Willa Cather, Paul Strand, Martha Graham, Ansel Adams and Aldous Huxley, as well as (above, from left) Robinson Jeffers, Andrew Dasburg, Jack Hunter Young and Frieda Lawrence.

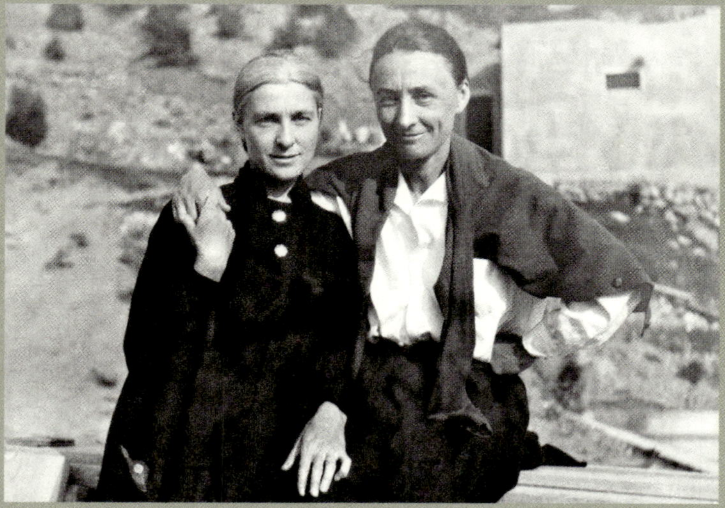

On Mabel's invitation, Georgia O'Keeffe (above, right) visited Taos in 1929. She fell in love with the open skies and sun-drenched landscape. When her husband, Alfred Stieglitz, died in 1946, O'Keeffe took up permanent residence in nearby Abiquiu.

Mabel's son, John Evans, found a mentor, father-figure and friend in Tony Luhan, the only other man in his mother's life he would ever accept and respect.

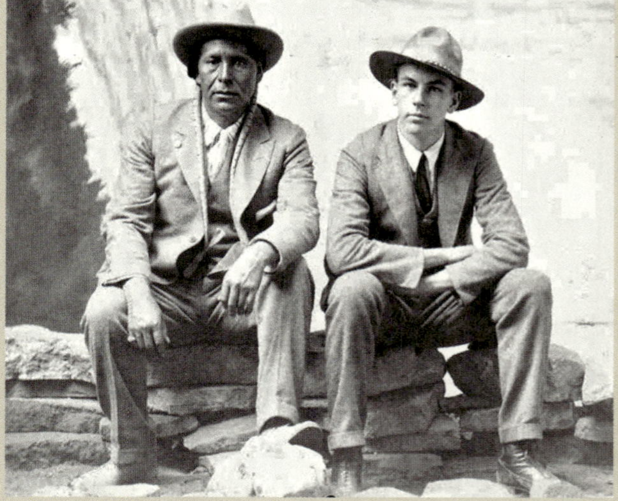

By the time Mabel had invited D.H. Lawrence to Taos she was 41 years old. She had finally found love and was now on a mission to transform the world, convinced that Taos was the chosen landmark for the remaking of Western civilization. Mabel believed that the native Indian culture held the soul's cure against modern-day society and its ills. After reading *Sons and Lovers* and *Psychoanalysis and the Unconscious*, Mabel intuited that D.H. Lawrence had the power to divine the secret of Pueblo life. She was convinced that he would understand how the Indians' relationship with the natural world could restore a modern world beleaguered by war and bereft of faith—and that it was he who could reveal it to the world through his writing. She felt Lawrence could best speak "Taos" for her: He "would take my experience, my material, my Taos and...formulate it all into a magnificent creation." [4]

Mabel resorted to everything, including witchcraft, to make sure that the Lawrences would accept her ceaseless invitations to come to Taos. They finally accepted in 1922, traveling to New Mexico via Australia and San Francisco. D.H. and Frieda returned again in 1924 with their good friend, the Honorable Dorothy Brett, an English painter. During their first year in Taos, the Lawrences exchanged the original handwritten manuscript of *Sons and Lovers* for a small ranch house on Mabel's property. Lawrence was completely transfixed by the landscape and—for a time—found it an inspiring place to paint and write. But he never grew to share his host's enthusiasm for Pueblo Indian culture. Mabel never got the treatise for the redemption of humanity that she had summoned him to write. And so, a contentious relationship developed between Lawrence and his patron. Never before had he fantasized about wanting to actually murder someone like he did Mabel. [5]

Their volatile relationship lasted for the next six years, until Lawrence's untimely death in 1930. While his time in Taos was fraught, in the end it benefitted them both. Mabel was the inspiration for Lawrence's novel *The Plumed Serpent,* and she wrote the definitive book detailing Lawrence's time in New Mexico—and her most famous tome—*Lorenzo in Taos*.

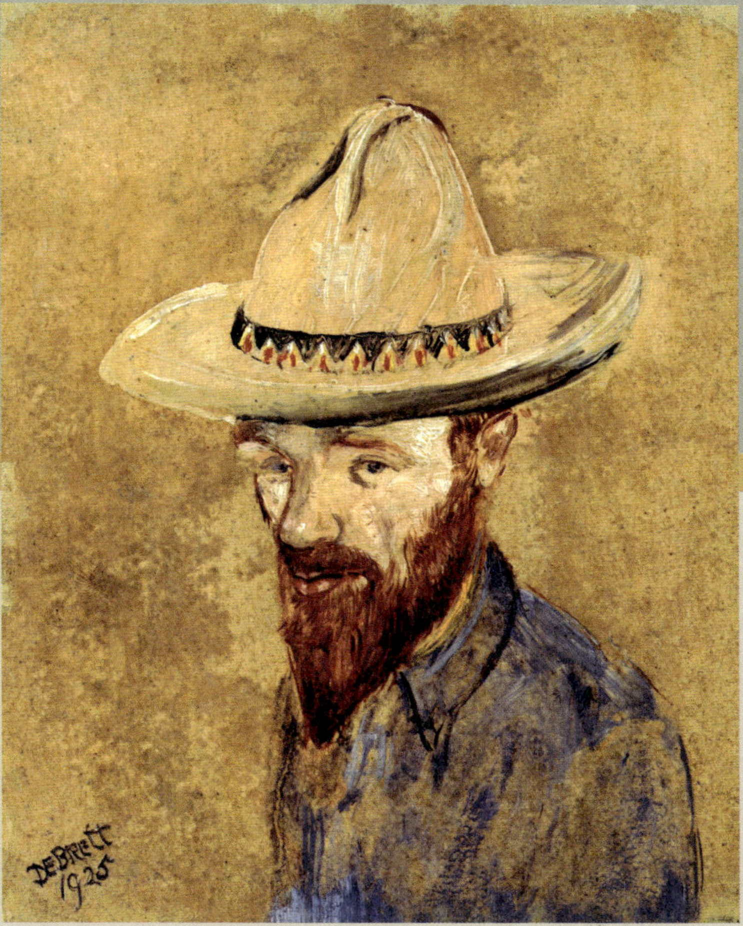


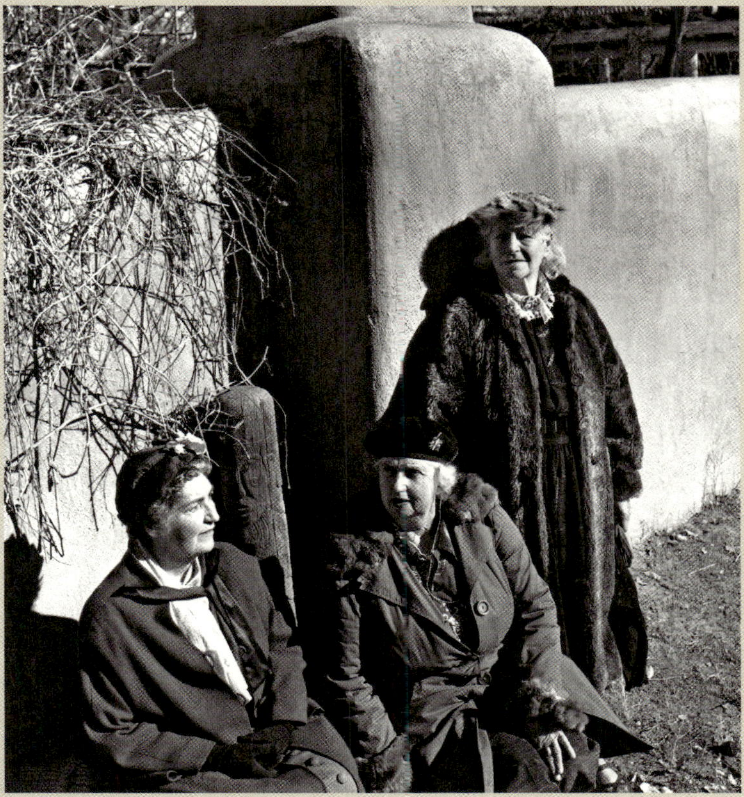

The friendship of Mabel Dodge Luhan, Frieda Lawrence, and the Honorable Dorothy Brett—three women who at one time were forced to share the attention, affection, and respect of D.H. Lawrence—suffered a terrible blow by the late 1920s due to jealousies and betrayal. They found one another again, long after Lawrence's death, and reunited to form a new friendship that would last the remainder of their lives.

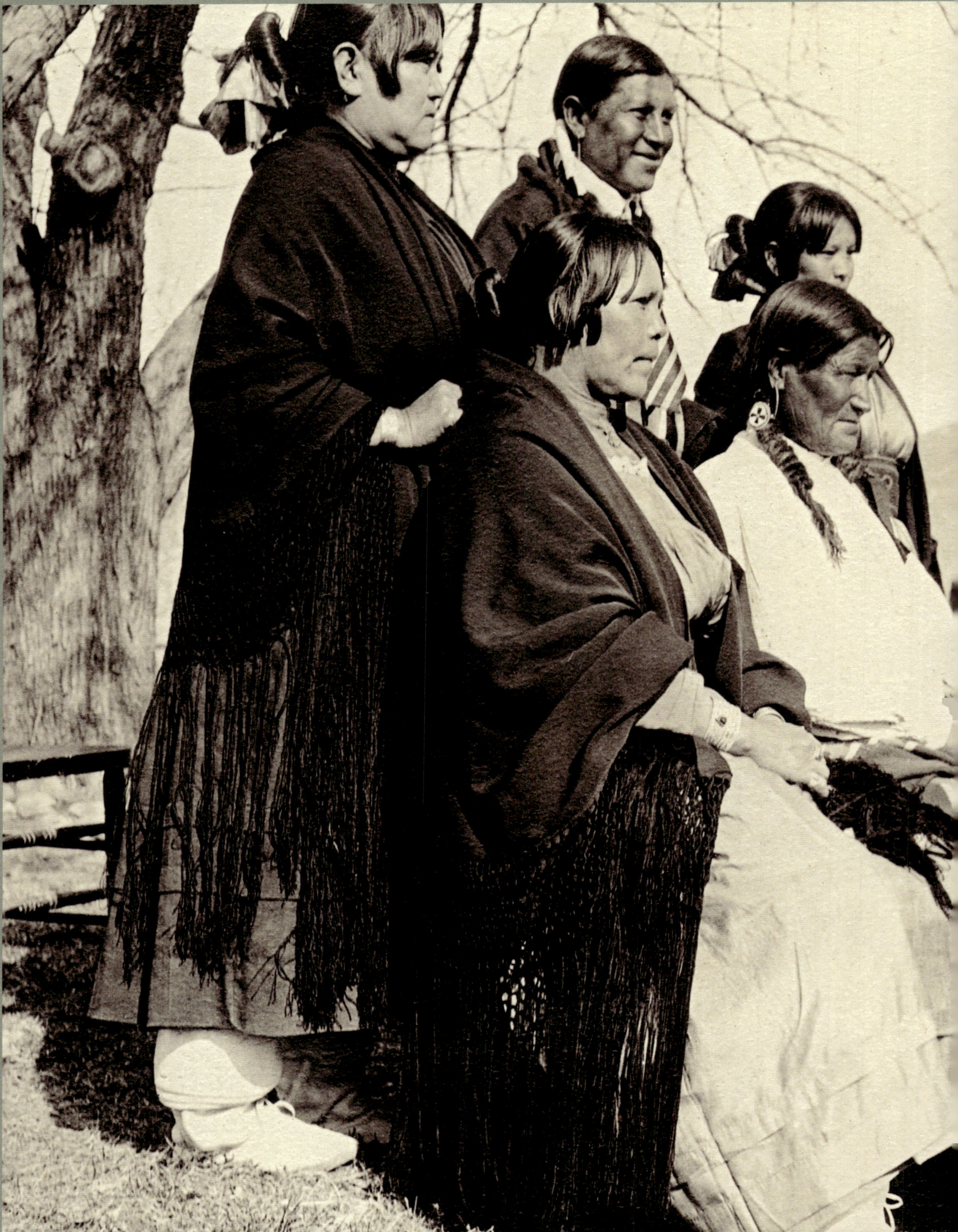

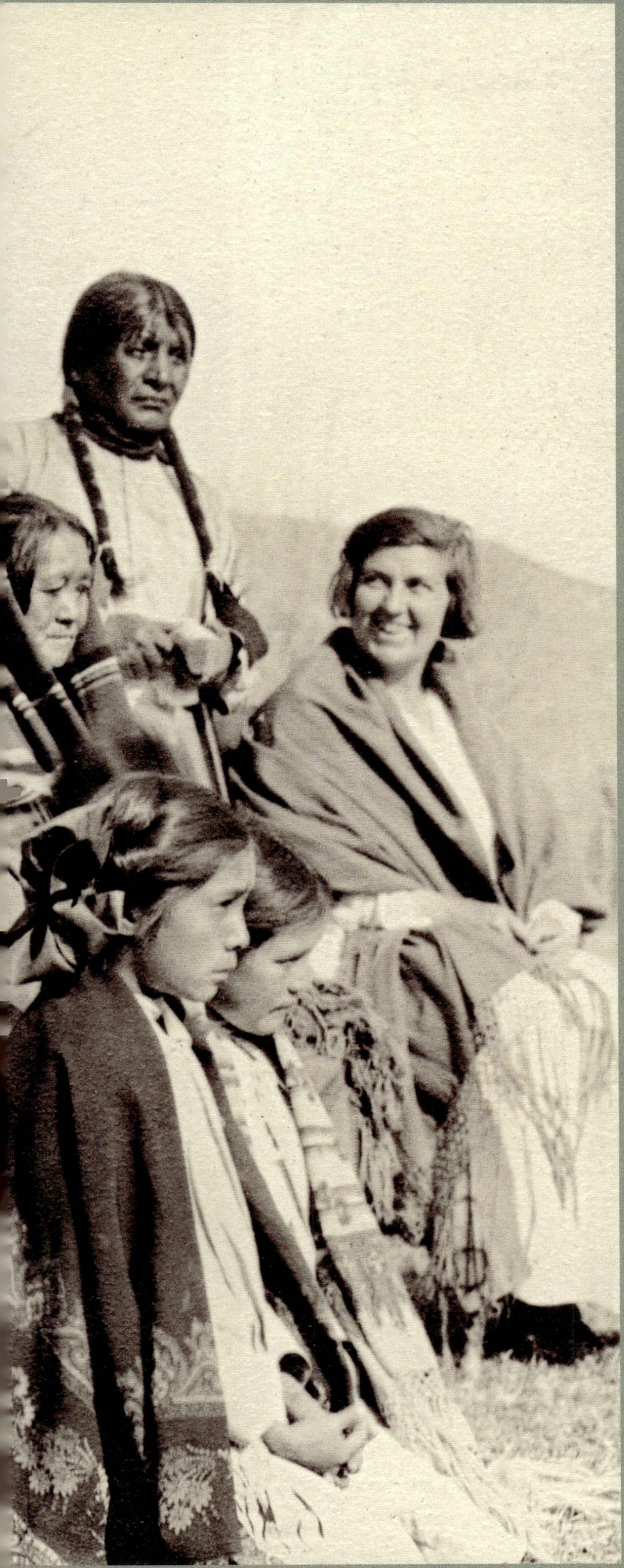

Mabel had been transformed by Tony's presence in her life and felt a deep connection to his tribe: "It was the Indian life I was entering, very slowly, a step at a time. I was becoming acquainted with a kind of living I didn't know existed anywhere. I had heard, of course, of the Golden Age, and of the Elysian fields, but those had only been words to me. Now I found out what they meant."[6] A prophetic reading in 1919 with her occultist, Mrs. Lotus Dudley, convinced Mabel that her alliance with Tony would function as a "bridge between cultures" and serve as the model to educate the world. In addition to disseminating the earth-based spiritual tenets of the Pueblos around the world, Mabel wanted to make sure that their lands were protected and honored by the government.

To that end, Mabel began to work feverishly through her political and cultural contacts, bringing artists and reformers together to influence federal policy. Their cultural politics blended Indian and Anglo concerns, combining music, poetry, and art with appeals and lobbying efforts. Everyone from the Boy Scouts of America to a group of elite social scientists took up Mabel's cause. Her most important ally was reformer John Collier. During the 1920s, Tony Luhan showed Collier the poor living conditions in American Indian communities. As a result, Collier formed the American Indian Defense Association. He worked tirelessly for the next 10 years on Indian reforms, preserving Pueblo lands and promoting the benefits of their social system. Tony Luhan was instrumental to Collier's efforts, serving as his interpreter and liasion to the various pueblos in New Mexico. Tony also led a delegation of Indians to New York City and Washington, D.C. to advocate for their rights to ancestral lands, which had been inundated with squatters. Franklin Roosevelt appointed Collier in 1933 as the Commissioner of Indian Affairs. In 1934, Collier created what was known as the Indian New Deal, a piece of federal legislation that permanently secured the right to tribal self-rule for all Native Americans and allowed them to privatize communal holdings. Mabel, Tony, and Collier also launched a campaign to free the sacred Blue Lake from government control. A 30-year battle ensued that they finally won in 1970, when President Nixon signed the lake back to its rightful owners, the Taos Pueblo Indians.

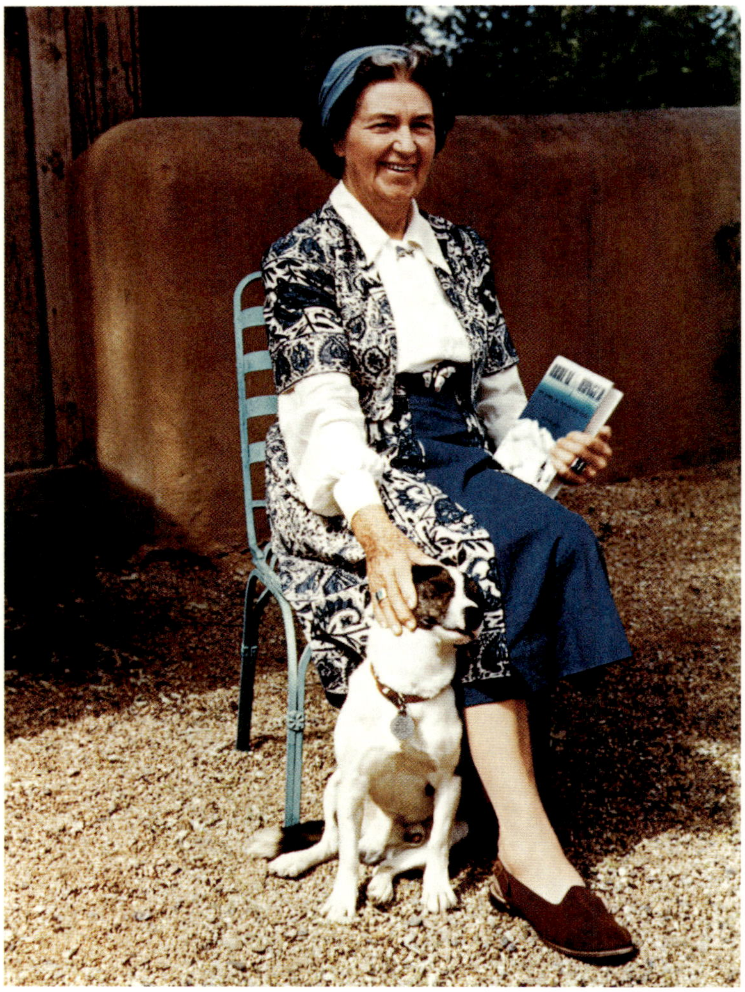

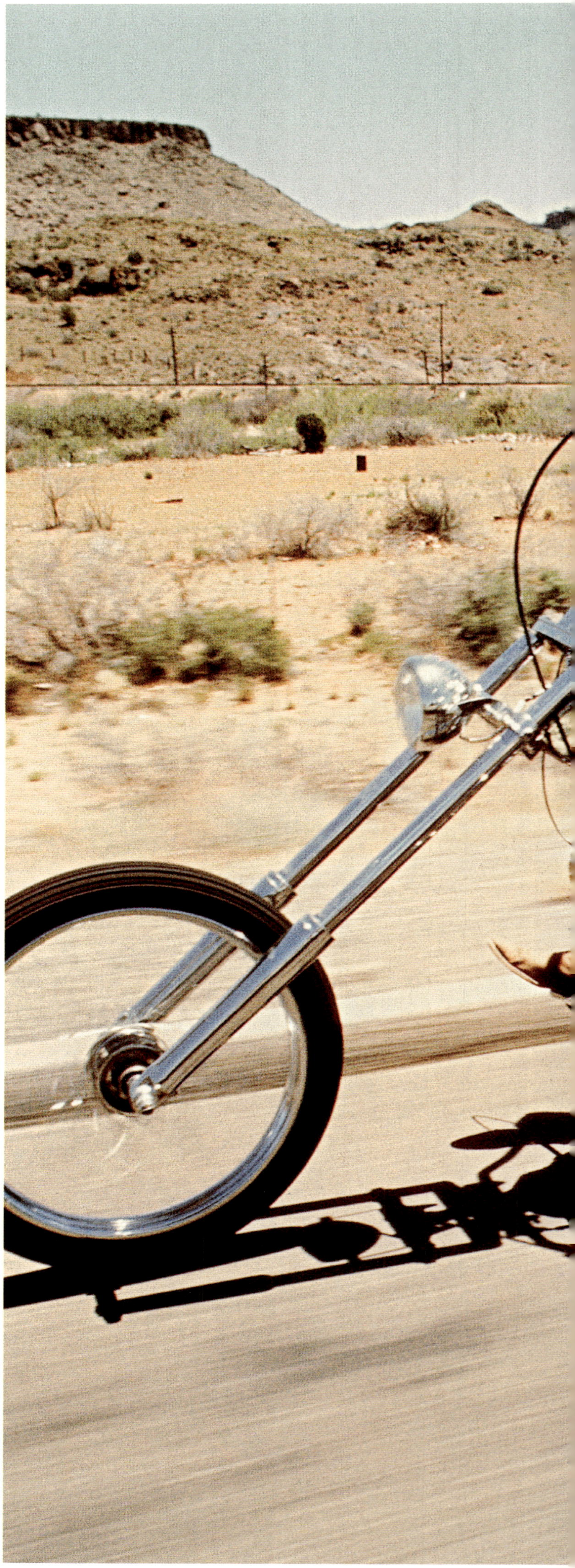

Mabel Dodge Luhan died on August 13, 1962, of coronary thrombosis after a decade of battling illness. She was buried, ironically, next to Kit Carson, a frontier lawman who had spent his life killing Indians. After Mabel's death, Tony's health suddenly declined. He died six months later, and his body was buried in the family plot on the Taos Pueblo. After their passing, John Collier wrote: "in their joined lives there has been beauty, generosity, naïveté, human goodness, and a luminousness whose dying sundown gleam is around them still."

The legacy of Mabel and Tony continues to this day through the lifeline of Los Gallos. The actor and director Dennis Hopper discovered Taos by accident during a scouting trip through the Southwest for his seminal film *Easy Rider*. He initially rejected the idea of filming there, since he was looking for an actual commune, not an artist community. But then—"I just suddenly fell in love with it. It was very mystical to me. I kept trying to get out of town, and an Indian would come and say *the mountain is smiling on you…*" Hopper ended up staying to film for two weeks in Taos and returned to buy Los Gallos from John Evans with the revenue from *Easy Rider* a year later. He then created his own artist retreat and film production studio at the house. Los Gallos has since been designated a national historic landmark. Today it is owned by an angel investor and is run as a private hotel and retreat.

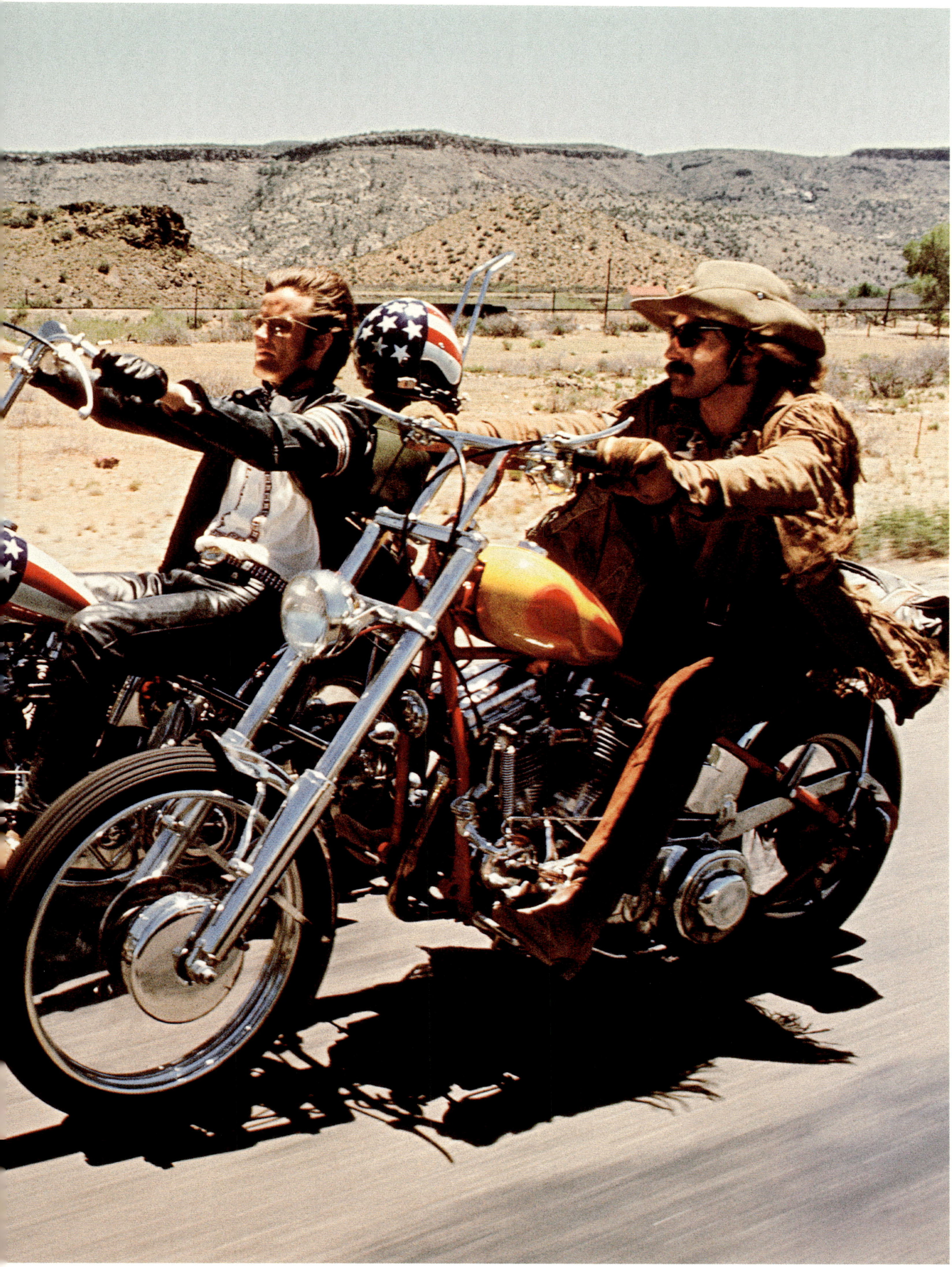

IN PRAISE OF

# DANIELLE FAITH GREEN

Danni Green is an 18-year-old writer from Boerum Hill, Brooklyn. She recently graduated from the Academy for Young Writers in Williamsburg. Her favorite writers include the Beat poet Bob Kaufman and author John Michael Green. Writing may well be in her blood—over the course of her portrait sitting, she mentioned that Gil Scott-Heron was her distant relative. When Danni was in 11th grade, her English teacher, Adam Faulkner, encouraged her to apply to Girls Write Now, a mentorship program that pairs promising young women writers with professional women who work in writing and media. Danni's mentor, Kathleen Scheiner, encouraged her to explore genres aside from poetry, so she began experimenting with prose. We met Danni after the annual Girl's Write Now Chapters reading series, where she presented the following piece.

"Letter to Kanye, January 14, 2012, 7:45 p.m." is part of a series of works Danni has been developing over the past year. It was written at a moment when she thought she would not be able to attend college this fall. "It terrified me. I couldn't find a way around the money aspect of school." To confront her feelings of helplessness, Danni put pen to paper and—as she does sometimes when she feels overwhelmed—wrote a letter to hip-hop artist Kanye West. She had been thinking about one of her favorite songs by him, "Spaceship." "I really related to the idea in his lyrics: 'I wish I could buy me a spaceship and fly me away.'" Danni is drawn to the honesty of West's music, the fact that he expresses genuine emotion without reservation or fear. She aspires to the same degree of openness and honesty in her writing.

Danni continues to work on her "Letters to Kanye" series. She will be attending Lewis and Clark College in Portland, Oregon, this fall.

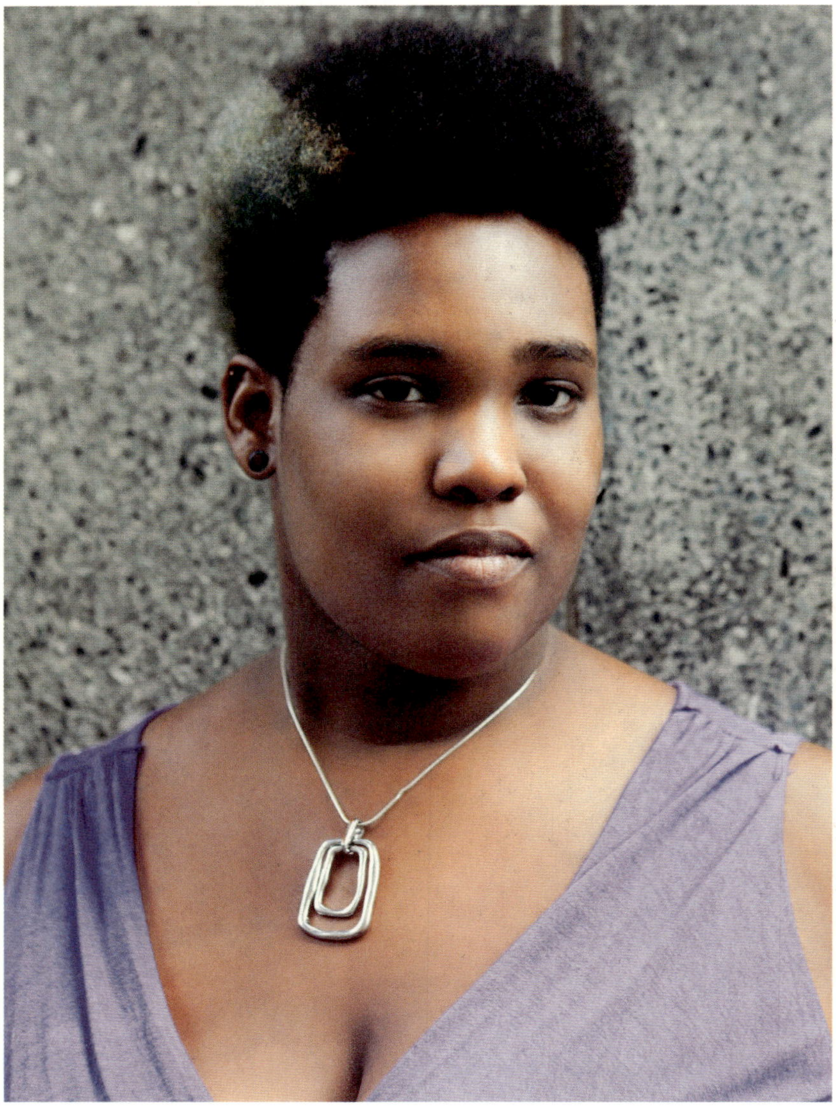

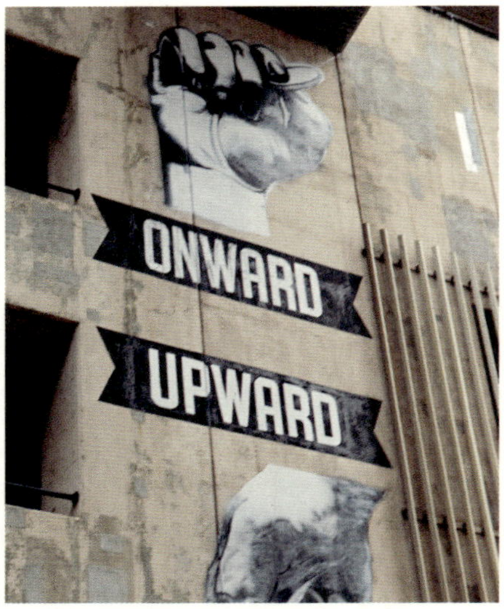


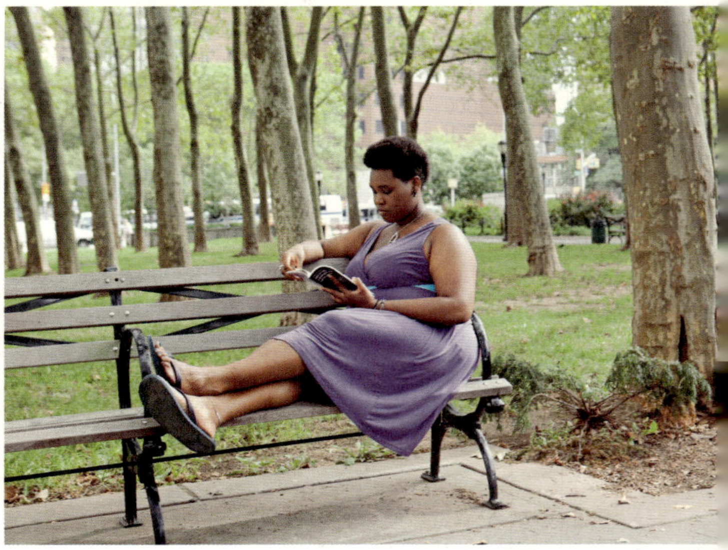

PHOTOGRAPHS BY POPPY DE VILLENEUVE

*January 14, 2012, 7:45 p.m.*

Dear Kanye,

Nine days ago I called the financial aid office of every college I applied to. Told them I had to submit my FAFSA without parental information. Told them Shawn—the man I don't call daddy and who has only ever been 23 chromosomes won't give me his information. Raises his voice to shout like Otis Day. Hurls "You're stupid" from the bottom of his throat. Every time my mom and I try.

Each college said my parents are married and the boy I refuse to call daddy lives in the house so they can't help me. Said I was in a tough situation like I didn't know. And like I don't see the lives of the people I live with and how Content like a snake has opened its mouth wide and swallowed their lives whole. My brother Robert is jobless. Almost 30. Has an associate's degree and no direction. My sister, Jessica, is sleeping with the man she loves and isn't her husband. She just got laid off. Has four children and no more food stamps. My brother Darius made a house out of my grandfather's room to avoid everything that's on the outside of his door. My younger brother Philip has taken the Geometry Regents three times. Smokes weed and wonders what he'll do with his life. My mother. Had she gone to UCLA would be a doctor right now. The closest Aunt Carla has gotten to being an actress is flipping the pages of her celebrity tabloids looking for herself.

My family has redefined happiness to make their life mean something. This isn't about college, Kanye. This about being Here. I don't mean here in Brooklyn, but Here. This place where dead dreams lurk in the footprints of everyone you're close to. Where your future stares at you through the eyes of a parent. It looks like a husband I don't love, an affair to revive what's in my coffin-chest, a job that reminds me of what I never achieved, a checking account with a zero balance and children whose faces ask, *What's for dinner?*

It's 7:54 right now. The 14th day of 2012. But Here barriers between days have dismantled themselves and morphed 24 hours into one long minute. Because it feels like 2011 and 2010 and '09 and '08 and every year that made me wish my feet would move. College was a step toward being a published writer.

For the past two years the contempt in my soul pushed me to get A's. I lost sleep to write essays, didn't hang out with friends to do homework. But now it's slowly sinking in. There isn't an escape from what dirties the dishes and puts the dust between the floor boards of my house. Not pursuing your dreams is a sickness. My mom and the giver of 23 chromosomes are carriers. It is in my plasma. And sometimes I cry like a dying man of a terminal illness. Because everything has just gotten so hard. Like breathing. Like having faith in myself. Like believing I won't stay Here. This place reeks of settling, and I'm starting to get used to the odor.

I'm too full of fear that I'm going to be My Family. I've seen the way their muscles fold, how their joints crack. What's in Them has infected me. I'm losing hope and determination. There are times when I ask myself, *Who am I kidding thinking that I'll be different? That I'll do something with my life?*

What makes me think I can get There? There. The place people are referring to when they say "You've made it" or "You're on your way." I feel I'm not on my way. That I'm such a failure. Because I strived for college but likely won't go, and my friends will leave and I'll stay. I don't know who or what can help me get There. I just know I'm not There. If I were There I wouldn't know another hungry night. I wouldn't be scared to pray. I wouldn't wake up feeling so weak. I'd be progressing toward my goal. I'd... I'd...

Ever feel you're not There, Kanye? Does the question, *How do I get There?* swim laps in your pool of thoughts? If so. What is your answer?

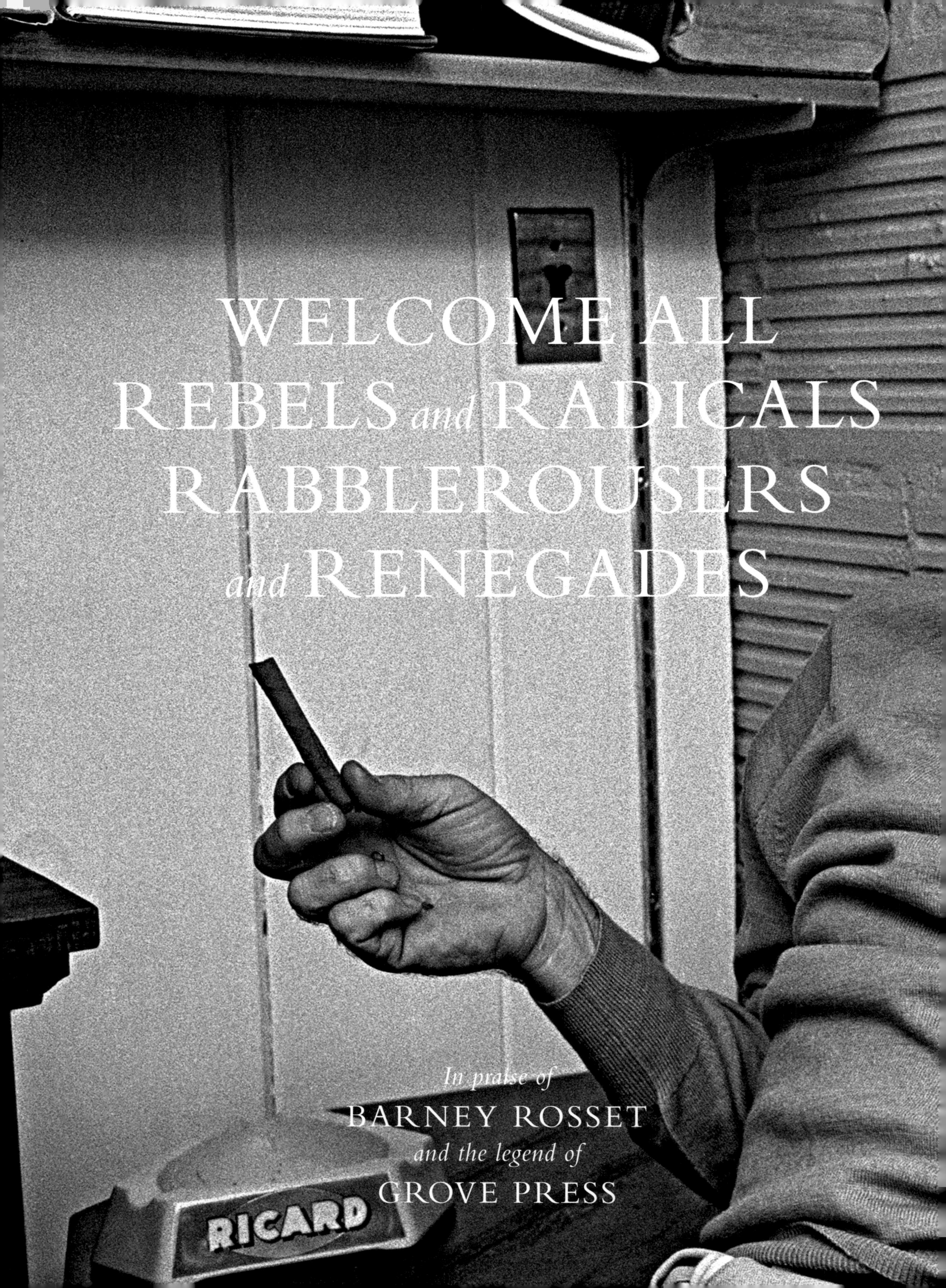


# WELCOME ALL REBELS *and* RADICALS RABBLEROUSERS *and* RENEGADES

*In praise of*

BARNEY ROSSET

*and the legend of*

GROVE PRESS

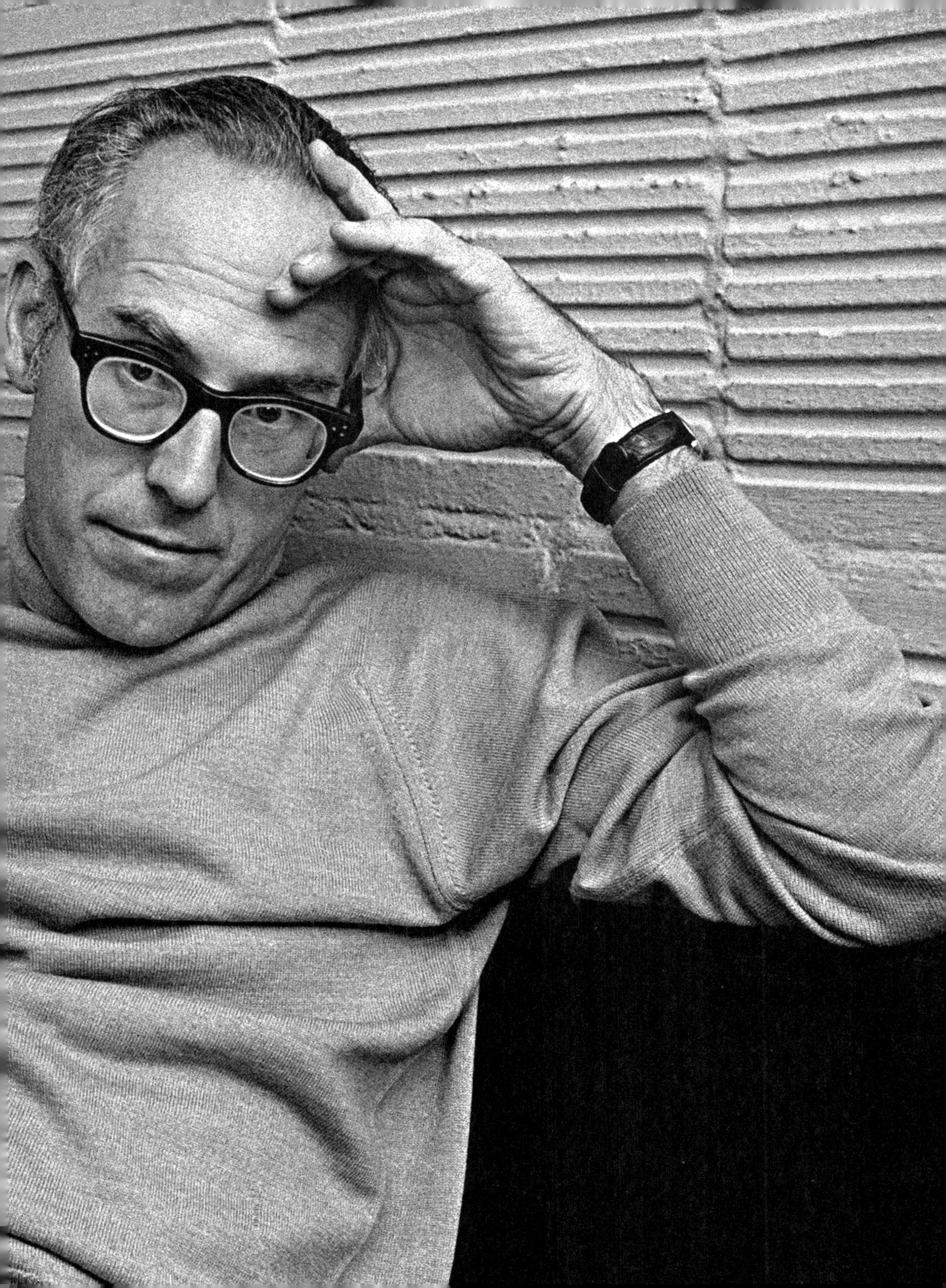

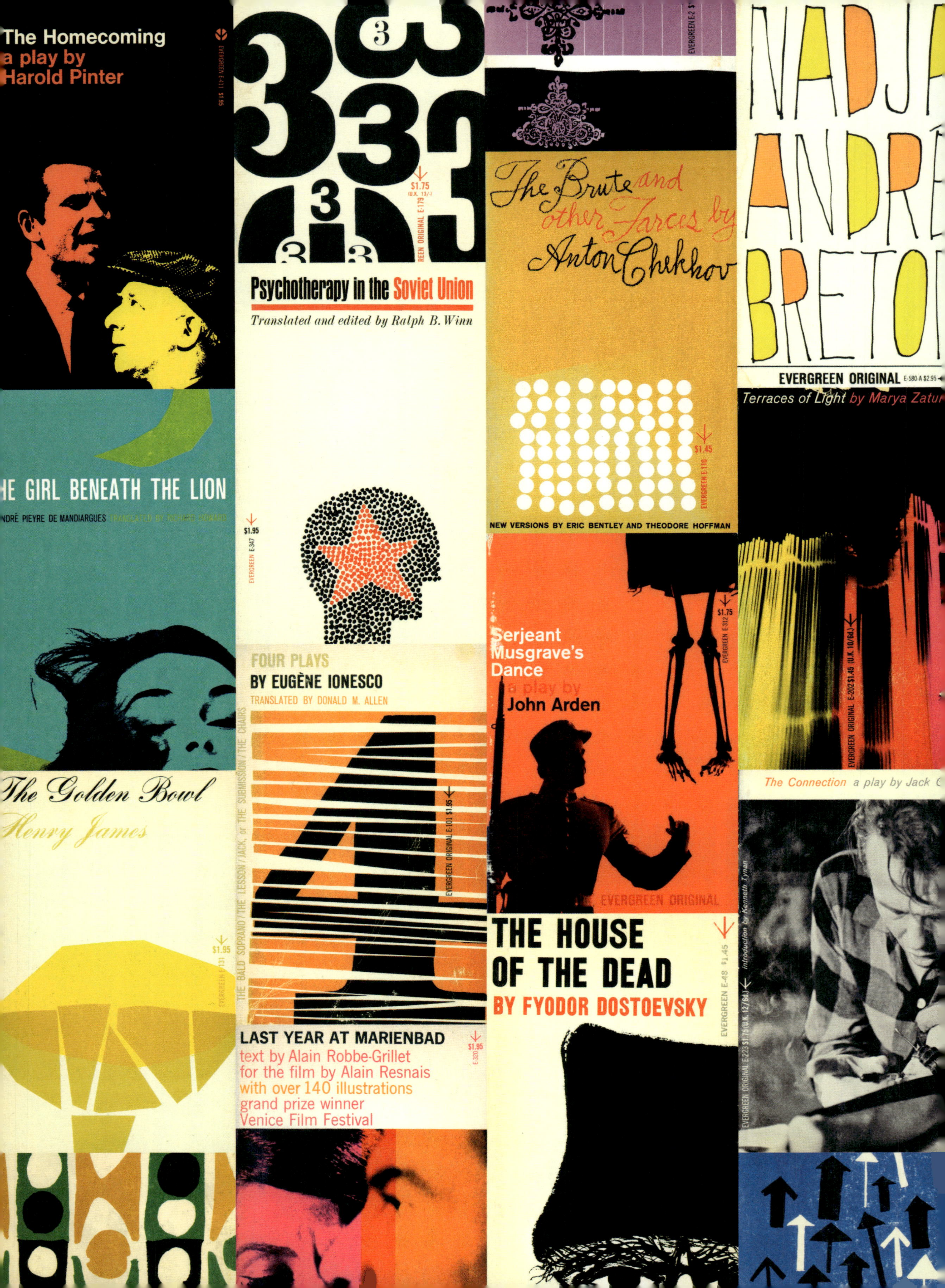
The Homecoming
a play by
Harold Pinter
EVERGREEN E-411 $1.95
Psychotherapy in the Soviet Union
Translated and edited by Ralph B. Winn
$1.75
EVERGREEN E-347 $1.95
The Brute and other Farces by Anton Chekhov
NEW VERSIONS BY ERIC BENTLEY AND THEODORE HOFFMAN
$1.45 EVERGREEN E-110
NADJA ANDRÉ BRETON
EVERGREEN ORIGINAL
Terraces of Light by Marya Zatur
HE GIRL BENEATH THE LION
NDRÉ PIEYRE DE MANDIARGUES
FOUR PLAYS
BY EUGÈNE IONESCO
TRANSLATED BY DONALD M. ALLEN
THE BALD SOPRANO / THE LESSON / JACK, or THE SUBMISSION / THE CHAIRS
EVERGREEN ORIGINAL E-101 $1.95
Serjeant Musgrave's Dance
a play by
John Arden
$1.75 EVERGREEN E-312
EVERGREEN ORIGINAL
EVERGREEN ORIGINAL E-202 $1.45 (U.K. 10/6d.)
The Connection a play by Jack G
introduction by Kenneth Tynan
The Golden Bowl
Henry James
$1.95 EVERGREEN E-131
THE HOUSE OF THE DEAD
BY FYODOR DOSTOEVSKY
EVERGREEN E-48 $1.45
LAST YEAR AT MARIENBAD
text by Alain Robbe-Grillet
for the film by Alain Resnais
with over 140 illustrations
grand prize winner
Venice Film Festival
$1.95 E-320

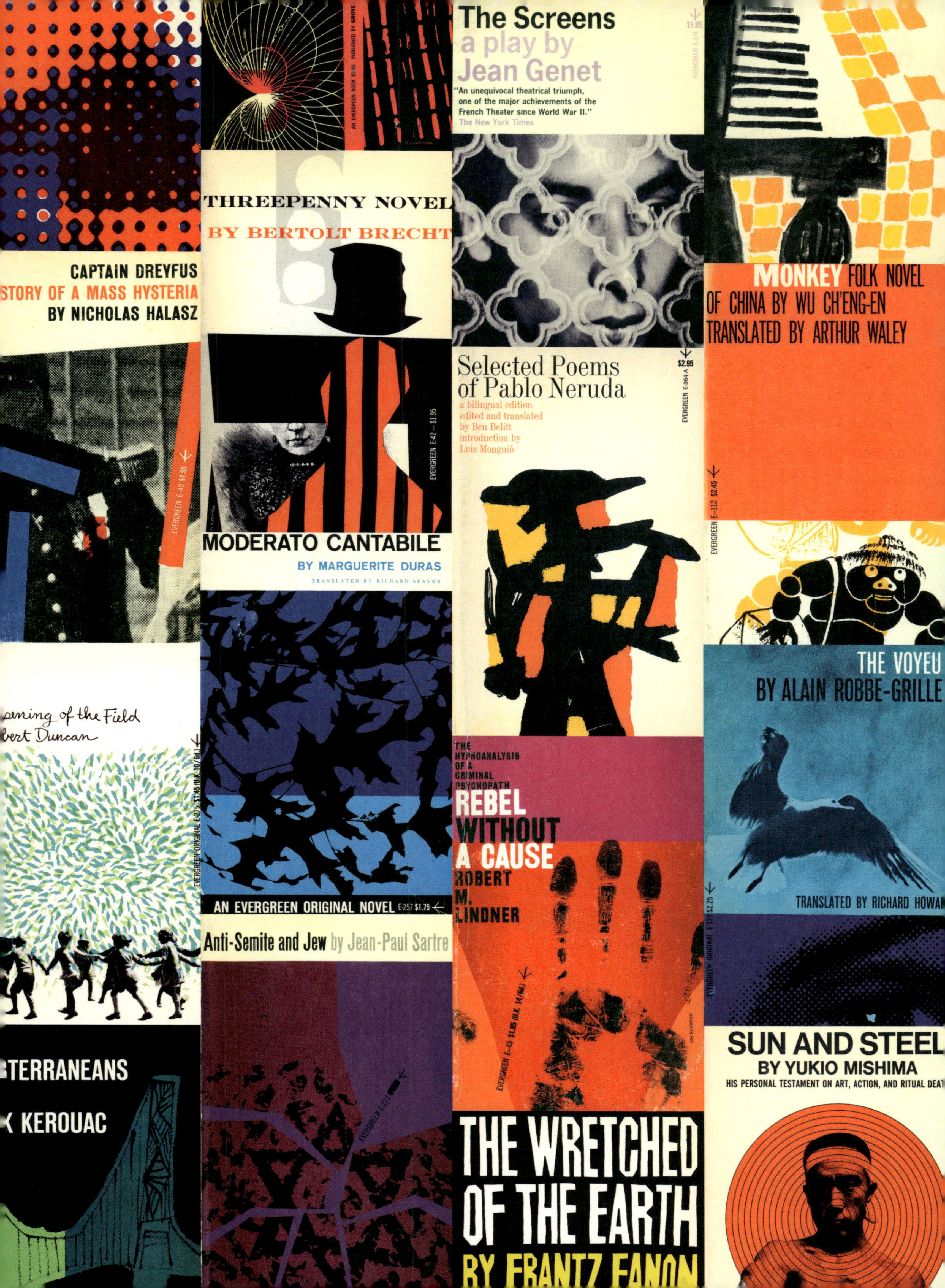
CAPTAIN DREYFUS
STORY OF A MASS HYSTERIA
BY NICHOLAS HALASZ
EVERGREEN E-49 $1.95
THREEPENNY NOVEL
BY BERTOLT BRECHT
EVERGREEN E-42 — $1.95
The Screens
a play by
Jean Genet
"An unequivocal theatrical triumph, one of the major achievements of the French Theater since World War II."
The New York Times
$1.95
MONKEY FOLK NOVEL
OF CHINA BY WU CH'ENG-EN
TRANSLATED BY ARTHUR WALEY
EVERGREEN E-112 $2.45
Selected Poems
of Pablo Neruda
a bilingual edition
edited and translated
by Ben Belitt
introduction by
Luis Monguió
$2.95
EVERGREEN E-364-A
MODERATO CANTABILE
BY MARGUERITE DURAS
TRANSLATED BY RICHARD SEAVER
THE VOYEU
BY ALAIN ROBBE-GRILLE
TRANSLATED BY RICHARD HOWA
THE HYPNOANALYSIS OF A CRIMINAL PSYCHOPATH
REBEL WITHOUT A CAUSE
ROBERT M. LINDNER
AN EVERGREEN ORIGINAL NOVEL E-257 $1.75
Anti-Semite and Jew by Jean-Paul Sartre
SUN AND STEEL
BY YUKIO MISHIMA
HIS PERSONAL TESTAMENT ON ART, ACTION, AND RITUAL DEA
THE WRETCHED
OF THE EARTH
BY FRANTZ FANON
TERRANEANS
K KEROUAC

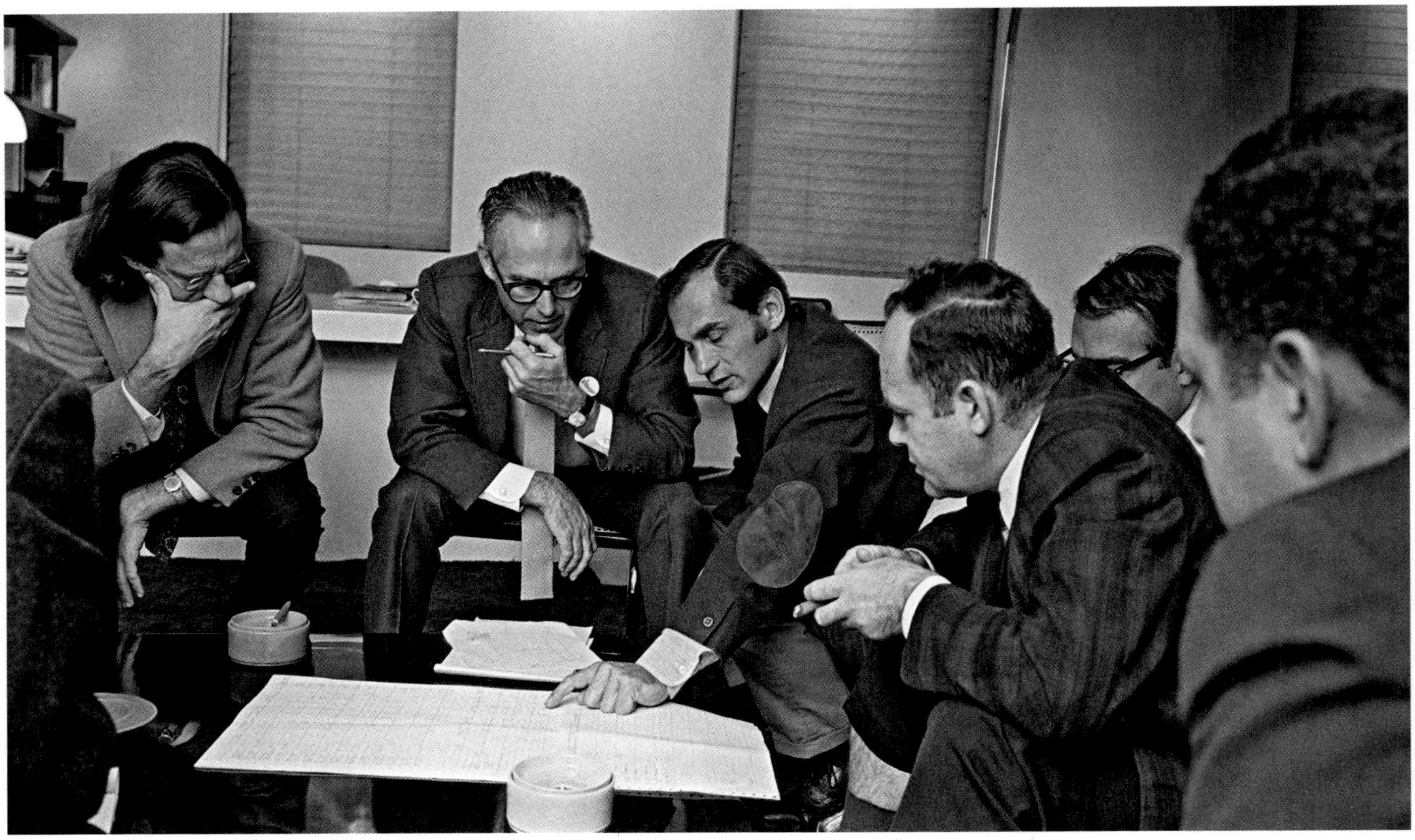

It is easy for us to take the freedoms we enjoy for granted, but to do so is a dangerous slight to history. We rarely question the freedoms we feel entitled to, and sometimes neglect our responsibilities to them. But if we look closely at the boundaries of freedom—what is or is not actually allowed—we might find something more is required of us. Freedom is not passive—it demands action.

Barney Rosset was a man of action and mischief. As the publisher of the hugely influential Grove Press, he spent his life challenging America's commitment to its basic constitutional rights of free speech and free press. Born into a wealthy family in Chicago in 1922, Barney attended a number of progressive schools, including Francis Parker, where he became increasingly politically minded and outspoken. In the eighth grade, he printed a Communist newsletter called the *Anti-Everything* with his friend (and future cinematographer) Haskell Wexler, and later campaigned for the pardon of John Dillinger, a childhood hero. After graduating, Barney discovered his contrarian views were out of sync with the rigid expectations of Swarthmore and the University of Chicago, two traditional colleges he attended. He abandoned each in turn and joined the Army, where he served in the Photographic Signal Corps.

Barney developed a lifelong passion for film while traveling through India and China documenting civilian life for the Army. When he returned to the States after WWII, he bristled at the hypocrisy of his country fighting a war for freedoms that many of its own citizens were denied. Barney spent a small fortune making *Strange Victory*, a film that examined the prejudices faced by African-American soldiers returning from combat. The film was a commercial flop, but its themes of freedom, justice, and the paradoxes of American life would define Barney's agenda from then on.

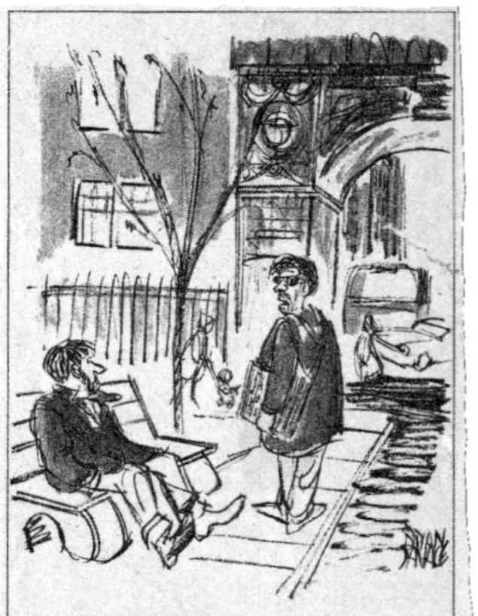

"Hey, man, which way to Grove Press?"

In 1949, Barney married the painter Joan Mitchell and became immersed in the avant-garde scene in New York. It was a heady time—the city crackled with art and music that broke with tradition; revolutionary political movements emerged that would transform America in the years to come. In the midst of all this change, Barney found his calling when Joan introduced him to the original owners of Grove Press. He purchased the company and set about signing new writers who expressed the emergent spirit of dissent and non-conformity he admired. His first real success was found in the Irish playwright Samuel Beckett. Barney did not shy away from Beckett's abstract language and absurdist themes, persuading the reticent playwright to publish *Waiting for Godot* with Grove in 1954. It was the start of a life-long friendship.

With the success of such an unconventional writer under

his belt, Barney created *Evergreen Review,* a literary journal that showcased the radical forms and anti-establishment attitudes of the Beat Generation. From the very beginning, Barney wanted to challenge what was acceptable to publish according to the letter of the law. After Allen Ginsberg's "Howl" caused the arrest of its original publisher, Lawrence Ferlinghetti, Barney re-released it in *Evergreen*, thereby expanding the banned poem's national readership. For Barney, the mission of Grove Press and *Evergreen Review* was clear—to support the literary experimentation of cutting-edge writers while fighting censorship of any kind.

Barney began challenging America's commitment to the ideals of the Constitution in earnest as early as 1954, when Grove Press imported and distributed copies of D. H. Lawrence's notorious novel, *Lady Chatterley's Lover.* The book had been banned in the States for its explicit presentation of sexuality, and Grove Press had to defend its actions in court. In 1959, Barney went a step further—Grove Press used the postal service to ship a new printing of *Chatterley* in a direct challenge to obscenity laws. Another lengthy court battle ensued, with a federal judge eventually lifting the ban on the book. Barney had used the Lawrence novel as a test case for his real passion project—a domestic printing of the even more shocking *Tropic of Cancer.*

Henry Miller had been a rebel hero to Barney since his college days, when as a freshman he wrote a paper about *Tropic of Cancer.* He had long dreamed of publishing the banned book in the States, and finally did so in 1961, setting off a dramatic legal furor. Miller's book was banned in cities and states across the country. Grove Press financed legal battles to challenge these bans and defend booksellers state-by-state. Though the controversy made *Tropic of Cancer* a bestseller, it also came at great personal

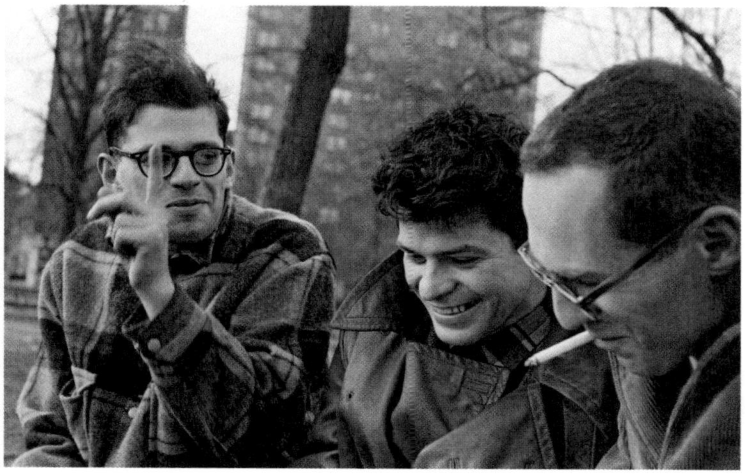

OPPOSITE: BARNEY DELIBERATES WITH THE GROVE PRESS STAFF • THIS PAGE: ALLEN GINSBERG, GREGORY CORSO AND BARNEY IN NEW YORK CITY • FOLLOWING SPREAD: GROVE BOOK DESIGNS BY ROY KUHLMAN

cost to Barney. He was forced to sell off a large tract of land in Southampton to pay Grove's ever-mounting legal fees. In 1964, the Supreme Court finally ruled in Barney's favor—*Tropic of Cancer* could not legally be banned as pornography.

By that point, Grove Press was firmly established as the publisher of the counterculture and continued releasing lightning rod titles throughout the 60s—William Burroughs' *Naked Lunch*, Malcolm X's *Autobiography*, and Pauline Réage's *Story of O.* Grove Press entered its boom period—*Evergreen Review* commissioned original journalism and published new photographers; Black Cat was created, an imprint of Grove devoted to the publication of erotica. With these profits, Barney returned again to cinema, releasing the Swedish semi-erotic film *I Am Curious (Yellow)* in 1968. It caused a public outcry from conservative quarters and the theatrical run was eventually shut down, but not before the film became a financial success.

Even with these court victories, Grove's titles were still not completely accepted by the mainstream. Many took offense to Barney's determined assault on the status quo, making Grove Press a target. In 1968, a grenade exploded at their offices on University Place. It was suspected that Cuban exiles were responsible, as *Evergreen Review* had published an excerpt from Che Guevara's diaries a short time before. Then, in 1970, the Grove staff attempted to unionize. These disruptions took a toll on the company. Barney attempted to hold on for a while, but the financial setbacks proved too great. He sold Grove Press to Ann Getty and George Weidenfeld in 1985. It was not an easy exchange, and within a year Barney was forced out of the company he had brought to international prominence.

The legacy of Barney Rosset's tenacious advocacy on behalf of writers must not be underestimated. Under Barney's stewardship, Grove Press signed numous writers who became Nobel laureates—Samuel Beckett, Kenzaburo Oe, Pablo Neruda, Harold Pinter and Octavio Paz—as well as a host of late-20th-century literary giants—Jack Kerouac, Jean Genet, Eugene Ionesco, LeRoi Jones, and Marguerite Duras. But perhaps more important than Grove's literary roster were the lasting effects of Barney's personal investment in free speech and his willingness to push the buttons of the establishment, regardless of consequence. Barney Rosset shifted the dialogue about free speech in America. Controversial texts are no longer seen as an affront to our way of life, but rather an incontestable right. On behalf of the writers and readers who have inherited the freedoms he fought for, we say, simply, *Thank you, Barney.*

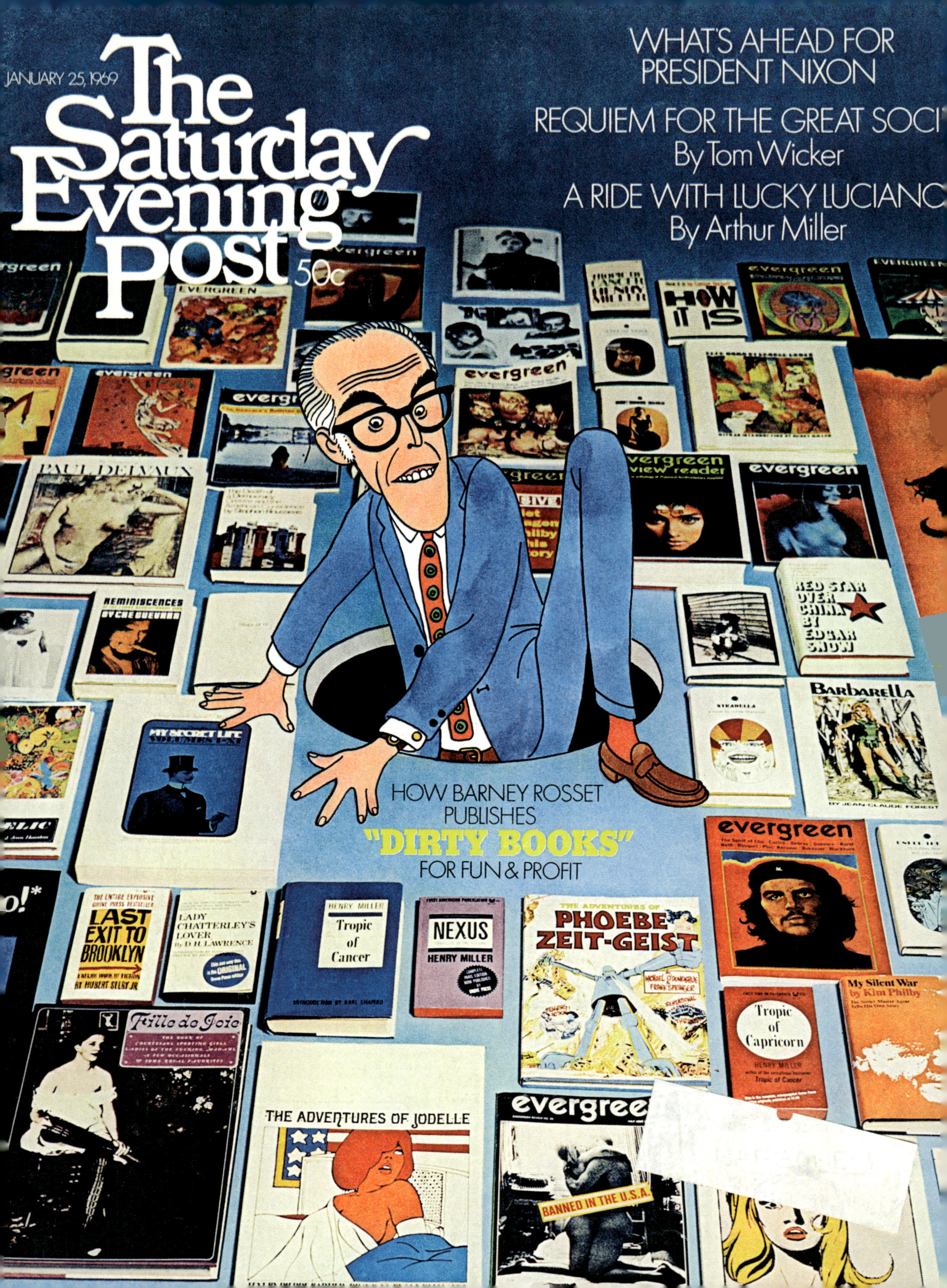
JANUARY 25, 1969
The Saturday Evening Post
50c
WHAT'S AHEAD FOR PRESIDENT NIXON
REQUIEM FOR THE GREAT SOCI
By Tom Wicker
A RIDE WITH LUCKY LUCIAN
By Arthur Miller
HOW BARNEY ROSSET PUBLISHES "DIRTY BOOKS" FOR FUN & PROFIT
evergreen
HOW IT IS
PAUL DELVAUX
evergreen review reader
REMINISCENCES BY CHE GUEVARA
RED STAR OVER CHINA BY EDGAR SNOW
MY SECRET LIFE
BARBARELLA
BY JEAN-CLAUDE FOREST
LAST EXIT TO BROOKLYN
BY HUBERT SELBY JR
LADY CHATTERLEY'S LOVER
By D. H. LAWRENCE
HENRY MILLER
Tropic of Cancer
NEXUS
HENRY MILLER
THE ADVENTURES OF PHOEBE ZEIT-GEIST
Tropic of Capricorn
HENRY MILLER
My Silent War
by Kim Philby
Fille de Joie
THE ADVENTURES OF JODELLE
BANNED IN THE U.S.A.

# evergreen

EVERGREEN REVIEW NO. 81

AUGUST 1970 / ONE DOLLAR

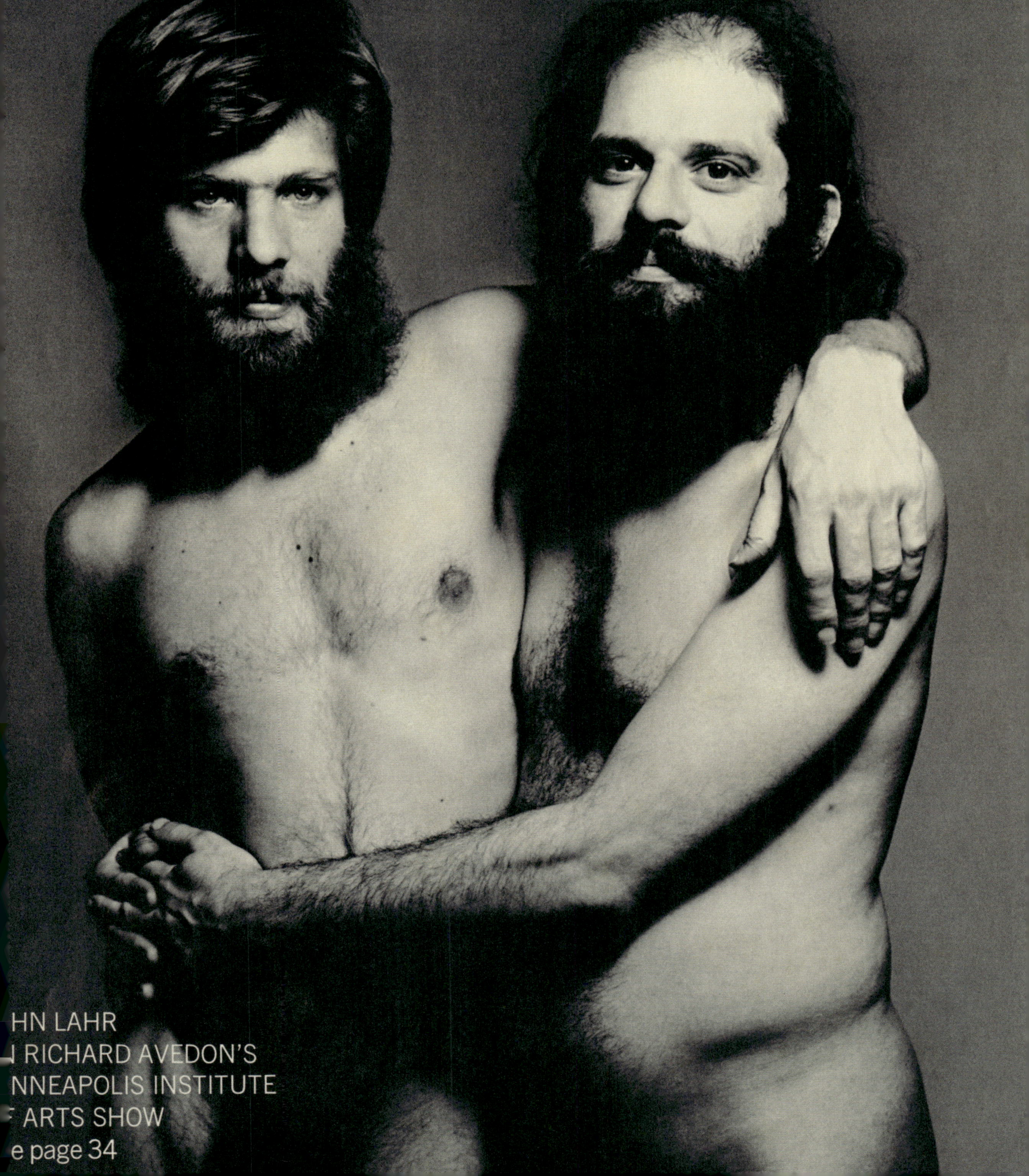

HN LAHR
I RICHARD AVEDON'S
NNEAPOLIS INSTITUTE
F ARTS SHOW
e page 34

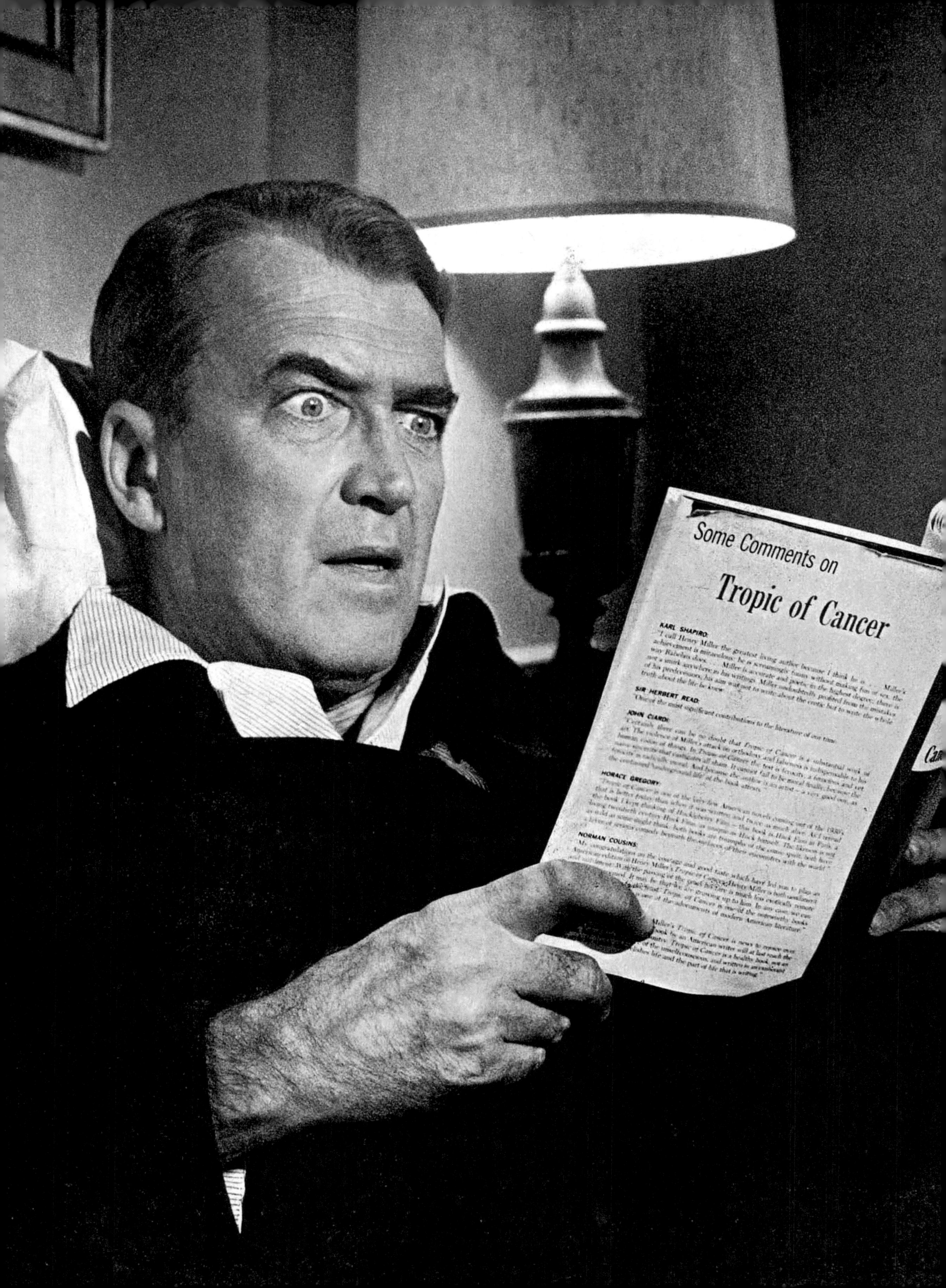
Some Comments on
Tropic of Cancer
KARL SHAPIRO:
SIR HERBERT READ:
JOHN CIARDI:
HORACE GREGORY:
NORMAN COUSINS:

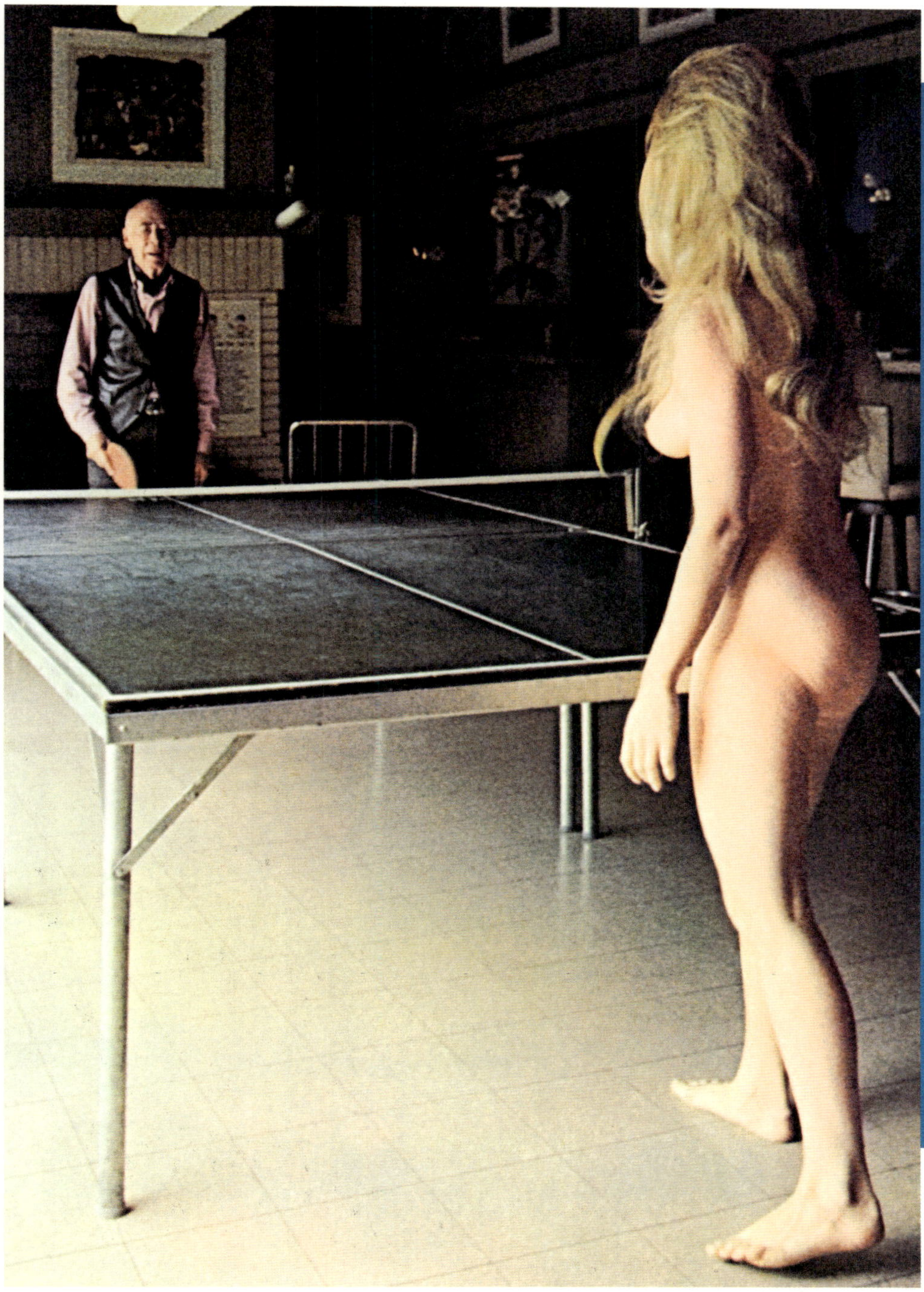

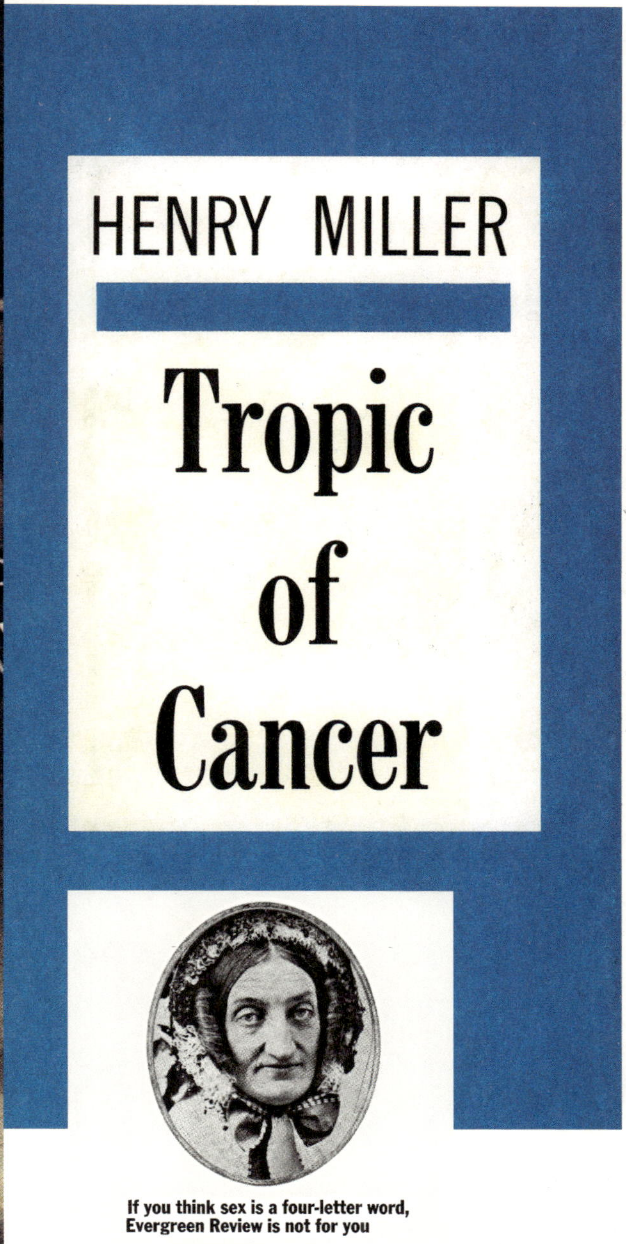


"This is not a book. This is libel, slander, defamation of character. This is not a book, in the ordinary sense of the word. No, this is a prolonged insult, a gob of spit in the face of Art, a kick in the pants to God, Man, Destiny, Time, Love, Beauty…what you will. I am going to sing for you, a little off key perhaps, but I will sing."

—*Henry Miller,* Tropic of Cancer

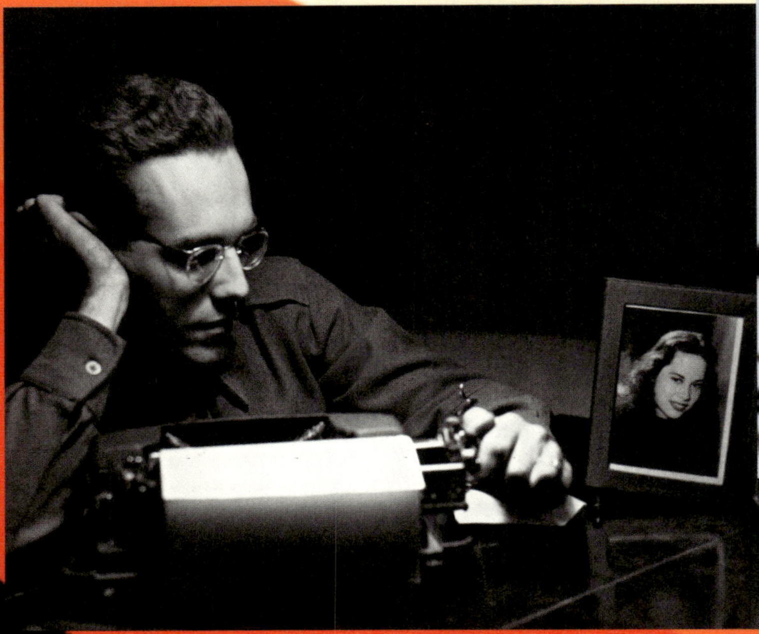

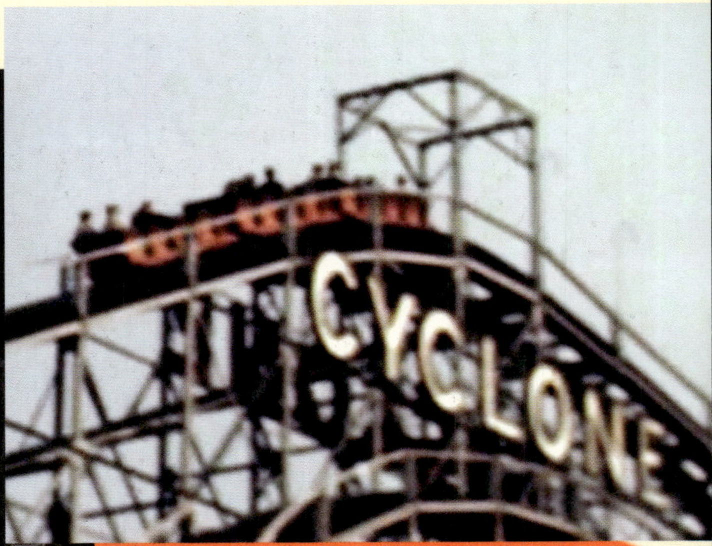


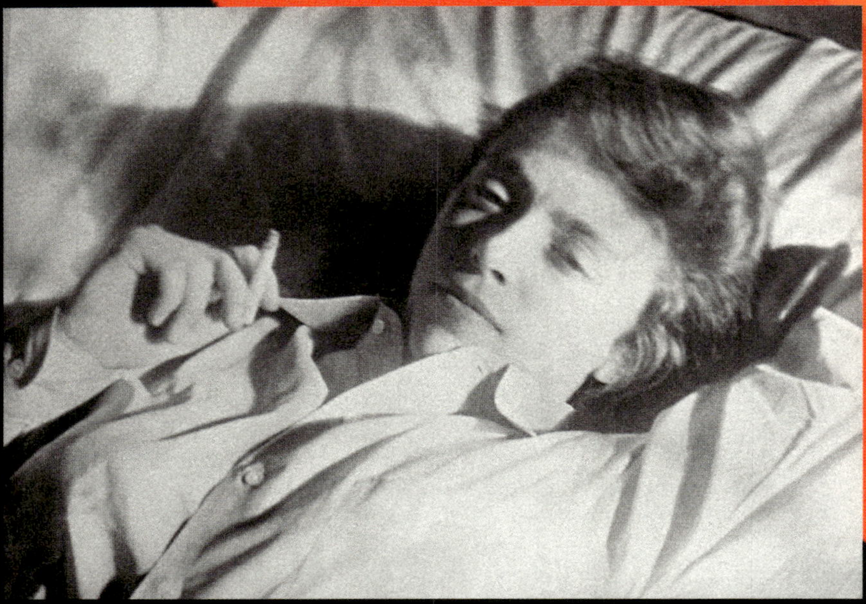

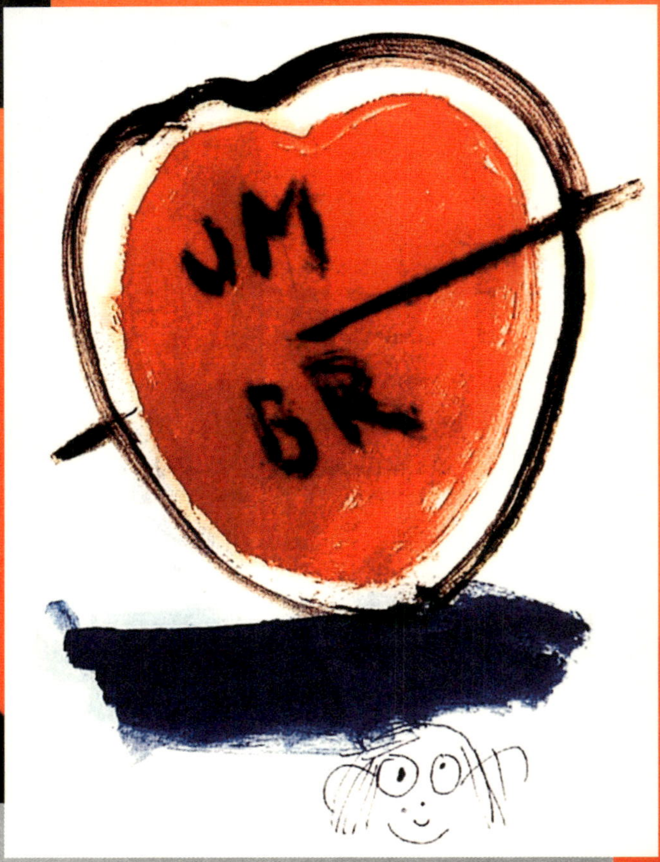


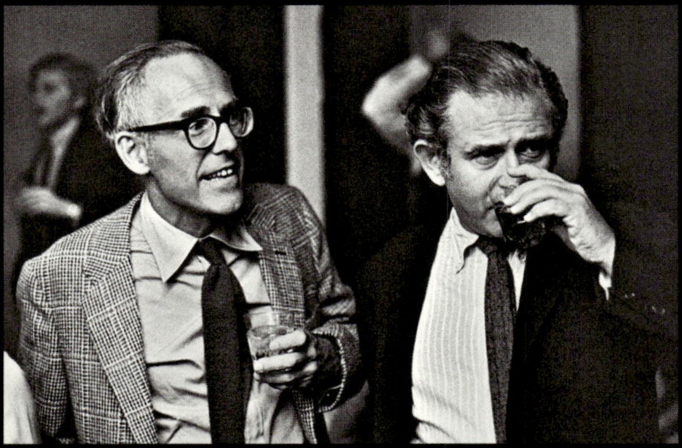

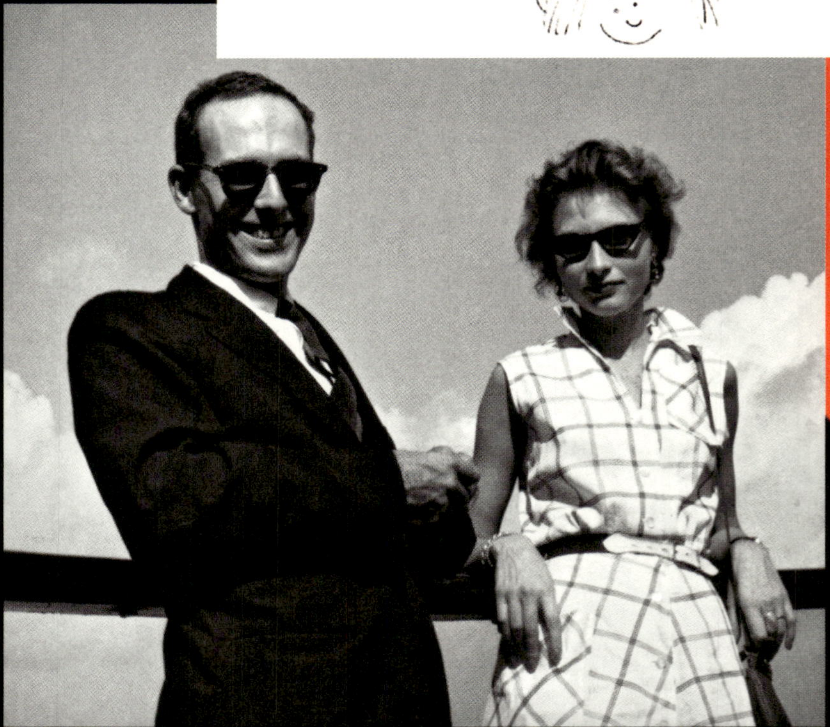

CLOCKWISE FROM TOP LEFT: BARNEY ROSSET IN HIS ARMY DAYS WITH A PHOTO OF HIS GIRLFRIEND • STILL FROM A TEST FILM BARNEY SHOT AT CONEY ISLAND • VALENTINE BY JOAN MITCHELL, BARNEY'S FIRST WIFE • BARNEY WITH HIS SECOND WIFE, LOLY • BARNEY WITH NORMAN MAILER • JOAN MITCHELL, PHOTOGRAPHED BY BARNEY ROSSET

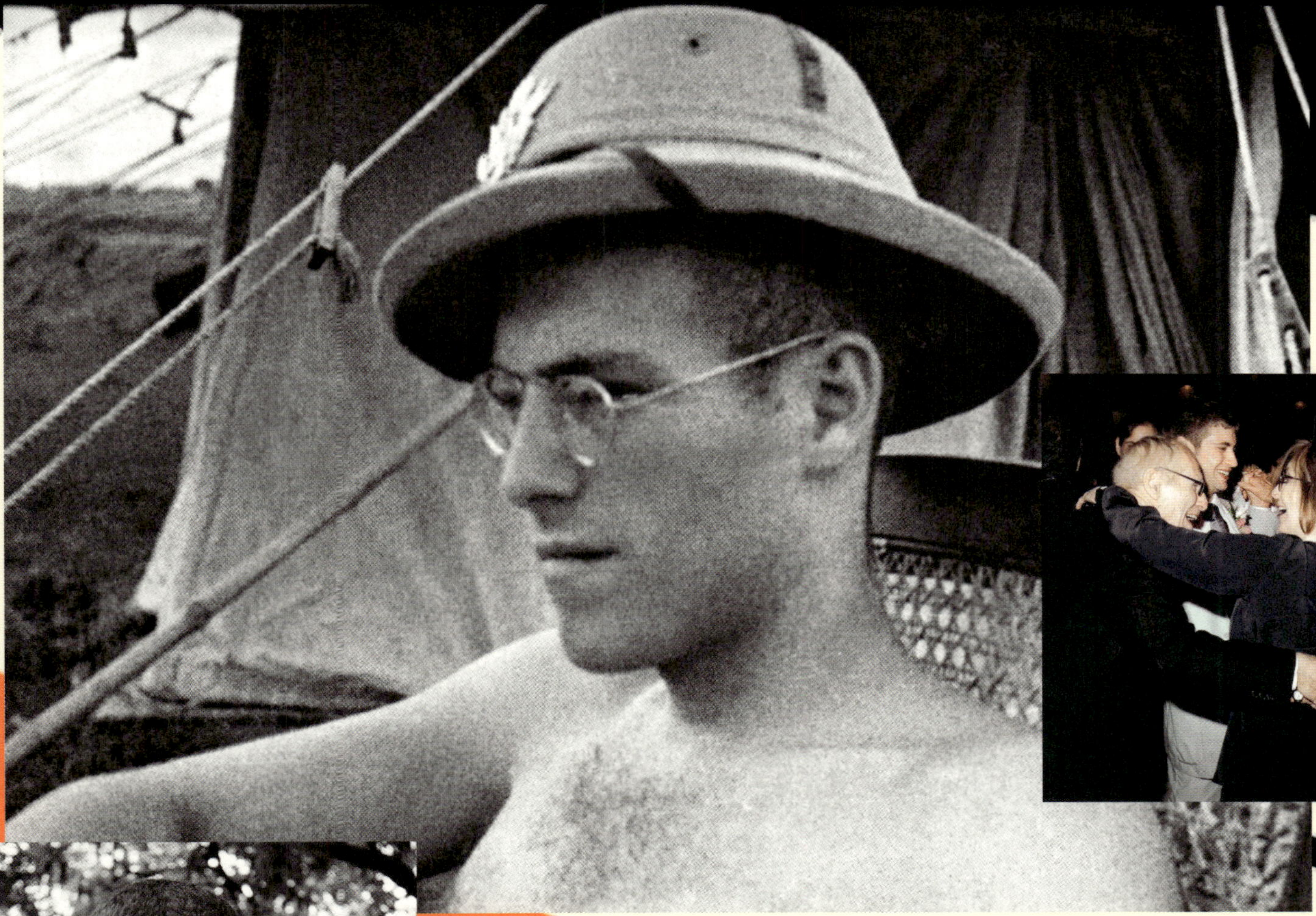

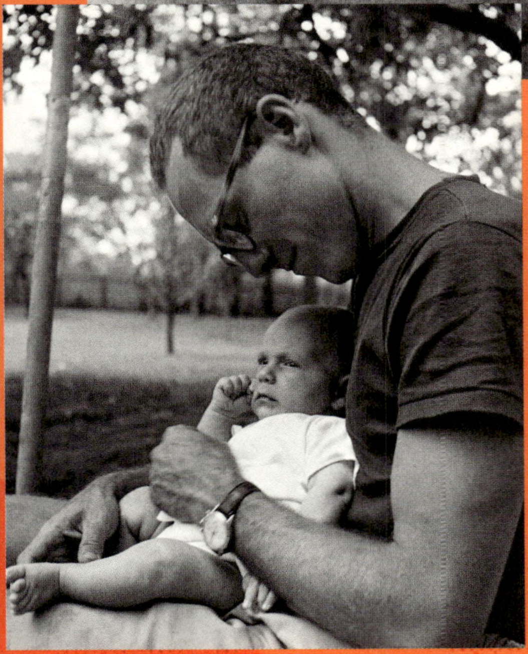

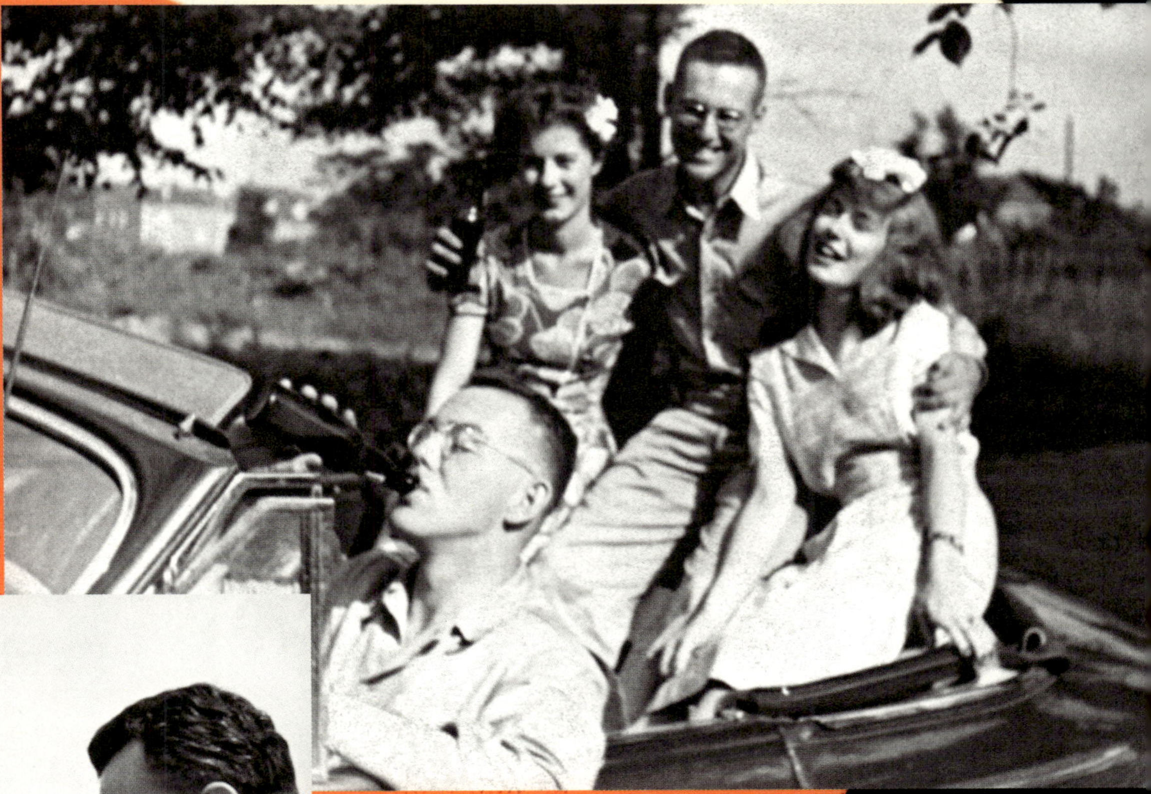

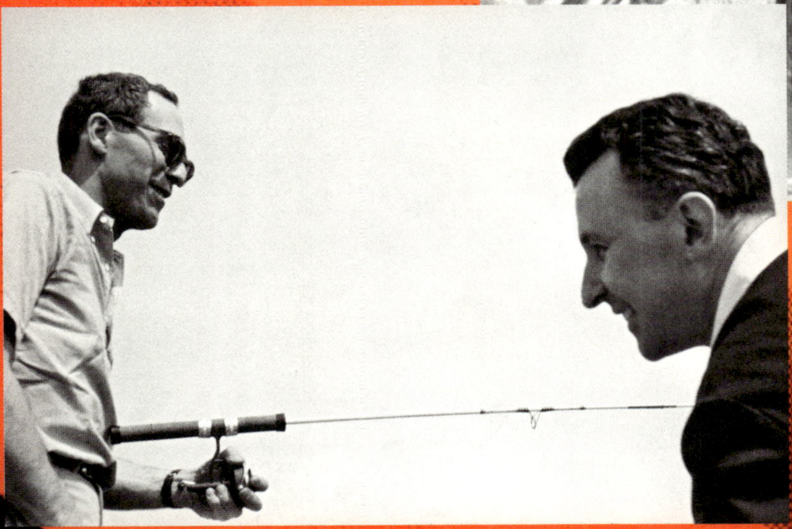

CLOCKWISE FROM TOP LEFT: BARNEY ROSSET IN THE ARMY • BARNEY DANCING WITH HIS FIFTH WIFE, ASTRID • BARNEY CELEBRATING WITH FRIENDS WHILE ON LEAVE FROM THE ARMY • BARNEY FISHING IN EAST HAMPTON WITH OLYMPIA PRESS PUBLISHER MAURICE GIRODIAS, THE ORIGINAL PUBLISHER OF *TROPIC OF CANCER* • BARNEY WITH HIS FIRST SON, PETER

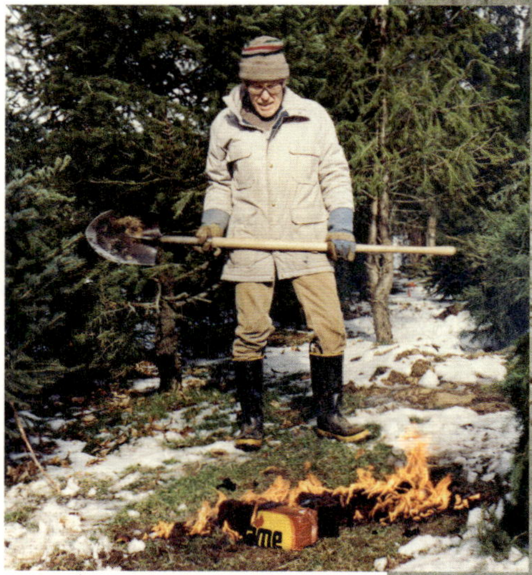

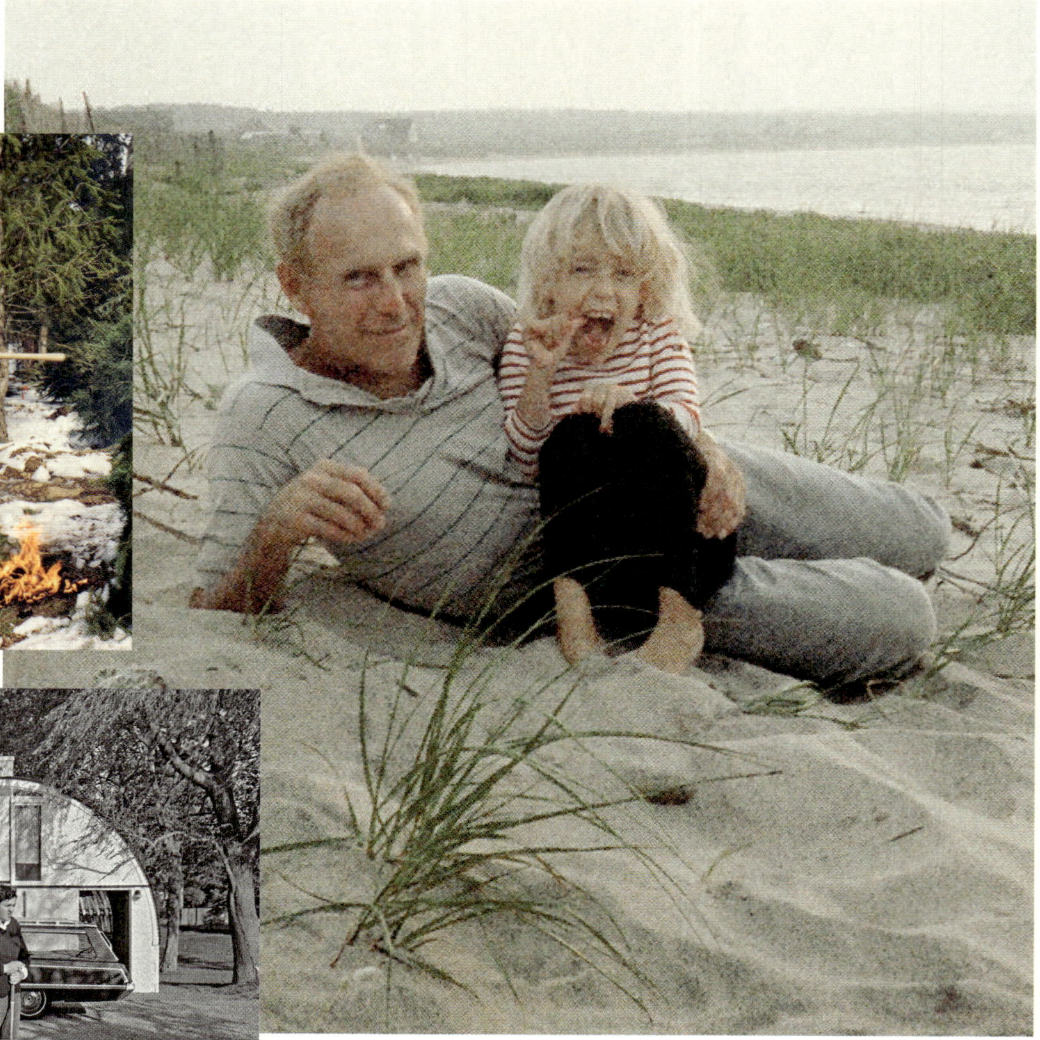

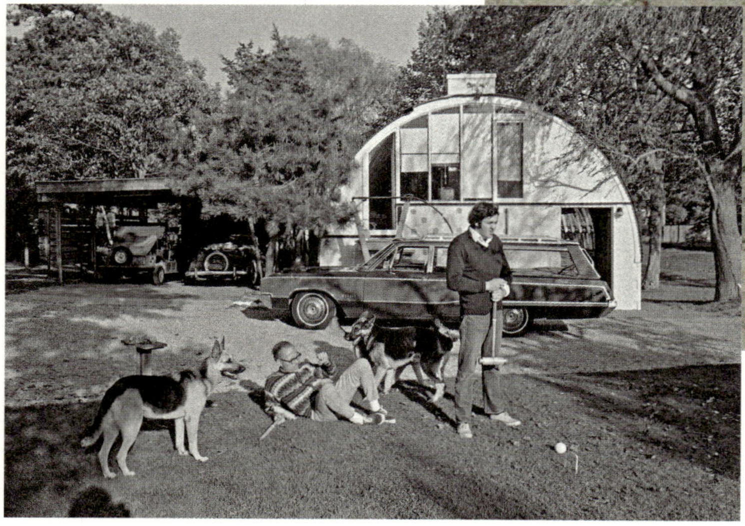

CLOCKWISE: BARNEY DOING HIS "WINTER PLANTING" AT HIS HOME IN EAST HAMPTON • BARNEY WITH HIS DAUGHTER CHANTAL IN SOUTHAMPTON • BARNEY PLAYING CROQUET WITH JOHN NATHAN OUTSIDE HIS QUONSET HUT IN EAST HAMPTON

"Ours is essentially a tragic age, so we refuse to take it tragically. The cataclysm has happened, we are among the ruins, we start to build up new little habitats, to have new little hopes. It is rather hard work: there is now no smooth road into the future: but we go round, or scramble over the obstacles. We've got to live, no matter how many skies have fallen."

—*D.H. Lawrence,* Lady Chatterley's Lover

# LADY CHATTERLEY'S LOVER

*BY*

# D. H. LAWRENCE

IN ITS ORIGINAL UNEXPURGATED EDITION

INTRODUCTION BY MARK SCHORER

PREFACE BY ARCHIBALD MACLEISH

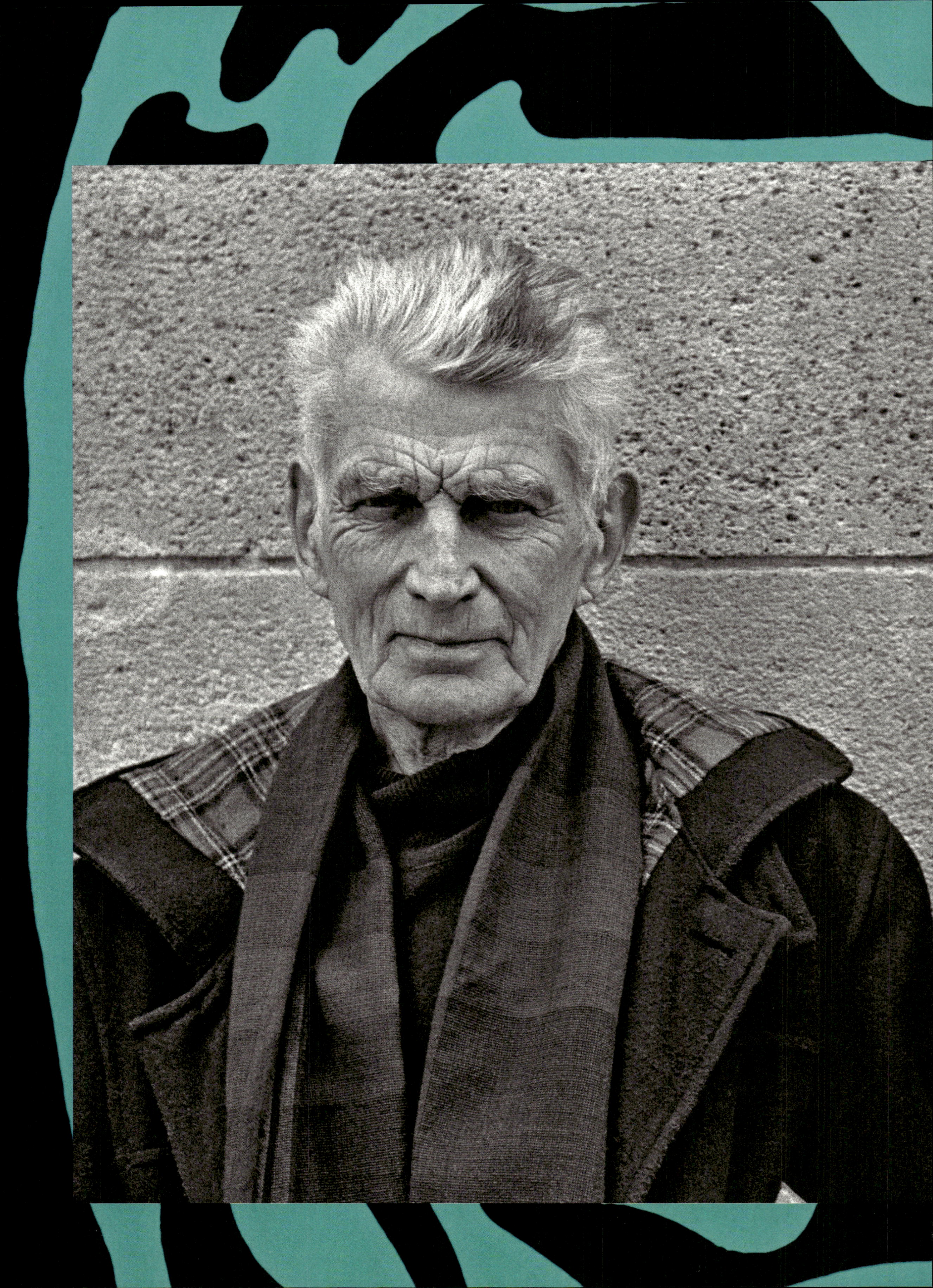

"I remember the exact moment [I met Beckett]. It was in the bar of the Pont Royal Hotel, which is next door to Gallimard. And at that time Sartre hung out there, as did Camus, and so on. I was with Loly, my wife at the time, and we were to meet Beckett at six for a drink. This very handsome gentleman walked in wearing a raincoat and said, 'Hi, nice to meet you. I've only got forty minutes.' He was all set to get rid of us! At four that morning he was buying us champagne."

—*Barney Rosset, from his* Paris Review *interview*

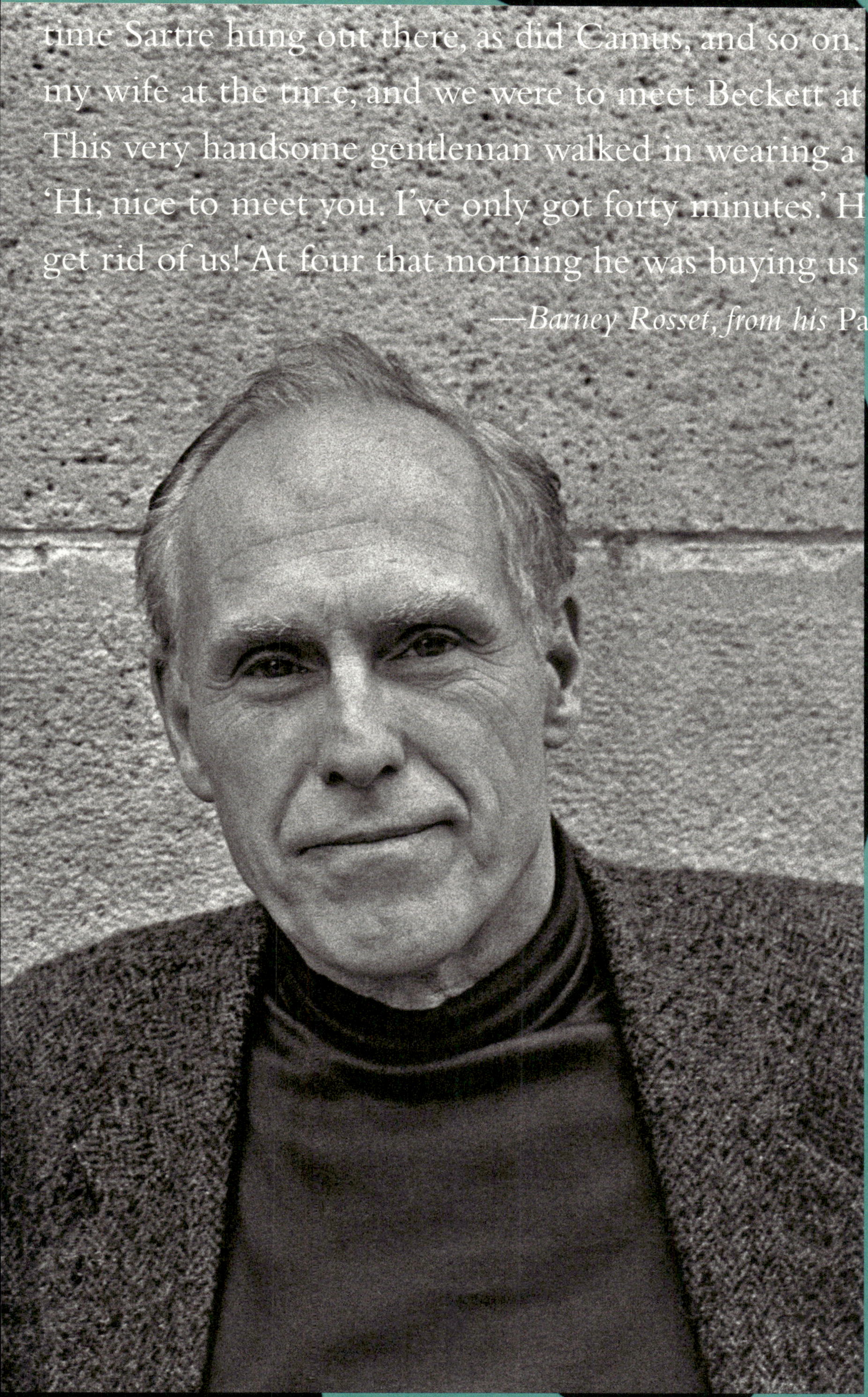

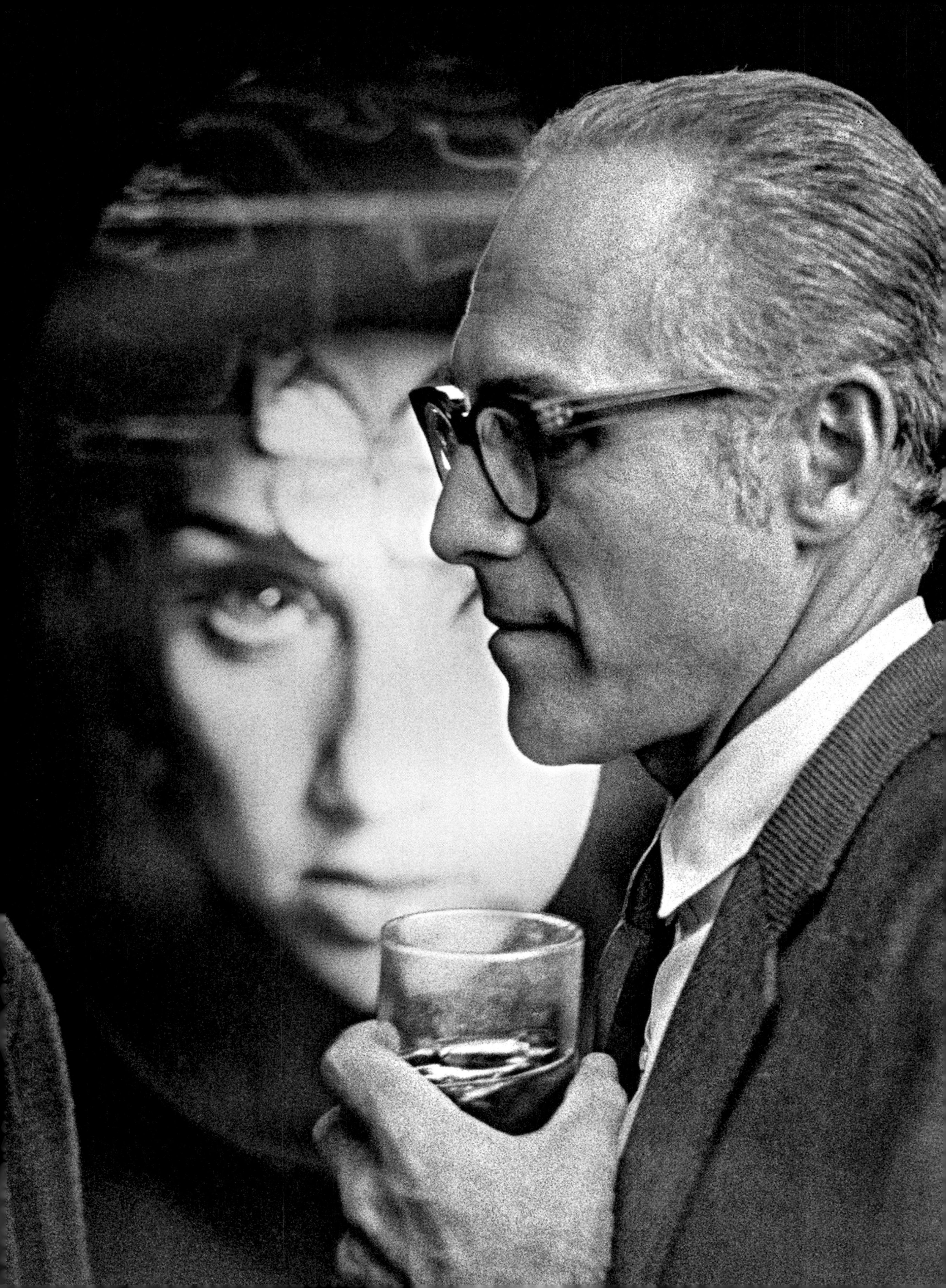

"For a moment, imagine a world without Barney Rosset's influence, and you will get a sense of his tsunami-like impact on modern culture. Of course, this was a decades-long tsunami that invigorated as it swept away. Whatever your feelings about the incredibly, staggeringly diverse roster of authors and books on the Grove Press list he published—from *Naked Lunch* and *The Wretched of the Earth* to *One Hundred Dollar Misunderstanding* and *Games People Play*, and so much else—there's probably no other single person in recent memory who's played a greater role in how we perceive our intellectual world. For it was not only the act of publishing books which no one else would have dared touch, but it was the particular mix of these books—to put Che Guevara side by side with Samuel Beckett, and Ionesco next to John Rechy, and the Marquis de Sade next to John Kennedy Toole—that is the masterpiece legacy that Barney Rosset has given all of us. He had no patience for snobbism, or compartmentalization, and for that matter little patience for any rulebook, and we are more fortunate because of it."

— *John Oakes, publisher*

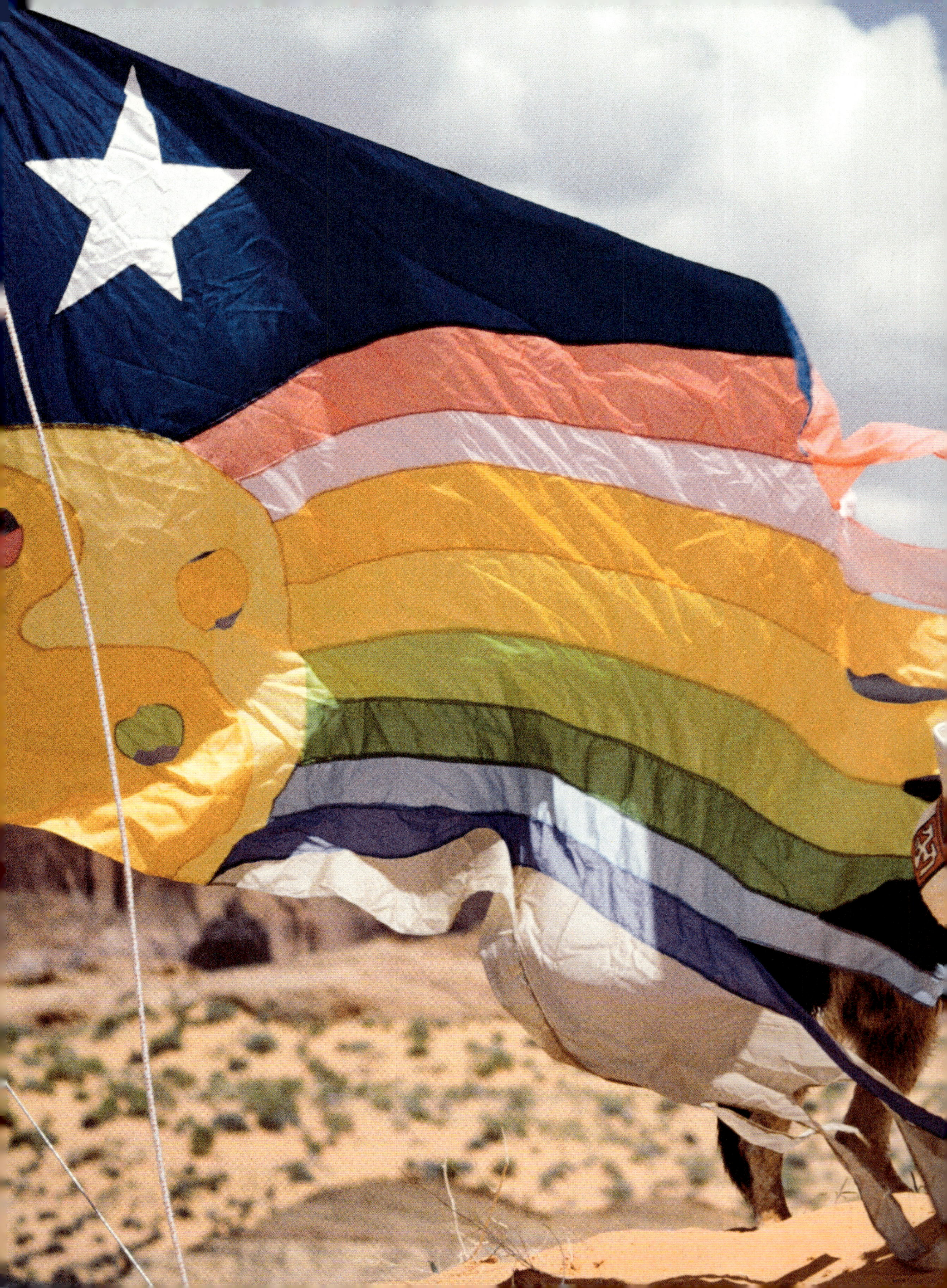

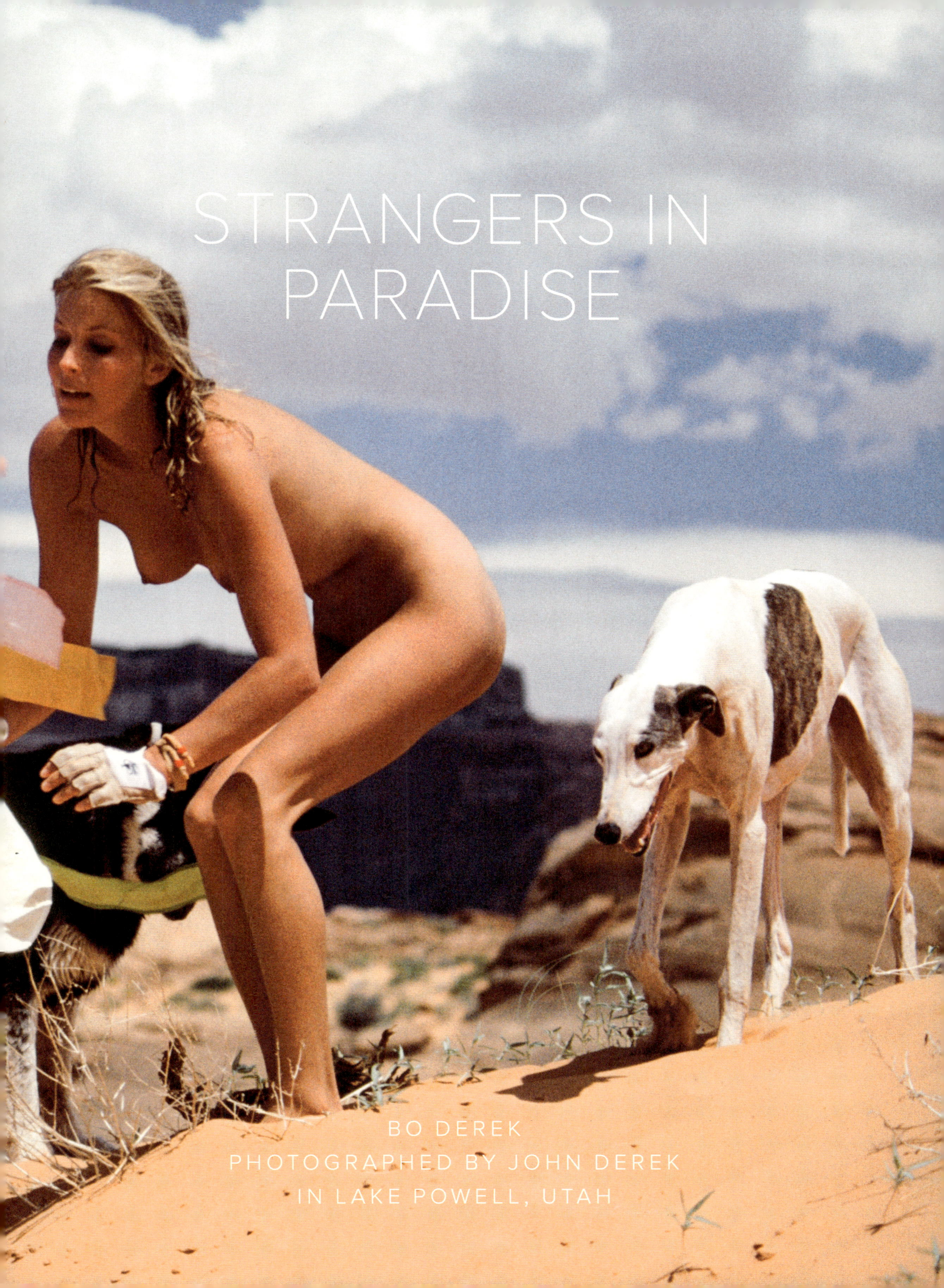

# STRANGERS IN PARADISE

BO DEREK
PHOTOGRAPHED BY JOHN DEREK
IN LAKE POWELL, UTAH

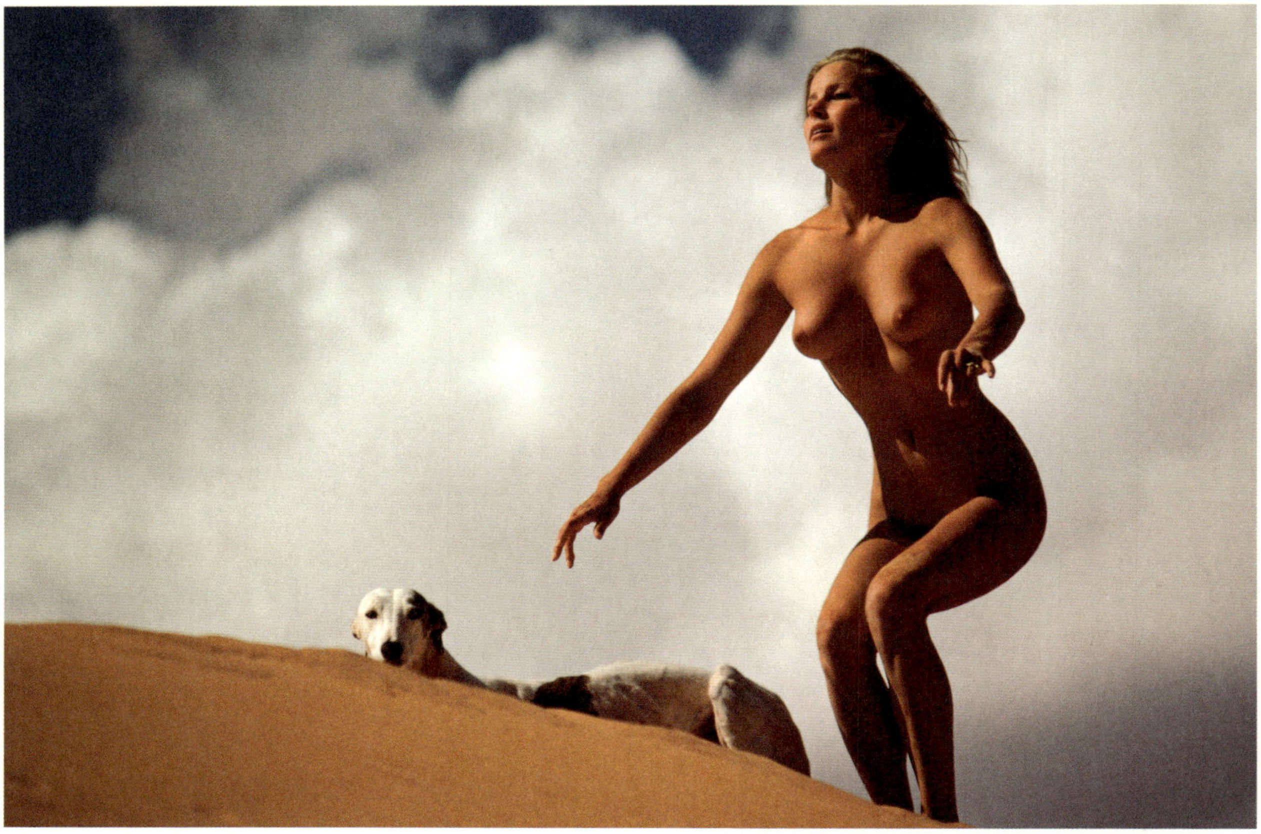

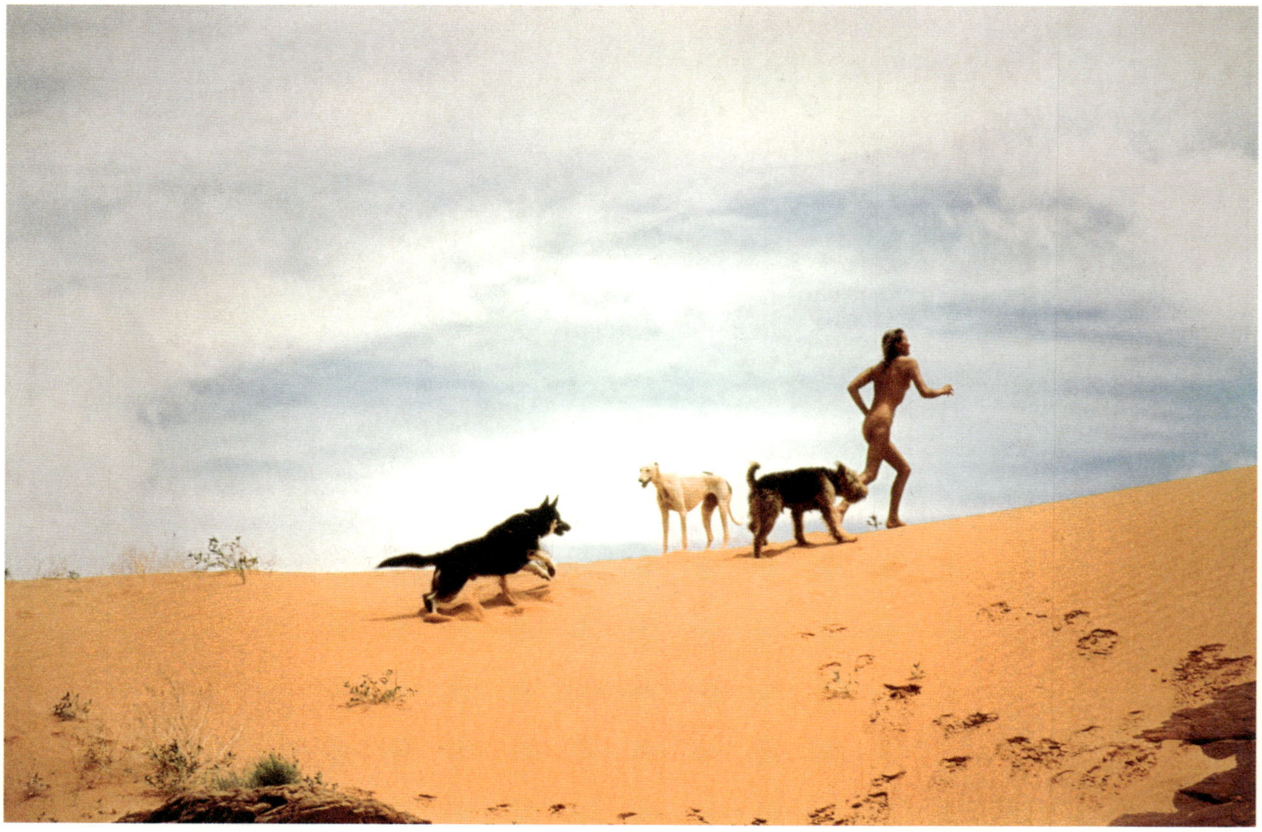

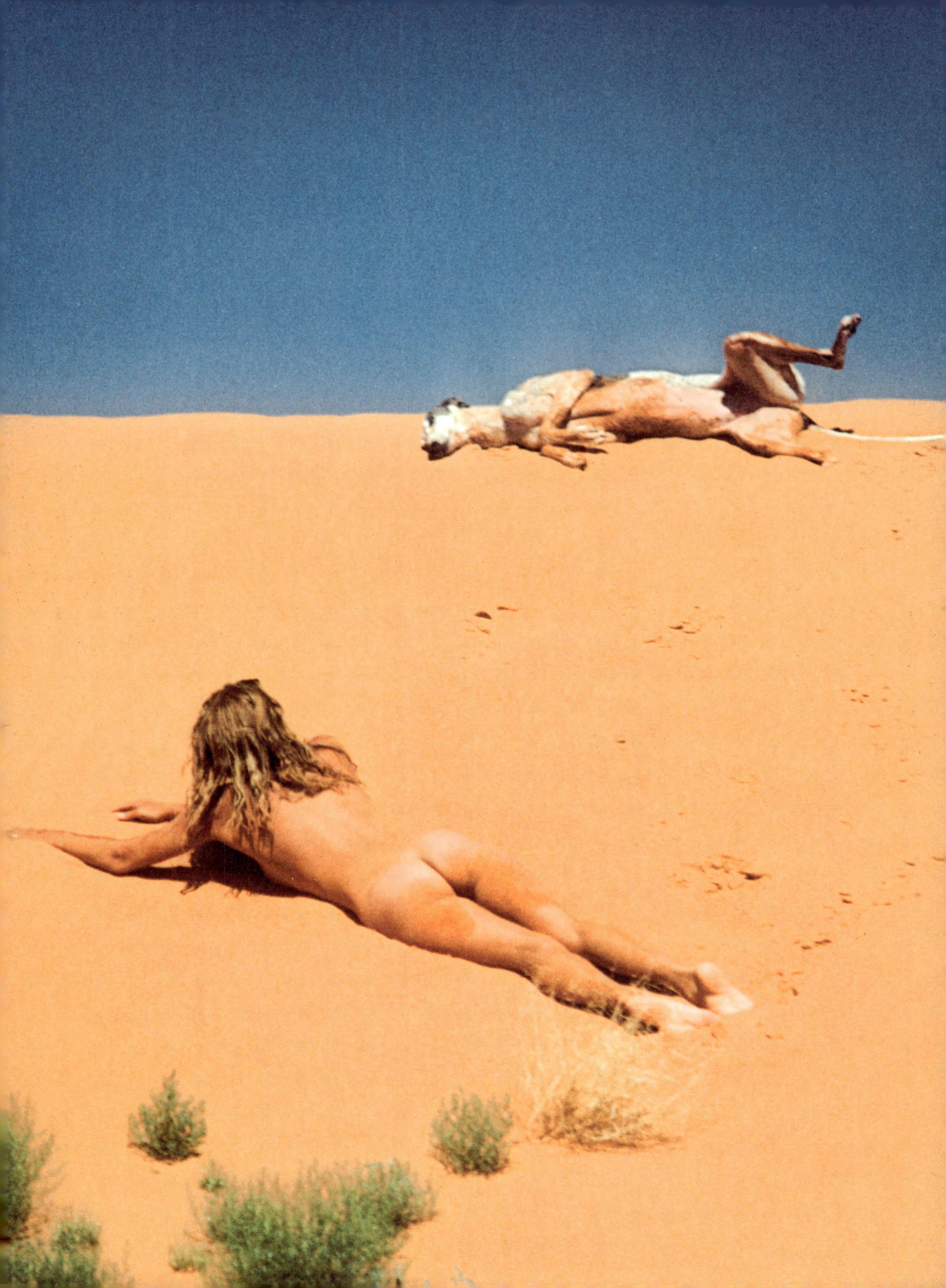

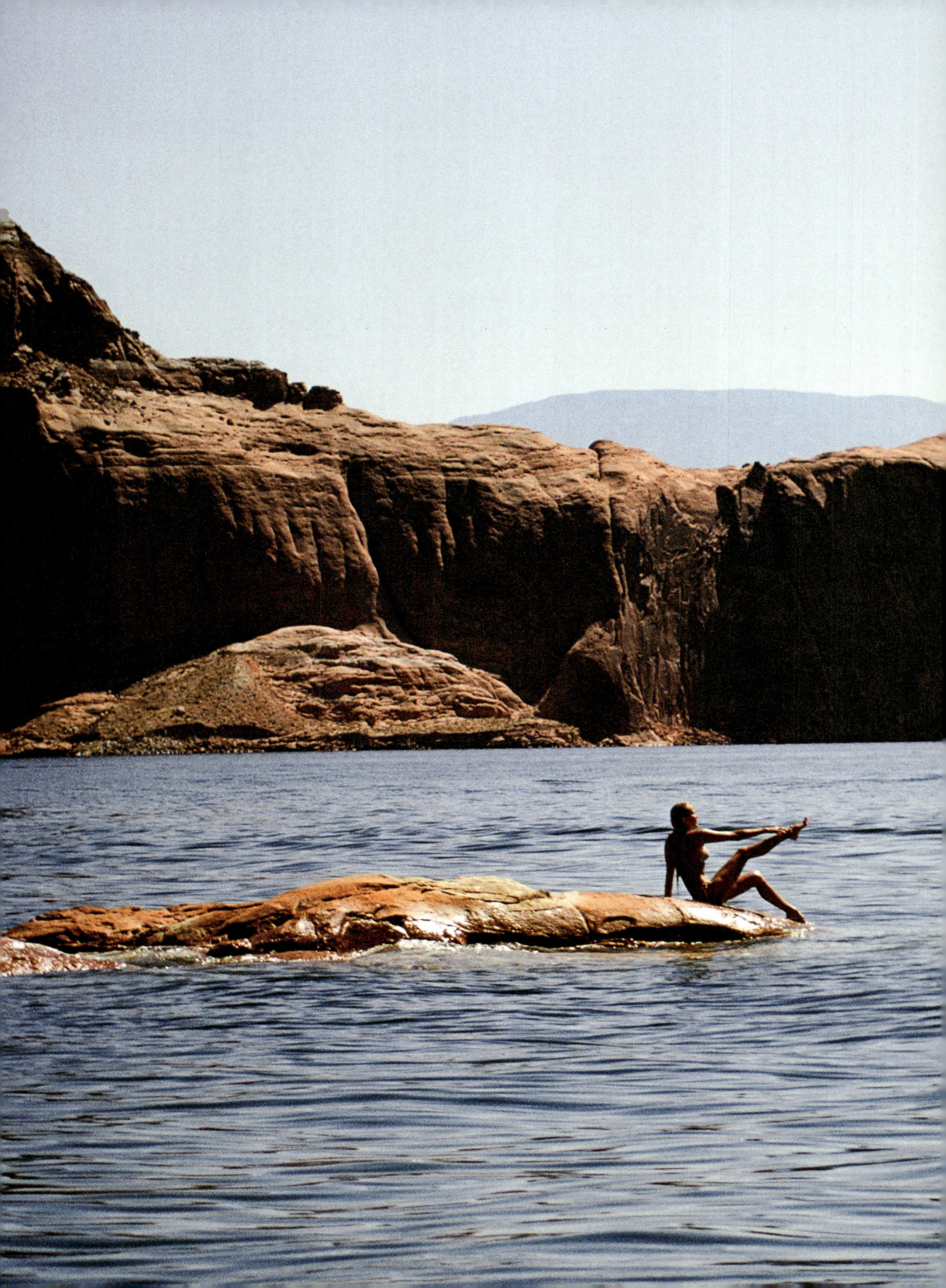

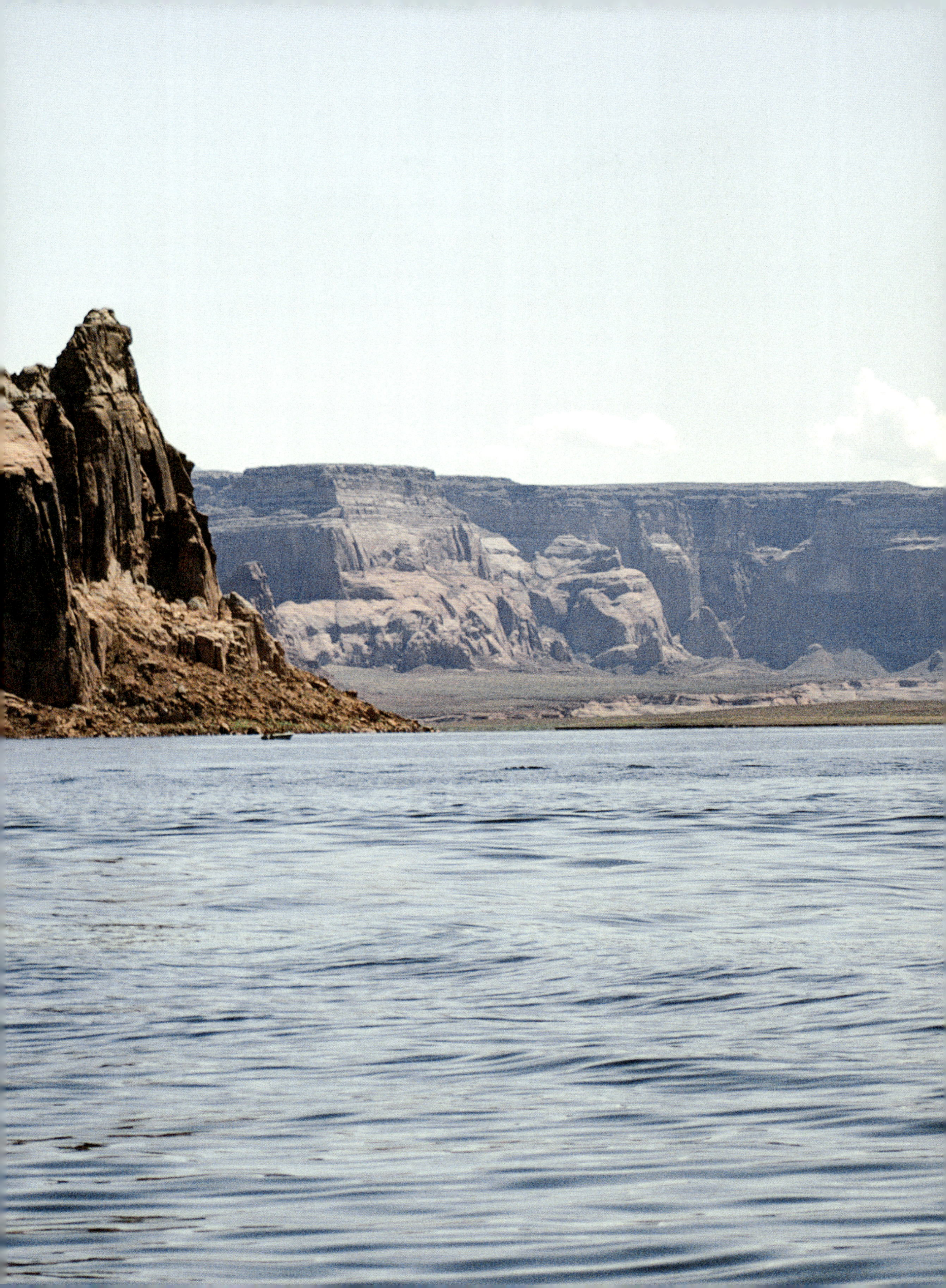

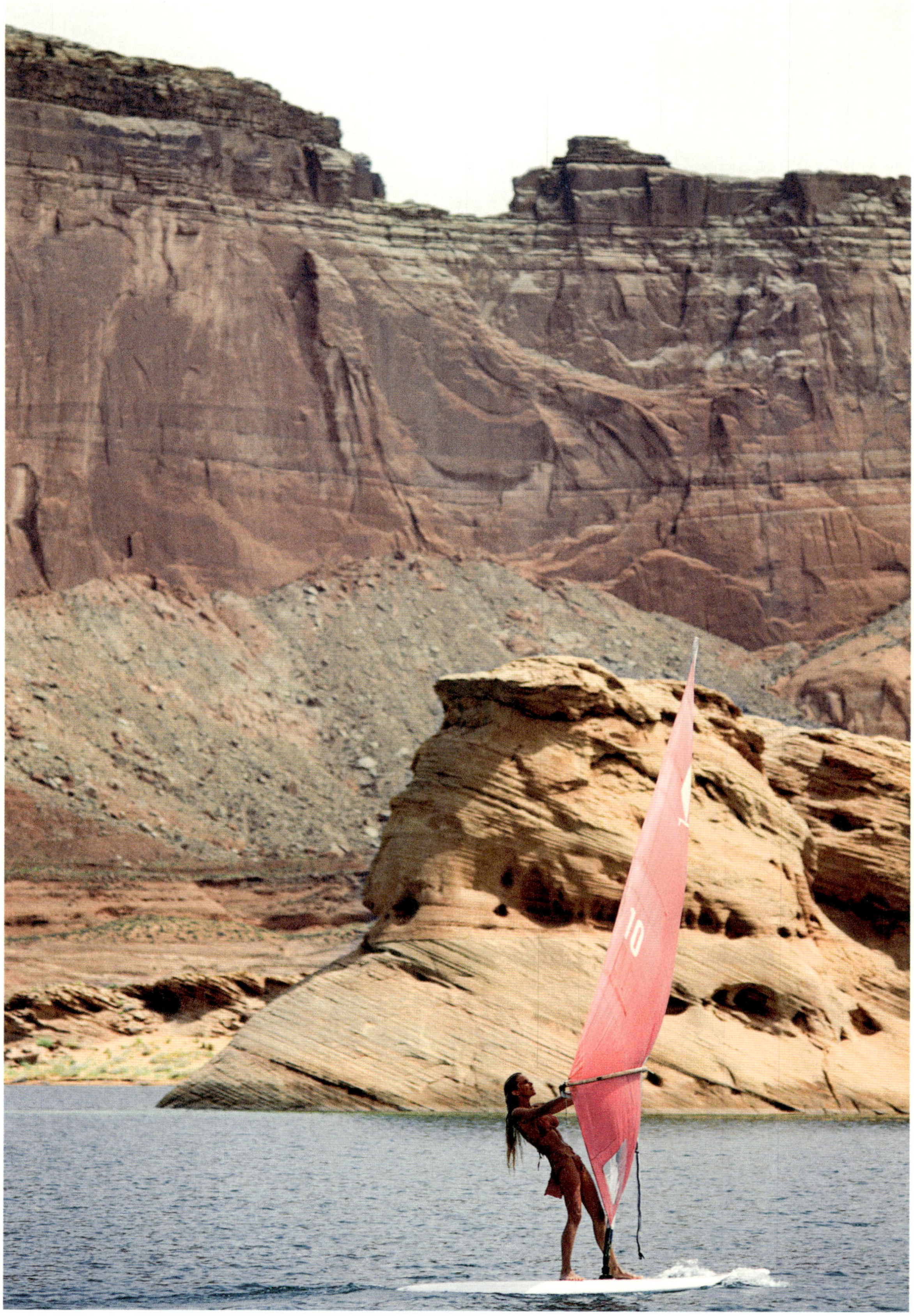

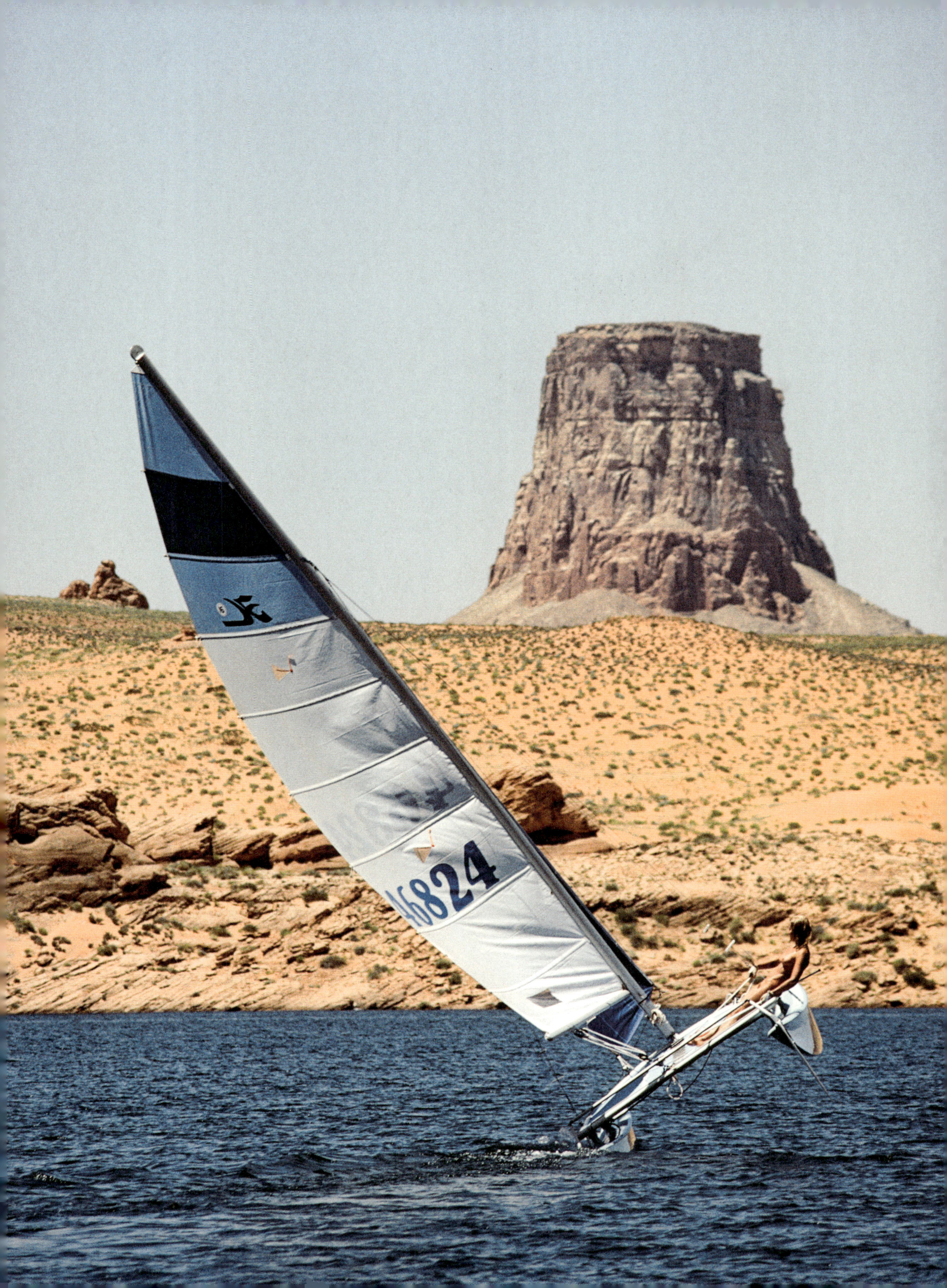
46824

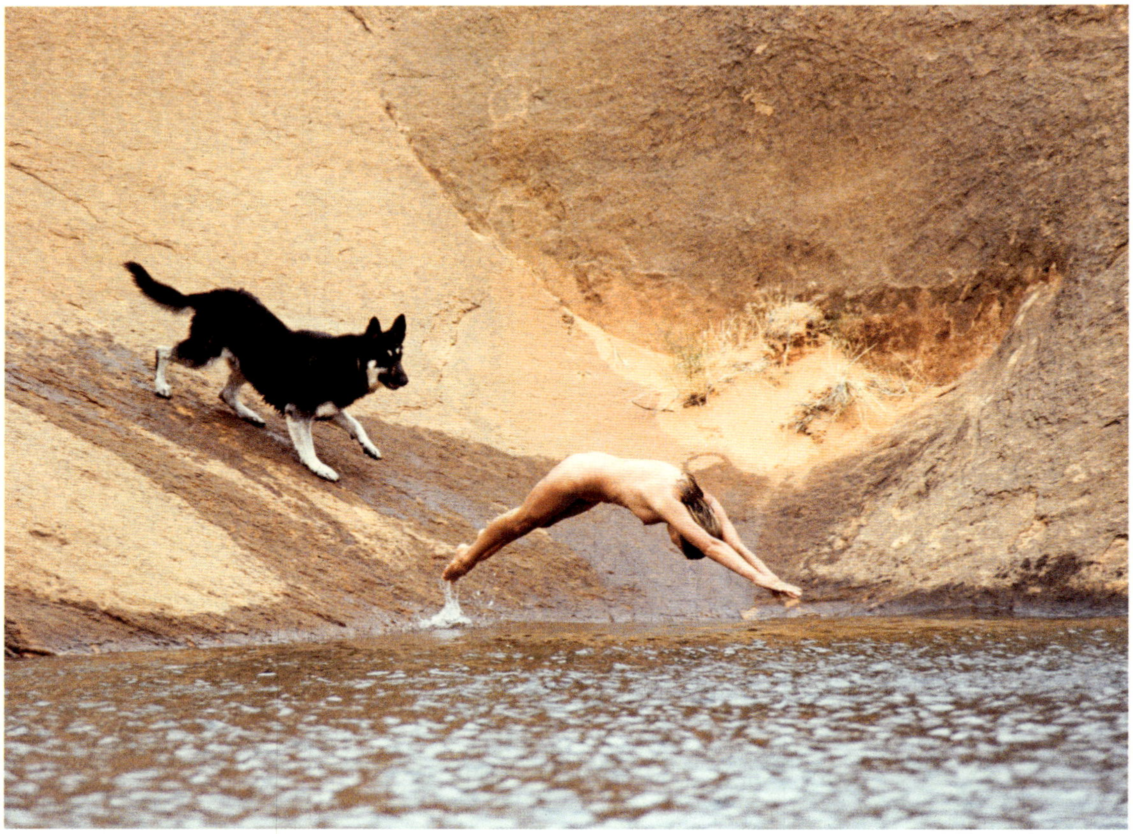

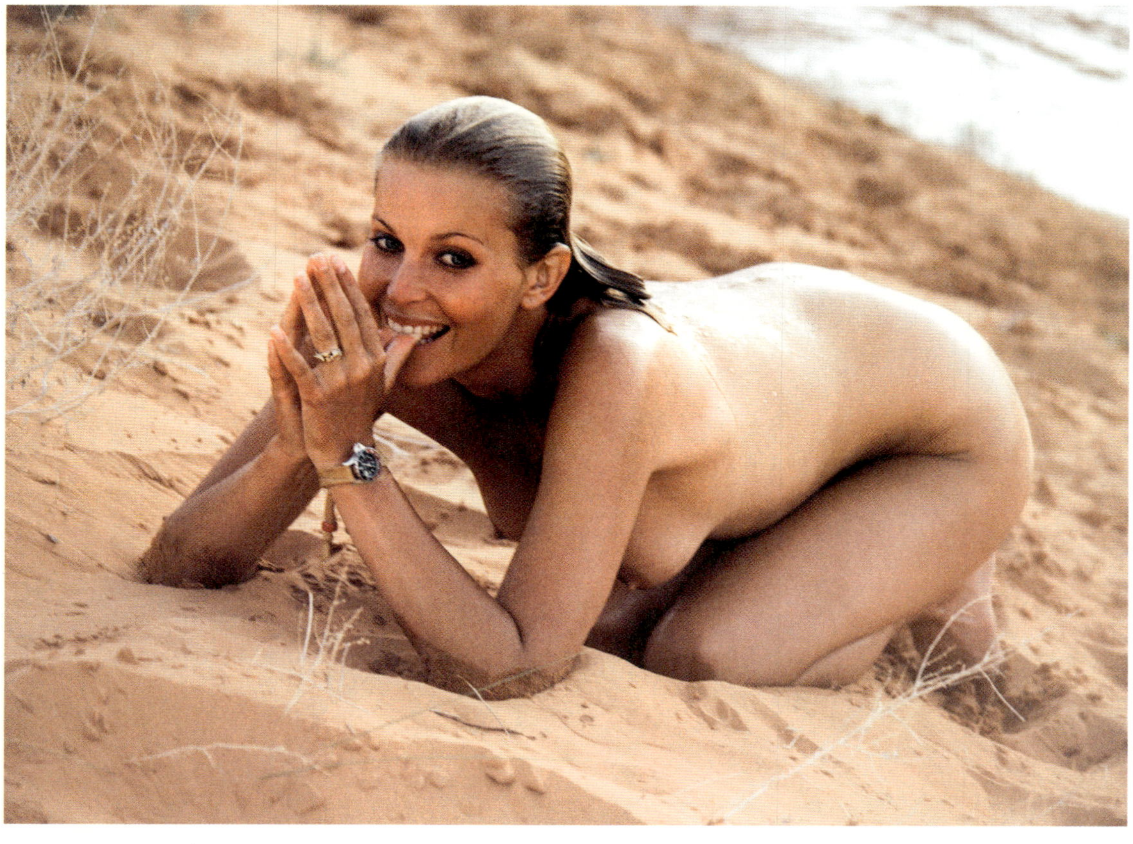

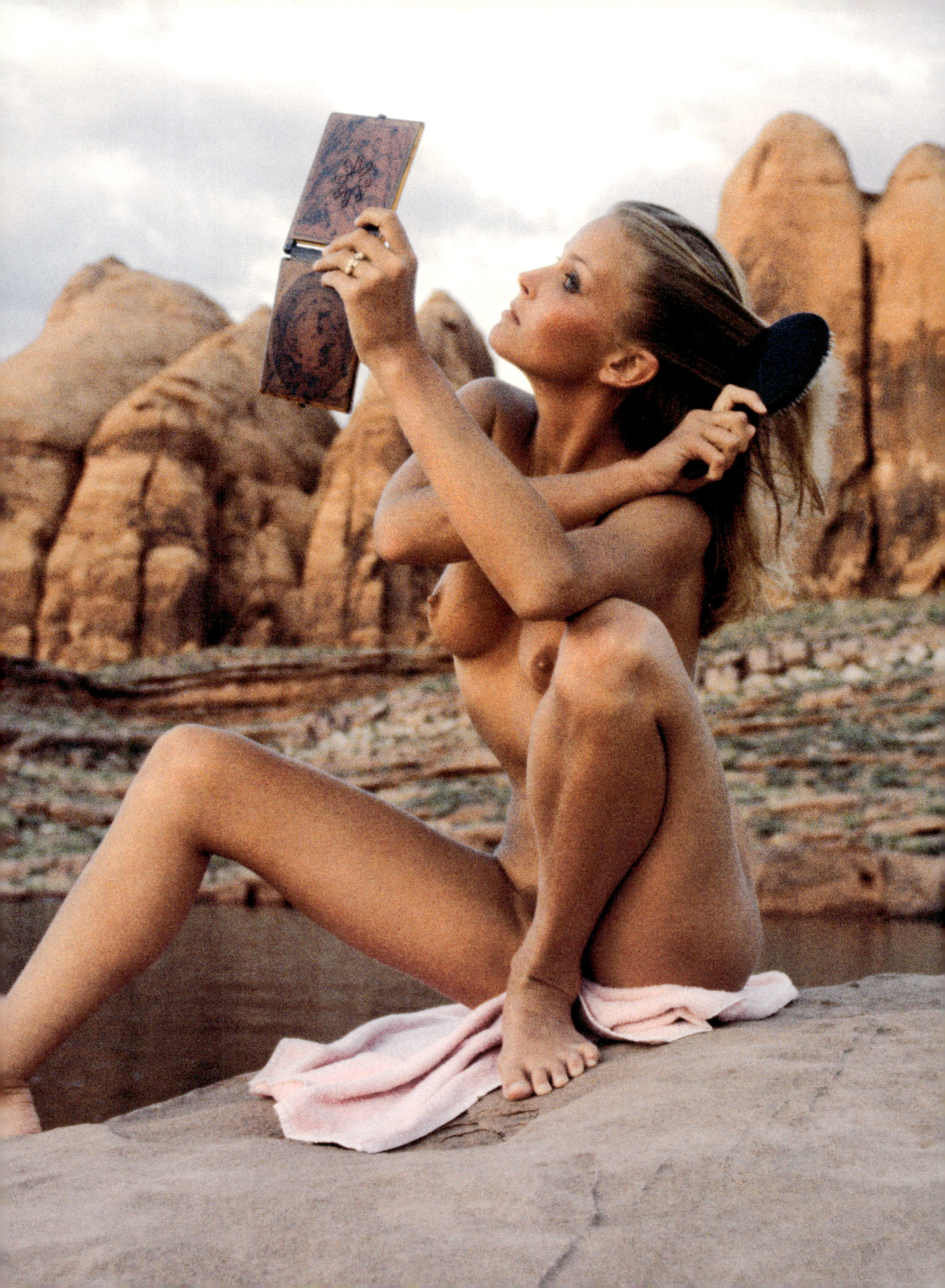

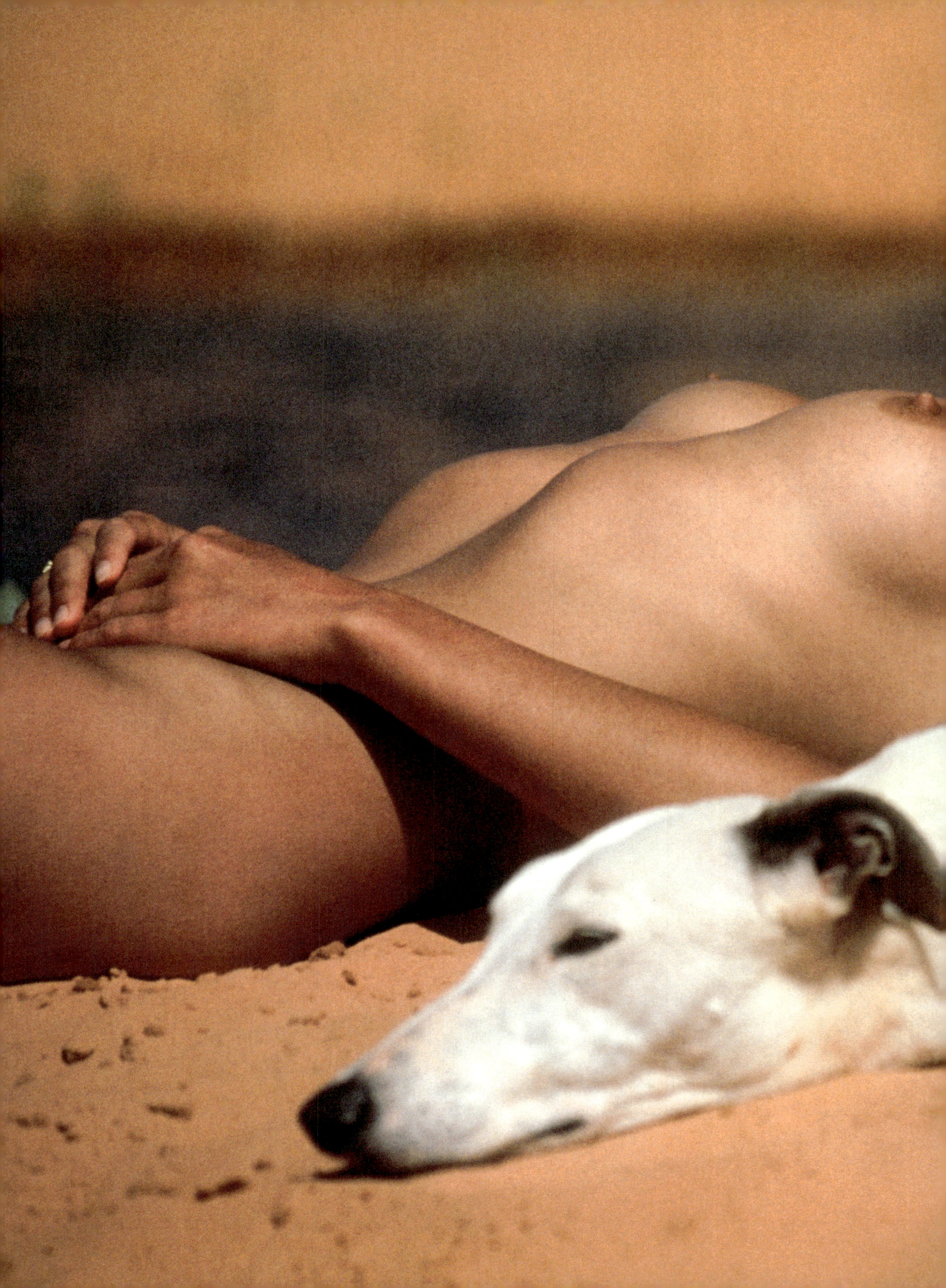

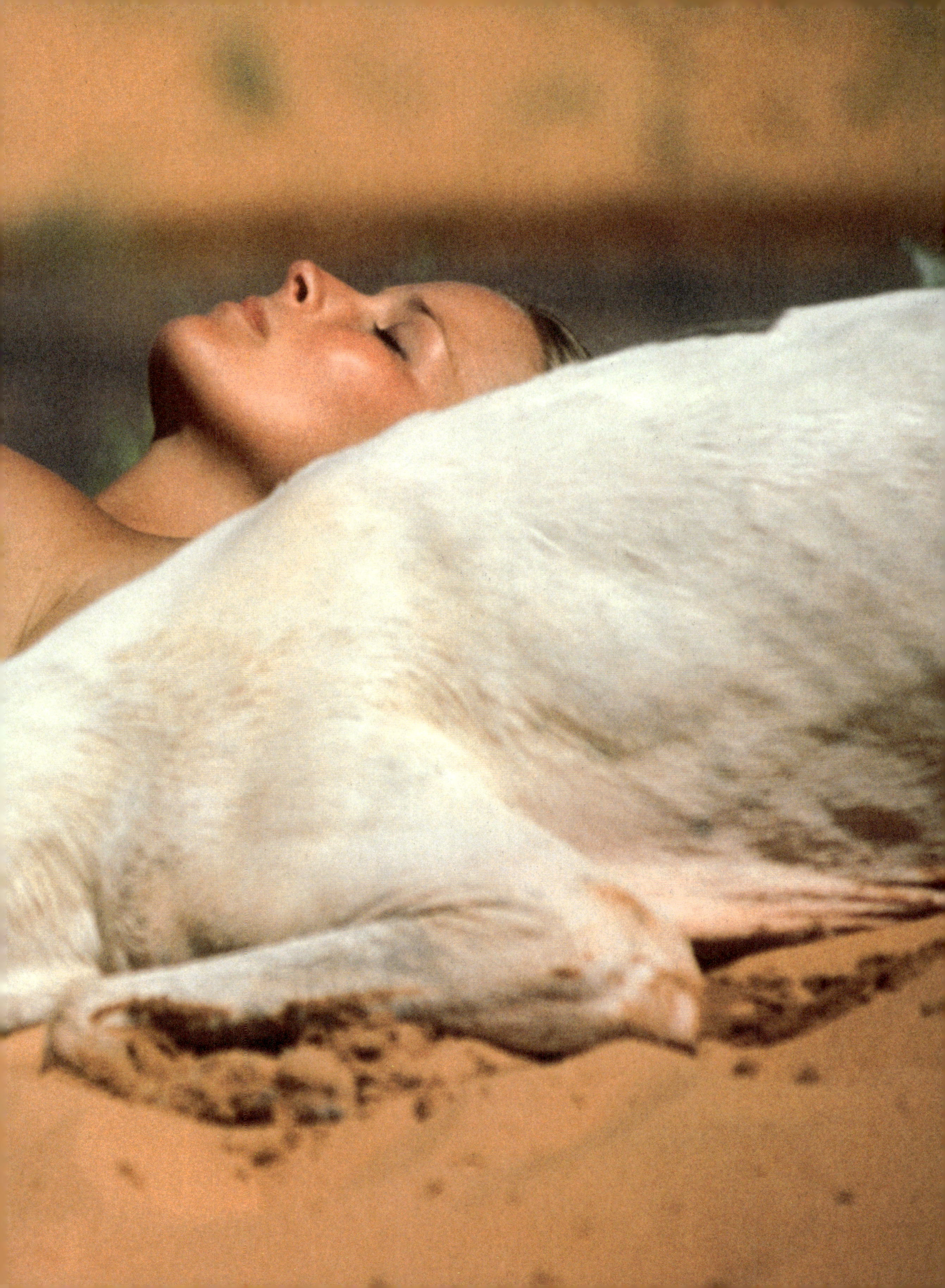

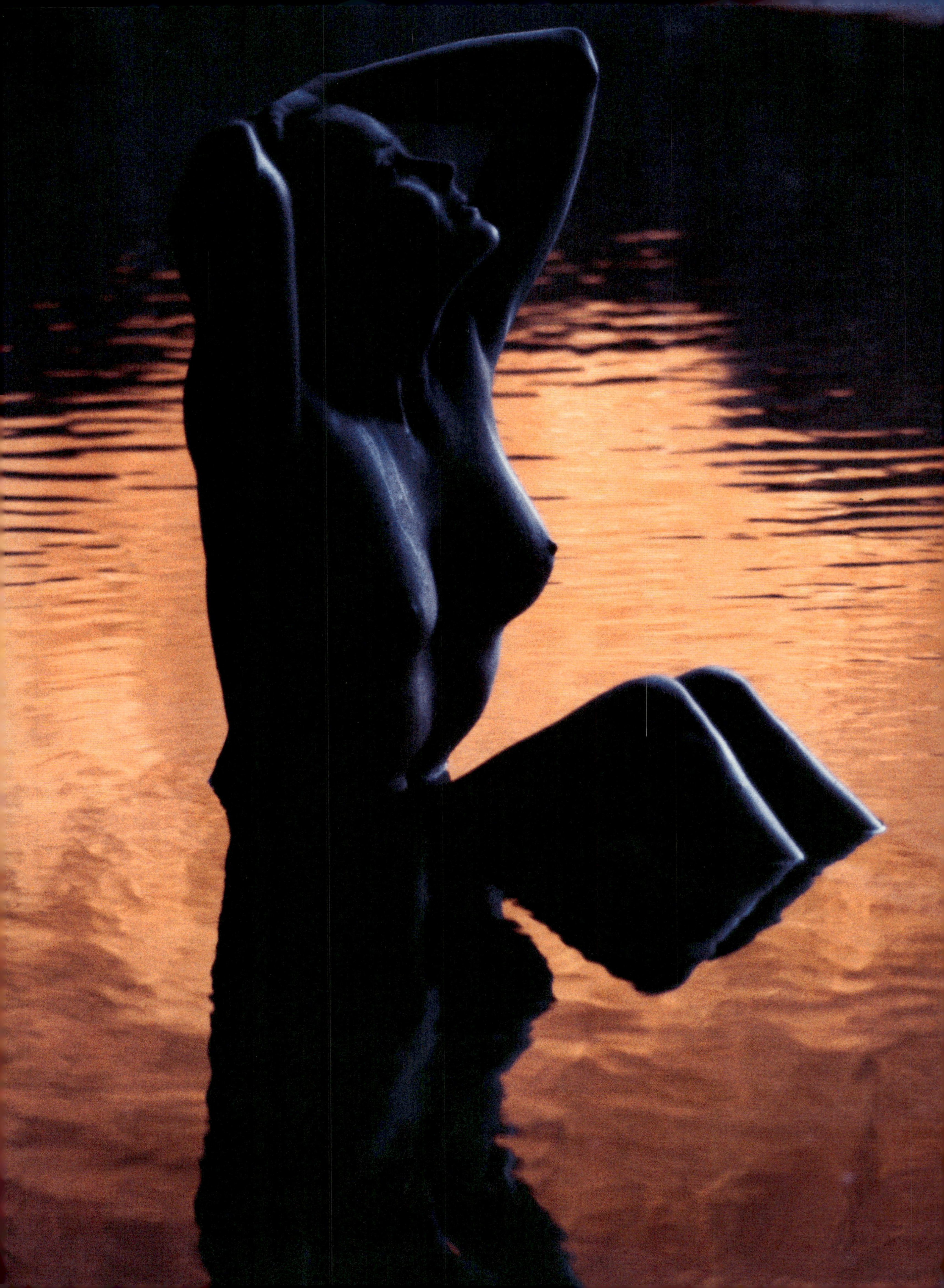

# A BEDTIME STORY

*It's way past your bedtime, so promise me that after you read this, you'll get some shut-eye.*

Once upon a time, in a far-off land called California, there lived a young maiden with blond hair down to her waist who breathed adventure and loved animals (especially dogs and horses) and wide-open spaces. What else could her mom call her but Bo (it stood for "beautiful one"). Little did Bo know that one day she would meet the most handsome knight in the world—not wearing a suit of shining armor, just a pair of torn jeans and a T-shirt. He had raven black hair, sported a tan, and his face resembled the men on the covers of those romance novels. This knight went by the name of John Derek. He was an actor, director, photographer, and friend of all two and four-legged creatures. A fan magazine once wrote that "everything in his house was made by his own hands." John was older than Bo and much wiser in the ways of the world. He lived a truly bohemian lifestyle, and his garden was filled with fruit trees, ferocious bumblebees, multicolored butterflies, and his most prized flowers—three voluptuous women, all backlit by the sun.

The first fair maiden was named Ursula Andress, a striking beauty from the mountains of Switzerland. She became known throughout the land when she walked out of the ocean wearing nothing but a white bikini and a knife for her role as Honey Ryder in the James Bond film *Dr. No.* John saved Ursula's life one day when he persuaded her not to go off with James Dean, another knight of heroic proportions, in his Porsche on that tragic ride to Salinas. Ursula and John married, and their lives were recorded daily by his camera for *Playboy*. She knew all about light, and he knew how to be in front of the camera. Most of the time, her clothes were thrown aside as quickly as the wind comes before the storm.

Just as the birds fly south when the days get shorter, John met another fair maiden, a blond actress named Linda Evans, who was the a star of television's *The Big Valley*. Ursula moved far away to Rome and continued to make movies, but she left her belongings behind, and there was always a welcome mat for her on the drawbridge leading to their castle. Once again, John didn't let a day pass without photographing Linda. He would even hand-tool Ursula and Linda's names into leather bags, diaries, and frames.

John's hair had begun to turn silver when he first met the shy maiden named Bo. They went off to Spain to just "live it up" as they used to say way back then. Wherever Bo and John traveled together, you could hear the heralding of trumpets. They eventually returned to Los Angeles and shared their castle with Ursula and Linda for an idyllic time as one big family.

This tale doesn't end there. Bo acted in many films with John's encouragement and became a reluctant star in the constellation above the Hollywood Planetarium with a movie called *10*. She braided her hair and looked like a blond Heptone from the Jamaican band that played sometimes with the legendary rasta Bob Marley. Bo and John would just hang out and take pictures without a care in the world. *Was that the sound of a flirtatious dragon passing overhead, or just the sail on Bo's windsurfing board as she raced by in the nude?* John and Bo would sometimes pile their dogs Harem Scarem, Smoke, and Amber into a camper, hook up their 14-foot ski boat and set off to Lake Powell with only a pair of those torn jeans for him and a suede bikini—designed by John—for her. All Bo would cook on their little hibachi stove were tiny hot dogs that John and the pups devoured. They would end each day tired and sun-kissed, his knapsack filled with rolls of Kodachrome 25. As Bo tells it, "I was his fantasy—20 years old, and he was 49." Years later, when John the gallant knight took ill, all three women gathered together again to care for him and love him as they had when they were young. Even after John died, they still remained the closest of friends.

You can't find this love story in any children's book, but I think it is one of the greatest in the volumes of unwritten romances. We only wish our dads had read it to us when we were just kids, falling fast asleep into dreamland with the covers over our heads. Just imagine how different our lives would have been! *—Bruce Weber, Montauk, New York, 2012*

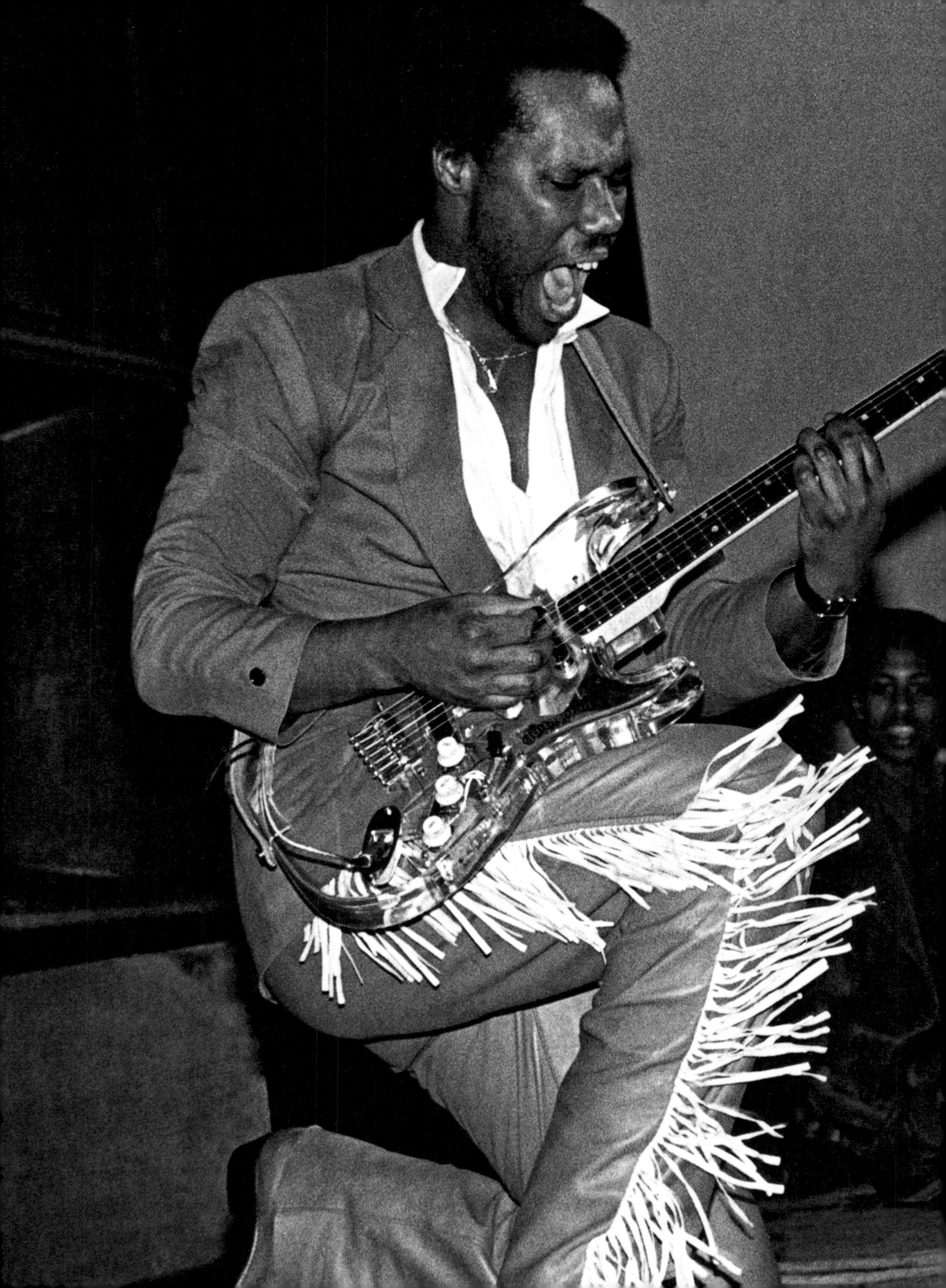

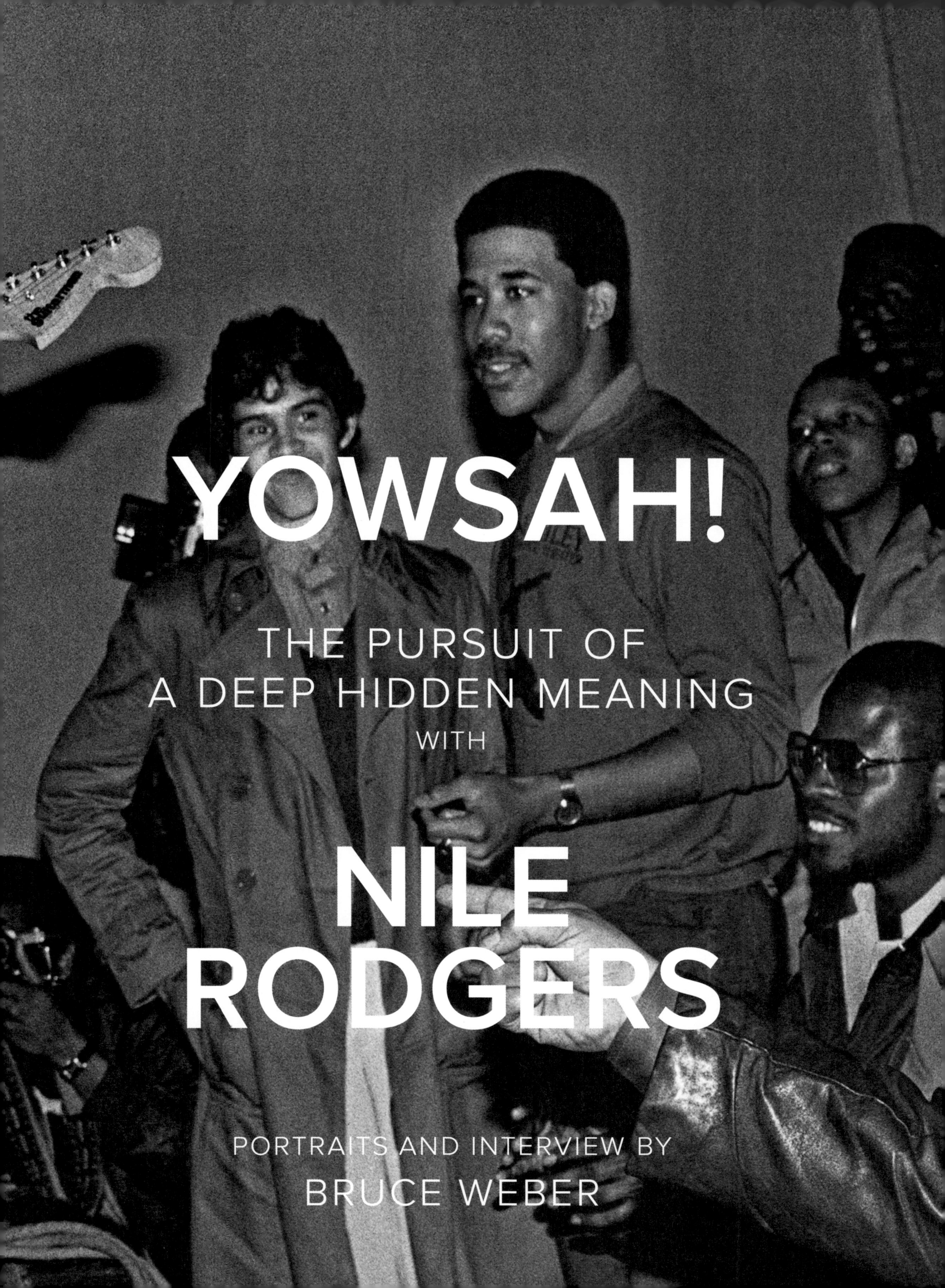
YOWSAH!
THE PURSUIT OF
A DEEP HIDDEN MEANING
WITH
NILE
RODGERS
PORTRAITS AND INTERVIEW BY
BRUCE WEBER

e's one of the great unsung heroes of pop music, a man with a deep soul connection to the history of jazz and a magical funk sensibili hat gets people up and dancing. A wild child of the Greenwich Village counterculture, Nile Rodgers formed the seminal disco band Chic with his friend Bernard Edwards and stormed the charts with hits like "Everybody Dance" and "I Want Your Love." They then went on to produce music that defined the sound of an era: David Bowie's album *Let's Dance*, Diana Ross' post-disco smash *Diana*, Madonna's *Like A Virgin*, and countless others. Nile's recent book biography, *Le Freak: An Upside Down Story of Family, Disco and Destiny* chronicles his unconventional family life, rise to music stardom, rock 'n' roll antics, struggle with drug addiction, battle with cancer, and charitable vision for the We Are Family Foundation. Nile sat down with us in his uptown apartment to talk about his amazing journey.

**BRUCE WEBER:** I want anyone who is interested in music or art or photography or painting to read your book. Because it's really about making…

**NILE RODGERS:** Something from nothing.

**BW:** Exactly, it's about making things. I felt that so much. And I didn't know so many of the crazy things that had happened to you when you were a kid! And in spite of it all, you have an openness and warmth in your eyes and a desire to help people. I wonder how you had the strength to face the world that way.

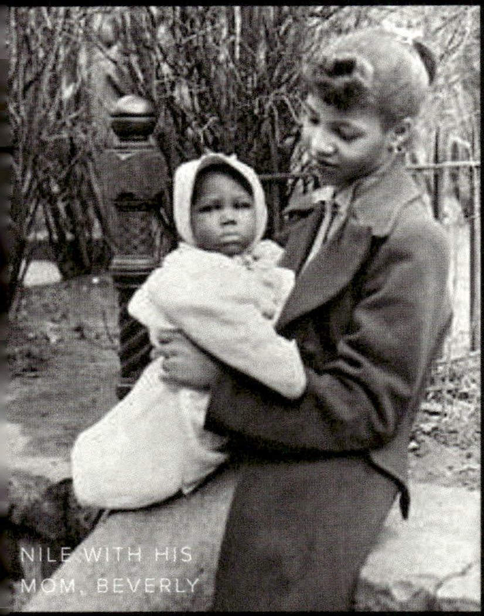

NILE WITH HIS MOM, BEVERLY

**NR:** In my heart I think it's the way that I was socialized, the way that I came up. I grew up in downtown New York. It was just an incredible place, so exciting for a child like myself living among adults. My stepfather was *the* beatnik, almost like a caricature. Thelonious Monk and Lenny Bruce and people like that would just hang out at my parents' crib. I never knew anything else. Even though many people around me were junkies, they were also artists and intellectuals, altruistic people with huge hearts. They wanted to give to people. I had to find my own way, but the people around me were always very loving.

Around the time I was a kid, the city asylums were putting lunatics out on the street, because the state was cutting back on hospital budgets. That made New York City a very colorful place. But it also felt completely safe. I would run into people like that on the street all the time, and they might do something interesting like recite the libretto to an opera or something. You could say "Papageno" to a dude and he'd start singing *The Magic Flute* on the street. It was a fantasy.

But New York City has changed so much. When we go to the Bitter End now, I'm walking along and it sort of looks like Bleecker Street. I find myself wondering, *What happened to all the fire escapes?* There are a few things that look the same because they're historical landmarks. But the Meatpacking District is completely gentrified now. It has the sense of a neighborhood, but it's a brand-new neighborhood. A friend of mine lives in a building that used to be The Boys' Club when I was a kid. It's got the auditorium in there and everything. I don't even recognize the Bowery anymore.

**BW:** Tell me more about your family, Nile. I know they were so important to you.

**NR:** My stepfather was one of the coolest and most loving people I have ever known. The three of us, him, my mother and I lived in an apartment on Greenwich Street. I was fascinated as a kid with science—chemical kits and Erector sets and all that sort of thing. I was in the Cub Scouts and wanted to learn how to make a perfect campfire. I remembered seeing the badge for it—a perfect circle of logs. So while still in the apartment, I made a nice circle of matches and lit the center. Of course, there was an intense flame and a strong sulphur smell. I couldn't even put it out at first—eventually I did, but the windowsill of the apartment was scorched. When my stepfather got home, he sat me down and stared at me silently for five minutes. It was very

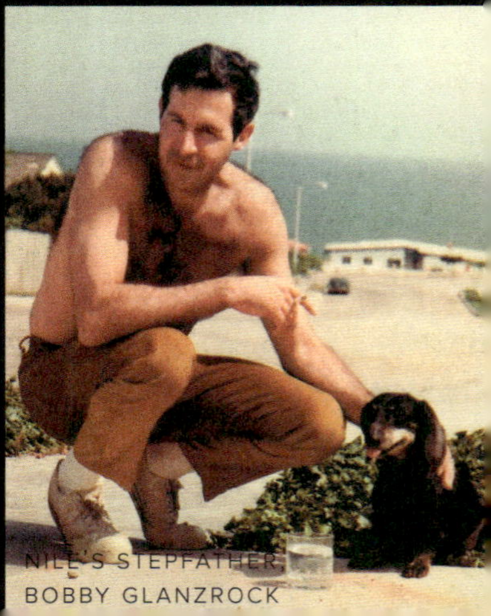

NILE'S STEPFATHER BOBBY GLANZROCK

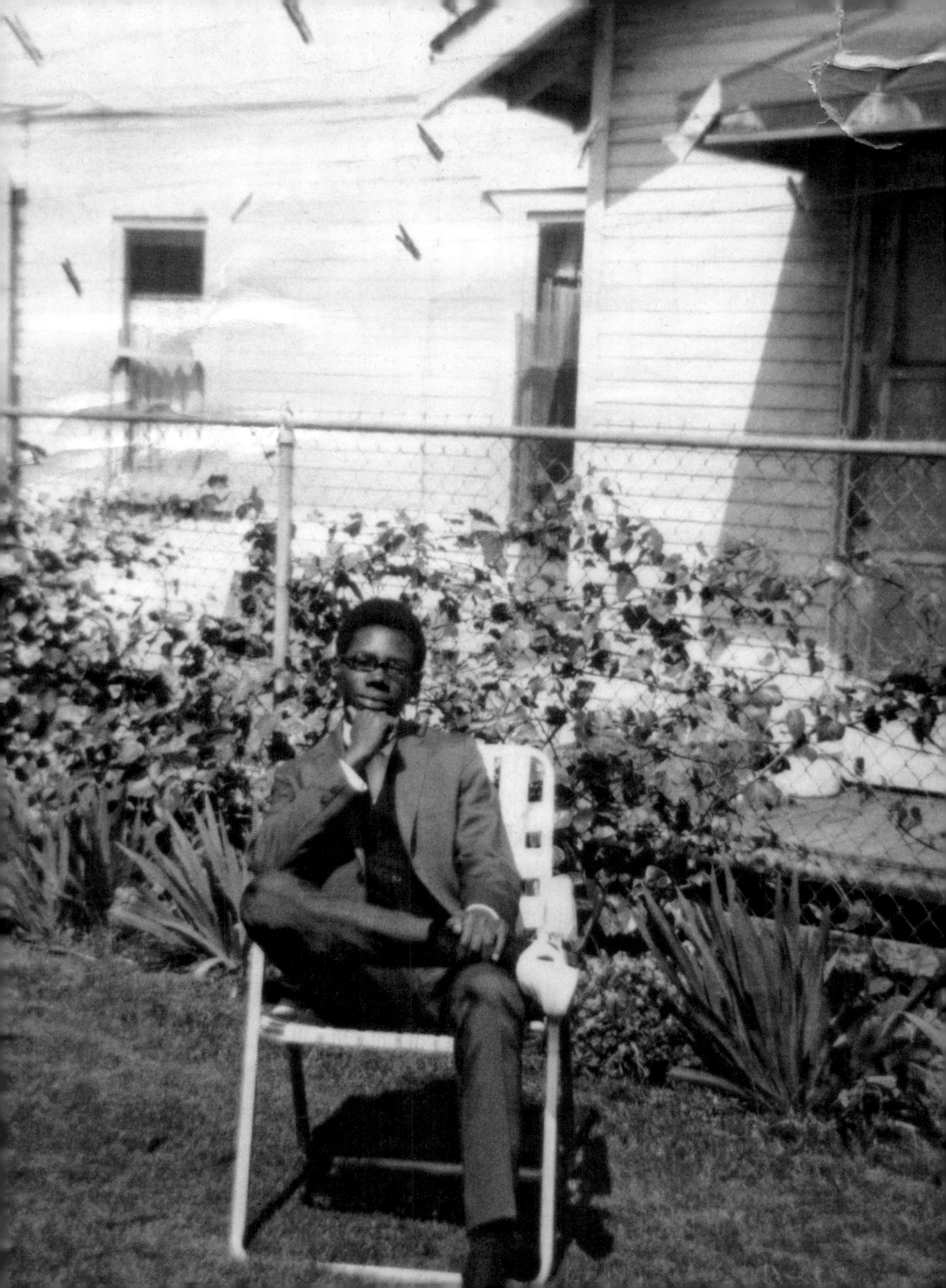

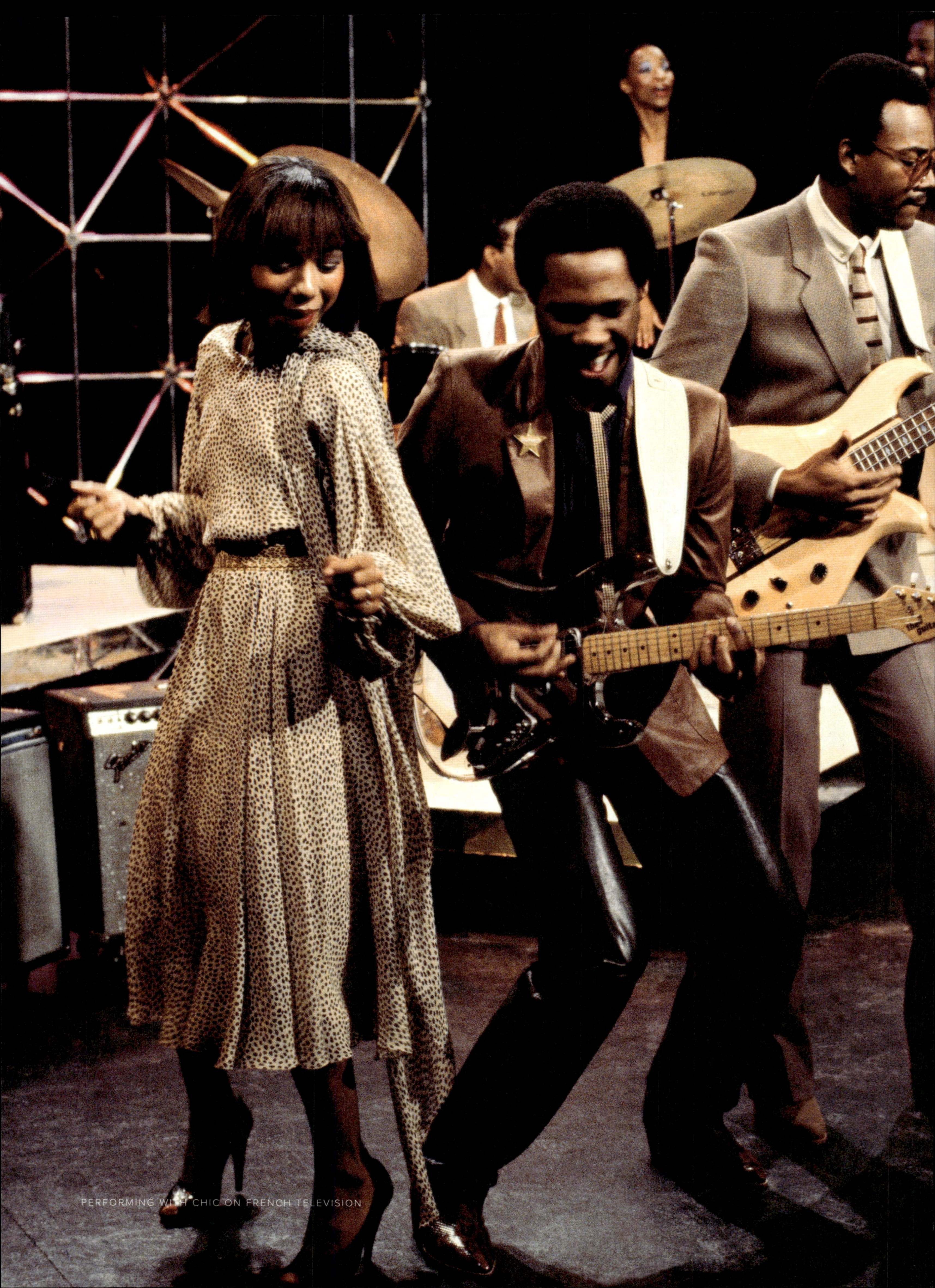

PERFORMING WITH CHIC ON FRENCH TELEVISION

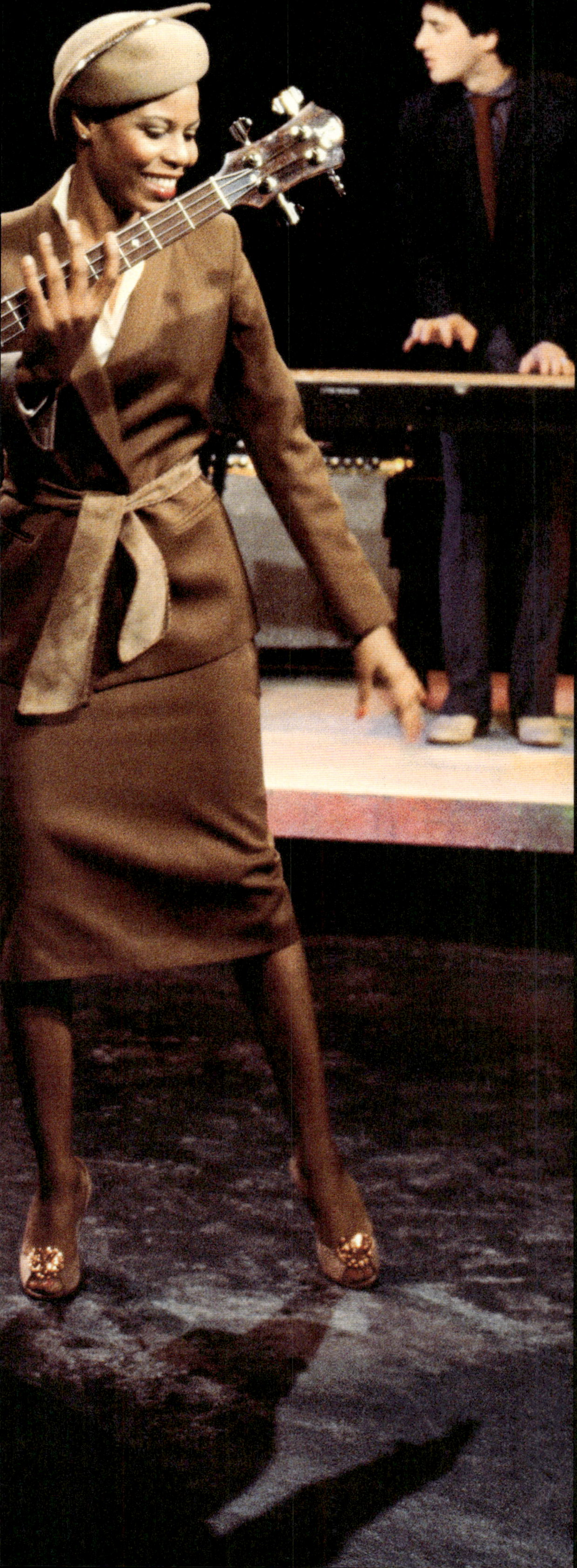

contemplative, because he wanted me to understand the depth of what I had done wrong. After all that silence, he said, "Pud, dig yourself." That was the most serious disciplinary action that he ever doled out. He just wanted me to dig myself.

I kept being a Cub Scout even after we moved to Alphabet City. That was the hardcore hood. In those days, there were no hippies in Alphabet City yet—it was still beatnik. Tompkins Square Park was a major spot for copping heroin, the downtown version of Needle Park. Kids who were in organizations like the Cub Scouts, instead of being picked on, got a pass in a strange way. The gangs wouldn't bother us. They must have thought, *Wow, these kids are sort of cool, they're doing stuff for the community*. We were always good kids, helping little old ladies cross the street and such.

**BW:** Did you have a nickname as a kid?

**NR:** It was actually Pud, short for Pudding Pie. It's cute in one sense but strange and a bit tough for my family in another. My great-great-great grandmother was half white. She enjoyed privileges that were not afforded to dark-skinned Africans. So she tried to keep that fair-skinned look in the family. Everybody in my family is light-skinned except for me, because of my dad. My mom was 13 when she got pregnant with me. Her friend was in the next room having sex with my father's buddy while my father and mother were just sitting there on the couch. At some point, he suggested, like all good guys would, "Maybe we should go for it." So they did. She literally had had one period at that point, and he talked her into having sex. Nine months later I popped out. So "Pud" refers to the color of my complexion, chocolate pudding. Even though it may have started as a semi-derogatory nickname, everyone to this day calls me Pud.

**BW:** What did you want to communicate as you were writing your book?

**NR:** I was very aware of not trying to be a writer. I didn't want to get caught up in wordplay to try to dazzle people with my use of the English language. That's just not where I was coming from. I was trying to tell the story of my life in my own voice, as if I was having a conversation with the reader. And I wanted to tell the truth of every story, exactly as it happened. For example, when I was a kid, everyone believed this cat Alice Cooper was the reincarnation of a witch by the

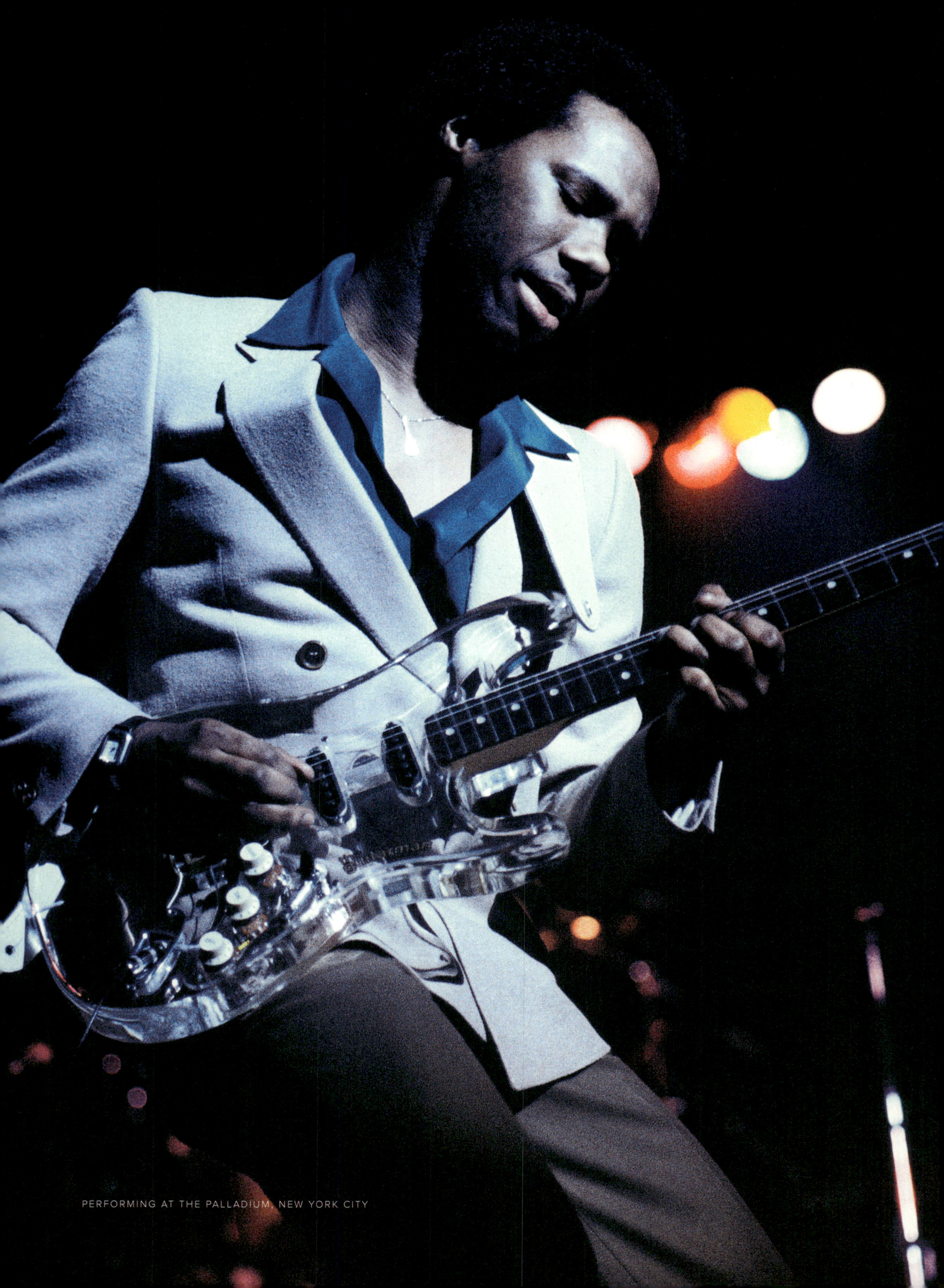

PERFORMING AT THE PALLADIUM, NEW YORK CITY

same name. That was his rap, probably some bullshit he made up. Part of the myth of Max's Kansas City was that The Velvet Underground played there and Alice Cooper followed them on stage. Well, that was almost correct. My band—New World

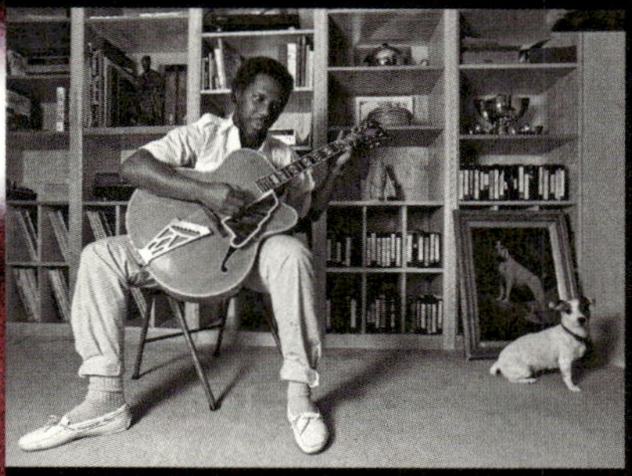

Rising—played after The Velvet Underground, and *then* Alice Cooper. But because we were a bunch of teenagers who never became famous, no one remembers that we were part of the story. When I was writing the book, I asked Alice, "Would you go along with my side of the story or what the rock 'n' roll historians say?" He said, "Yours is exactly right—how the fuck did you remember that?" Of course I remembered—it was a huge deal to me to play at Max's Kansas City right after The Velvet Underground!

**BW:** I flipped out when you wrote about Brett Ratner's mom. I've known Brett since he was a kid. What's his mom like?

**NR:** Brett is tame compared with his mom. When I started to play music, I was the shyest person in the world. I was a good player, but I felt like the ugly duckling in this gorgeous family. So I had stage fright. Because I was a jazz guy, I'd play sitting in a chair, not facing the audience. It was Brett's mom, Marsha, who came up to me and said, "Nile, you're so fucking good, you need to turn around and face the people! You need to show your guitar playing!" So I tried it one night and people got into it. Then Marsha told me, "Now, why don't you dance around?" I was like, "Wait a minute, Marsha. Yesterday I was playing in a foetal position, and now you want me to dance?!" She helped me out in that way, pushed me a bit. I started dancing in front of people and got great jobs after that.

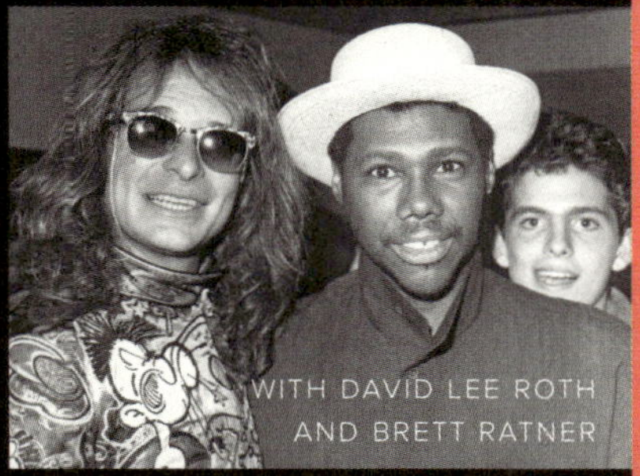

WITH DAVID LEE ROTH AND BRETT RATNER

**BW:** It's hard to think of you as shy, because you always had such amazing style. I don't care how hip the times were, not everyone dressed like you did.

**NR:** I guess that's true. Even when I was the poorest guy in the world, living on the subway, or the streets, in crash pads or communes, if I got any dough, even a little bit extra, I was going to a clothing store. I used to go to shops like Granny Takes a Trip or Limbo. I knew every store on St. Mark's Place. I wanted to be a fashionable hippie, because I wanted to look like I was in a band that was making money.

The hippie movement was cool, because it was really an alternate universe. Kids took everything about how their parents were raised and what society expected and did their own take on it. I was into the extreme of everything. As a super hippie, I always liked doing stuff to my hair. My family was so pretty, I had to do something to be noticed. So I'd use chemical relaxer and braid my hair, then comb it out to get it to stand straight up like Kathleen Cleaver or Michael Jackson. Then my buddies and I

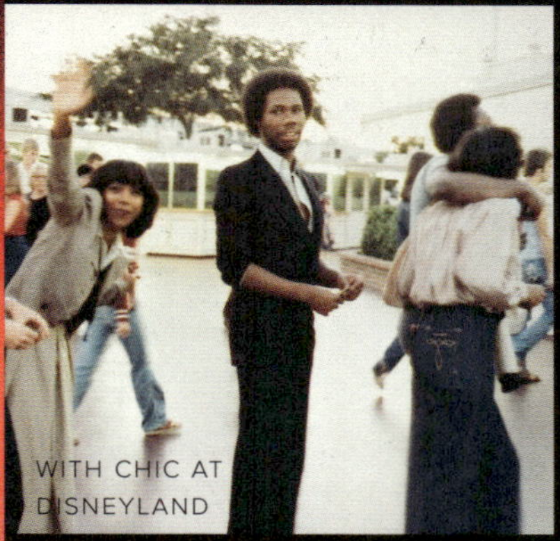

WITH CHIC AT DISNEYLAND

would color our hair using vegetable dye. I realized that it was almost impossible to get the light colors to show up in my hair, but the dark colors like green or blue would work. In normal light, you couldn't see it. But if I stood out in the sunlight, people would say, "Man, his hair is green!" I'd walk down the street looking like broccoli.

**BW:** Even today, if your dreadlocks were green, you'd be stared at!

**NR:** My stepfather Bobby was central-casting handsome, and he came from a long line of haberdashers. So he was a hip beatnik who had the whole Cary Grant thing going. Even when my stepdad went collegiate, he still had flair—the corduroy suit with the patches, always with a pocket square, no matter what. My mom wanted me to dress to look like him, so I'd be seen rolling around Little Italy looking like Thomas Wolfe in a suit with glasses. It was ridiculous, but I thought it was cool. Everybody in the family was into fashion. My grandmother always used to say, "If you want to get ahead, get a hat."

**BW:** I like how you describe your parents in such a glamorous way. My dad looked like Paul Newman and my mom like Grace Kelly, and I was this geeked-out kid. But I loved music, and I know it helped you as a kid too.

**NR:** Music is what made us cool, even when I was playing classical. My parents were the most amazing role models. We didn't listen to pop music so much—my parents were more into what we used to call bebop. While everybody else was listening to "Who Wears Short Shorts?" my parents were playing records like "Have You Got a Penny, Benny?" I used to sit at home when I was 6 or 7 listening to Nina Simone and Miles Davis. The very first present I ever got in my life was the Elvis Presley 45 "Blue Suede Shoes" and a pair of blue suede shoes to go with it. Then I got a navy blue sharkskin suit, and that was my outfit for my first holy communion. I walked into the church looking like *Ocean's Eleven*.

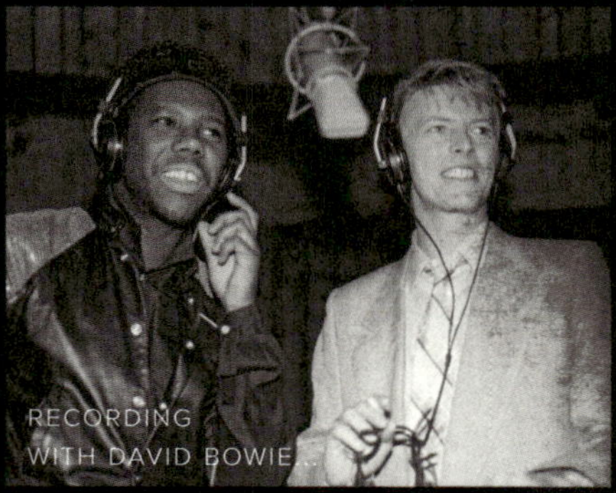
RECORDING WITH DAVID BOWIE...

**BW:** That influence clearly continued, because you incorporate all kinds of visual influences into the music you make. Whether you're referencing the hippie community or the jazz community, you bring everything together in your music and style. Not many musicians have that visual sensibility.

**NR:** I try to explain this idea to people all the time. When I was working on *Let's Dance* with David Bowie, we did tons of research. Bowie has such a rich artistic sense, and when it comes to music he's a real jazzer. We looked at everything, different types of music and iconography. After about two weeks of visiting museums, going to different people's houses and looking at art collections, David showed me an album cover with a picture of Little Richard in a red suit getting into a red Cadillac and said, "Nile darling, this is rock 'n' roll. This is what I want my album to sound like." And I knew exactly what he meant. If you look at the cover of *Let's Dance*, David's in a yellow suit, he's got yellow hair, the only thing that's missing is the Cadillac. It wasn't just rock 'n' roll, it was the early '80s and the beginning of the whole metrosexual thing. We didn't have a name for it then, but David was a pioneer, that ultra-male, good-looking super-dude. It just shows you how forward-thinking certain artists can be.

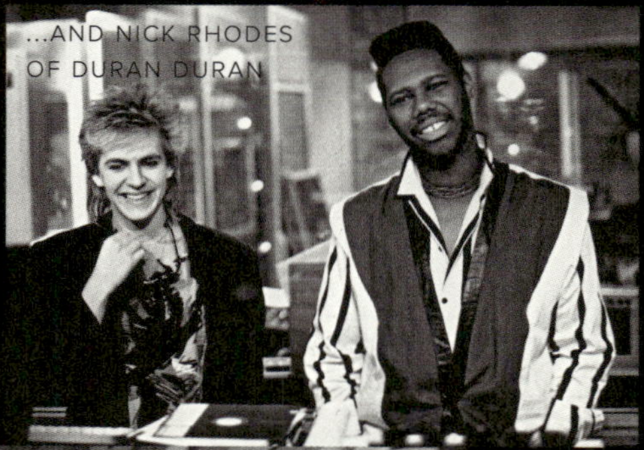
...AND NICK RHODES OF DURAN DURAN

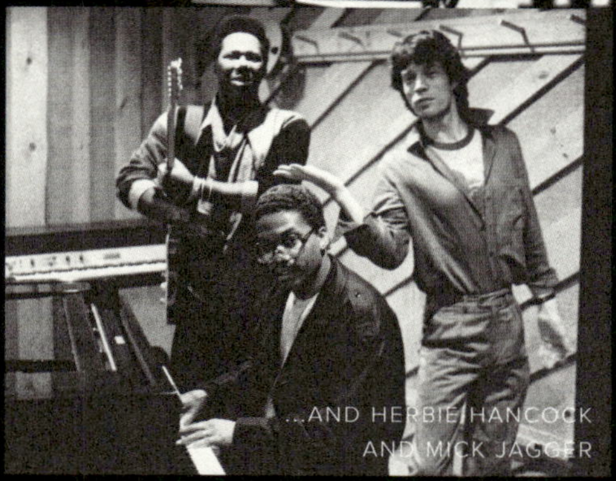
...AND HERBIE HANCOCK AND MICK JAGGER

**BW:** You wrote that your songs are kind of like your children. I don't have kids either, but I sometimes feel the same way about my photographs. I understand that connection to your work.

**NR:** I never had kids, but I was a babysitter for a little while.

**BW:** Really, for whom?

**NR:** John Lennon and Yoko Ono. Actually, it was my girlfriend's job at the time. But she was studying primal scream therapy with this theater guy named Alec Ruben at a workshop just around the corner. I would babysit for Julian while she was at her classes. Julian and I always laugh about it now—he says, "Man, you were the weirdest babysitter ever." I took the same approach with him as my parents did with me—Jules could do anything he wanted as far as I was concerned.

**BW:** That's so crazy! I want to ask you now about Luther Vandross, because I love his voice and his interpretation of songs. What was he like?

**NR:** If it weren't for Luther, I wouldn't be the musician that I am today. We started out together—I met him when I got the job in the *Sesame Street* band right after high school. Then I worked with Luther as part of the Radio City Music Hall band, during which time I recorded "Everybody Dance," the first record I wrote for Chic. Typically there were two shows a night at Radio City. We did the first show, then ran over to the studio during intermission to record "Everybody Dance." I had all these famous musicians singing on it, for free, during their break. That record only cost $10 to make—the money needed to bribe the elevator operator not to tell the boss that we were in there after-hours. To this day, it has made over $8 million.

That night, Luther made me realize that I was the guy in charge. He kept saying, "Well, Nile, you wrote the music, you did this, so you're the producer." He taught me about varying the speed of a recording, overdubbing, multitracking, vocal arrangement and just from that one session, I learned so much. I would do the same thing for every subsequent session I did after that.

**BW:** Chic is such a great name for a band. How did you come up with it?

**NR:** Because I grew up in a jazz household, it was common knowledge that when black jazz musicians made it, they would go to France like Nina Simone where they'd be treated like

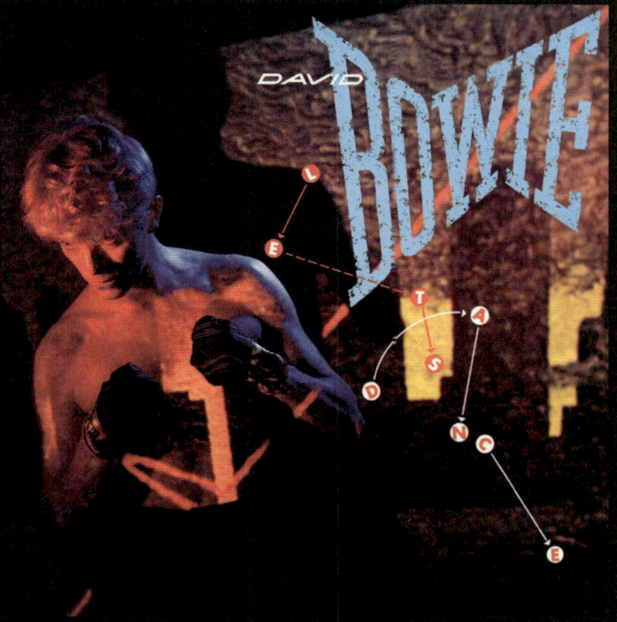
DAVID
BOWIE

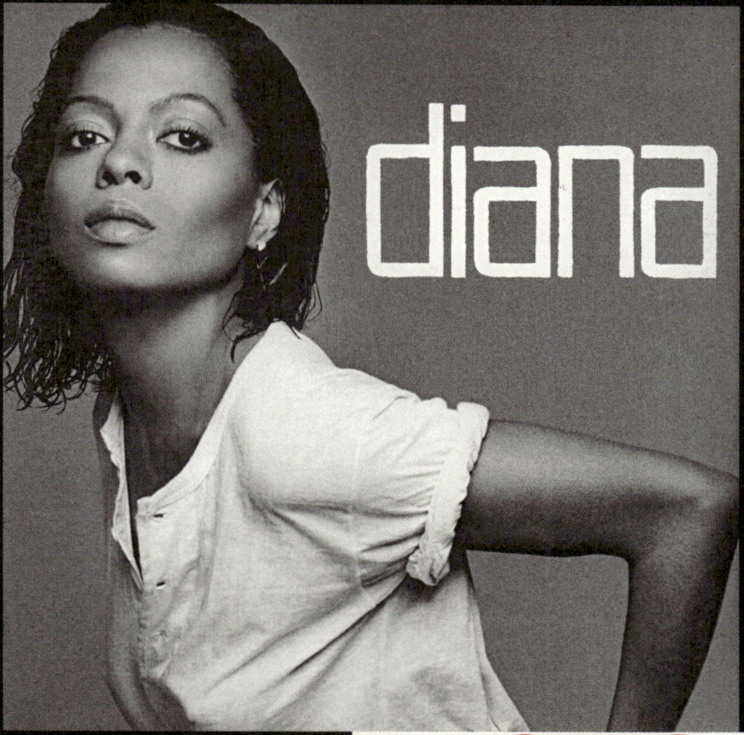
diana

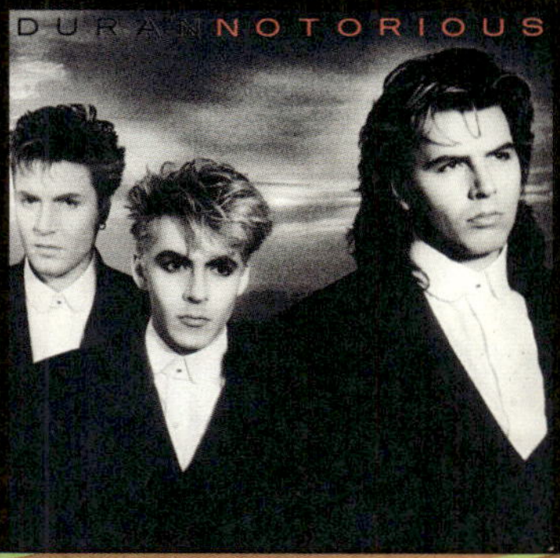
NOTORIOUS

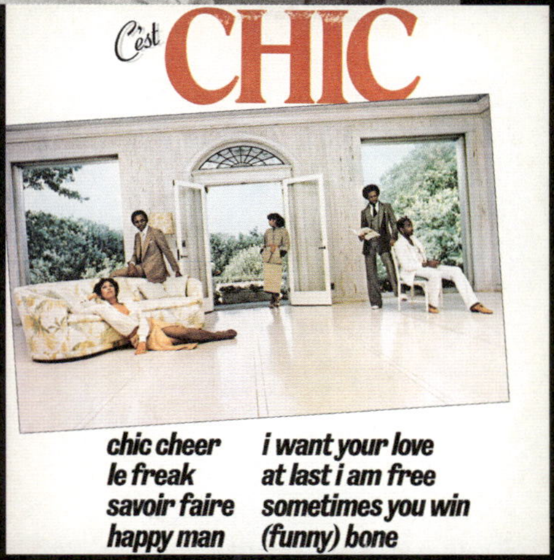
C'est CHIC
chic cheer
le freak
savoir faire
happy man
i want your love
at last i am free
sometimes you win
(funny) bone

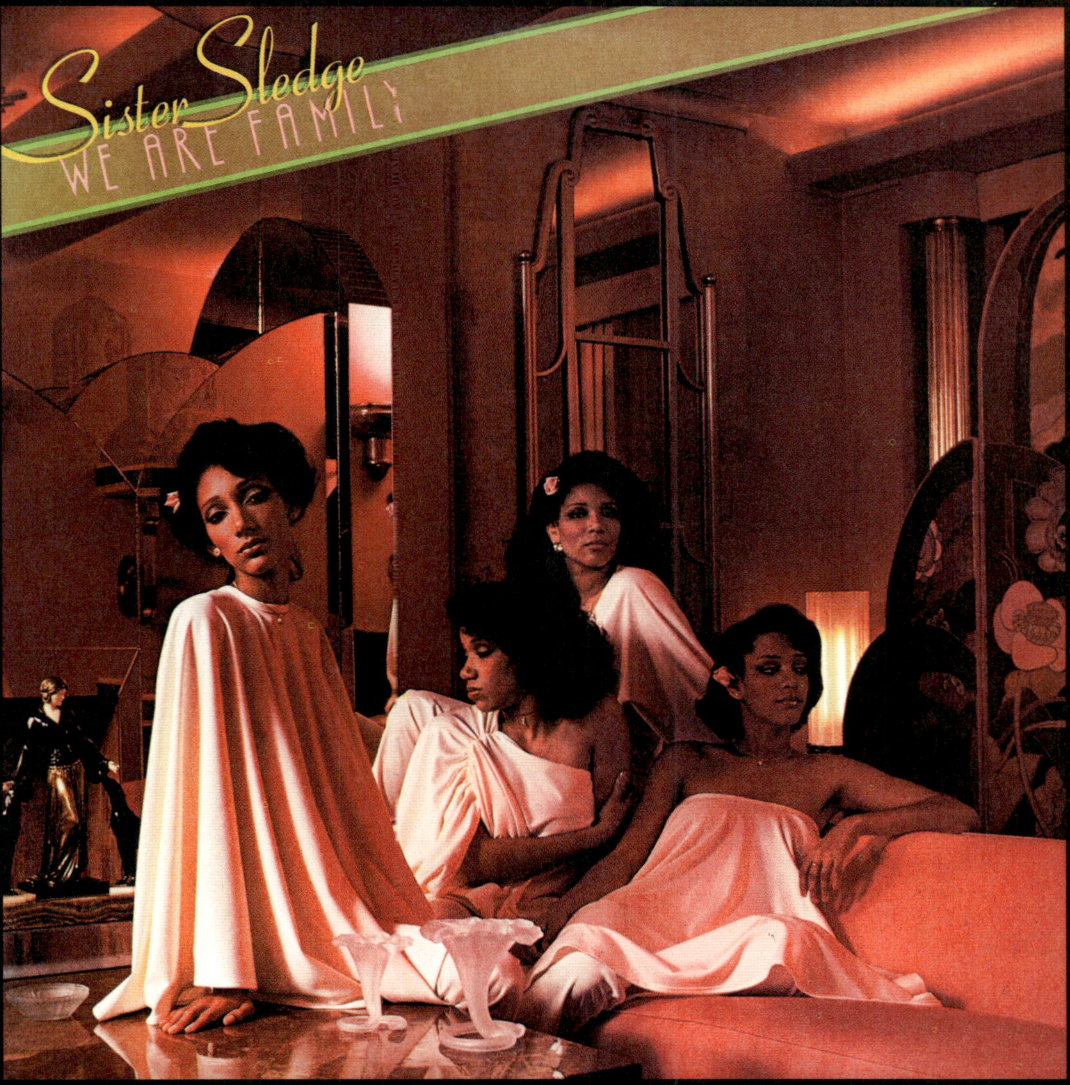
Sister Sledge

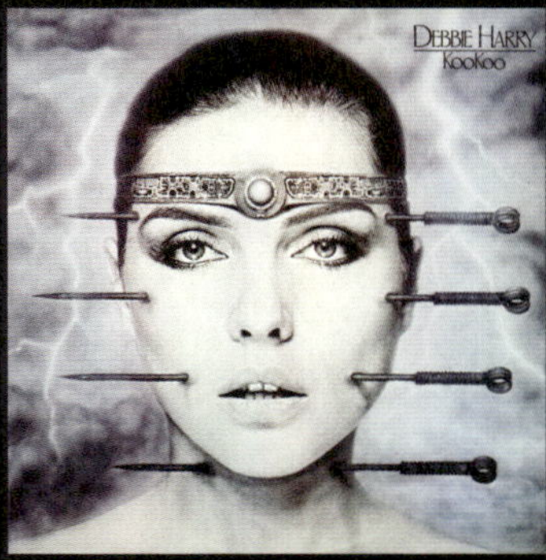
DEBBIE HARRY

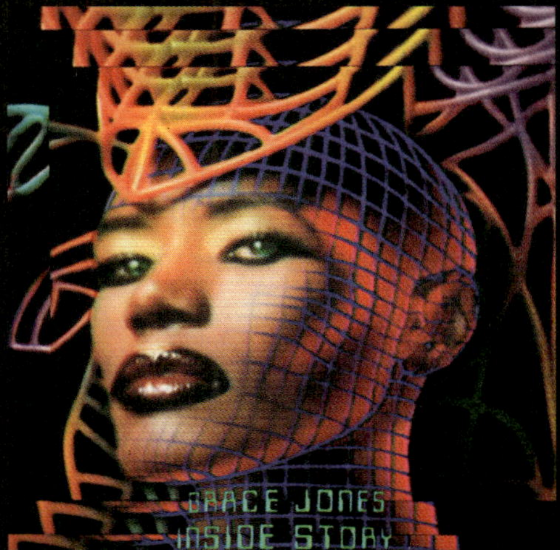
GRACE JONES

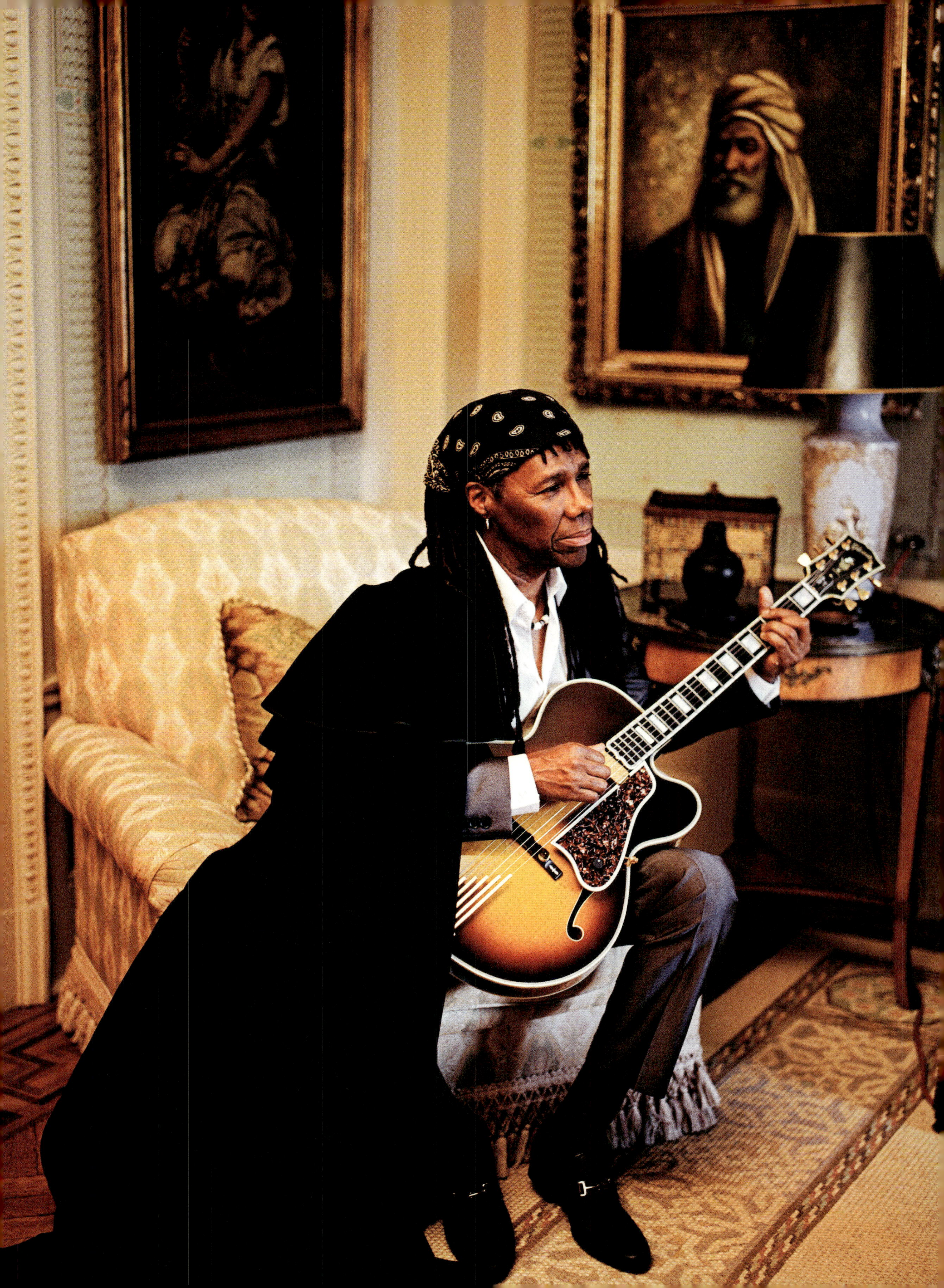

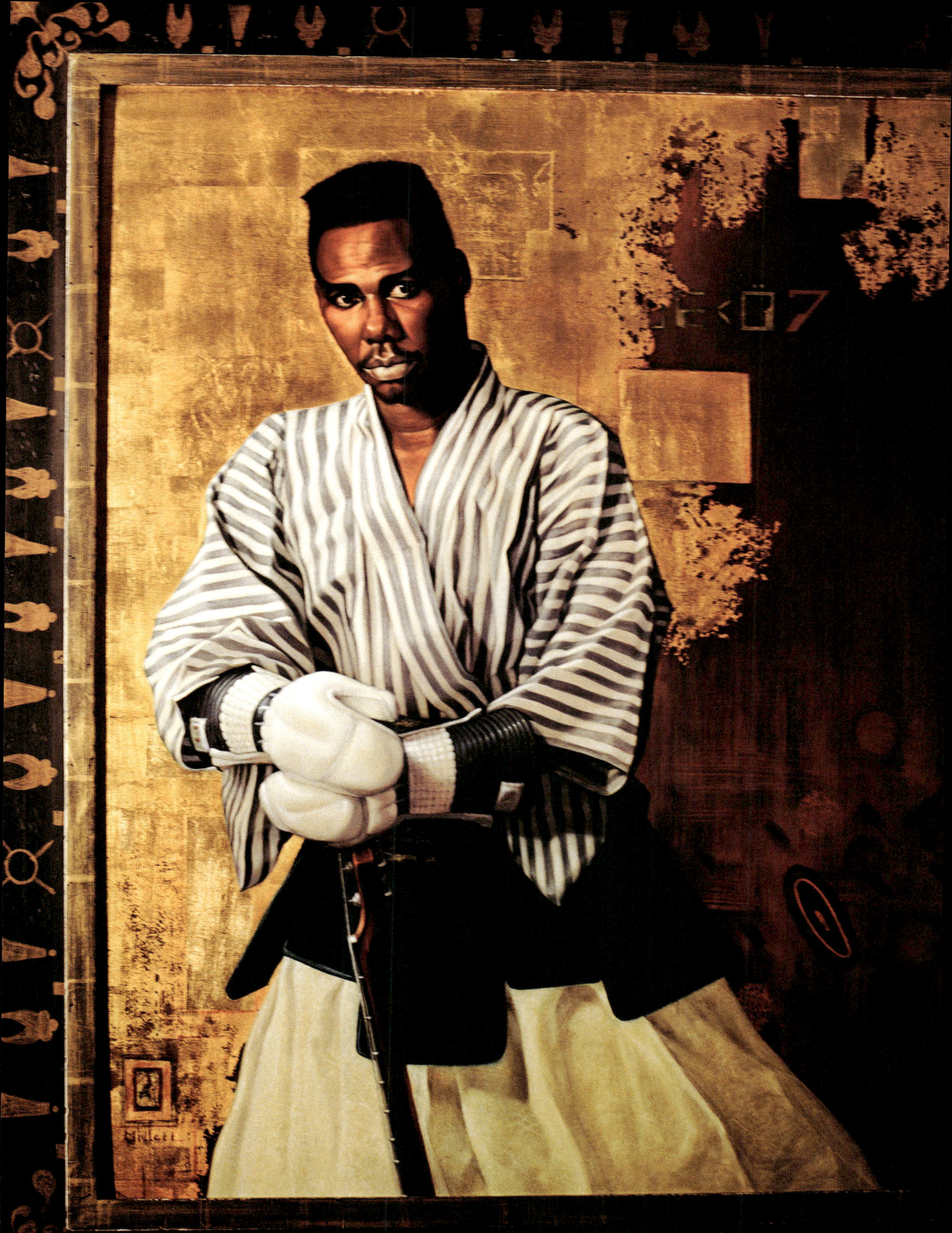

human beings. So when we started out, I thought, *Why don't we pretend to be these sophisticated cats from France right from the beginning?* We set out to be more than a funk band—we wanted to be a funk, sophisto French band. Seriously, our first album had songs like, "Est-ce que c'est Chic?" We didn't even know what we were talking about. My girlfriend at the time was from Belgium, and I said, "Here, baby, write some lyrics." But we had a vibe and it was cool so people bought into it.

"Everybody Dance" has all these complicated, jazzy, chromatic chord progressions. When I wrote the song, I thought it was cool but not commercial. So I kept the lyrics super simple.

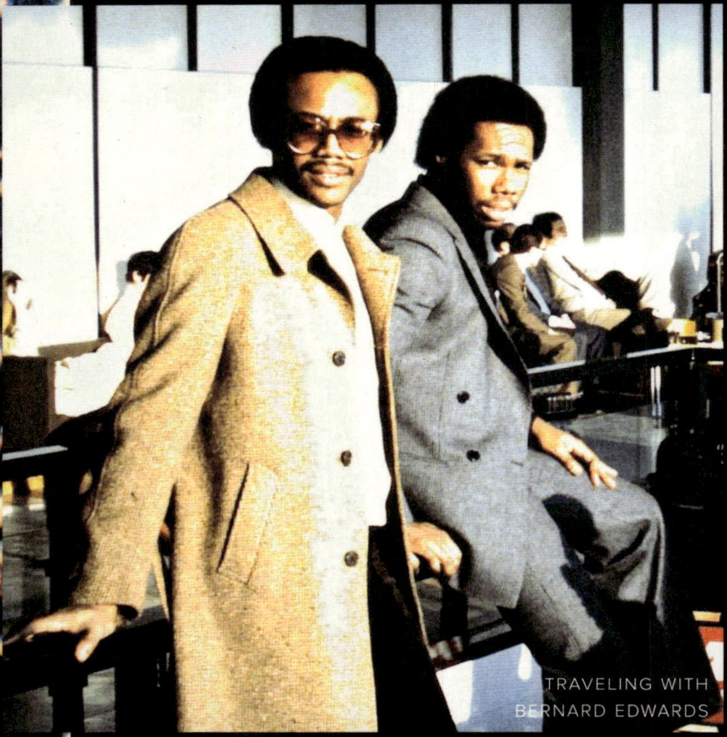
TRAVELING WITH BERNARD EDWARDS

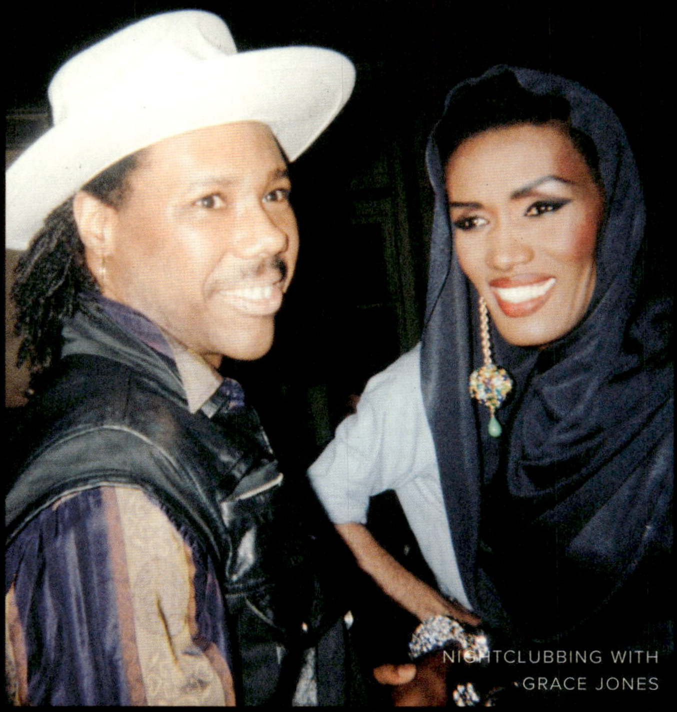
NIGHTCLUBBING WITH GRACE JONES

I remember playing it for Bernard the first time. His listened to it and said, "The chord changes are cool. But what the fuck does 'doo-doo-doo-doo' mean?" I said, "Listen, every disco record out there has a la-la-la-la chorus. 'Doo-doo-doo-doo' is technically the same, but it's hip."

**BW:** Do you remember the first time you heard it on the radio?

**NR:** The very first time I heard my music outside of a recording studio was at a club called The Night Owl. My friend was deejaying there, and he called me to say, "Nile, you've got to come over and see this." I didn't know it at the time, but he had made two acetates of our first recording of "Everybody Dance." When I walked into the Night Owl, the record was playing. I was shocked to see people dancing and singing and going crazy. "Everybody dance, clap your hands…" It was just amazing, unlike anything I've ever felt before—like my first high, sex, whatever. It's never been like that again since.

**BW:** Who were some other people who inspired you and Bernard early on?

**NR:** When Bernard and I were putting together our band, this Puerto Rican keyboardist Rob Sabino told us about his friend Ace Frehley, who had a band named KISS. We went to check them out—they didn't have a record deal at that time. It was the most amazing thing I had ever seen. The audience was all wearing face paint and platform shoes, and the band and the audience were screaming "Fuck you!" at each other. I thought, *This is great!* It was a totally immersive artistic experience in music like I had never seen before. It felt like I was in a whacky sideshow. It was similar when I saw Brian Ferry and Roxy Music. It was like being at a fashion show, but they were playing music and these beautiful girls were dancing in military outfits. I said to Bernard, "We've got to do the black version of this."

Some R&B guys, like the Ohio Players, had done it—they had pictures of these beautiful models on the cover instead of the band. So as we defined Chic, we knew what we had to do. I think that's why the formula worked so well. We weren't naturally those guys, but we could actually pretend to be.

**BW:** I've known Suzanne de Passe for a long time. How did she get you to work with Diana Ross?

**NR:** Diana is and was a super, super, super star. Chic was playing at the Santa Monica Civic Auditorium, and we were killing it. It was 1979, our year, and the place was packed. We'd done "Good Times," "Le Freak," and "I Want Your Love." It was complete mayhem—people were screaming. We ran backstage, covered in sweat, and Diana Ross was there. Suzanne had brought her to meet us. Diana said to us, "Wow, that was so cute." We didn't even know what to say to her but, "Thank you, Miss Ross."

**BW:** I remember buying that record you did with Diana like it was yesterday. Listening to "Upside Down" for the first time...

**NR:** There are a couple of things that Bernard and I did that I would say are close to perfect, and that was one of them. The record company didn't hear it that way at first. We had to sue them to put out the biggest record of Diana Ross' life. This story didn't make my book, but it's really funny. Berry Gordy and Motown didn't pay us at first for the Diana album. They were all pissed off with me. Berry had made God knows how many millions off of it. So we finally decided we couldn't take it anymore and set up a meeting with our lawyers to get our money. We drove to Berry's house in Bel Air. He walks us to the playroom and then to the den, the bar, the swimming pool. He's doing everything but talk about the money he owes us—which was, by then, a million three for our share of the royalties.

Bernard always had a gift for saying the right thing at the right time. So Berry shows us a horse race with a horse that he owned running in it. It was the Santa Anita Handicap, and his horse won. Berry said, "You know, I bought that horse for $25,000 but after that race he's worth about $3 million." And without dropping a beat, Bernard replied, "Well, excuse me, Mr. Gordy, can you cut three legs off that motherfucker and pay us?" It was great. Berry hit the floor laughing, and he said, "Alright, I've got it guys, I understand."

**BW:** Was there anyone you wish you'd had a chance to work with and didn't?

**NR:** Donna Summer was the one artist that I always thought I would make the perfect record with. She was the queen of disco. I had to force Diana Ross to go there, force Sister Sledge to go there. What would have happened with the woman who had done "Bad Girls" and "Love to Love You Baby"? I mean, she just had that thing. We had meeting after meeting after meeting, and I don't know why it never came together.

The other match made in heaven that never made music was with Miles Davis. It's the one thing I really lament not doing. We met at a photo session for Issey Miyake and became great friends. We saw each other all the time and he used to say to me, "Nile, write me a motherfucking 'Good Times.'" Knowing his sense of humor, I always thought he was bullshitting me. So I'd write him "Bitches Brew Part II" and he'd say, "Marcus can do that—don't do that shit. Give me 'Good Times,' man!" Looking back, I can see it so clearly. Miles was going for a hit.

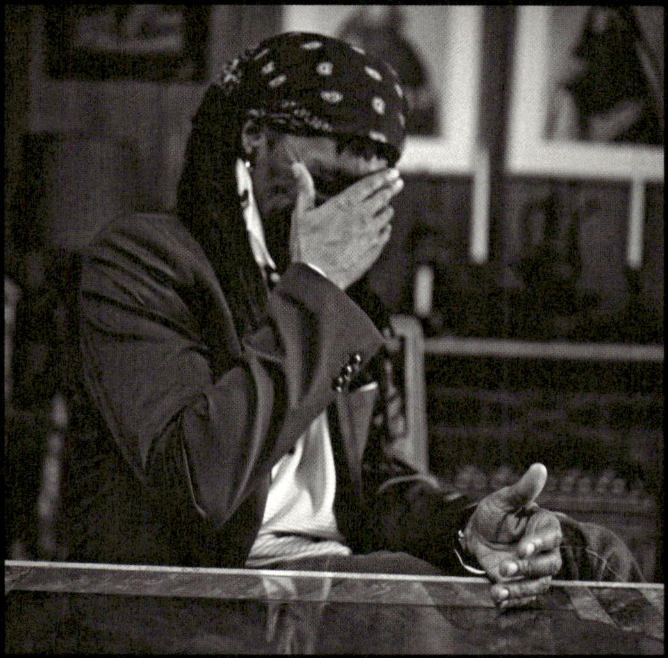

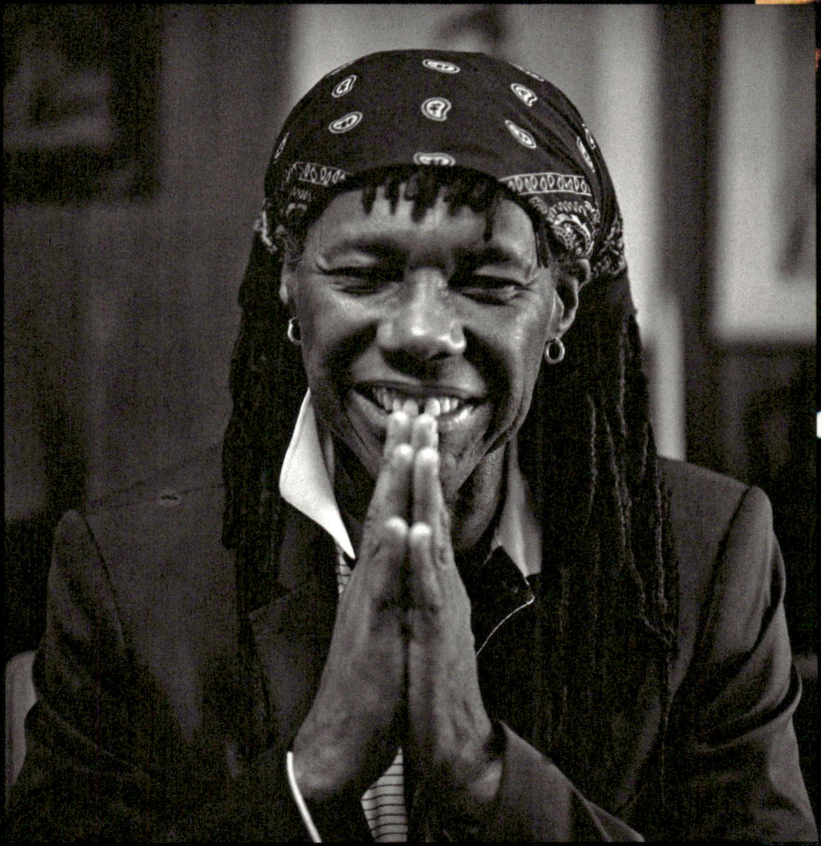

Herbie Hancock was in the pop charts with "Rockit" and "Chameleon." Miles had been dead serious, and it breaks my heart that I didn't realize it at the time. It just seemed so absurd.

**BW:** But that's what makes you a great producer. Musicians trust you because they believe in the music that you've made yourself.

**NR:** The artists usually do, but the powers that be don't necessarily. I'm working right now with this girl Elly Jackson from a group called La Roux. She's hip, but she's in that really weird spot where the record company wants her to

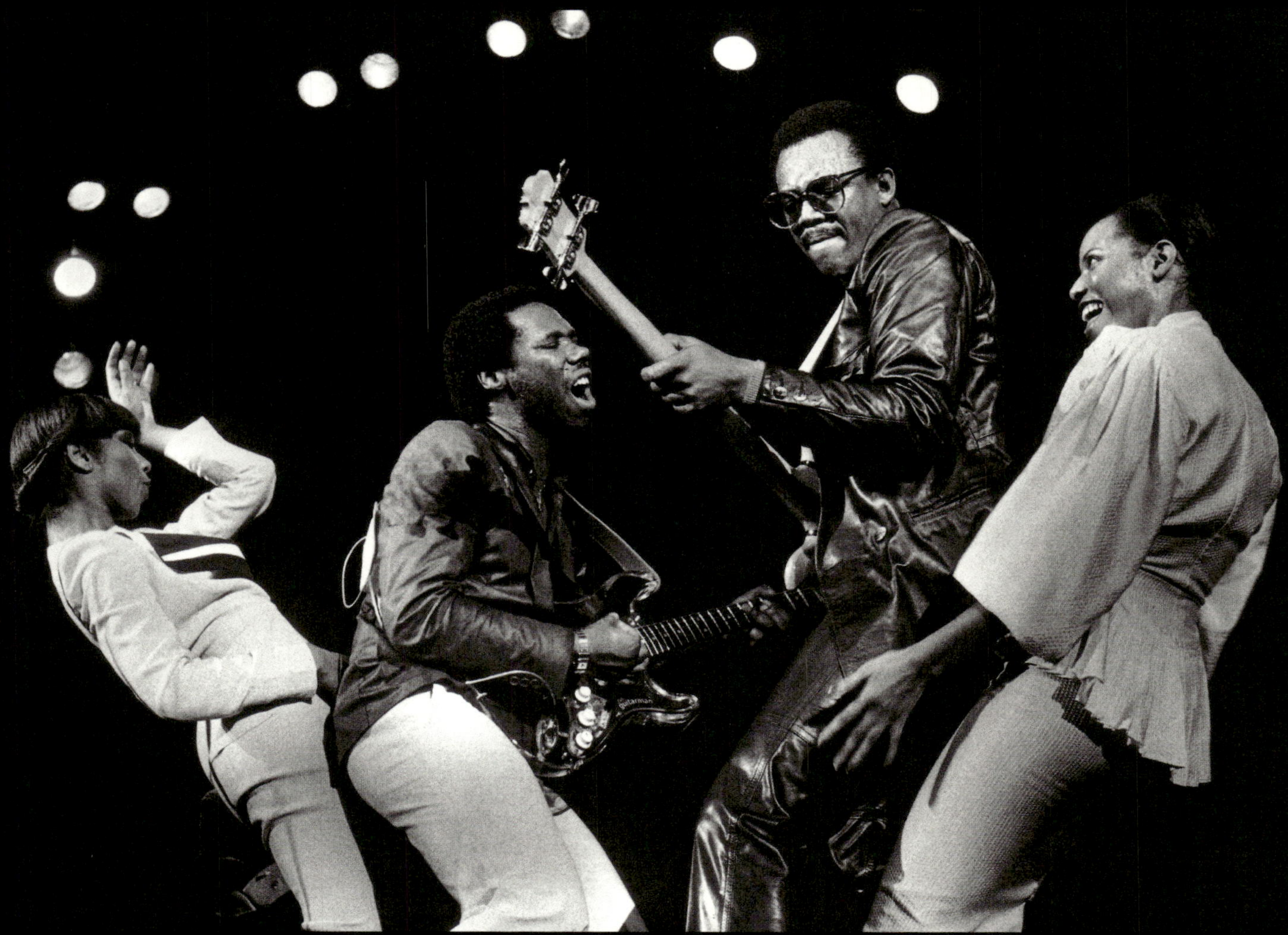

be something and she's smarter than they are. I understand both points of view—I tell her, "Elly, you're on this natural path as a musician. But you can't do something that's so amazing but alienates your fan base to a point that your record company has no idea how to promote it. You've just got to believe in somebody to help you see your vision through. Because at the end of the day, that's all you've got." It's a hard thing to explain to people, the balance between being commercial and being artistic. Bowie said it to me perfectly: "Nile darling, if you come from art, you'll always be associated with art." He meant if you're in an artistic place, you can do commercial shit but it's still going to be arty and cool—so don't be afraid of it.

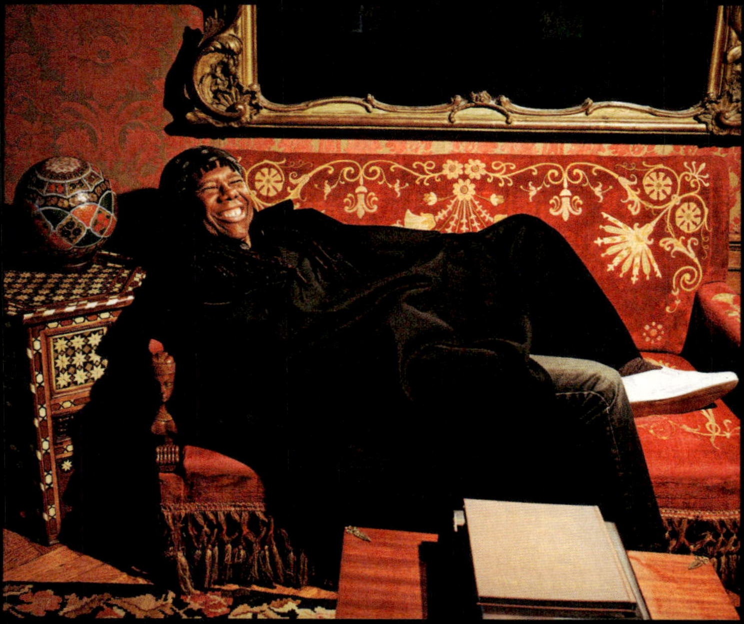

**BW:** I want to ask you one more thing. On my way here today I spoke to a friend and she just got a bad diagnosis from her doctor. I just didn't know what to say to her. Based on your own battle with cancer, do you have any suggestions for me?

**NR:** The one thing I never do is give people advice in these situations. All I can talk about is what I do because experiences with illness are so unbelievably personal. I always tell myself, "Keep swimming, keep going forward." I let the doctors do what they need to, and I do everything in my power to help myself. That's as valid as what anyone else might do. I act as if there's no cancer—I never miss any jobs, do all the gigs I'm supposed to. I'm probably working now more than I ever have, because I can say to myself, *This is the life I built.* I'm lucky enough to have an artistic life, so I want to just keep going.

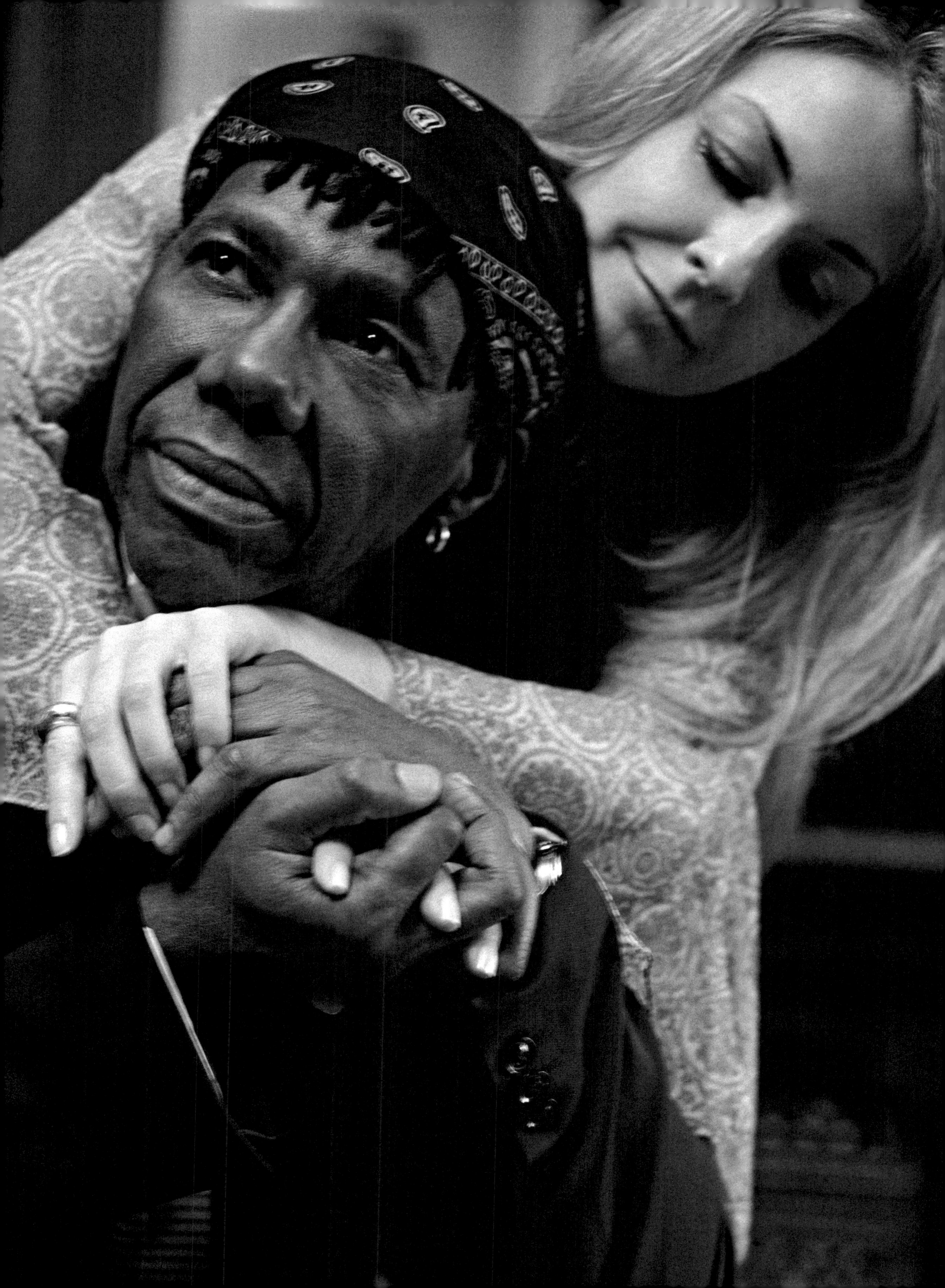

YOU HAVE TO

# BE BRAVE

ENOUGH TO

# BELIEVE IN

WHAT YOU ARE

LOOKING AT

MRS. POLLY MELLEN

PORTRAITS BY BRUCE WEBER

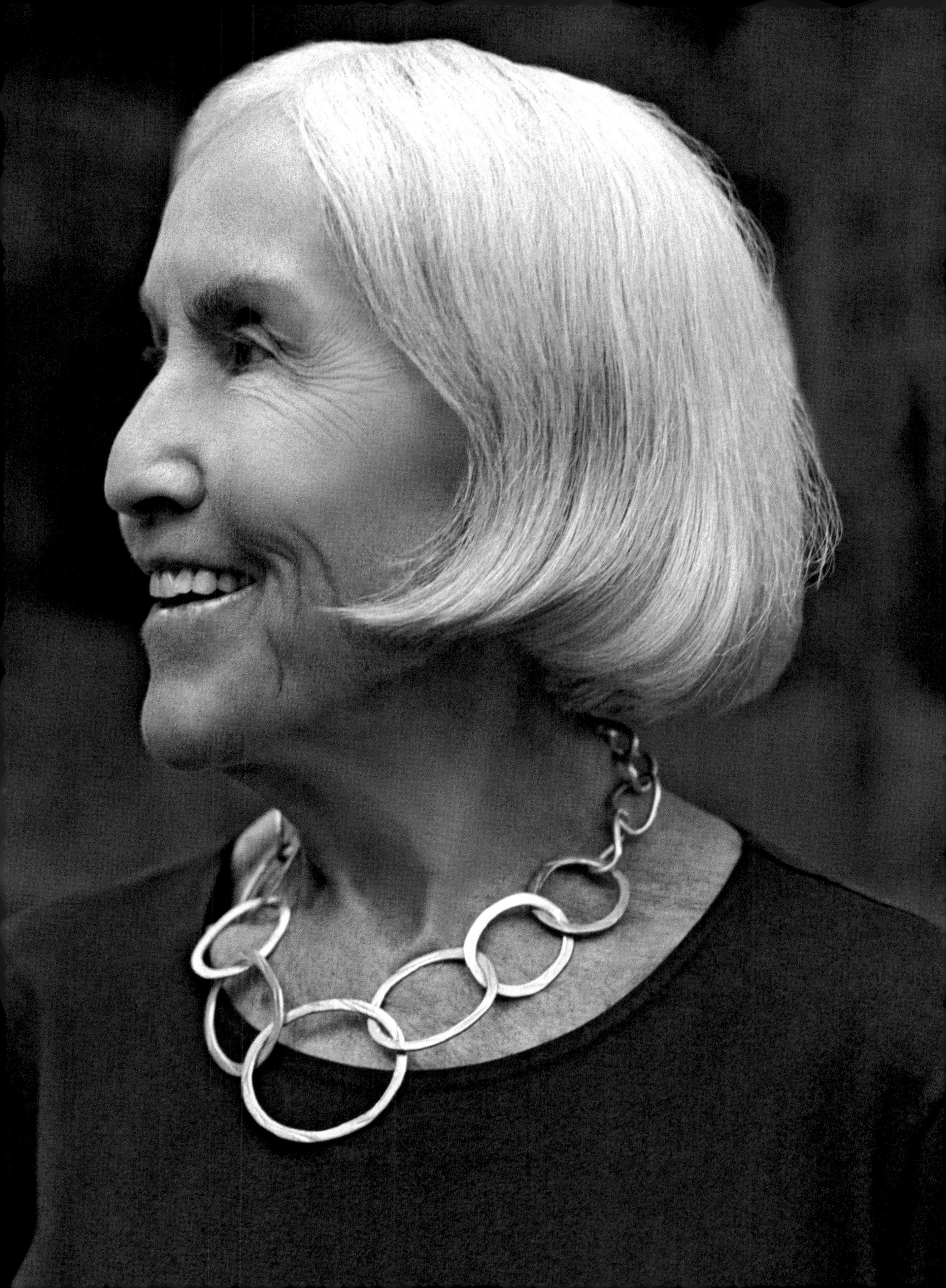

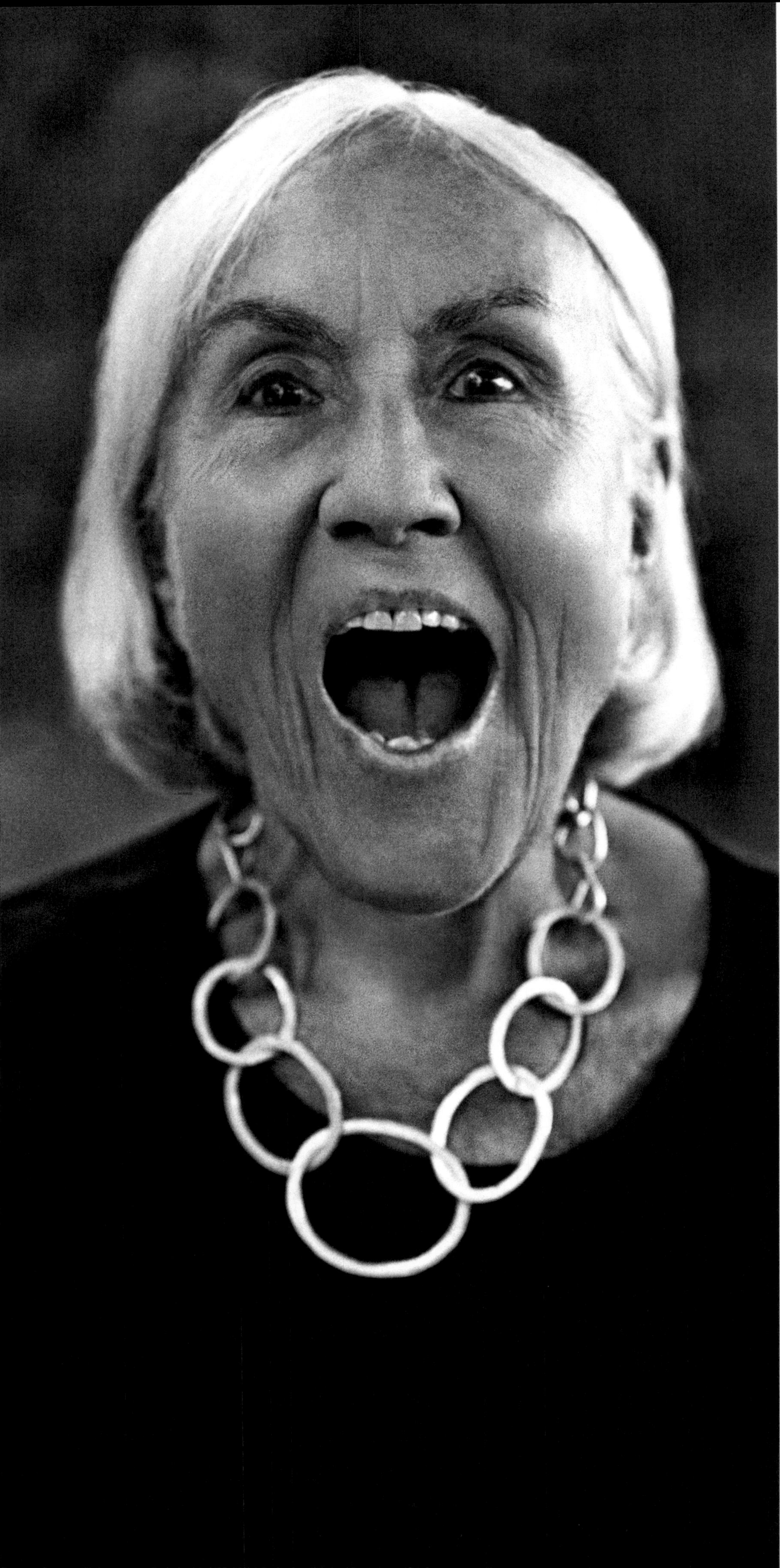
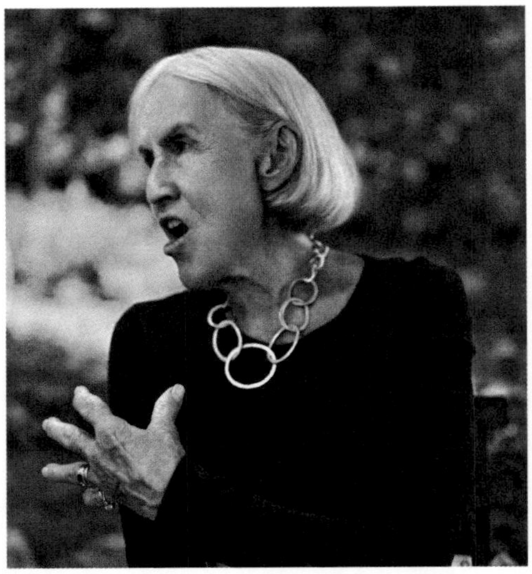
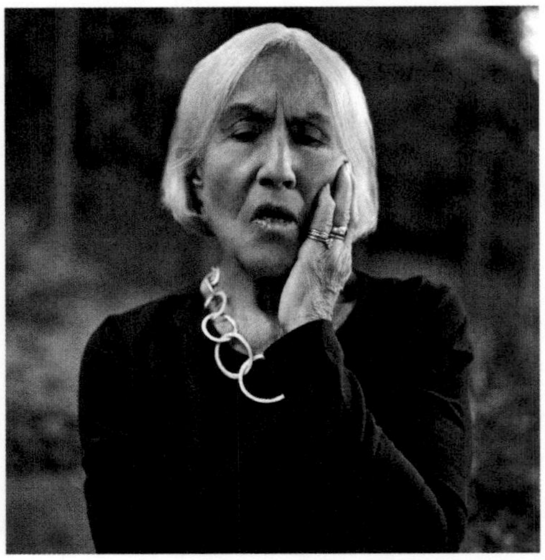
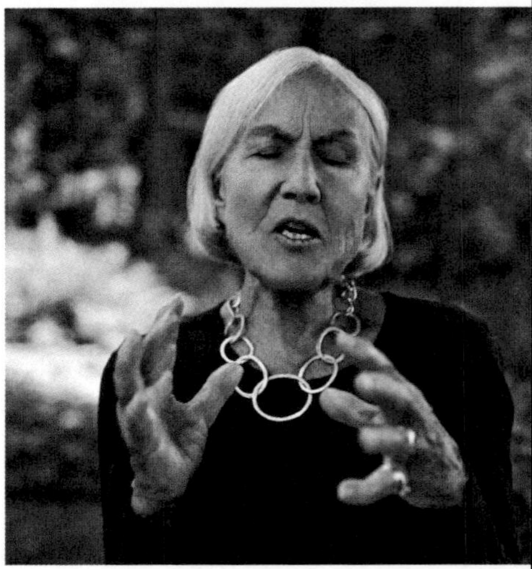
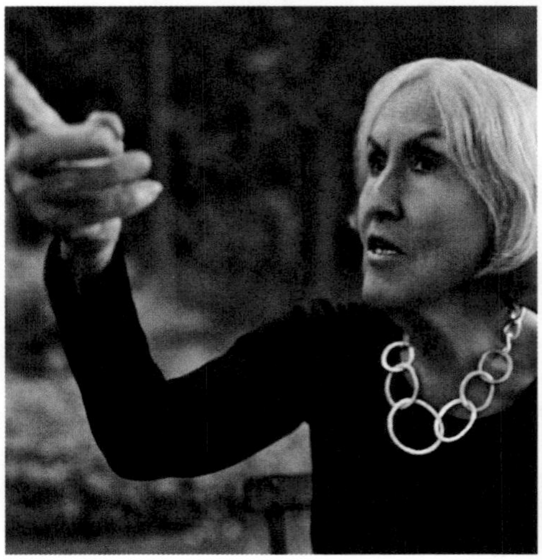

## "Nothing venture, nothing win."—*Sir Edmund Hillary*

Polly Mellen started her career as an editor at *Harper's Bazaar* under the watchful eye of Diana Vreeland, Carmel Snow, and Alexey Brodovitch. In an interview with Nicolas Ghesquière, she described her nervousness the first time she met Mrs. Vreeland, the fashion editor, "She wore Mainbocher, and her hair was pulled back so tightly that it looked like it was lacquered a navy blue." After working together at *Harper's Bazaar,* Mrs. Vreeland brought Polly to *Vogue* and introduced her to Richard Avedon, who became her mischievous confidant. Years later, Avedon gave her a photograph of the two of them on set, and on the print he wrote, "Dear Polly, Just dancing through life together, Love Dick." It was a perfect expression of their rich, complicated, decades-long collaboration. When Mrs. Vreeland left *Vogue*, Polly continued to work there with Grace Mirabella and Alexander Liberman. She eventually left *Vogue* to become creative director at *Allure*.

Polly is retired now and lives in a place in Connecticut too beautiful to mention, for fear her fans will move there en masse. She still skis in the winter and swims laps in her pool all summer. Polly lives with her husband of 47 years, Henry Wigglesworth Mellen, and has four children and five grandchildren. Her curiosity about the world and her lust for the next big thing are her magic.

Time flies fast in the fashion world. It doesn't seem that long ago, but in the early '70s, magazine editors and designers were still called Mr. and Mrs. before their proper names. Models would say, "I had a sitting at Mr. Penn's today." As a young photographer, you wished for the day when this powerhouse of fashionable attitude—who a select few called "Polly"—would be pulling up your model's skirt or putting on her jacket inside out while you loaded your trusted camera with film. Many of my friends at that time worked as assistants to the fashion editors at Condé Nast. They were all from good families, and they inhabited the infamous fashion closets of *Vogue, Mademoiselle,* and *Glamour*. There was Kezia Keeble, Vera Wang, Sarah Foley, Helen Murray, Barbara Bersell, Julie Britt, Nonnie Boylan, and Jade Hopson. It was a little like the play *The Prime of Miss Jean Brodie*, but Frances Patiky Stein, Carrie Donovan, Babs Simpson, and especially Polly Mellen were all vying for the lead role made famous by Maggie Smith. I can't tell you how many nights I spent drinking glasses of scotch on the rocks with beer chasers at Elaine's, P.J. Clarke's, or even Max's Kansas City listening to these young fashion editors desperately crying their hearts out, swearing like truck drivers and asking, "Why doesn't Polly love me?"

So that's why I was trembling when I first worked with Polly for a sitting with Farrah Fawcett for *Vogue*. At that time, the poster of Farrah with her Garren haircut hung on every young man's wall. Polly's first words to me and the hairdresser Bob Fink that day were so dramatic that for a moment we considered running out the door. Bob had fallen asleep on the couch, so Polly gently tapped him on the shoulder and said, "Mr. Fink, are we going to do *any* work today? Throw that ACE comb with all the missing teeth away and let's start anew!" Bob looked up and said, "Sure, what's the diff?" Polly just stared him down, so he quickly jumped up and started fixing Farrah's hair with a new comb. "*Darling*, just try this on for me," Polly whispered as she put Farrah in a grey cashmere hooded sweatshirt. I could tell that Farrah was feeling a little insecure that day—maybe it was because her hairdresser was sound asleep and her photographer was so nervous he could barely lift the camera. I watched Polly talk to her in such a warm, intimate way—like a mother, with lots of encouragement. This naturally gave Farrah the strength and presence to feel special in front of the camera. Taking my leave of Polly, I knelt down and looked into Farrah's eyes. We smiled at each other, and when she grabbed my hand gently as I held the camera, I could literally feel her icy fingers get warm. I started taking pictures, when suddenly Polly said, "*Dear* Bruce, step over here for a moment and *see what I'm seeing*." Even though I was young and a bit headstrong, I was hungry to learn and knew that I had the best professor in the business. So I stood next to Polly and pointed my camera down at what she was seeing. Damn, she was right! Farrah's head, her chest, her hips, made a beautiful composition like a Noguchi sculpture. The day passed too quickly, for I wanted to learn more.

Years later, as we sat in her living room, I said, "Polly, your garden looks like a beautiful green-on-green wardrobe—a different shade for the sweater, the pants, the shirt, the overcoat... and let's not forget the hat! It looks like it was tailor-made in Ireland." We laughed, and for that moment I was sitting next to her at a fashion show, and she was the only person in the room standing up, applauding and yelling, "Bravo! Bravo!" Polly once said, "It is a privilege to be able to do what we do. Always remember to be a good sport and be humble—and know that someday you have to give that privilege back. It belongs to the madding crowd." —*Bruce Weber, Montauk, New York, 2012*

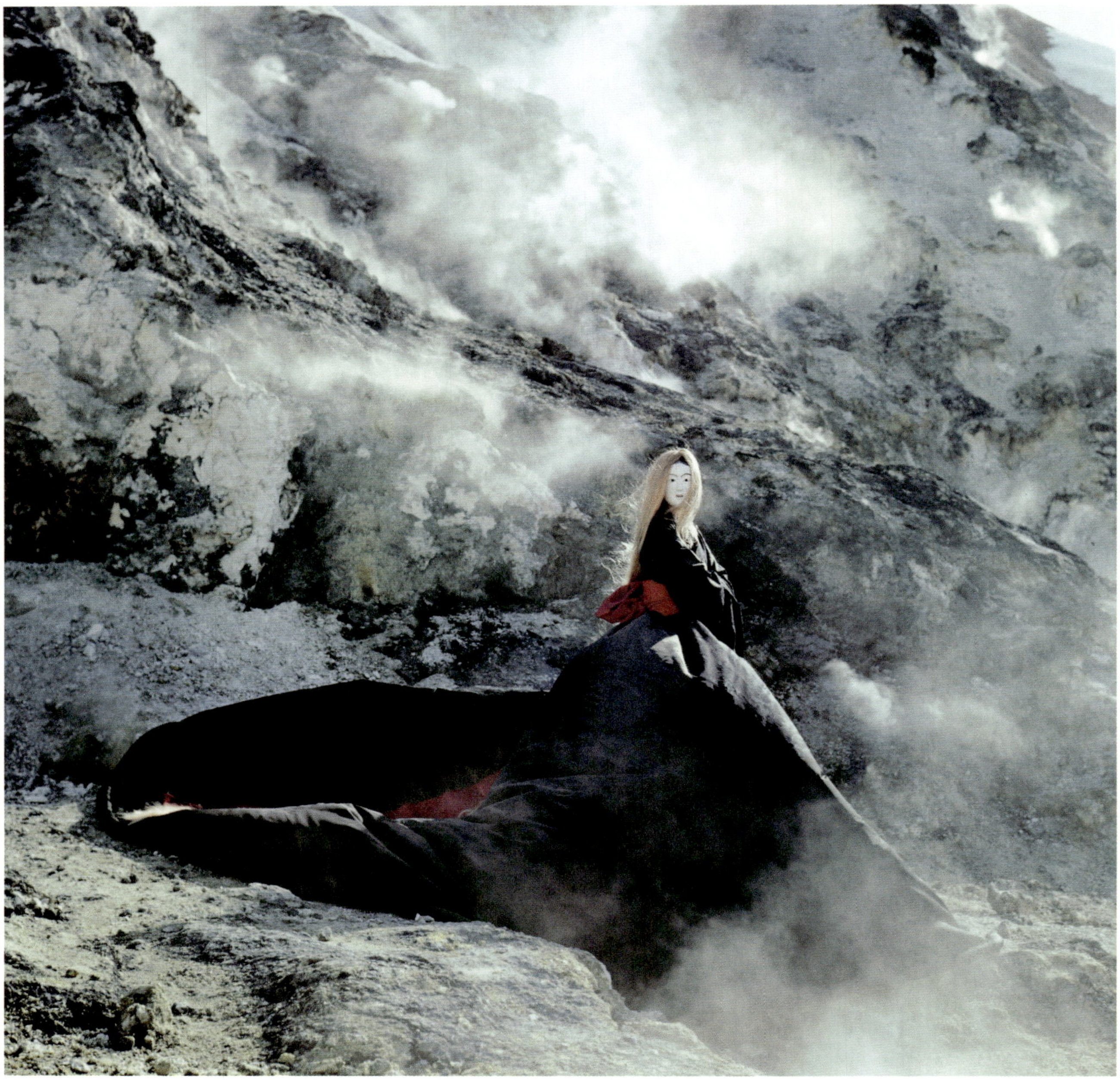

**WHEN I STARTED WORKING AT *VOGUE*,** the first shoot I went on was to Japan with Dick Avedon and Veruschka. It meant I didn't have a friend at *Vogue*, because everyone was wondering why I got the plum shoot when I was the new girl—I had just come from *Harper's Bazaar*. Two editors had gone to Mrs. Vreeland to complain, so I said to her, "I feel a certain hostility, and it's getting very hard for me." Mrs. Vreeland looked me straight in the eye and said, "Who needs friends right now? Right now you just go out and you do what I know what you can do." She believed in me, so I had to put it behind me, and went for five weeks to Japan.

It was a huge privilege, that whole trip, and I just immersed myself in it. That's the way you take things further and learn. We went to a sumo wrestling stable to find a man who could work with Veruschka. We went to a tea house where you spend the night, and then we went to a monastery. I didn't get up for first prayers but I got up for second prayers at 5 o'clock in the morning. At one point in Hokkaido, we were up on a cliff, with the Japan Sea on one side and Russia on the other. We suddenly heard this wonderful a cappella chanting. A group of women came marching over the hill with straw wrapped around their feet and navy and white fabric draped around their bodies in different ways. It was the chicest thing I'd ever seen, and all of a sudden they took everything off. Underneath they wore white gauze, and it was wrapped around their heads too. They had obviously been greased with something because the gauze was sticking to them. The women went out onto a rock ledge in the wintertime and dove into the sea—they were pearl divers. It was simply fantastic. —*Polly Mellen*

ABOVE AND LEFT: VERUSCHKA, JAPAN, FEBRUARY 1966. PHOTOGRAPHS BY RICHARD AVEDON

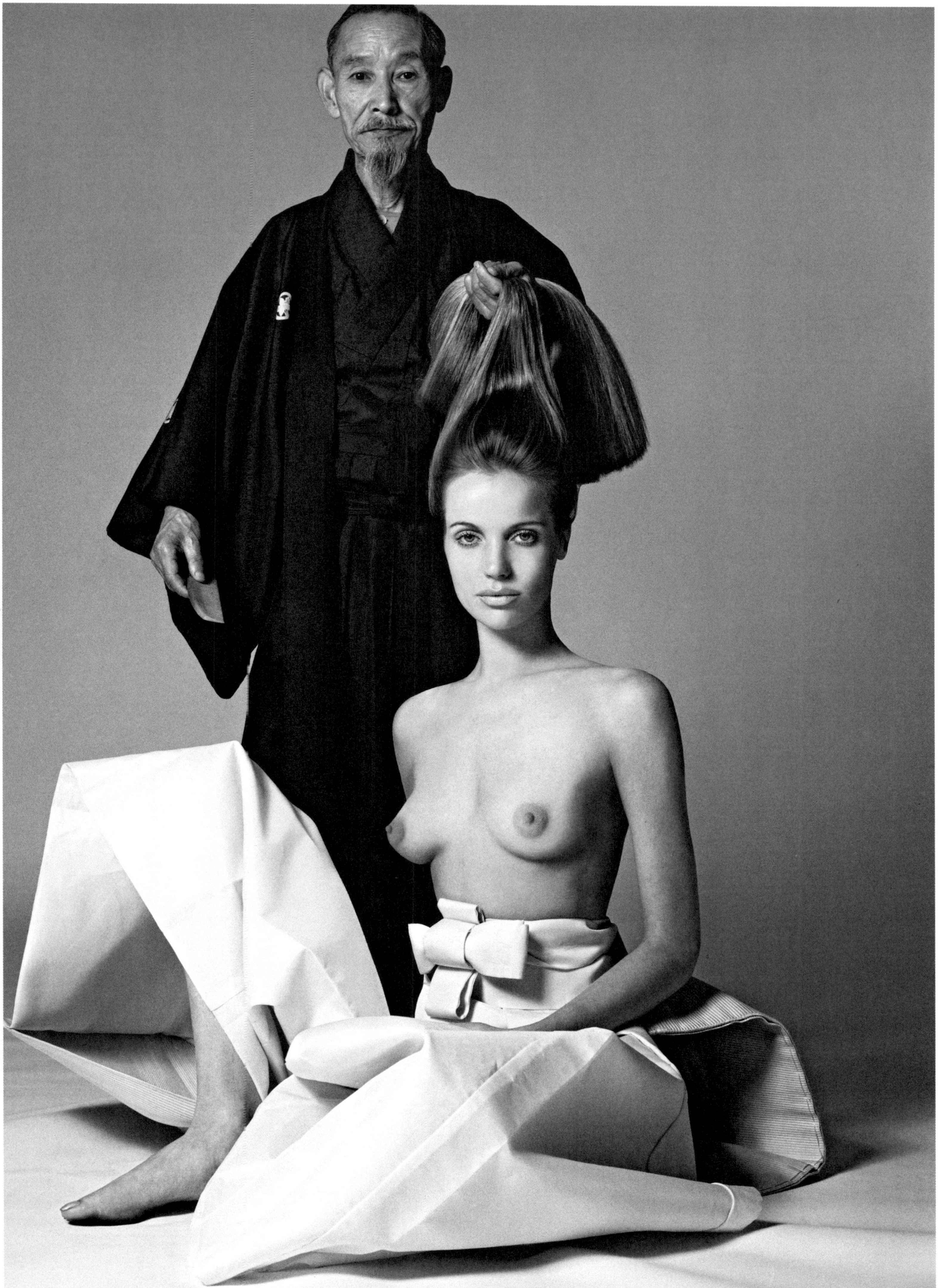

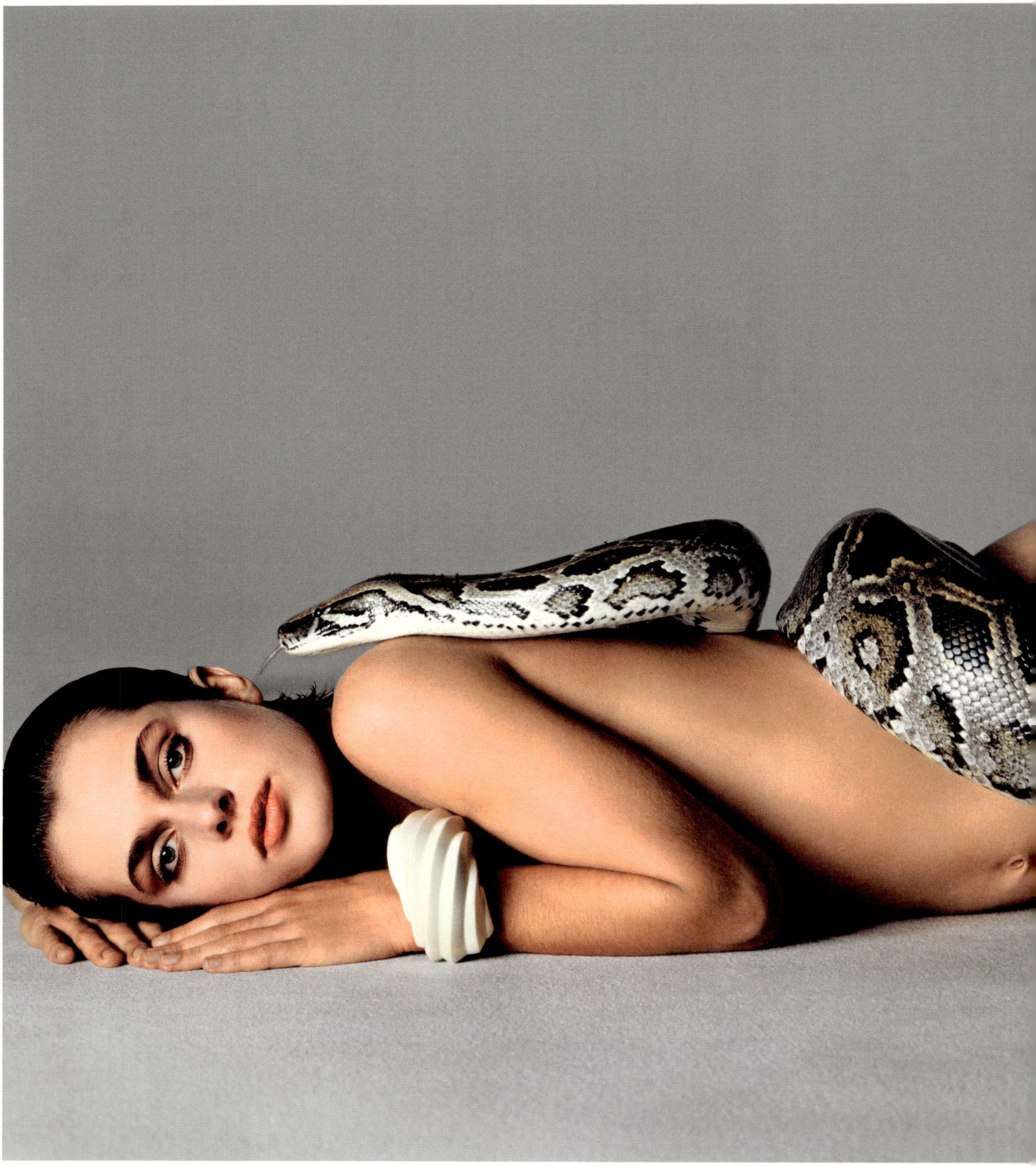

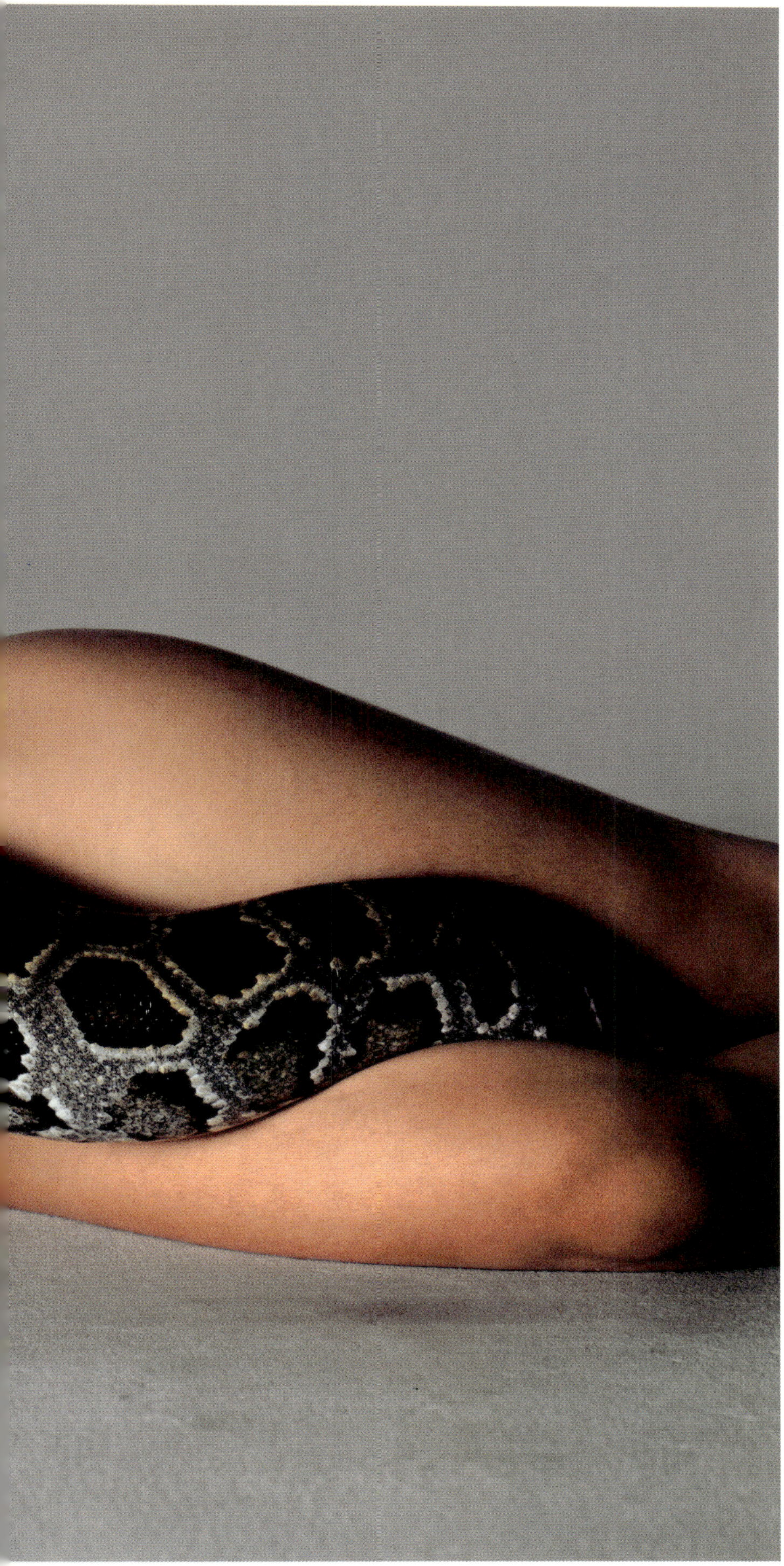

*An excerpt from Polly Mellen's conversation with Nicolas Ghesquière.*

GHESQUIÈRE: I think, in your work with Avedon, you invented a new kind of fashion picture.

MELLEN: Starting with Nastassja Kinski.

GHESQUIÈRE: Exactly.

MELLEN: No clothes. I wish I hadn't even put that bracelet on her.

GHESQUIÈRE: [laughs] Now today you want to take off the bracelet? I love that! I think that image you made with Avedon was one of the most remarkable ever.

MELLEN: You couldn't imagine being there. I mean, the snake kissed her! The snake wound up her little naked body and put its tongue in her ear, and the picture was done. I couldn't believe what I was seeing. The snake had been defanged, so there was no worry on that stance.

GHESQUIÈRE: But it was a big snake!

MELLEN: I loved it. I held it, which was a very erotic feeling. Have you ever held a snake? Well, let me tell you, it is so erotic.

NASTASSJA KINSKI. PHOTOGRAPH BY RICHARD AVEDON

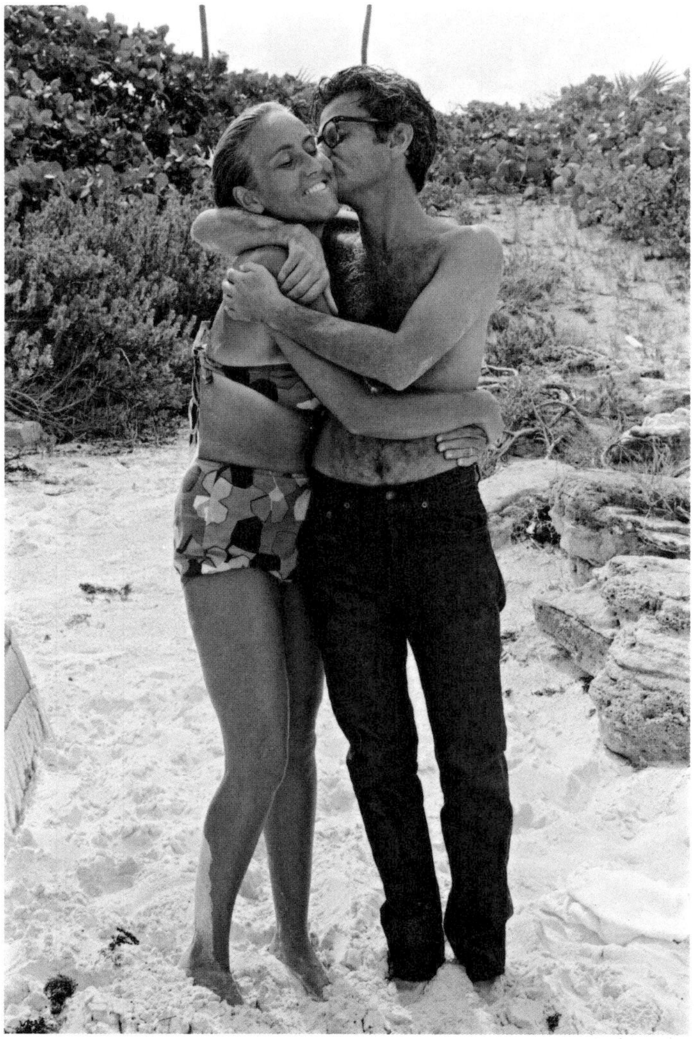

**POLLY MAKES A GORGEOUS FUSS,** and out of that sweet commotion comes the most precise order. She's funny about serious things and serious about button holes. She once said of a designer, "Dick, the man was a genius. There used to be mystery in every button hole, but now there isn't a secret in the whole goddamn place!"

Polly is the lion in the path. No one passes Polly, no one will surpass her. There will be sittings and studios for a long while, but there will never be another Polly Mellen. From Vreeland's rib came Polly Mellen, and from that day on, Eden never looked better."

*—Richard Avedon, presenting Polly's CFDA Lifetime Achievement Award*

ABOVE: POLLY MELLEN AND RICHARD AVEDON, GREAT EXUMA, THE BAHAMAS, OCTOBER 1988
RIGHT: LAUREN HUTTON AND ALAN LEWIS, GREAT EXUMA, THE BAHAMAS, OCTOBER 1988

PHOTOGRAPHS BY RICHARD AVEDON

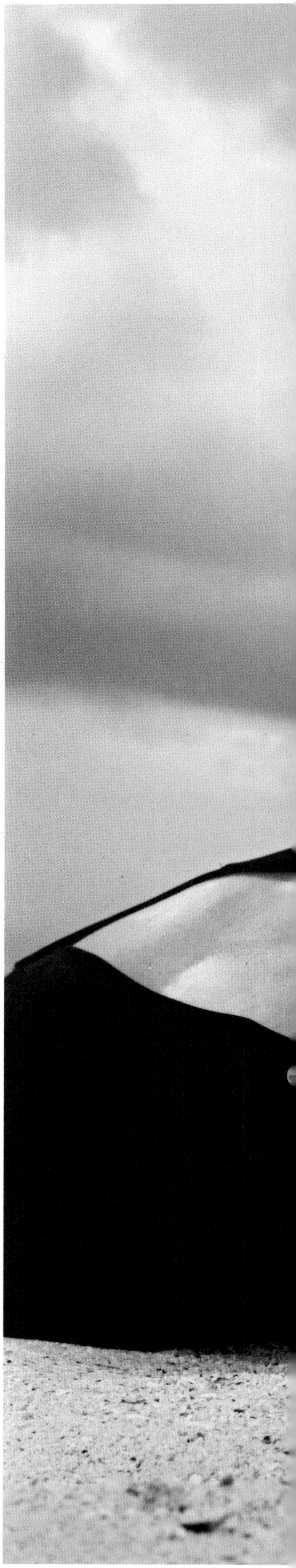

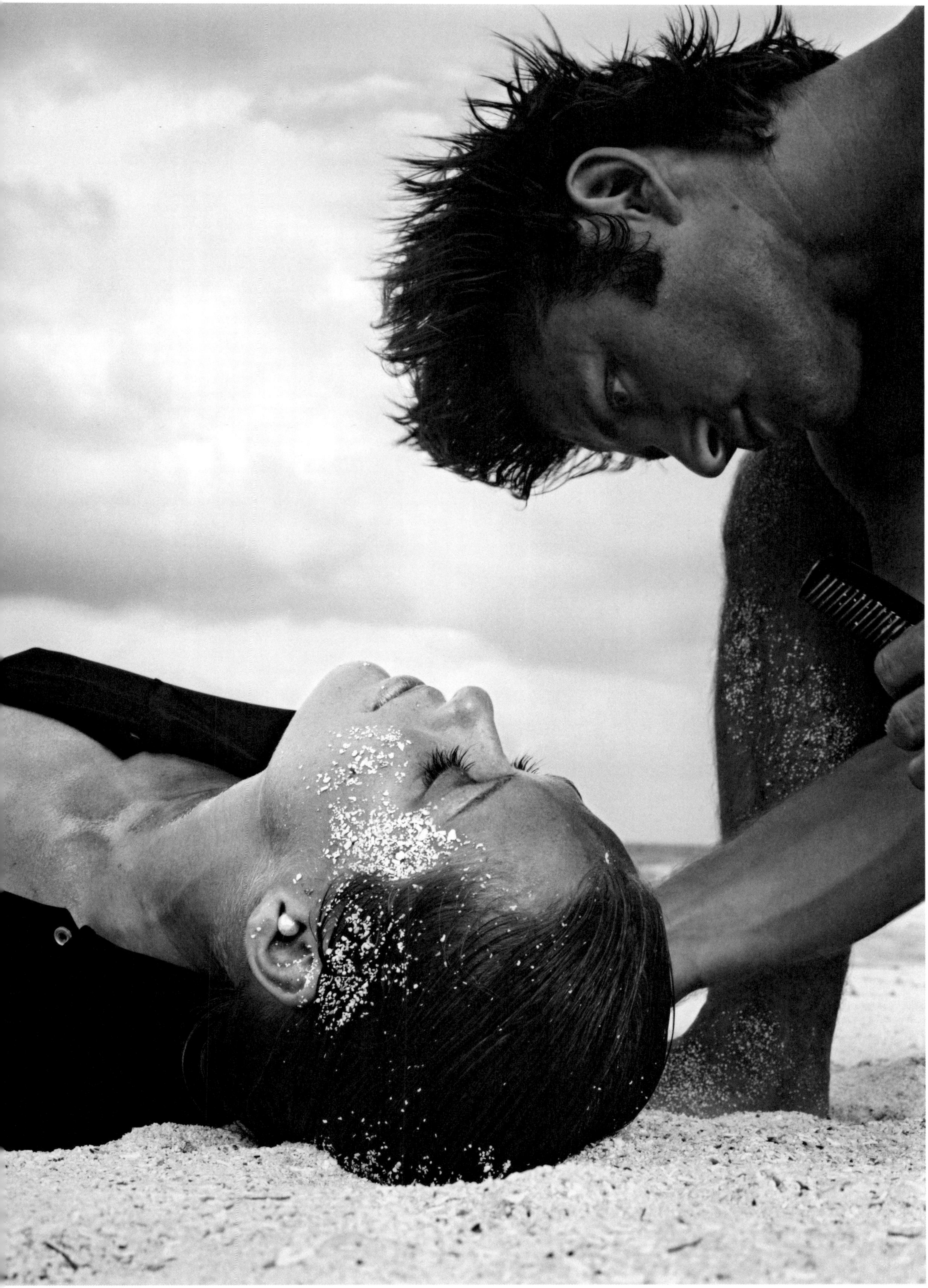

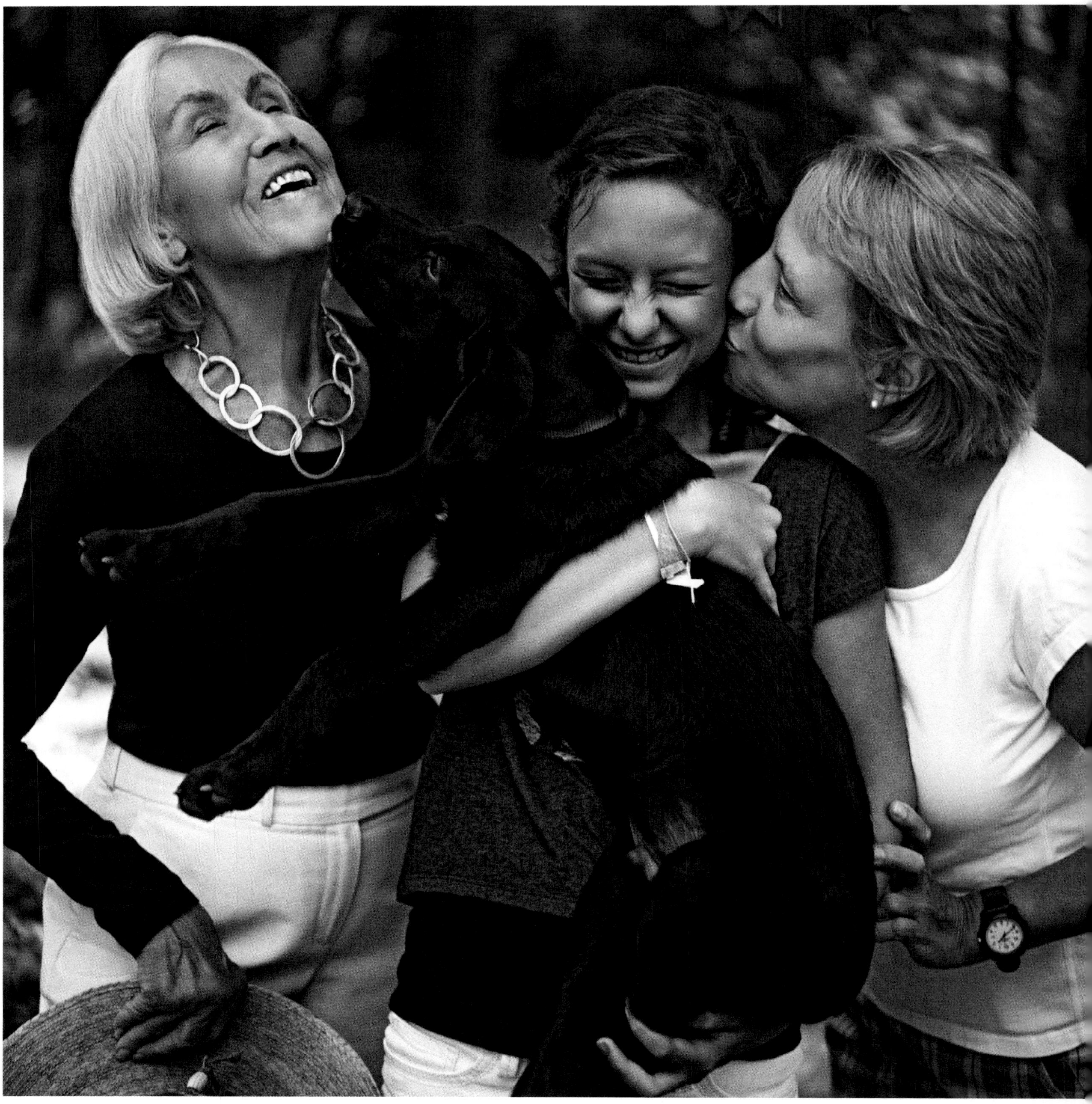

**YOU JUST CAN'T STOP DISCOVERING,** whatever it is, and you have to be open to it. Something very interesting happened to me the other day. I was at lunch with my granddaughter Molly (*pictured above*) at a special place called the Golden Wok, because we love the sushi. Molly had just returned from camp and had the terrible experience of losing her dog—the time had come for Bevy to be put down. But her new puppy came along with us, and as we sat there chatting, Molly said, "You know, I think I'm a little strange." I asked, "What makes you think you're strange?" She replied, "Well, I want to change my name." "You do?" "I don't really want to change my name, I just want to change the spelling to 'Mollie.'" I thought, *That's interesting.* It showed me individuality and personality and a little bit of daring. I think those things are very important to continue growing. It's very brave to do at 13, just at the beginning of everything. —*Polly Mellen*

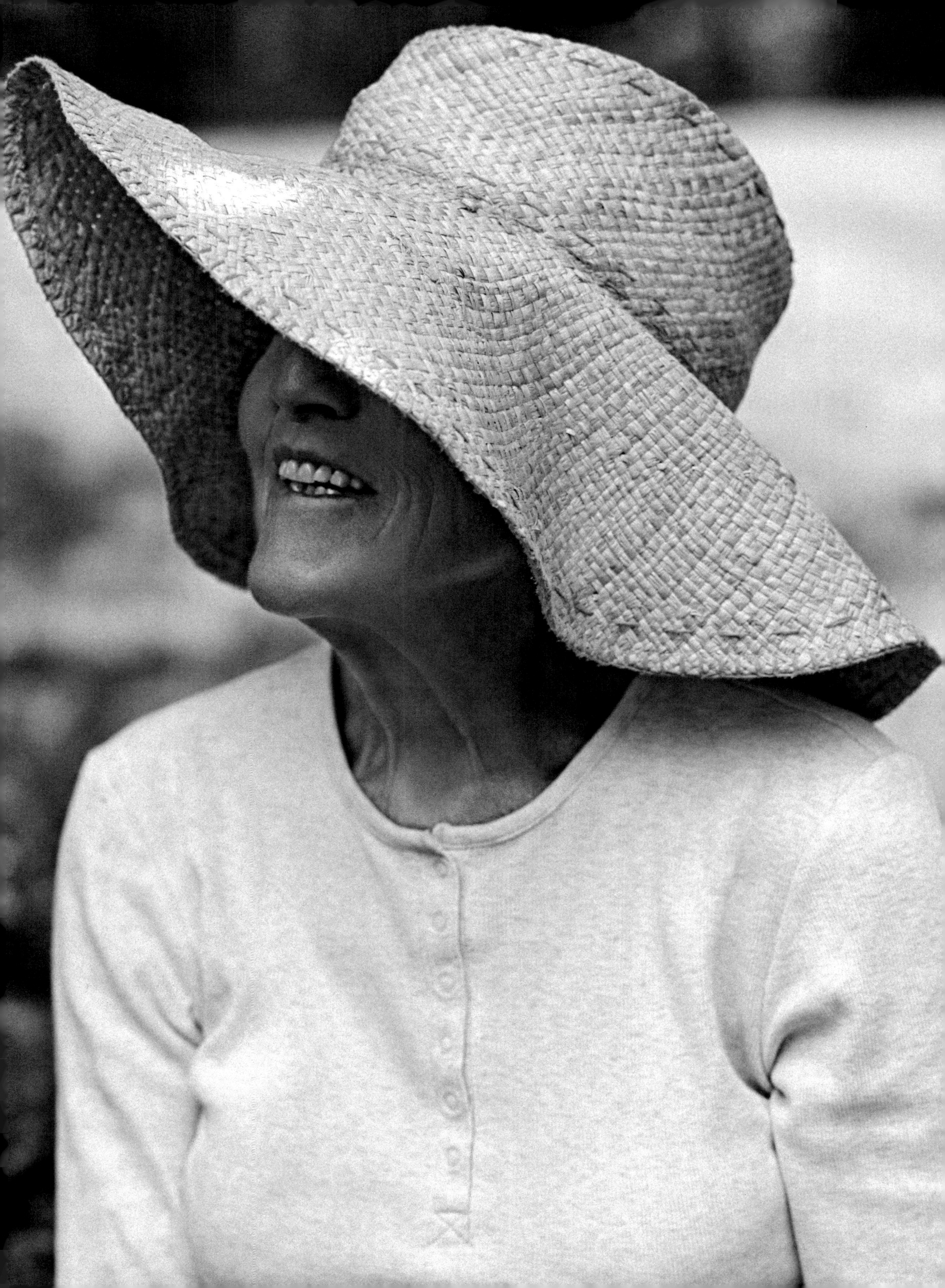

**PETER KEATING, THAT BAD BOY!** We did a shoot together with Helmut in Saint-Tropez called the "Story of Ohh." I said to him, "Peter, your hair! It's getting a little thin up top." He told me, "Polly, grass never grows on a busy street." We gave a party afterwards for Helmut in our apartment in New York. Peter said to him, "Thank you, Helmut, for making me one of your white women."

I think if Helmut were alive today, he would be exploring whatever the new thing might be. I mean, think of him—a photographer who got so disenchanted one time with a model who cancelled yet again that he said, "I'm not using models, I'm going to use mannequins." And then he did—he used store dummies. He had such an interesting mind. That model who cancelled took him so far away from what he'd ever done before. Photography is like exploring, and Helmut understood that. Nobody took pictures like him. —*PM*

PHOTOGRAPHS BY HELMUT NEWTON

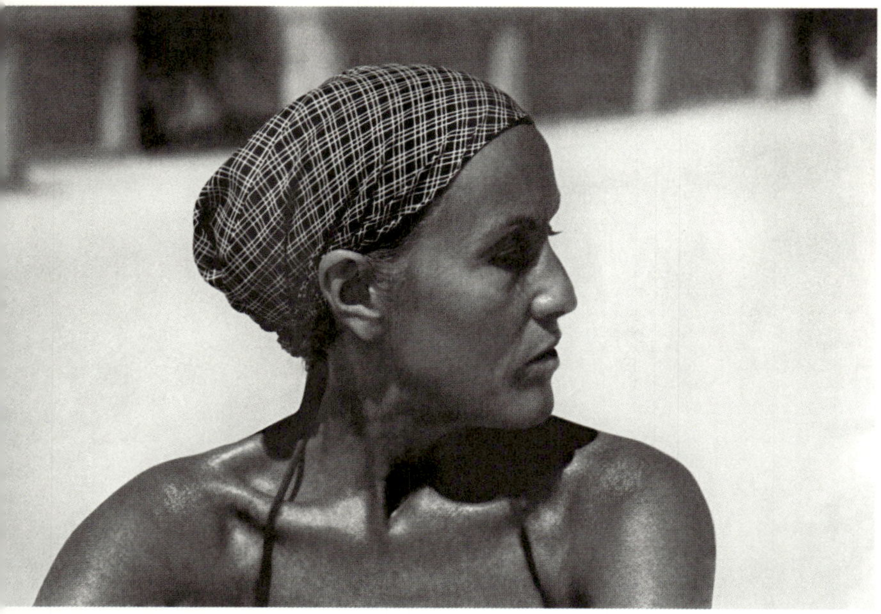

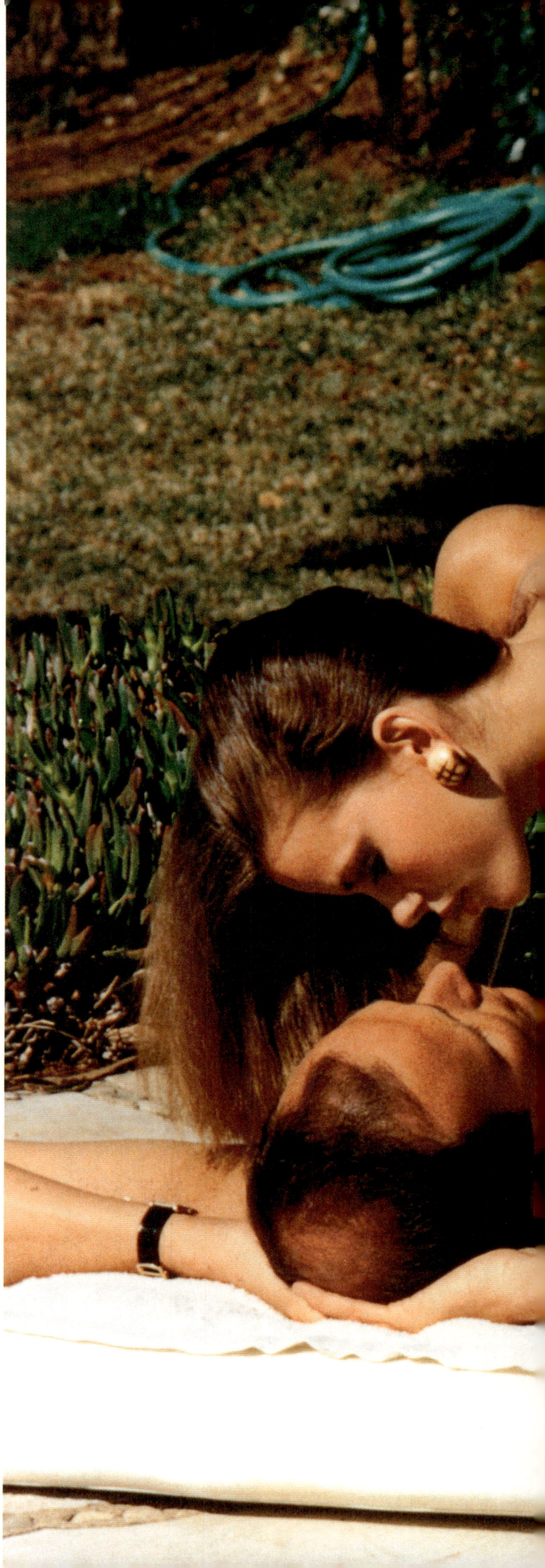

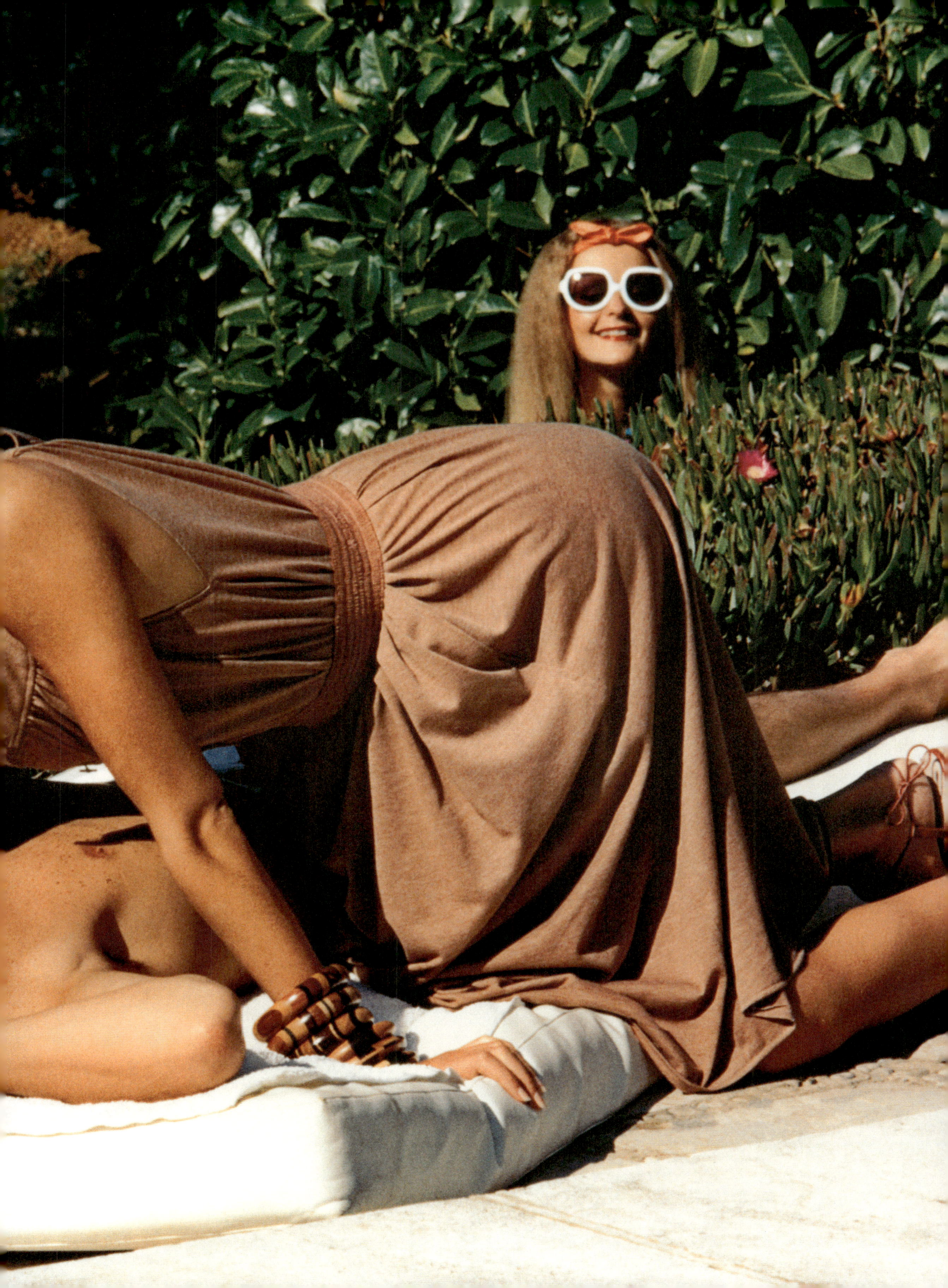

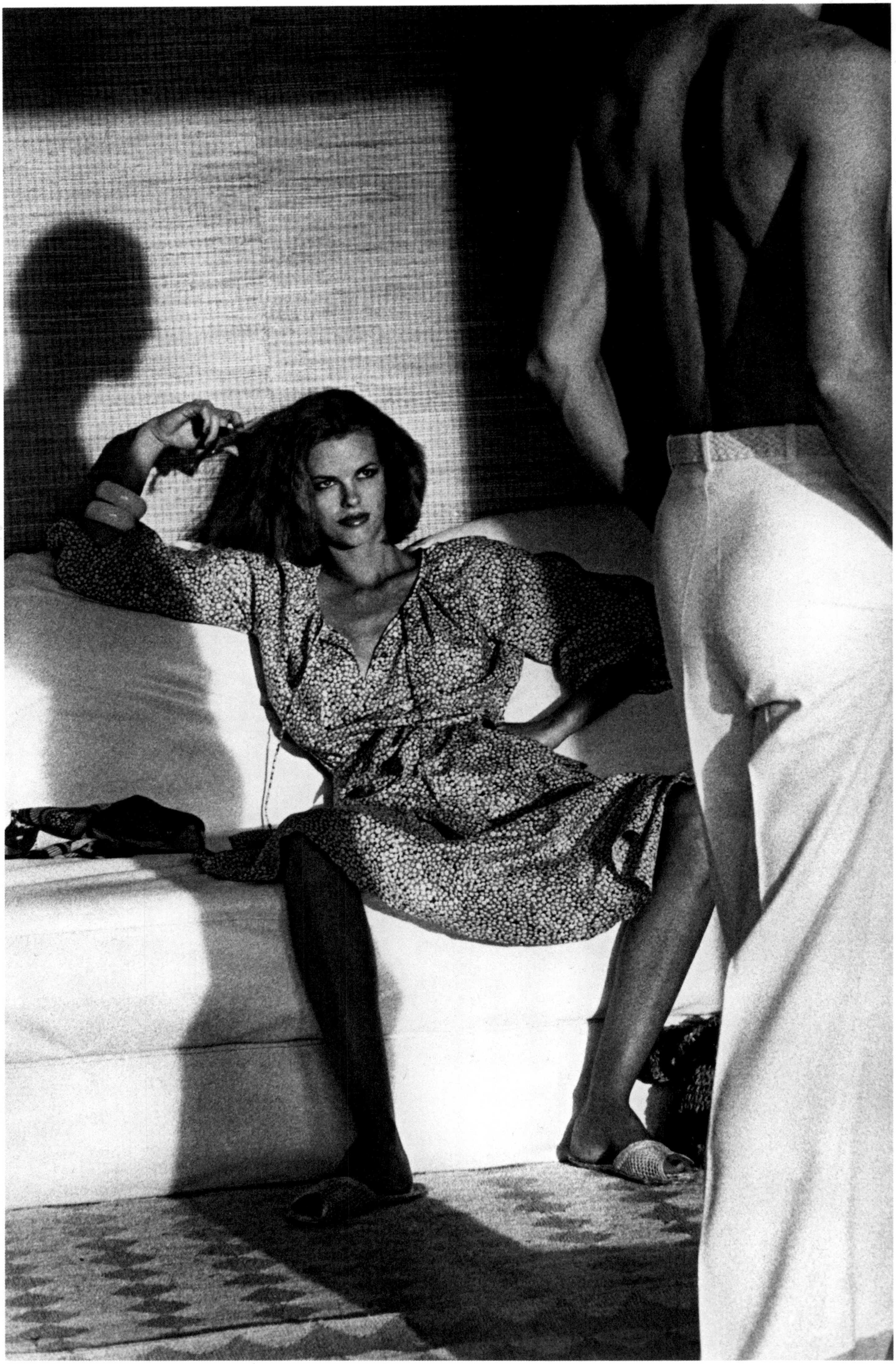

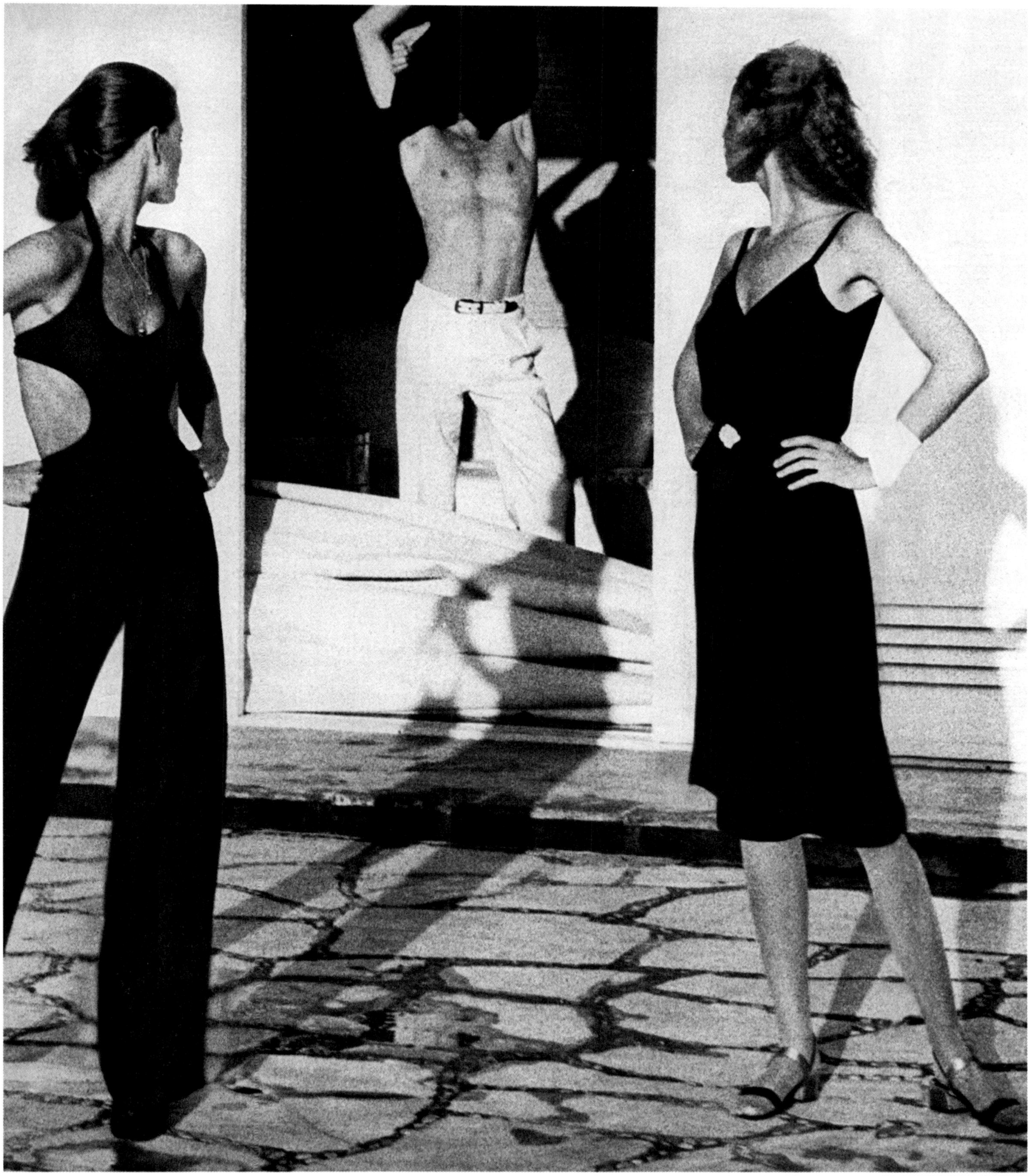

"Polly loved how I was sitting like a man on the couch. I was really just tired of waiting for Helmut to take my photograph. I guess I was a little spoiled." —*Lisa Taylor, remembering the "Story of Ohh" sitting*

"When I first met Mrs. Mellen I didn't like her and she wasn't very nice to me—always making me go into the fashion closet to look for this and that. But once I let her know I wasn't afraid anymore she brought me into her world and taught me everything I know. I ended up loving her, and I think of her even today as a force of nature." —*Helen Murray*

PHOTOGRAPHS BY HELMUT NEWTON

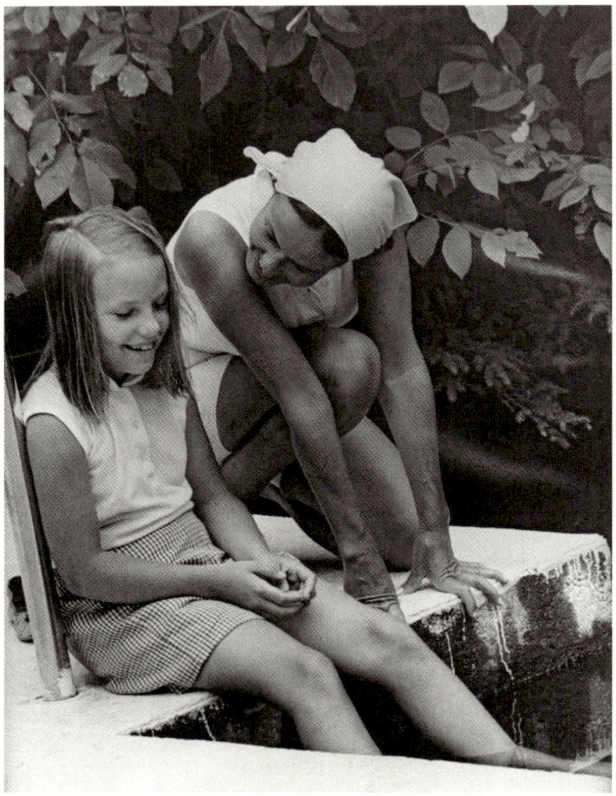

WITH LESLIE BELL, HER DAUGHTER, IN BERNARDSVILLE, NJ

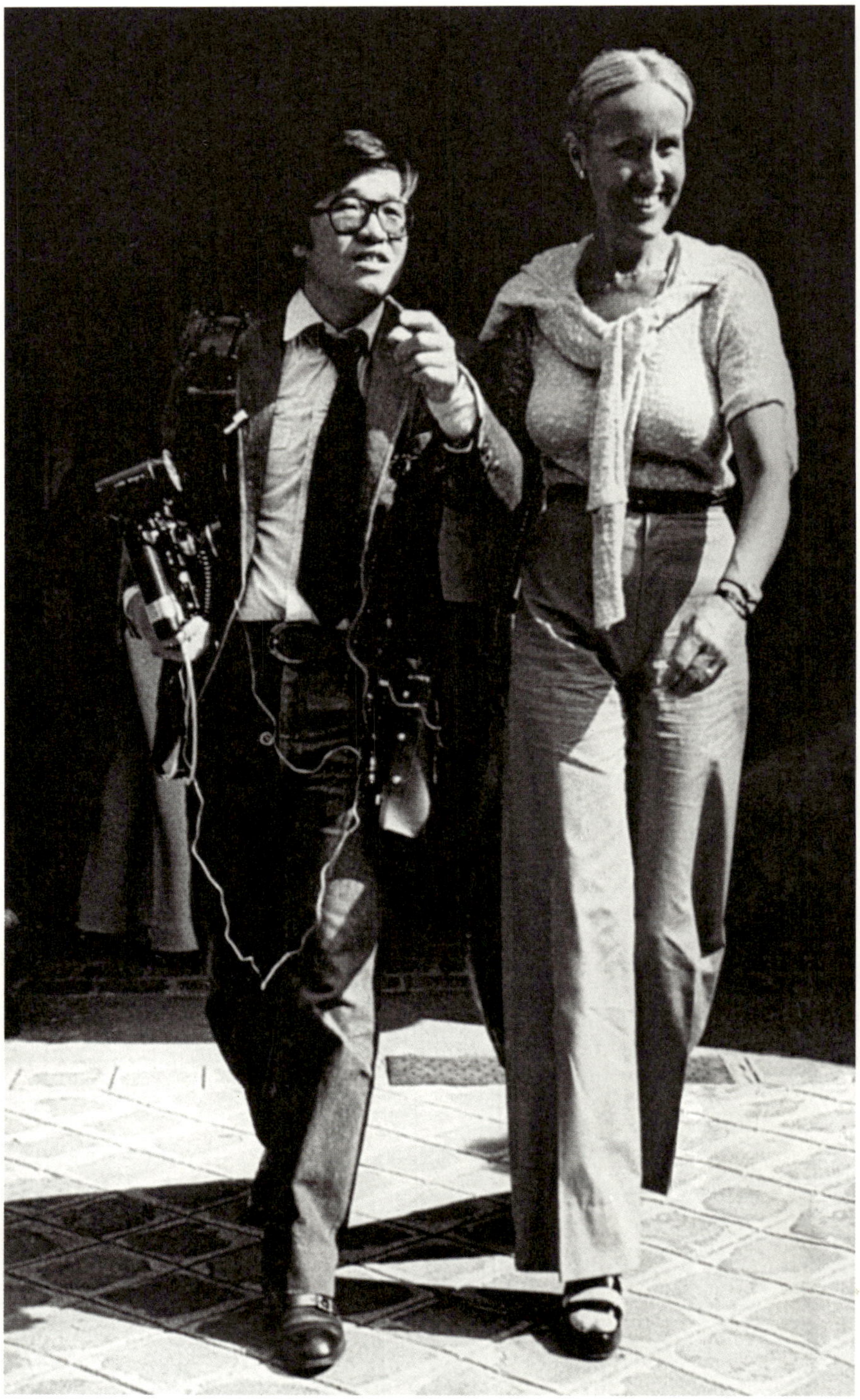

WITH HIRO, HEADED TO POLLY'S FAMILY HOME AT THE MILL REEF CLUB

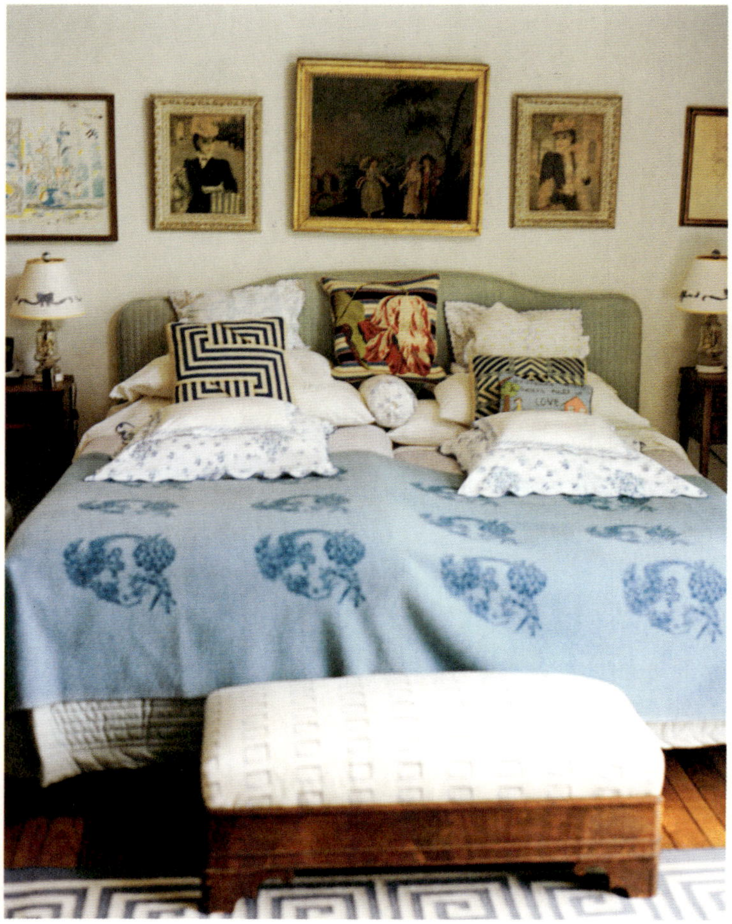

When Dick saw this room, he threw himself down on the bed and cried, "I found the place to have my nervous breakdown." I told him, "Get up dear, because if anyone has a breakdown it's going to be your dear friend Polly. So just forget it!"—*PM*

IN JAMAICA—PHOTO BY LOUISE DAHL-WOLFE

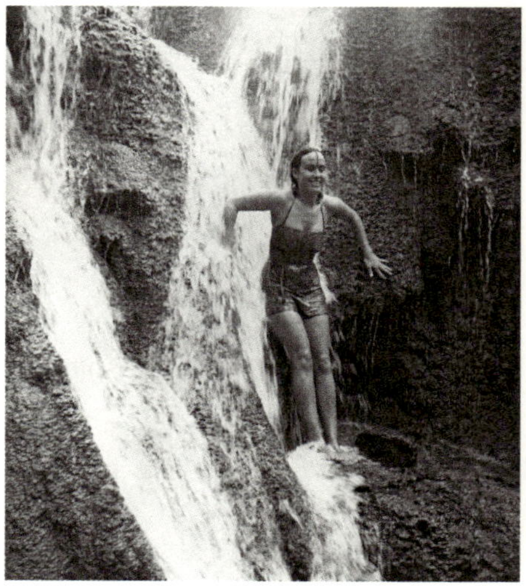

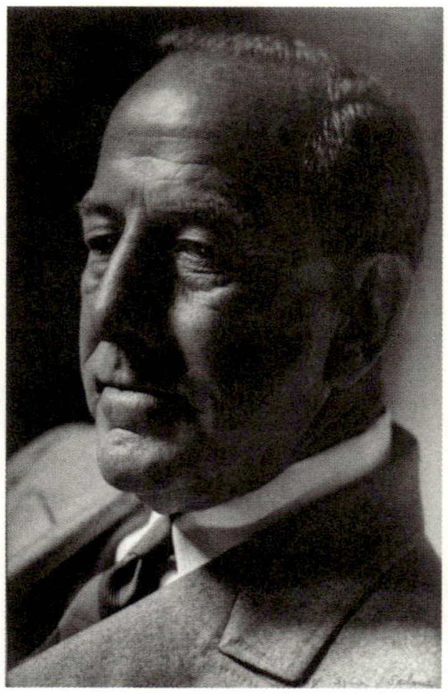

POLLY'S FATHER, WALTER B. ALLEN

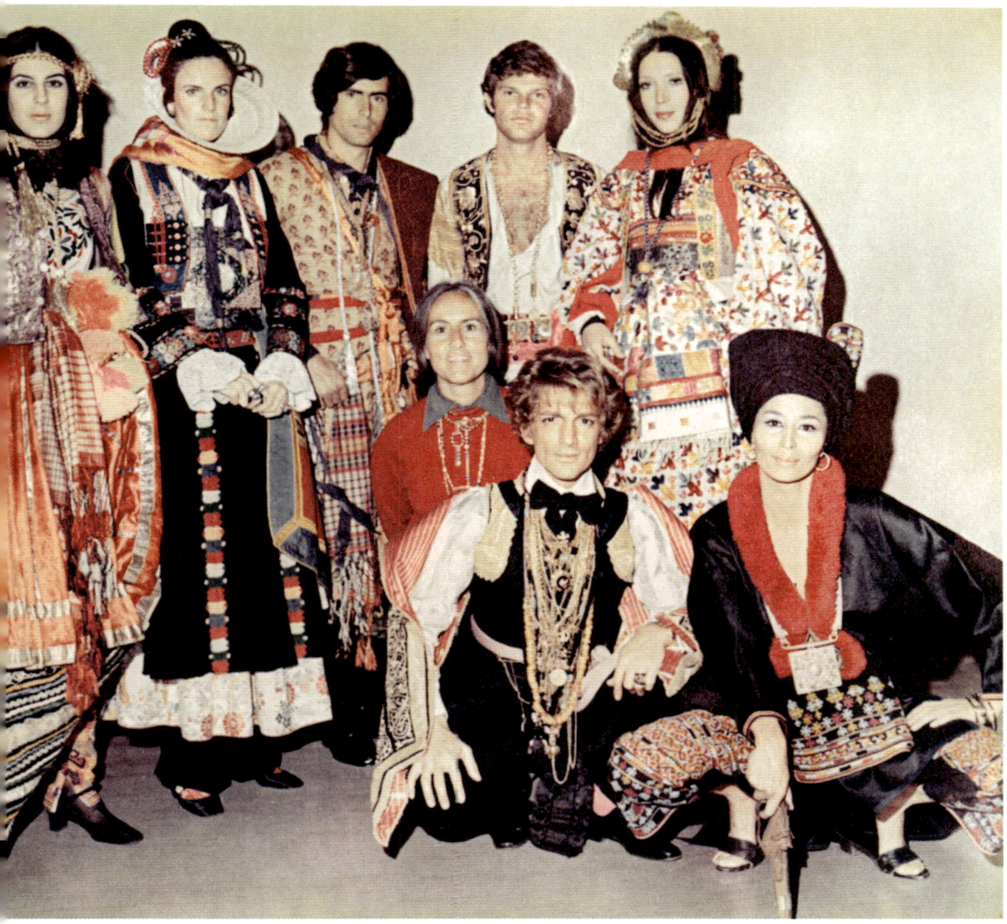

POLLY IN THE MIDDLE WITH FRIENDS AT A MET MUSEUM PARTY HOSTED BY DIANA VREELAND
FRONT ROW FROM LEFT: GIORGIO DI SANT' ANGELO, CHINA MACHADO / BACK ROW FROM LEFT: UNKNOWN, KEZIA KEEBLE, ALEX VALDEZ, EGON VON FÜRSTENBERG, MARINA SCHIANO

POLLY SKIING IN MÜRREN, SWITZERLAND

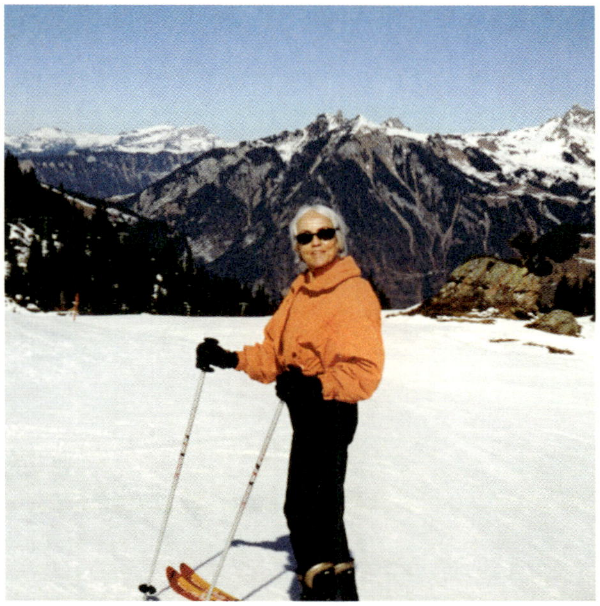

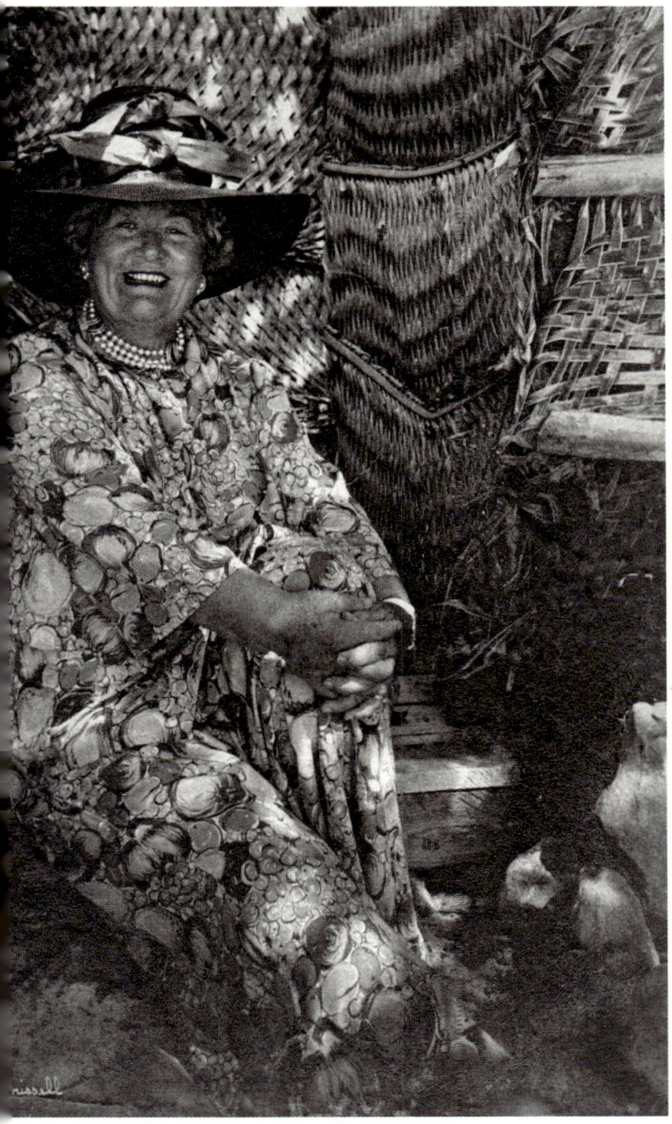

"At sunset at the Mill Reef Club in Antigua you could always find Polly's mother, Mrs. Allen (*pictured at left*), telling stories, surrounded by tons of children. She was one of the most wonderful people that I remember from my childhood."—*Lisa Taylor*

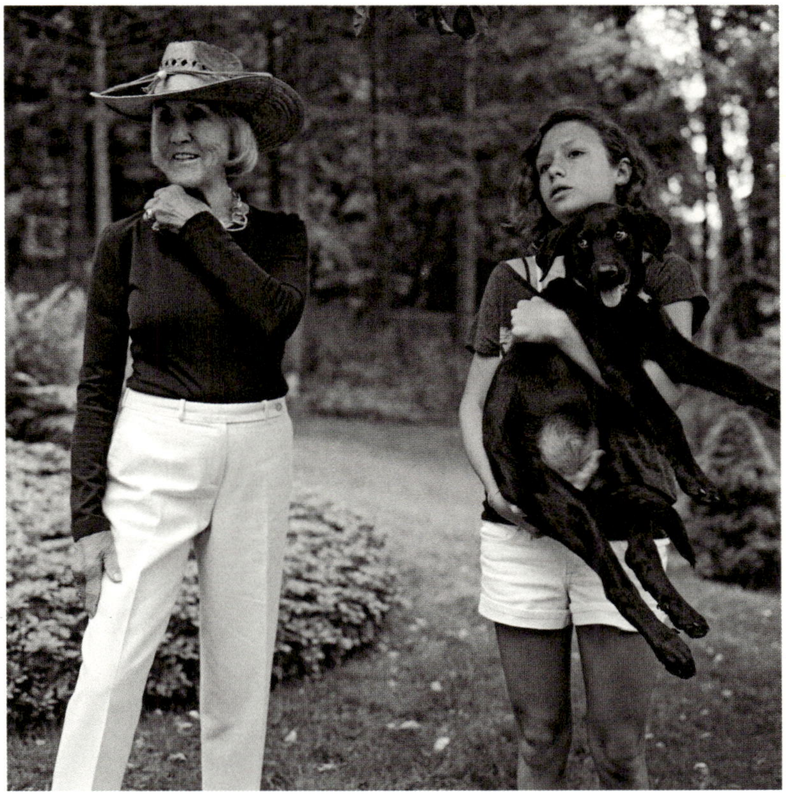

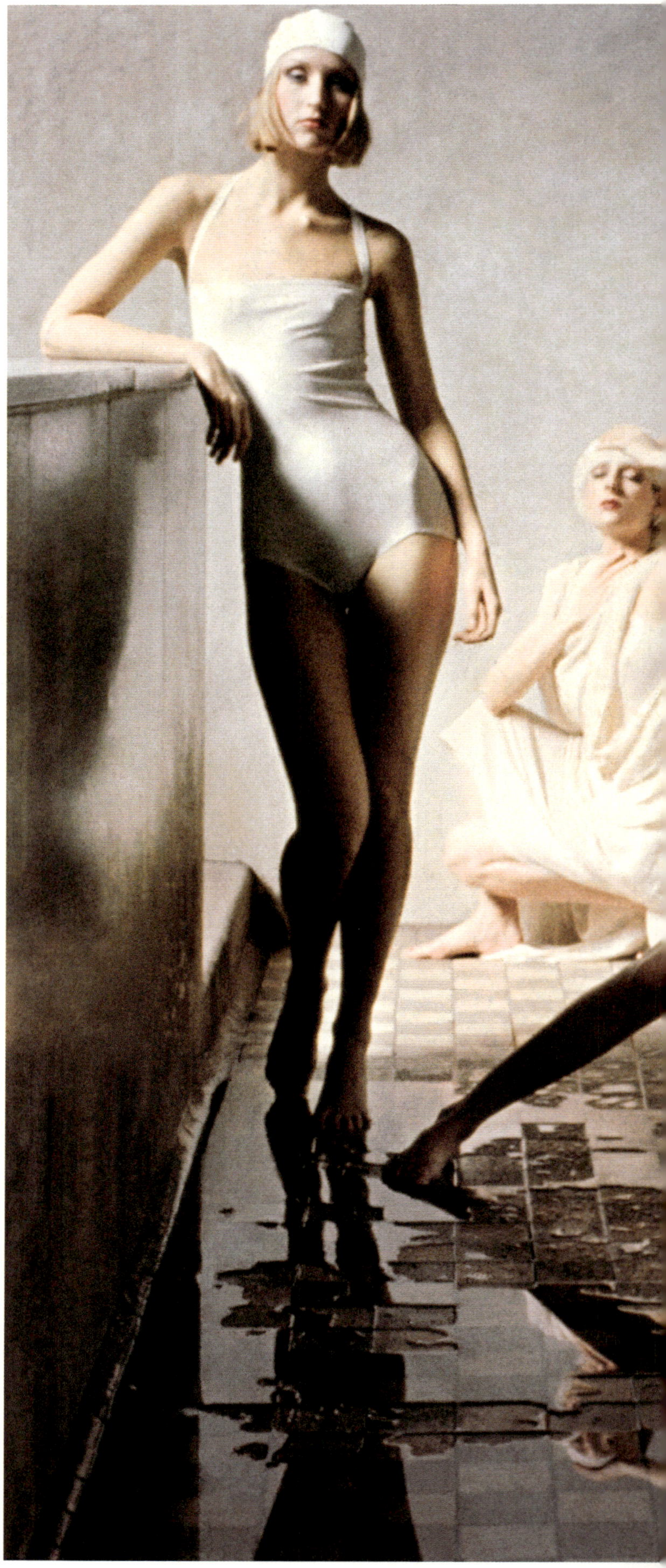

**WHEN DEBORAH'S PICTURES CAME IN,** people said, "This is not possible, we cannot publish them." I was there in the art department and Alexey Brodovitch said to me, "Go, Polly, get out." I left the building and went for a walk. When I got back, Alex had left a message to go and see him. I thought he was going to break it to me that they were killing the story, because I was extremely proud of the pictures.

He surprised me and said, "I don't want you to worry about anything, it's an incredible shoot. I'm so thrilled to have it for *Vogue*. It's going to be published and we'll just call it a feature or something." He was 100 percent for it. For me, all of it works. It's almost another kind of portraiture. It's the space between the figures and Deborah's positioning of them that are so important.

You have to know what your eye is trying to say. You give over to what you feel, if you're given the privilege of working with these kinds of talented women and men. —*PM*

PHOTOGRAPH BY DEBORAH TURBEVILLE

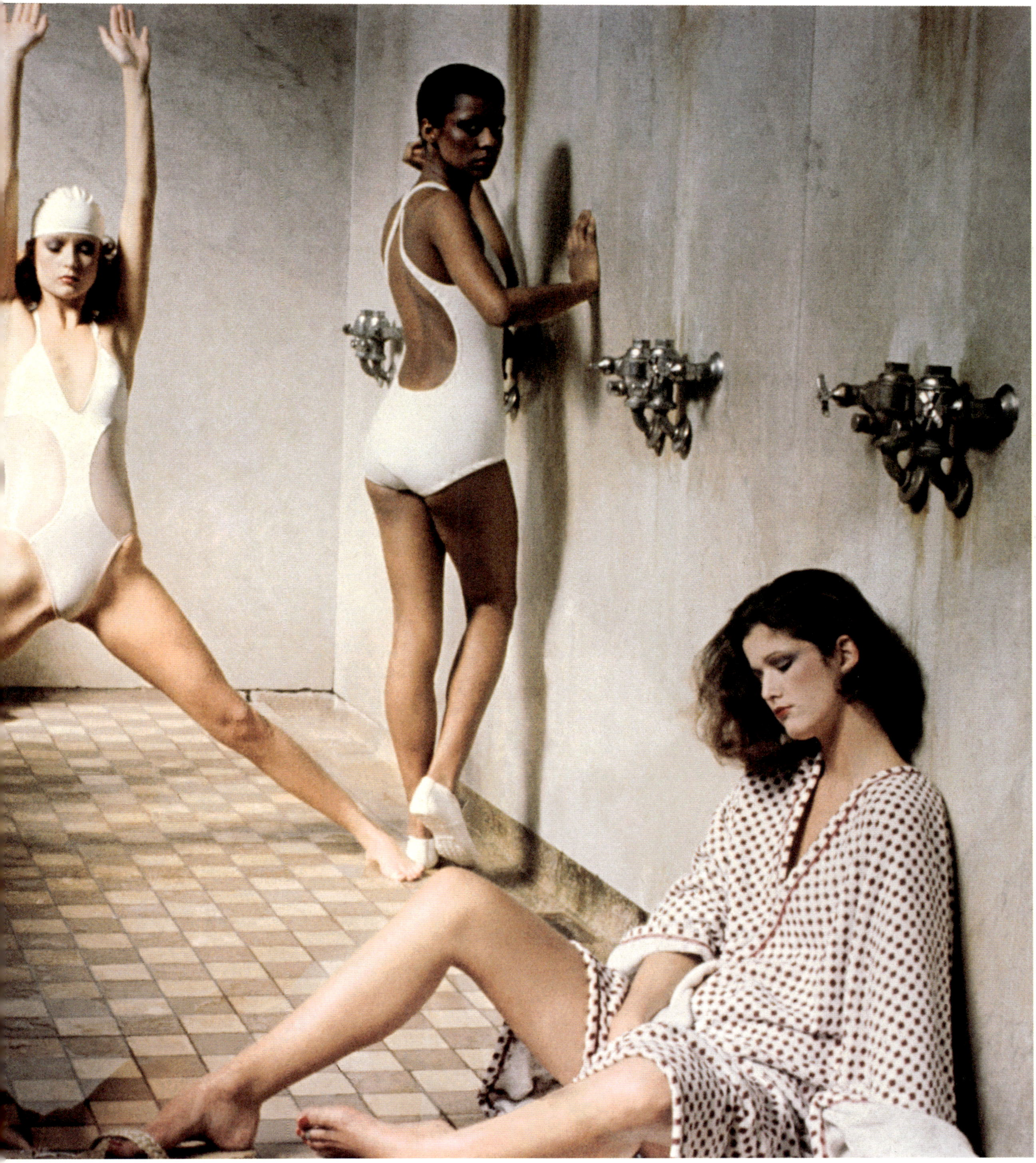

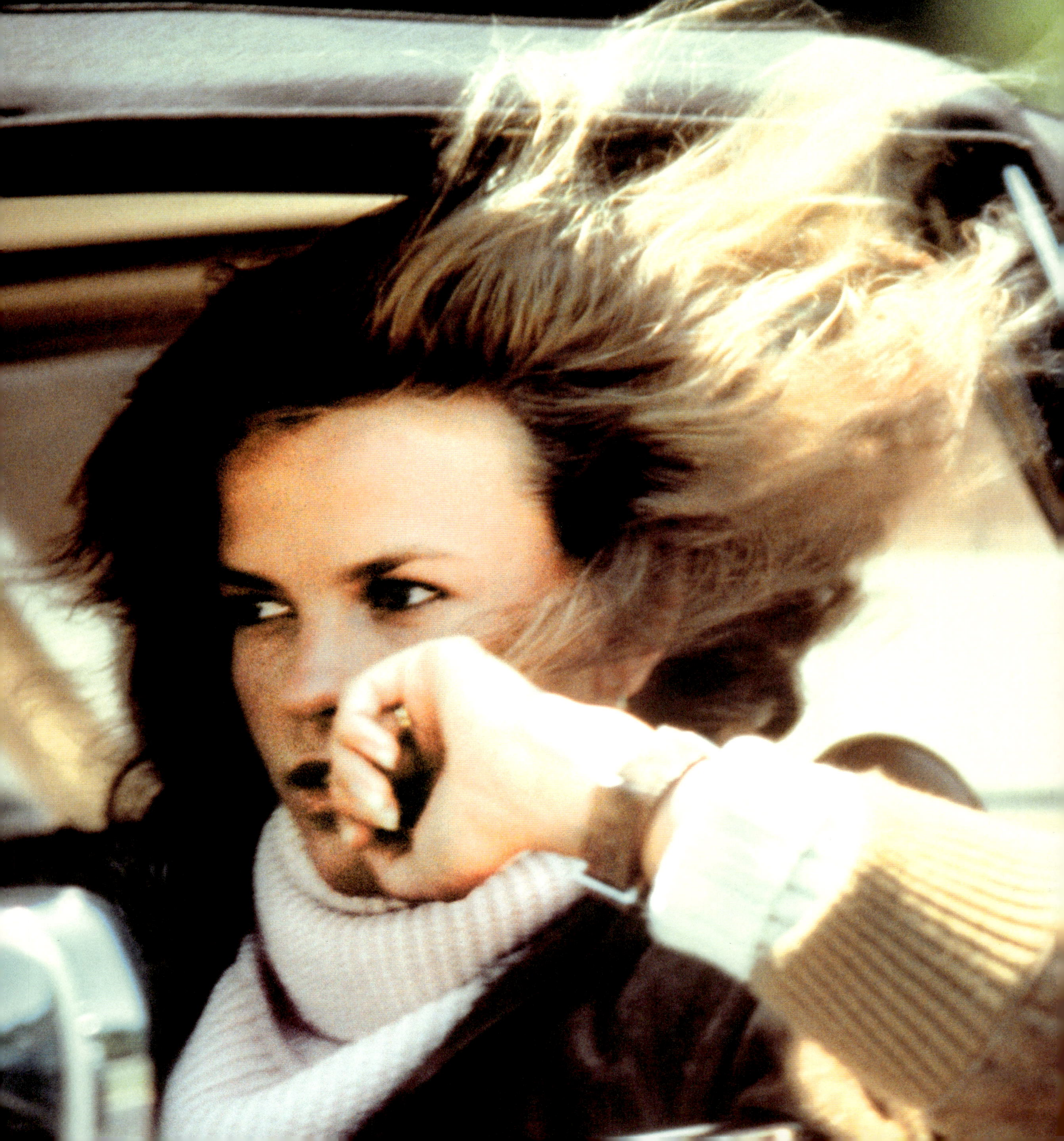

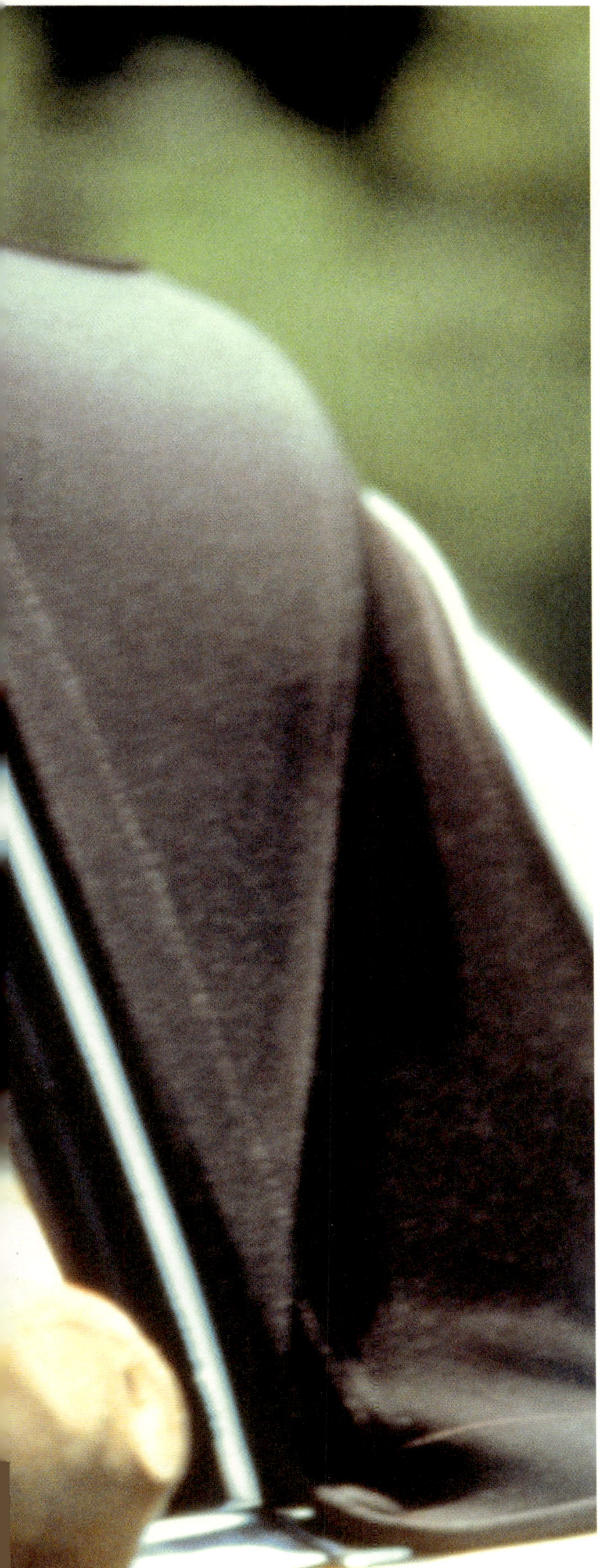

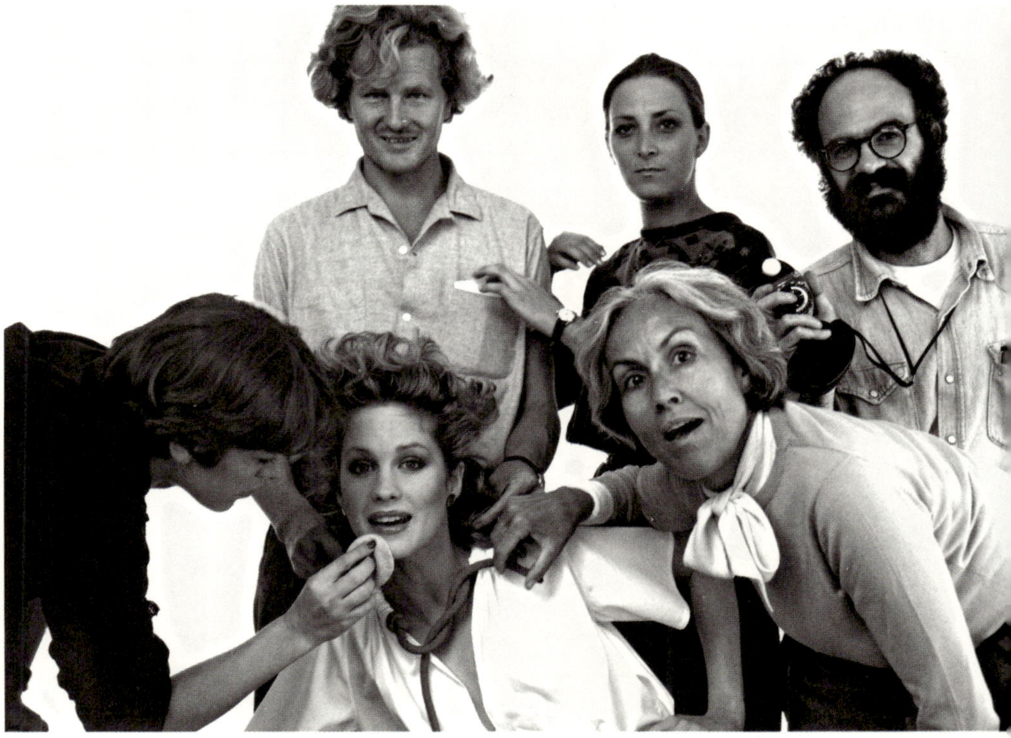

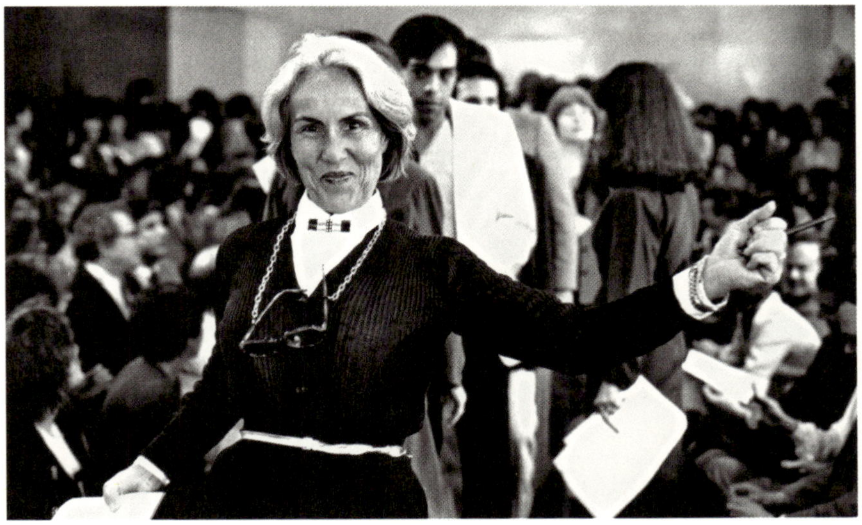

**WORKING WITH ARTHUR WAS ALWAYS A JOY.** He's such a great listener. Whenever we developed a project together he would be extremely enthusiastic from the start. In his pictures, Arthur was always dedicated to a certain kind of reality—he did lots of projects that were fanciful, but he always worked with natural light, whether on location or in the studio. I had such fun working with Arthur—he had this incredible studio on Grand Street and would always play wonderful music on his shoots. He is a jazz fiend, plays piano, and trumpet and—I can tell you from experience—he is a *great* person to dance with. —*PM*

PHOTOGRAPHS BY ARTHUR ELGORT

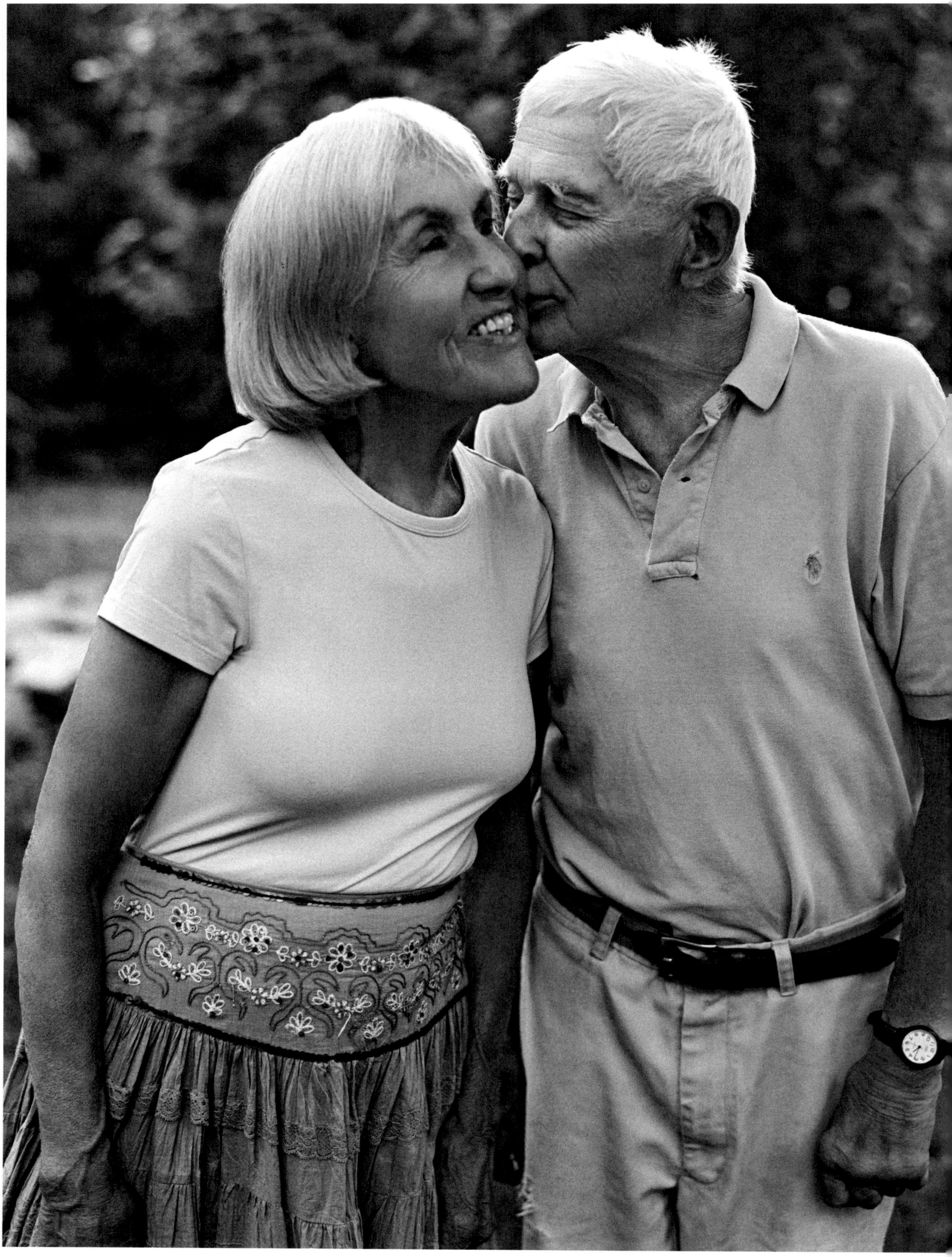

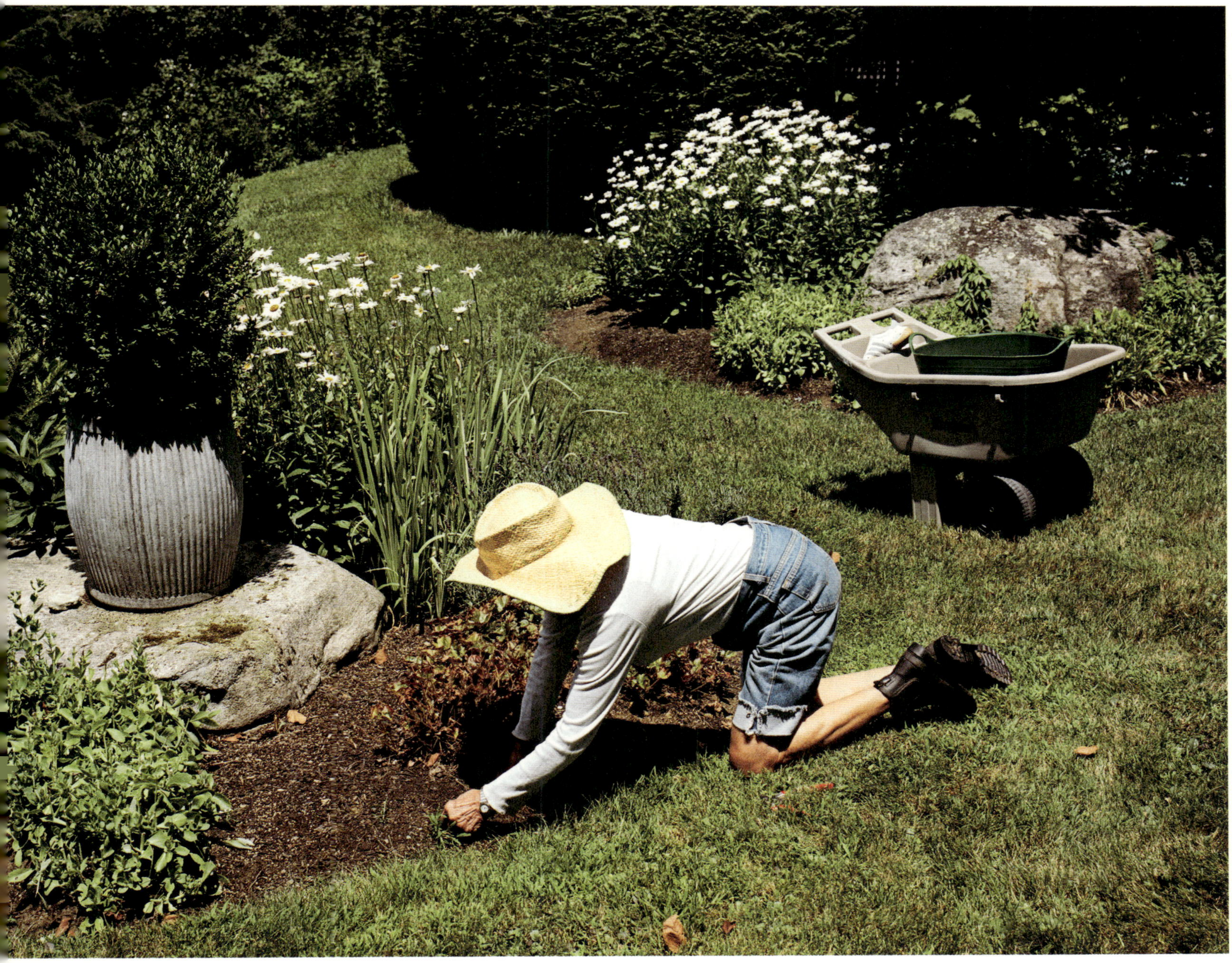

**HENRY LIKED MY SISTER PATTY,** so he took her out first. I married Louis Bell and had two children and lived on the Main Line in Philadelphia. That was a turbulent little marriage that lasted eight years. After my divorce, Mrs. Vreeland talked me into going back to *Harper's Bazaar.* I didn't really think I wanted to go back to fashion—I thought I wanted to do something *stronger.* She told me, "You have been gifted with a talent, Polly, and you owe something back to what you're lucky enough to have been given." So naturally I went back to *Harper's Bazaar.* Around that time, I got a phone call from Henry Mellen, who I had always had a little crush on. He said, "You've come back to New York City—so how is everything?" I thought he was going to ask me out, but he never did. So I thought, *To hell with him!* About a week later, Henry called again and asked, "How are you making out in New York City?" I said, "Henry, I'm making it out *just fine.* What do you want? Why don't you take me out to lunch or dinner?" "OK!" he said, and it accelerated from there, thank goodness. I gave a party for my mother, and Henry came and played the piano. The night ended and he started to leave, and I said, "Where are you going? Don't go yet." And we were married that January. He's my support system—he makes my breakfast and my dinner. We've been married for 47 years. He's a wonderful, gentle man. —*PM*

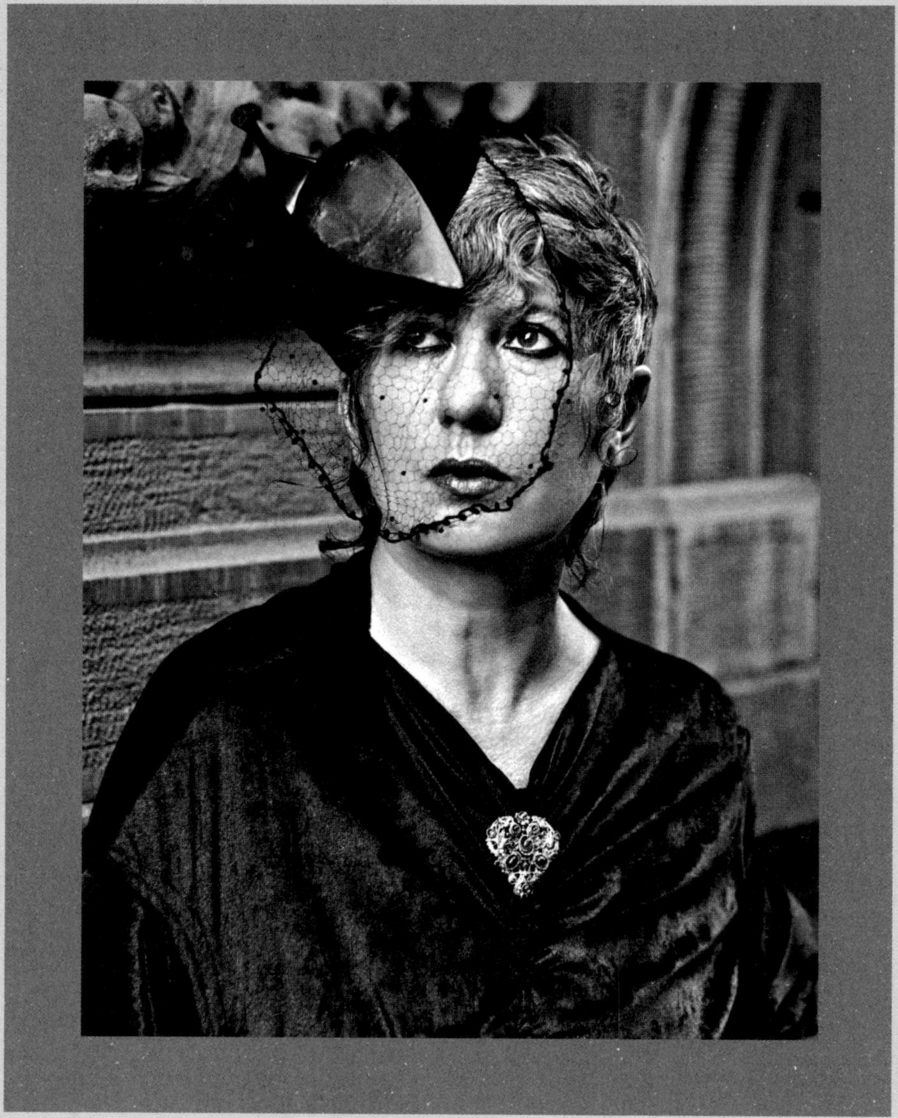

THIS VOLUME IS DEDICATED
TO THE MEMORY OF

# ANNA PIAGGI

Did the Italian flags fly at half-mast the day our blue-haired love child left us? Did the bells of the Duomo ring so loudly that they could be heard all the way across the Atlantic, reaching every art, design, or journalism school in America? Did these students know that their freedom of expression in the arts is partially due to the eccentricities and fantasies of this fashion editor, Signora Piaggi? Yes, I hope so. For all the reasons that Americans love Italy—pasta, wine, films, architecture—we must now add Anna Piaggi to the list.

On my first visit to Milan to photograph for *Vogue Italia*, Franca Sozzani and Luca Stoppini arranged for me to have tea at the home of Anna. Her husband, the photographer Alfa Castaldi, was there too, and their friend, the fashion historian Vern Lambert. I don't remember the tea, or the Milanese pastries. But I can't forget the darkness of the room as we all sat around the table just gossiping and trying to translate their Italian. Anna would get up every 15 minutes and go into the other room, closing the door behind her. Then she would return, wearing a different dress. After the fourth change of clothes, I couldn't take it anymore, all this flirtation! So I told Anna, "Please, come out onto the street and let's take a walk and do some portraits." Now, years later, I still have a print to give her and as I look around my room, everything I see in it she could turn into a hat. But I can only send her a big kiss and laugh about how she's turned her palazzo in heaven into the Land of Oz. —*Bruce Weber*

THIS VOLUME IS DEDICATED
TO THE MEMORY OF

# DASH SNOW

A merry prankster in love and art. A merrier prankster to those who only saw the outside. Dash's sketches, writings, photographs, paintings, and all the other beautiful, random things he made out of nothing will be missed by his friends and even his foes—but I don't think he had any. The enduring memory of Dash in the hearts of his ragtag band of minstrels, rabblerousers, and artists can only be compared to this exchange between Elizabeth Taylor and Richard Burton in *Cleopatra*:

CLEOPATRA: What has happened?
ANTONY: To me? You have happened to me.

I didn't know Dash until I photographed him. I went to his studio in an old loft building on the Bowery, and as soon as the lock clicked and the door opened to a collage of out-of-body experiences, I thought, *What fun!* And later I thought, *What sadness.* It's not fair that he's not here to give us a wink. —*Bruce Weber*

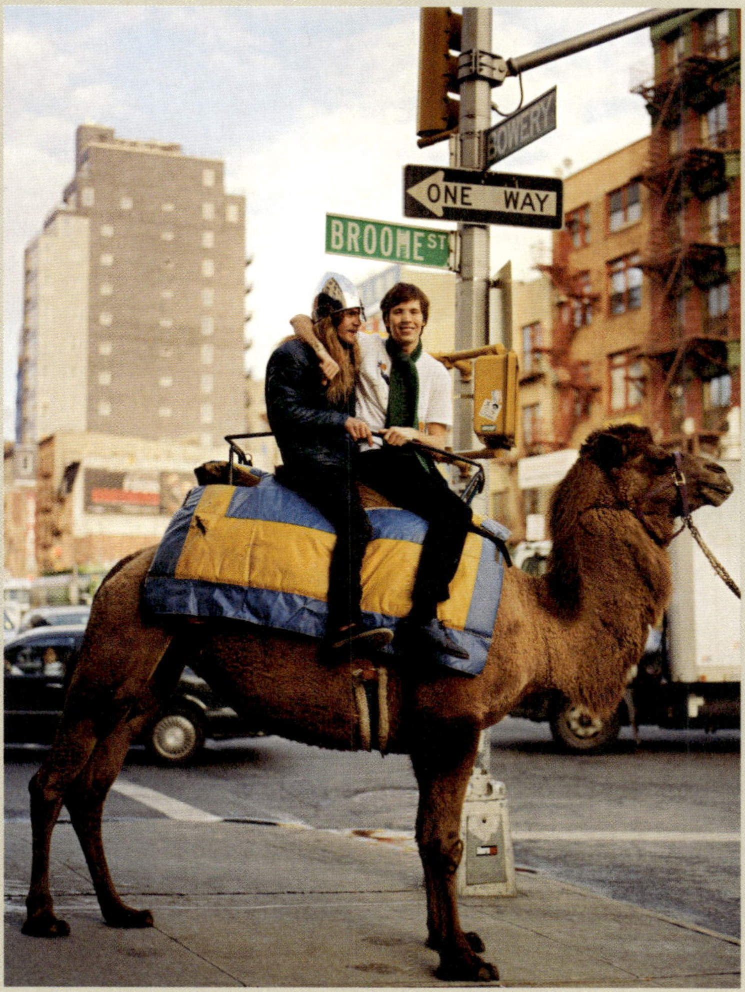


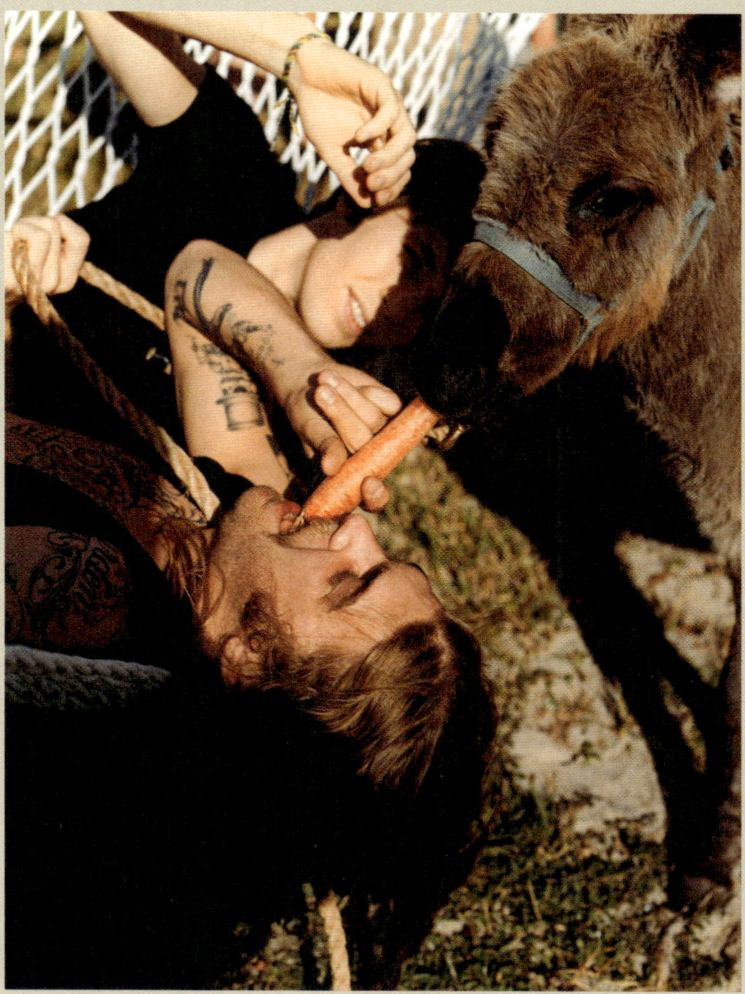

DASH SNOW WITH HIS FRIEND RYAN MCGINLEY IN NEW YORK AND MIAMI, 2005

**EDITORS** BRUCE WEBER · NAN BUSH · NATHANIEL KILCER
MATTHEW RICHARDS · SKYLAR PITTMAN

**ART DIRECTOR** NATHANIEL KILCER

**CONTRIBUTORS** DANIELLE GREEN • DAVID HUTCHINGS • EVA LINDEMANN
CARLOS CHARLIE PEREZ • POPPY DE VILLENEUVE

**ACKNOWLEDGEMENTS** Hendrik teNeues • Christina Burns • Alwine Krebber • Sandra Klimt • Vicki Dwight, Michael Amoruso & Chelsea Photographic
Bo Derek • Lillian Firestone • Danny Trejo • Kaffe Fassett • Astrid Rosset • Polly & Henry Mellen • Nile Rodgers & Nancy Hunt

Gloria Honojosa • Brandon Mably • Erin Gafill • Douglas Booth • Dan Terkel • Balthazar Korab • Felicia Molnar & Cranbrook Academy of Art • Mark Dineen Francisco Alonzo • Charles Talbot • Matt Glass • Sharan Elran • Alex Solomon • Jackie Laurita • Katherine Wood • Amy Weiks • Mohamed Thiam • Hermann Tauchert Rebecca Mazzei, Marsha Miro & MOCAD • Olayami Dabls • Jeff Nolan, Brittny Andrews, Ivan Gamboa, Ashley Cook, Katherine Craig & North End Studios Philip Cooley, Steve Coy & Pony Ride • OmniCorp • Judi Jordan • Anne Marie Menta, Nancy Kuhl, Mary Ellen Budney & Beinecke Rare Book and Manuscript Library, Yale • Steven Brower • Bob Adelman • Emmanuel Cris • Morgan Entrekin & Grove/Atlantic • Joan Mitchell Foundation • Mara Vivat • Michael Shulman & Magnum Photo • Leigh Montville, Shawn Waldron, Cynthia Cathcart & Condé Nast Archive • Michele Franco, Erin Harris & The Richard Avedon Foundation
June Newton • Arthur Elgort • Sally Taylor • Bruce Gilden • Pirkle Jones Foundation • Jean Bubley

Michael Murphy • Jeff Tautrim • Joseph DiGiovanna • Chris Domurat • Roberto Patella • Hillery Estes • Jeannette Shaheen • Dawn Boller • Elizabeth Murphy Dawn Tomassone • Gwen Walberg • Jeanine Morick • Jonathan Bernstein • Suze & Julio Mazzei • John Scott • Louis Rivera • Richard Amaro • Christine Agro
Mark Mulitz • Reynaldo Herrera • Boris McNertney • Natalia Ortega • Gioia Bini • Jenna Lanoff

Dale Slomoff • Paul Jasmin • Sam Shahid • Betty Eng • Dimitri Levas • Allan Mindel • Francis Grill • Franca Sozzani • Graydon Carter • Gelila & Wolfgang Puck Carla Sozzani • Kris Ruhs • Ingrid Sischy • Sandy Brant • Helmut Lang • Edward Pavlick • Victor Alfaro • Pablo Alfaro • Derek & Sophie Craighead & Family
*Always* Elizabeth Taylor

Dr. Ibraheem • Paul Martino • Dr. Lannie & Behna Gardner • Dr. Patrick Dalton • Carrie Hunt & Noe, Jasper & Beau Dewitt • Jeremy, Kathy, Oscar & Lucia Dewitt Ron, Nancy, Jamie & Meghan Bush • Tommy Marengo • Deguinaldo Da Costa • Cece Mota • Julia Villanueva • Soledad Villanueva • Michele Porto • Beth Tavernier Paulo Cruz • Javier & Maria Cuevas • Fabiola Arredondo • Tommy Lee • Dr. Tom Sessa • Dr. Gerald Johnson • Dr. Wayne Winnick • Pat & Tom Downing
Barbara & Ernie Tompsett • Dr. Mike Farber • Dr. Steve Withrow & Colorado State University Animal Cancer Center

*Billie Holiday • Little River • Dream Catcher • Kodiak • Tao • Hud • Elvis • Hope • Jazz*

**PLEASE SUPPORT** WE ARE FAMILY FOUNDATION [http://www.wearefamilyfoundation.org] GIRLS WRITE NOW [http://www.girlswritenow.org]

ALL-AMERICAN VOLUME TWELVE – A BOOK OF LESSONS



PUBLISHED BY TENEUES PUBLISHING GROUP [www.teneues.com]

**EDITORIAL COORDINATION** CHRISTINA BURNS, TENEUES PUBLISHING COMPANY **PRODUCTION COORDINATION** ALWINE KREBBER, TENEUES VERLAG **COLOR SEPARATIONS** ORT MEDIENVERBUND

teNeues Verlag GmbH + Co. KG
Am Selder 37
47906 Kempen, Germany
Phone: +49-(0)2152-916-0
Fax: +49-(0)2152-916-111
e-mail: books@teneues.de

Press department: Andrea Rehn
Phone: +49-(0)2152-916-202
e-mail: arehn@teneues.de

teNeues Digital Media GmbH
Kohlfurter Straße 41–43
10999 Berlin, Germany
Phone: +49-(0)30-7007765-0

teNeues Publishing Company
7 West 18th Street
New York, NY 10011, USA
Phone: +1-212-627-9090
Fax: +1-212-627-9511

teNeues Publishing UK Ltd.
21 Marlowe Court, Lymer Avenue
London SE19 1LP, UK
Phone: +44-(0)20-8670-7522
Fax: +44-(0)20-8670-7523

teNeues France S.A.R.L.
39, rue des Billets, 18250 Henrichemont, France
Phone: +33-(0)2-4826-9348

ISBN 978-3-8327-9667-9

Library of Congress Control Number: 2012942041

Printed in Italy.

While we strive for utmost precision in every detail, we cannot be held responsible for any inaccuracies, nor for any subsequent loss or damage arising.

Bibliographic information published by the Deutsche Nationalbibliothek. The Deutsche Nationalbibliothek lists this publication in the Deutsche Nationalbibliografie; detailed bibliographic data are available in the Internet at http://dnb.d-nb.de.

**teNeues Publishing Group**
Kempen
Berlin
Cologne
Düsseldorf
Hamburg
London
Munich
New York
Paris

teNeues

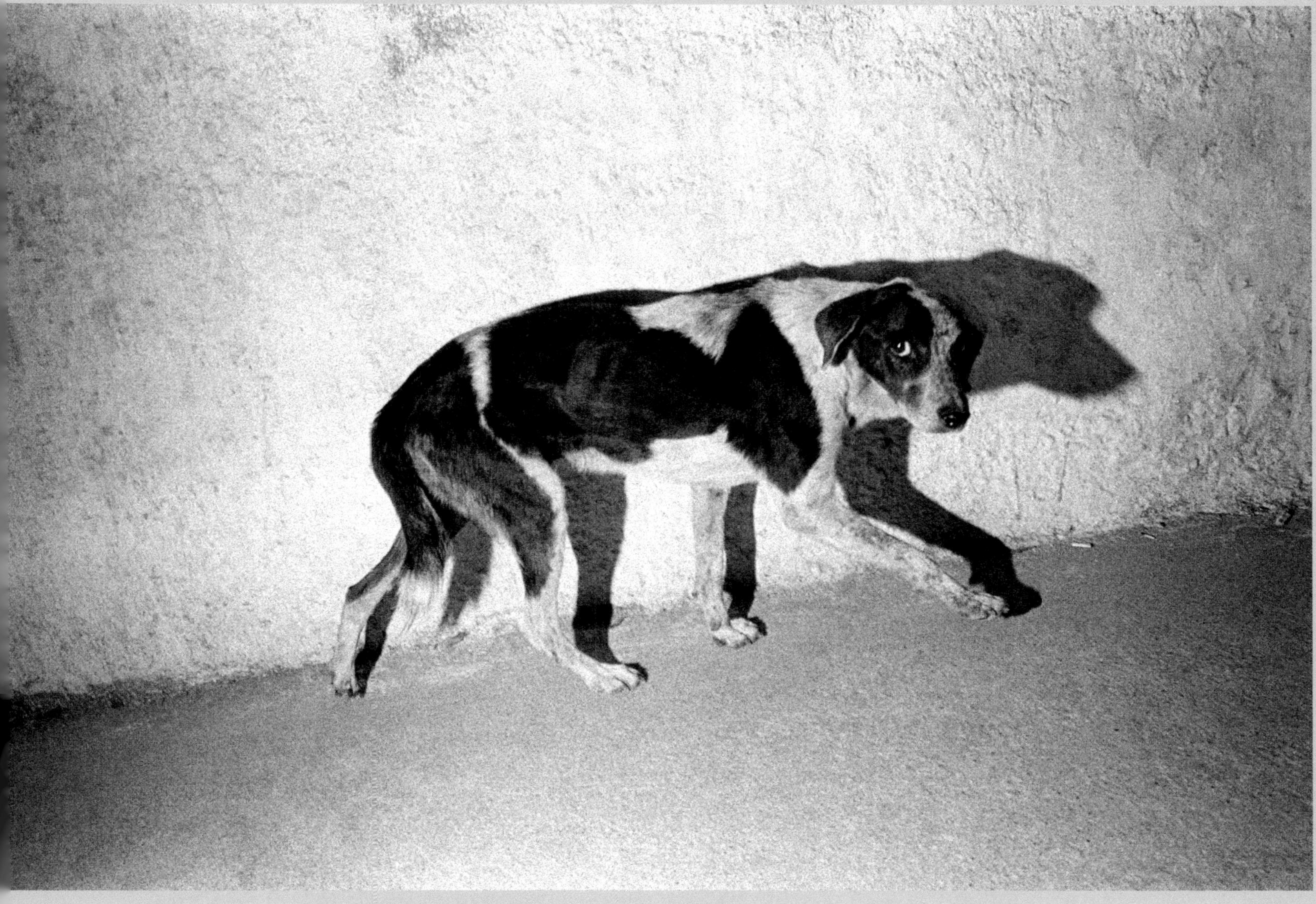

PHOTO BY BRUCE GILDEN

# PLATE LISTING

## COVER & INTRODUCTION

[slipcase image] *Chapel at Cheltenham Ladies College, Gloucestershire, England 1954* by Esther Bubley [cover image] *Bo Derek, Santa Ynez, California 1994* by John Derek [inside front cover-p. 1] *Bo Derek, Santa Ynez, California 1994* by John Derek [p.2] *Bo Derek, Santa Ynez, California* 1994 by John Derek

## FRANKLIN FARMS

[p. 4-5] *Students from Franklin Farms on a camping trip* by photographer unknown [p.6] *Building a mobile, Armonk 1970* by photographer unknown [p.8] *Boys carrying a table, Armonk 1970* by photographer unknown [p. 9] *Girls Dancing, 1966* by photographer unknown [p. 10] *Boy hammering a nail at Corey Lane, 1958* by photographer unknown [p.11] *Children's Work, Corey Lane c.1960s* by photographer unknown [p. 12] *Living chess pieces from the play* The Art of Asha *performed at ABS studios in NYC 1971* by photographer unknown [p. 13] *Boys dancing the Capoeira, Franklin Farms 1966* by photographer unknown [p. 14] *George Ivanovitch Gurdjieff with a student* by photographer unknown [p. 15 clockwise from top left] *The main hall at Franklin Farms, c. 1960* by photographer unknown • *Students at Franklin Farms* by photographer unknown • *Hiking the Long Trail, 1978* by photographer unknown • *Elders of the Gurdjieff Foundation at a children's picnic, Franklin Farms, 1962* by photographer unknown • *Buddha from the play* Monkey *performed at Armonk, 1969* by photographer unknown

## THE CHAMP—DANNY TREJO

[p. 16] *Danny Trejo, Arleta, California 2012* by Bruce Weber [p. 17] *Danny Trejo, Arleta, California 2012* by Bruce Weber [p. 18] *Danny Trejo, Arleta, California 2012* by Bruce Weber [p. 20-21] *Danny Trejo and friends unload his custom* Machete *bicycle, Arleta, California 2012* by Bruce Weber [p. 22] *Family photograph at Alice Trejo's home, Arleta, California 2012* by Bruce Weber [p. 23] *Danny Trejo praying* by photographer unknown [p. 24] *Danny Trejo, boxer* by photographer unknown [p. 25] *Family photograph at Alice Trejo's home, Arleta, California 2012* by Bruce Weber [p. 26-27] *Still from* Machete *(2010)* [p. 28 clockwise from top left] *Still from* Marked for Death *(1991)* • *Danielle Trejo, Mia Brito and Danny Trejo having lunch, Arleta, California 2012* by Bruce Weber • *Gilbert Trejo holding a* Machete *poster, Arleta, California 2012* by Bruce Weber • *Still from* Machete *(2010)* • *Danny Trejo, Arleta, California 2012* by Bruce Weber • *Danny at the taco stand, Arleta, California 2012* by Bruce Weber [p. 29 clockwise from top left] *Danny Trejo, Arleta, California 2012* by Bruce Weber • *Alice and Danny Trejo, Arleta, California 2012* by Bruce Weber • *Danny Trejo on his* Machete *motorcycle, Arleta, California 2012* by Bruce Weber • *Danny Trejo with a baby, Arleta, California 2012* by Bruce Weber • *Danny Trejo, Arleta, California 2012* by Bruce Weber • *Still from* Machete *(2010)* • *Still from* Ranchero *(2008)* [p. 30-31] *Trejo Family portrait, Arleta, California 2012* by Bruce Weber [p. 32] *Danny Trejo at Big G's Classic Cars, Los Angeles, California 2012* by Bruce Weber [p. 32 clockwise from top left] *Bel Aire at Big G's Classic Cars, Los Angeles, California 2012* by Bruce Weber • *Big G's Classic Cars, Los Angeles, California 2012* by Bruce Weber • *Car show poster at Big G's Classic Cars, Los Angeles, California 2012* by Bruce Weber • *Big G's Classic Cars, Los Angeles, California 2012* by Bruce Weber • *Big G's Classic Cars, Los Angeles, California 2012* by Bruce Weber [p. 33] *Big G's Classic Cars, Los Angeles, California 2012* by Bruce Weber • *Gilbert Trejo and Mia Brito at Big G's Classic Cars, Los Angeles, California 2012* by Bruce Weber • *Big G's Classic Cars, Los Angeles, California 2012* by Bruce Weber • *El Camino at Big G's Classic Cars, Los Angeles, California 2012* by Bruce Weber • *Big G's Classic Cars, Los Angeles, California 2012* by Bruce Weber • *Big G's Classic Cars, Los Angeles, California 2012* by Bruce Weber [p. 34] *Danny Trejo, Arleta, California 2012* by Bruce Weber [p. 35] *Danny Trejo's shoes, Arleta, California 2012* by Bruce Weber [p. 36-37] *Danny Trejo mural, Los Angeles, California 2012* by Bruce Weber

## ALL SMILES—KAFFE FASSETT

[p. 42-43] *Kaffe Fassett, Douglas Booth and Brandon Mably, London, England 2012* by Bruce Weber [p. 44] *Kaffe Fassett in London* by Steve Lovi [p. 46] *Kaffe Fassett in Big Sur* by photographer unknown [p. 47] *Douglas Booth wearing a shawl by Kaffe Fassett, London, England 2012* by Bruce Weber [p. 49 clockwise from top left] *Kaffe Fassett on the deck at Nepenthe* by photographer unknown • *Kaffe Fassett on Pfeiffer Beach in Big Sur* by photographer unknown • *Kaffe with his sister Holly on the Café Kevah deck at Nepenthe c. 1972* by photographer unknown [p. 50] *Kaffe Fassett in his painting studio in Big Sur* by photographer unknown [p. 51] *Kaffe Fassett with Bill Gibb in England* by photographer unknown [p. 53 clockwise from top left] *Kaffe Fassett at home, London, England 2012* by Bruce Weber • *Kaffe Fassett's home, London, England 2012* by Bruce Weber • *Kaffe Fassett's home, London, England 2012* by Bruce Weber • *Kaffe Fassett painting, London, England 2012* by Bruce Weber [p. 54-55] *Hats designed by Kaffe Fassett, London, England 2012* by Bruce Weber

## STUDS TERKEL

[p. 57] *Studs Terkel, Chicago 1992* by Steve Kagan [p. 58 clockwise from top left] *Studs Terkel and his wife Ida, Chicago* by photographer unknown • *Studs Terkel working in his study, Chicago 1992* by Steve Kagan • *Studs Terkel conducting an interview, Chicago c. 1950* by Stephen Deutch

## LIVING ART IN DETROIT—CRANBROOK

[p. 60-61] *Cranbrook Academy of Art Campus* by Balthazar Korab [p. 62] *Sculpture on the campus of the Cranbrook Academy of Art* by Balthazar Korab [p. 64] *Cranbrook Academy of Art Library, Bloomfield Hills, Michigan 2012* by Carlos Charlie Perez [p. 65] *Interior of the Cranbrook Academy of Art Library, Bloomfield Hills, Michigan 2012* by Carlos Charlie Perez [p. 66-67] *Untitled* by Alex Solomon [p. 68] *Ceramicist Maija Grotell with her students in the Cranbrook Academy of Art Ceramics Studio, 1939* by Richard Askew [p. 69 top] *Sheran Elran, Cranbrook Academy of Art, Bloomfield Hills, Michigan 2012* by Carlos Charlie Perez [p. 69 bottom] *Sheran Elran's* Unlimited Edition *installed at the Cranbrook Academy of Art Gallery, Bloomfield Hills, Michigan 2012* by Carlos Charlie Perez [p. 70] *Carol Wald with a cat, 1968* by Barry Edmonds [p. 71] *Reverie, 1987* by Carol Wald [p. 72] *"Horse" Series, The Gray Mare, 1977* by Carol Wald [p. 73] *The Dream, 1989* by Carol Wald [p. 74] *James Scripps Booth in his painting studio, 1918* by photographer unknown [p. 75] *Matt Glass with a puppet from his film* Citadel, *Cranbrook Academy of Art, Bloomfield Hills, Michigan 2012* by Carlos Charlie Perez [p. 76] *John Burnett in Cranbrook's Iron Shop with Francis Faus, 1930* by J.W. Hughes [p. 77 top] *Mohamed Thiam's artwork* Trading Faces, *Cranbrook Academy of Art, Bloomfield Hills, Michigan 2012* by Carlos Charlie Perez [p. 77 bottom] *Mohamed Thiam, Cranbrook Academy of Art, Bloomfield Hills, Michigan 2012* by Carlos Charlie Perez [p. 78] *Fur Stool, 2012* by Mark Dineen [p. 79] *Charles and Ray Eames at their home, Pacific Palisades, CA 1974* by Wayne Miller [p. 80 clockwise from top left] *Toshiko Takaezu pot making series (detail) 1974* by photographer unknown • *Katie Wood, Cranbrook Academy of Art, Bloomfield Hills, Michigan 2012* by Carlos Charlie Perez • *Carl Milles in his studio with his assistant, Svea Klein, and models for the Fountain of Faith 1949* by photographer unknown [p. 81 clockwise from top left] *Charlie Talbot, Cranbrook Academy of Art, Bloomfield Hills, Michigan 2012* by Carlos Charlie Perez • *Harry Bertoia with a student, 1939* by Richard Askew • *Amy Weiks workspace, Cranbrook Academy of Art, Bloomfield Hills, Michigan 2012* by Carlos Charlie Perez • *Zoltan Sepeshy with students in the painting studio, Cranbrook Academy of Art painting department, 1942* by photographer unknown • (from left) *Elizabeth Edmark, Marie Bexell, Peggy Broberg, and Gerda Nyberg in the Loja Saarinen weaving studio, Cranbrook Academy of Art, 1935* by photographer unknown [p. 82] *Preying Monkey, 2012* by Francisco Alonzo [p. 83 left] *Francisco Alonzo, Cranbrook Academy of Art, Bloomfield Hills, Michigan 2012* by Carlos Charlie Perez [p. 83 right] *Sculpture studio, Cranbrook Academy of Art, Bloomfield Hills, Michigan 2012* by Carlos Charlie Perez [p. 84] *Cranbrook Academy of Art Campus* by Balthazar Korab [p. 85] *Cranbrook Academy of Art Campus* by Balthazar Korab

## LIVING ART IN DETROIT—DOWNTOWN CONVERSATIONS

[p. 86-87] *Olayami Dabls' Iron House, Detroit, Michigan 2012* by Carlos Charlie Perez [p. 88 left] *Olayami Dabls' Iron House, Detroit, Michigan 2012* by Carlos Charlie Perez [p. 88 right] *Olayami Dabls, Detroit, Michigan 2012* by Carlos Charlie Perez [p. 89] *Olayami Dabls'* Iron Teaching Rocks Table Manners, *Detroit, Michigan 2012* by Carlos Charlie Perez [p. 90 top] *Olayami Dabls'* Rocks Teaching Themselves How To Rust, *Detroit, Michigan 2012* by Carlos Charlie Perez [p. 90 bottom] *Façade of MOCAD, Detroit, Michigan* by photographer unknown [p.91 left] *Façade of MOCAD, Detroit, Michigan 2012* by Carlos Charlie Perez [p. 91 right] *Children of the Nataki Talibah Schoolhouse at MOCAD, Detroit, Michigan* by photographer unknown [p. 92] *Brittny Andrews, Jeff Nolan, Ivan Gamboa & Ashley Book, Detroit, Michigan 2012* by Carlos Charlie Perez [p. 93 left] *Façade of PonyRide, Detroit, Michigan 2012* by Carlos Charlie Perez [p. 93 right] *Philip Cooley at PonyRide, Detroit, Michigan 2012* by Carlos Charlie Perez [p. 94] *Untitled (Rooftop View), 1957 oil on masonite* by Hughie Lee-Smith [p. 95] *Hughie Lee-Smith sketching at a picnic, c. 1950* by photographer unknown [p. 96-97] *Street Scene, 1952 oil on canvas* by Hughie Lee-Smith

## HIGH DESERT HEIRESS

[p. 98] *Mabel Dodge Luhan's Los Gallos residence (main gate), Taos, New Mexico* by photographer unknown [p. 99] *Mabel Dodge Luhan standing in gateway* by photographer unknown [p. 100] *Mabel Dodge Luhan as a young woman (ca. 1890–1900)* by photographer unknown [p. 101] *Mabel Dodge Luhan as a young woman (ca. 1890–1900)* by photographer unknown [p. 102] *Mabel Dodge Luhan seated cross-legged and wearing a turban (ca. 1915)* by photographer unknown [p. 103 top] *Mabel Dodge Luhan button: "Mabel Lujan was Round and Square."* [p. 103 bottom] *Mable Dodge Luhan seated on bench* by Will Connell [p. 104-105] *Mabel Dodge Luhan with pinto pony, eyes closed* by photographer unknown [p. 106] *Mabel Dodge Luhan standing at door near birdhouse* by photographer unknown [p. 107] *Photographs of Mabel Dodge Luhan's residences mounted on album page. Photographs labeled as "Living Room Big House", "Dining Room," "Dining Room-Big House," "Finney Farm-Croton," "Studio," "Ranchos Church," "Taos Pueblo Church,"* by photographer unknown [p. 108 left] *Mabel Dodge Luhan seated with dog* by photographer unknown [p. 108 right] *Tony Luhan standing with rifle and dog* by photographer unknown [p. 109] Tony Luhan wearing blanket by photographer unknown [p. 110-111] *Mabel Dodge Luhan, Frieda Lawrence, Dorothy Brett at Mrs. Lawrence's porch, near Taos, 1938* by Cady Wells [p. 112 clockwise from top] *Robinson Jeffers, Angelino Ravagli, Mabel Dodge Luhan, John Young Hunter, and Frieda Lawrence* by photographer unknown • *Tony Luhan and John Evans 1918* by photographer unknown • *Rebecca James & Georgia O'Keeffe Taos, New Mexico* by photographer unknown [p. 113 left] *D.H. Lawrence's Three Women (Mabel Dodge Luhan, Dorothy Brett, Freida Lawrence)* by George Daniell [p. 113 right] *D.H. Lawrence* by Hon. Dorothy Brett [p. 114-115] *Mabel Dodge Luhan posing with group of Native Americans* by photographer unknown [p. 116 left] *Mabel Dodge Luhan sitting with book and dog, August 15, 1947* by photographer unknown [p. 117] *Dennis Hopper and Peter Fonda in a scene from the film* Easy Rider

## DANIELLE FAITH GREEN

[p. 118 left] *Danielle Faith Green, Brooklyn 2012* by Poppy de Villeneuve [p. 118 top right] *Brooklyn 2012* by Poppy de Villeneuve [p. 118 bottom right] *Danielle Faith Green, Brooklyn 2012* by Poppy de Villeneuve

## BARNEY ROSSET & GROVE PRESS

[p. 120-121] *Barney Rossett at the Grove Press offices, New York City* by Bob Adelman [p. 122-123] *Cover designs* by Roy Kuhlman [p. 124 top] *Grove Press annual report business meeting, New York City* by Bob Adelman [p. 124 bottom] *Grove Press cartoon* by unknown artist [p. 125] *Allen Ginsberg, Gregory Corso and Barney Rosset in Washington Square Park, New York City 1957* by Burt Glinn [p. 126] Saturday Evening Post *cover* [p. 127] Evergreen Review *cover photograph* by Richard Avedon [p. 128] *James Stewart reading Henry Miller's* Tropic of Cancer, *Hollywood, CA 1963* by photographer unknown [p. 129 left] *Henry Miller playing ping-pong with Candice Thayer, Big Sur, CA 1971* by Bradley Smith [p. 129 top right] Tropic of Cancer *cover* [p. 129 bottom right] *Cartoon* by artist unknown [p. 130-131 background] *Illustration* by Roy Kuhlman [p. 130 clockwise from top left] *Barney Rosset in his Army days with a photo of his girlfriend* by photographer unknown • *Still from a test film shot in Coney Island* by Barney Rosset • *Valentine drawing* by Joan Mitchell • *Barney with his second wife, Loly* by photographer unknown • *Barney Rosset and Norman Mailer* by photographer unknown • *Joan Mitchell* by Barney Rosset [p. 131] *Barney Rosset in the Army* by photographer unknown • *Barney dancing with his fifth wife, Astrid* by Terence Strick • *Barney celebrating with friends while on leave from the Army* by photographer unknown • *Barney Rosset fishing with Maurice Girodias* by photographer unknown • *Barney and his first son, Peter* by photographer unknown [p. 132 clockwise from top left] *Barney Rosset doing his winter planting in East Hampton* by photographer unknown • *Barney Rosset and his daughter Chantal in Southampton* by photographer unknown • *Barney Rosset with John Nathan outside his quonset hut in East Hampton* by Bob Adelman [p. 133] Lady Chatterley's Lover *cover* [p. 134-135 background] *Illustration* by Roy Kuhlman [p. 134] *Samuel Beckett and Barney Rosset, Paris, France 1986* by Bob Adelman [p. 136-137] *Barney Rosset at the Grove Press offices with an* Evergreen *cover in the background* by Bob Adelman

## STRANGERS IN PARADISE

[p. 138-139] *Bo Derek with Smoke and China, Lake Powell, Utah 1979* by John Derek [p. 140 top] *Bo Derek and China, Lake Powell, Utah 1979* by John Derek [p. 140 bottom] *Bo Derek with Smoke, China and Scarum, Lake Powell, Utah 1979* by John Derek [p. 141] *Bo Derek with China, Lake Powell, Utah 1979* by John Derek [p. 142-143] *Bo Derek, Lake Powell, Utah 1979* by John Derek [p. 144] *Bo Derek, Lake Powell, Utah 1979* by John Derek [p. 145] *Bo Derek, Lake Powell, Utah 1979* by John Derek [p. 146 top] *Bo Derek with Smoke, Lake Powell, Utah 1979* by John Derek [p. 146 bottom] *Bo Derek, Lake Powell, Utah 1979* by John Derek [p. 147] *Bo Derek with China, Lake Powell, Utah 1979* by John Derek [p. 149] *Bo Derek, Lake Powell, Utah 1979* by John Derek

## YOWSAH—NILE RODGERS

[p. 152-153] *Nile Rodgers and Chic, 1982* by Ebet Roberts [p. 154 left] *Beverly Goodman with her son Nile* by photographer unknown [p. 154 right] *Bobby Glanzrock* by photographer unknown [p. 155] *Nile Rodgers in Los Angeles* by photographer unknown [p. 156-157] *Luci Martin, Nile Rodgers, Tony Thompson and Alfa, Paris France 1980* by James Andanson [p. 158] *Nile Rodgers plays at The Palladium, New York City 1979* by Waring Abbott [p. 159 clockwise from top left] *Nile Rodgers at home playing guitar with dog* by Lynn Goldsmith • *Nile Rodgers with Chic at Disneyland* by photographer unknown • *David Lee Roth and Nile Rodgers with Brett Ratner* by photographer unknown [p. 160 from top] *Nile Rodgers and David Bowie recording "Let's Dance" at Power Station studios, New York City 1982* by Paul Hardy • *Nile Rodgers with Nick Rhodes of Duran Duran in Maison Rouge Studio, recording "Wild Boys," London 1984* by Virginia Turbett • *Nile Rodgers, Mick Jagger and Herbie Hancock at the Power Station, New York* by photographer unknown [p. 161 clockwise from top left] *David Bowie's "Let's Dance" album* photograph by Greg Gorman • *Diana Ross' "Diana" album* photograph by Francesco Scavullo • *Chic's "C'est Chic" album* photograph by Joel Brodsky • *Debby Harry's "Koo Koo" album* painting by H.R. Giger, from a photograph by Brian Aris • *Grace Jones' "Inside Story" album* artwork by Richard Bernstein • *Sister Sledge's "We Are Family" album* photograph by Jim Houghton • *Duran Duran's "Notorious" album* photograph by John Swannell [p. 162] *Nile Rodgers at home, New York City 2012* by Bruce Weber [p. 163] *Painting of Nile Rodgers by Jane Millett, New York City, 2012* by Bruce Weber [p. 164 top] *Bernard and Nile* by photographer unknown [p. 164 bottom] *Nile Rodgers and Grace Jones* by photographer unknown [p. 165 top] *Nile Rodgers, New York City 2012* by Bruce Weber [p. 165 bottom] *Nile Rodgers, New York City 2012* by Bruce Weber [p. 166 top] *Nile Rodgers playing with Chic* by photographer unknown [p. 166 bottom] *Nile Rodgers at home, New York City 2012* by Bruce Weber [p. 167] *Nile Rodgers and Nancy Hunt at their home, New York City 2012* by Bruce Weber

## POLLY MELLEN

[p. 169] *Polly Mellen, South Kent, Connecticut 2012* by Bruce Weber [p. 170 clockwise from left] *Polly Mellen, South Kent, Connecticut 2012* by Bruce Weber • *Polly Mellen, South Kent, Connecticut 2012* by Bruce Weber • *Polly Mellen, South Kent, Connecticut 2012* by Bruce Weber • *Polly Mellen, South Kent, Connecticut 2012* by Bruce Weber • *Polly Mellen, South Kent, Connecticut 2012* by Bruce Weber [p. 172] *Veruschka, Japan, February 1966* by Richard Avedon [p. 173] *Veruschka, Japan, February 1966* by Richard Avedon [p. 174-175] *Natassja Kinski with the serpent, Los Angeles, California 1981* by Richard Avedon [p. 176] *Polly Mellen and Richard Avedon, Great Exuma, the Bahamas, October 1968* by Richard Avedon [p. 177] *Lauren Hutton and Alan Lewis, Great Exuma, the Bahamas, October 1968* by Richard Avedon [p. 178] *Polly Mellen with Leslie Bell, Molly Bell, and Bentley, South Kent, Connecticut 2012* by Bruce Weber [p. 179] *Polly Mellen, South Kent, Connecticut 2012* by Bruce Weber [p. 180] *Polly Mellen* by Helmut Newton [p. 181] *Lisa Taylor kissing Peter Keating, Saint-Tropez, Vogue, May 1975* by Helmut Newton [p. 182] *Lisa Taylor watching Peter Keating, Saint-Tropez, Vogue, May 1975* by Helmut Newton [p. 183] *Lisa Taylor and Eva Neilson, Saint-Topez, Vogue, May 1975* by Helmut Newton [p. 184 clockwise from top left] *Polly Mellen and Leslie Bell, Bernardsville, New Jersey* by Jill Krementz • *Polly and Hiro at the Mill Reef Club* by photographer unknown • *Polly's father William B. Allen* by photographer unknown • *Polly in Ocho Rios, Jamaica* by Louise Dahl-Wolfe • *Bedroom at Polly Mellen's house, South Kent, Connecticut 2012* by Bruce Weber [p. 185 clockwise from top left] *Polly Mellen at Met Museum Party with Giogio Di Sant' Angelo, China Machado, Kezia Keeble, Alex Valdek, Egon von Furstenberg and Marina Schiano, New York City* by photographer unknown • *Polly skiing in Mürren, Switzerland* by photographer unknown • *Polly with Molly and Bentley, South Kent, Connecticut 2012* by Bruce Weber [p. 186] *Polly's mother, Leslie Smith Allen, at the Mill Reef Club, Antigua* by Toni Frisell [p. 186-187] *Five Women in pool shower room, Vogue, May 1975* by Deborah Turbeville [p. 188] *Lisa Taylor, 1976* by Arthur Elgort [p. 189 top] (from left to right) *Way Bandy, Rosie Vela, Christiaan, Polly Mellen, Debbie Dunmark and Jim Larson, New York City* by Arthur Elgort [p. 189 bottom] *Polly Mellen* by Arthur Elgort [p. 190] *Polly and Henry Mellen, South Kent, Connecticut 2012* by Bruce Weber [p. 191 *Polly Mellen in her garden, South Kent, Connecticut 2012* by Bruce Weber

## CLOSING

[p. 192] *Anna Piaggi, Milan, Italy 1982* by Bruce Weber [p. 193 left to right] *Dash Snow and Ryan McGinley, New York City 2005* by Bruce Weber • *Dash Snow and Ryan McGinley with a friend, Golden Beach, Florida 2005* by Bruce Weber [p. 195] *Dog outside a cemetery, Port-au-Prince, Haiti 1990* by Bruce Gilden [p.198-199] *Sun and Wave, San Francisco, California 1952* by Pirkle Jones [inside back cover] *A Photographer Washes his Negatives Among the Icebergs of Alaska* by Oscar Con Engeln

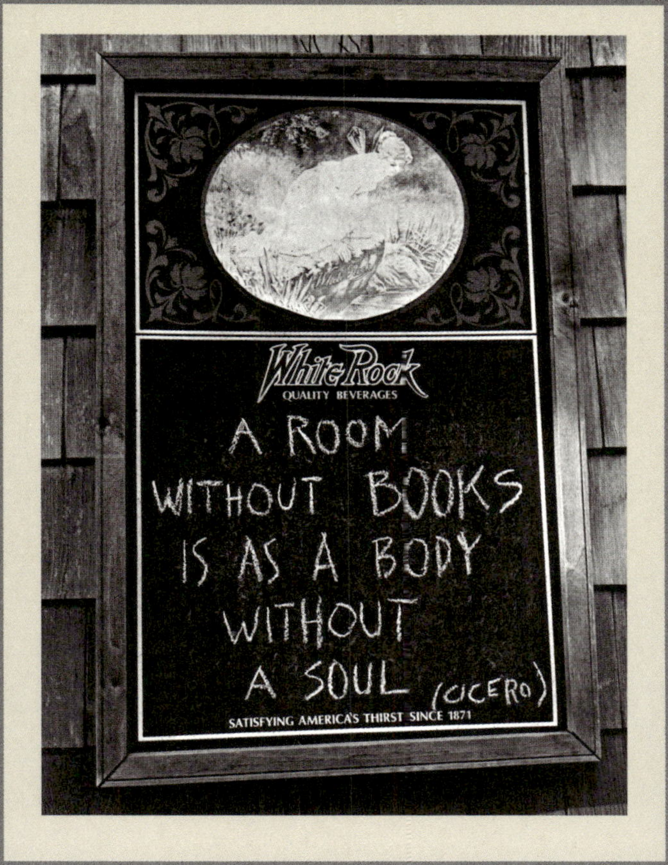


## CITATIONS [MABEL DODGE LUHAN]


1. Stern, Maurice. *Shadow and Light: The Life, Friends and Opinions of Maurice Stern*. New York: HBW, 1965. p. 112
2. Mabel Dodge Luhan. *Movers and Shakers* Albuquerque: University of New Mexico Press, 1985. p. 534-535.
3. Mabel Dodge Luhan. *Edge of Taos Desert: An Escape to Reality*. Albuquerque: University of New Mexico Press, 1987 p. 331-332.
4. Mabel Dodge Luhan. *Lorenzo in Taos*. NY: Knopf, 1932. p. 270
5. Knud Merrild. A Poet and Two Painters: A Memoir of D.H. Lawrence. New York: G. Routledge, 1938. p. 239-240


## CREDITS

[slipcase image] PHOTOGRAPH Copyright © The Estate of Esther Bubley

[cover, front inside cover, p.1-2, 138-150] PHOTOGRAPHS © The Estate of John Derek. Courtesy of Bo Derek

[p. 16-18, 20-22, 25, 28 top right, center left & right, bottom left, 29 top left & right, bottom left, center & right, 30-32, 34-39, 42-43, 47, 53-55, 162-163, 165, 166 center, 167, 169-170, 178-179, 184 bottom left, 185 bottom right, 190-193] PHOTOGRAPHS © Bruce Weber. All rights reserved. [p. 151, 171] TEXT © Bruce Weber. All rights reserved.

[p. 4-15] PHOTOGRAPHS & TEXTS Courtesy of Lillian Firestone / The Children's Work

[p. 23-24] PHOTOGRAPHS Courtesy of Danny Trejo [p.26-27] PHOTOGRAPH 20th Century Fox / The Kobal Collection [p. 28 top left] PHOTOGRAPH 20th Century Fox / The Kobal Collection [p. 28 bottom right] PHOTOGRAPHS Copyright © Photos 12 / Alamy [p. 29 center, top] PHOTOGRAPH Copyright © Indican Pictures / courtesy of Everett Collection [p. 29 center, bottom] PHOTOGRAPH Copyright © AF archive / Alamy

[p. 40-41] TEXT "A True Account of Talking to the Sun at Fire Island" copyright © 1971 by Maureen Granville-Smith, Administratrix of the Estate of Frank O'Hara, copyright renewed 1999 by Maureen O'Hara Franville-Smith and Donald Allen, from *The Collected Poems of Frank O'Hara* by Frank O'Hara, edited by Donald Allen. Used by permission of Alfred A Knopf, a division of Random House, Inc.

[p. 44, 50-51] PHOTOGRAPHS Courtesy of the collection of Kaffe Fasset [p. 46, 49] PHOTOGRAPHS Courtesy of the collection of Erin Gafill

[p. 57, 58 bottom right] PHOTOGRAPH Steve Kagan / Time Life Pictures / Getty Images [p. 58 top] Courtesy of the Estate of Louis & Ida Terkel [p. 58 bottom left] Stephen Deutch / Chicago History Museum / Getty Images [p. 56, 59] TEXT Excerpt from *Hope Dies Last* Copyright © 2003 by Studs Terkel. Reprinted by permission of The New Press. www.thenewpress.com

[p. 60-61, 84-85] PHOTOGRAPHS Courtesy of The Library of Congress [p. 64-65, 69, 75, 77, 80 top right, 81 top left & center right, 83, 86-89, 90 top, 91-93] PHOTOGRAPHS Copyright © Carlos Charlie Perez [p. 66-67] PHOTOGRAPH Copyright © Alex Solomon [p. 68] PHOTOGRAPH Copyright © Cranbrook Archive / Richard G. Askew 4855 [p. 70] PHOTOGRAPH Barry Edmonds, Carol Wald Papers, Archives of American Art, Smithsonian Insitution [p. 71, 74] ARTWORKS Copyright © The Estate of Carol Wald. Courtesy of Hermann Tauchert [p. 72] ARTWORKS Copyright © The Estate of Carol Wald. Courtesy of Karen Dunnam [p. 74] PHOTOGRAPH Copyright © Cranbrook Archive / JSB1024 [p. 76] PHOTOGRAPH Copyright © Cranbrook Archive / J.W. Hughes / CEC1360 [p. 78] PHOTOGRAPH Copyright © Mark Dineen [p. 79] PHOTOGRAPH Copyright © Wayne Miller / Magnum Photos [p. 80 top left] PHOTOGRAPH Toshiko Takaezu papers, Archives of American Art, Smithsonian Institution [p. 80 bottom] PHOTOGRAPH Courtesy Svea Klein [p. 81 top right] PHOTOGRAPH Copyright © Cranbrook Archive / Richard G. Askew / 4879-7 [p. 81 bottom left] PHOTOGRAPH Copyright © Cranbrook Archive / 5892-3 [p. 81 bottom right] PHOTOGRAPH Copyright © Cranbrook Archive / 2744 [p. 82] PHOTOGRAPH Copyright © Francisco Alonzo

[p. 90, bottom] PHOTOGRAPH Courtesy of Museum of Contemporary Art, Detroit [p. 94, 96-97] ARTWORK Copyright © Estate of Hughie Lee-Smith / Licensed by VAGA [p. 94] PHOTOGRAPH Courtesy of Swann Auction Galleries [p. 96-97] PHOTOGRAPH courtesy of June Kelly Gallery / Private Collection [p. 95] PHOTOGRAPH Courtesy of Pomegranate Communications, Inc.

[p. 98-99, 101-112, 114-115, 116 top left] PHOTOGRAPHS Courtesy of Yale Collection of American Literature, Beinecke Rare Book and Manuscript Library [p. 113 left] PHOTOGRAPH Copyright © The Estate of George Daniell, Dwayne and Gina DeJoy [p. 113 right] ARTWORK Copyright © National Portrait Gallery, London [p. 117] PHOTOGRAPH Copyright © Silver Screen Collection / Hulton Archive / Getty Images

[p. 118] PHOTOGRAPHS Copyright © Polly de Villeneuve [p. 119] TEXT Copyright © Danielle Green

[p. 120-121, 124 top, 132 center left, 134-137] PHOTOGRAPHS Copyright © Bob Adelman [p. 122-123] ARTWORK Cover designs by Roy Kuhlman. Courtesy of Arden Riodan [p. 124 center, 129 center right, 130 top left & right, bottom left & right, 131, 132 top left & right] PHOTOGRAPHS & ARTWORK Courtesy of Astrid Rosset [p. 125] PHOTOGRAPH Copyright © Burt Glinn / Magnum Photos [p. 126] ARTWORK Post cover © 1969 SEPS licensed by Curtis Licensing, Indianapolis, IN. All rights reserved. [p. 127] PHOTOGRAPH Copyright © The Richard Avedon Foundation. Cover courtesy of Astrid Rosset [p. 128] PHOTOGRAPH Copyright © Haynes Archive / Popperfoto / Getty Images [p. 129 left] PHOTOGRAPH Copyright © The Estate of Bradley Smith [p. 129] TEXT Excerpt from *Tropic of Cancer* by Henry Miller. Copyright © 1961 by Grove Press Inc. Used by permission of Grove/Atlantic, Inc. UK Rights secured through HarperCollins Publishers Ltd. Copyright © 1961 Henry Miller [p.130 center left & right] PHOTOGRAPH & ARTWORK Courtesy of Joan Mitchell Foundation [p. 130-131, 134-135] BACKGROUND ARTWORK Illustration by Roy Kuhlman. Courtesy of Arden Riodan [p. 132] TEXT Excerpt from *Lady Chatterley's Lover* by D.H. Lawrence. Copyright © 1959 by Grove Press, Inc. Used by permission of Grove/Atlantic Inc.

[p. 152-153] PHOTOGRAPH Copyright © Ebet Roberts / Redferns [p. 154-155, 159 center & bottom, 160 bottom, p. 164, 166 top] PHOTOGRAPH Courtesy of the collection of Nile Rodgers [p. 154-157] PHOTOGRAPH Copyright © James Andanson / Sygma / Corbis [p. 158] PHOTOGRAPH Copyright © Waring Abbott / Getty Images [p. 159 top] PHOTOGRAPH Copyright © Lynn Goldsmith [p. 160 top] PHOTOGRAPH Copyright © Phil Hardy / Gems. Courtesy of Phil Hardy [p. 160 middle] PHOTOGRAPH Copyright © Virginia Turbett / Redferns [p. 161] RECORD COVERS Courtesy of Nile Rodgers

[p. 172-173] PHOTOGRAPHS Copyright © The Richard Avedon Foundation [p.174-175] PHOTOGRAPH Copyright © 1981 The Richard Avedon Foundation p. 132] TEXT Excerpt [p. 176] PHOTOGRAPH Copyright © 2012 The Richard Avedon Foundation [p. 177] PHOTOGRAPH Copyright © 1978 The Richard Avedon Foundation [p. 180 bottom left] PHOTOGRAPH Copyright © Helmut Newton. Courtesy of June Newton [p. 180-183] PHOTOGRAPHS Newton / Vogue / Condé Nast Archive. Copyright © Condé Nast [p.184 top left & right, bottom center & left, 185 top left & right, bottom left] PHOTOGRAPHS Courtesy of Polly Mellen collection [p. 186-187] PHOTOGRAPH Turbeville / Vogue / Condé Nast Archive. Copyright © Condé Nast [p. 188-189] PHOTOGRAPHS Copyright © Arthur Elgort

[p. 195] PHOTOGRAPHS Copyright © Bruce Gilden / Magnum Photos

[p. 198-199] PHOTOGRAPH Copyright © 2011 Pirkle Jones Foundation

[p. 200] LYRICS "I May Never Pass This Way Again." Words and Music by Murray Wizell and Irving Melsher. Copyright © 1957 by Alley Music Corp., Trio Music Company and Cherio Music Publishers, Inc. Copyright Renewed and Assigned to Alley Music Corp and Trio Music Company. All Rights for Trio Music Company Administered by BUG Music, Inc., a BMG Chrysalis Company. International Copyright Secured. All Rights Reserved. Reprinted by Permission of Hal Leonard Corporation. [back inside cover] PHOTOGRAPH Copyright © National Geographic Stock

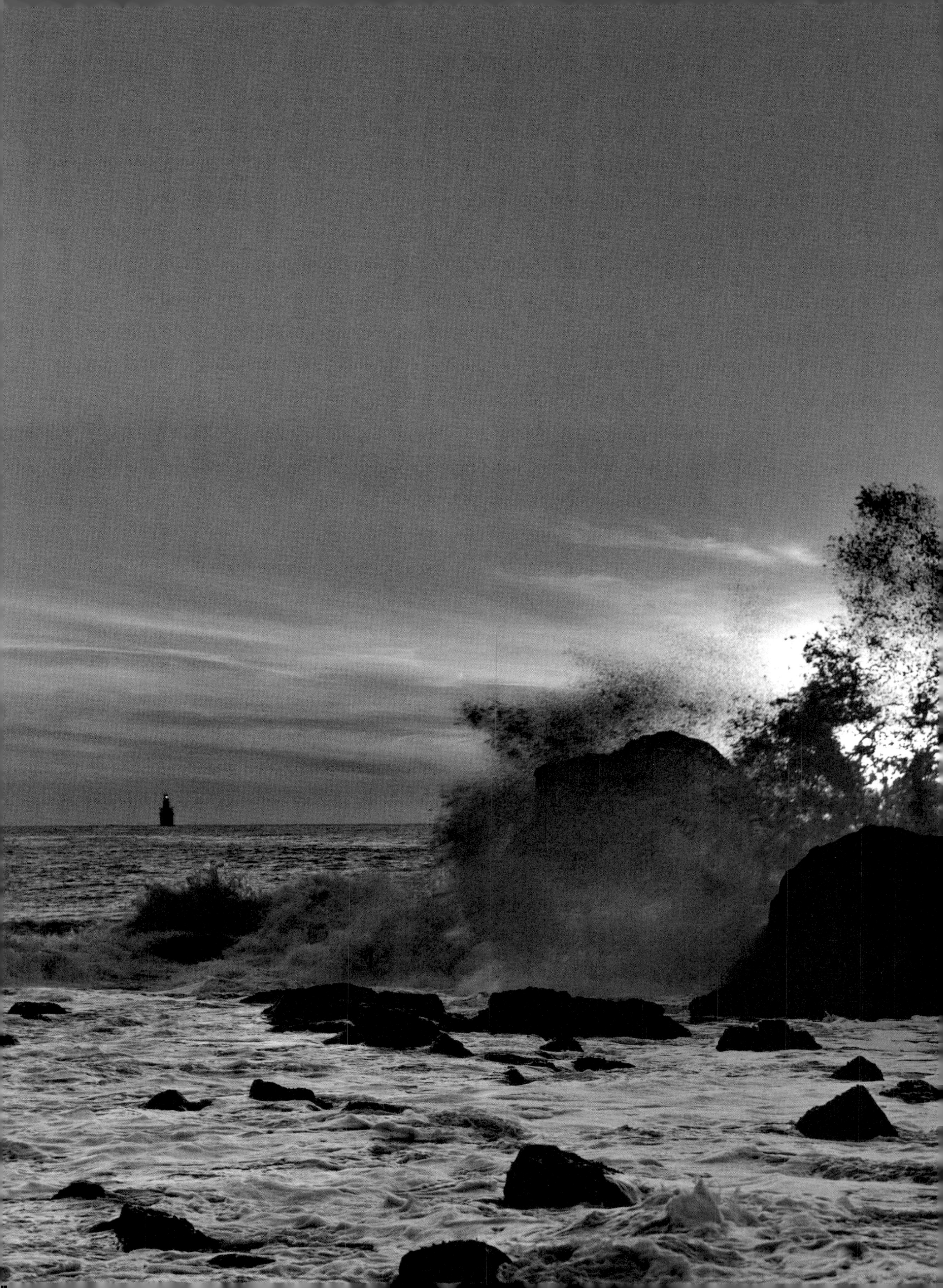

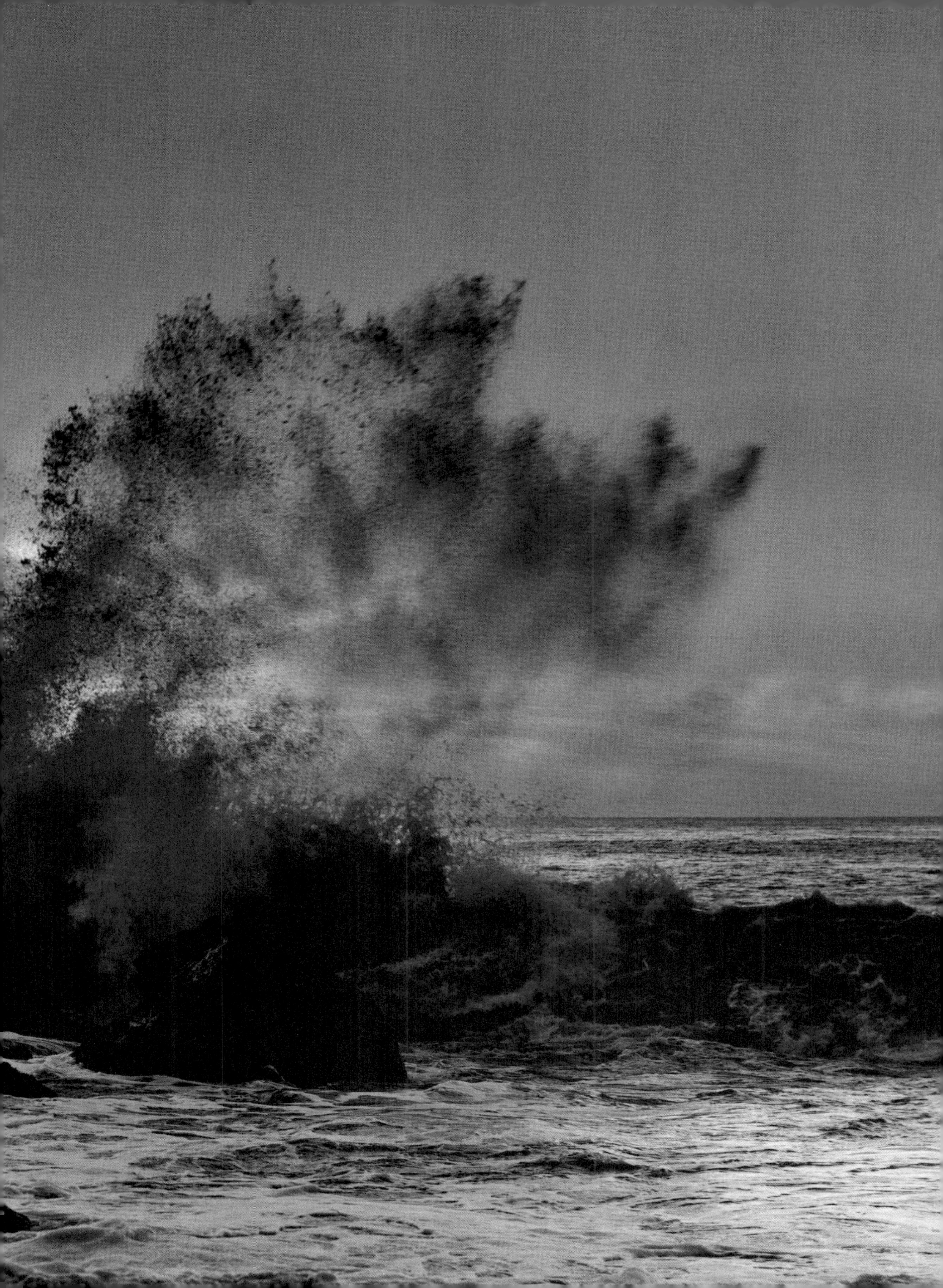

# *I May Never Pass This Way Again*

I'll give my hand
to those who cannot see
the sunrise or the falling rain.
I'll sing my song
to cheer the weary along
for I may never pass this way again.

I'll share my faith
with every troubled heart
so I shall not have lived in vain.
I'll give my hand.
I'll sing my song.
I'll share my faith
because I know
that the time is now
to fulfill each vow
for I may never pass this way again.

AS SUNG BY JONI JAMES ON HER ALBUM
*100 VOICES & 100 STRINGS*